California LEGAL ASPECTS OF REAL ESTATE

5TH EDITION, 4TH PRINTING

FRANK ZOTTER JR.
LEIGH CONWAY

Allied
Real Estate Schools
A Real Estate Express Company

This publication is designed to provide accurate and current information regarding the subject matter covered. The principles and conclusions presented are subject to local, state and federal laws and regulations, court cases and revisions of same. If legal advice or other expert assistance is required, the reader is urged to consult a competent professional in the field.

Real Estate Publisher
Leigh Conway

Academic Information Analyst
Laura King

Writers
Nicole Thome, Senior Technical Writer
Sue Carlson, Technical Writer

Editor
Emily Kazmierski

Production Designer
Susan Mackessy Richmond

©2017 by Allied Real Estate Schools, a division of Allied Business Schools, Inc.
5th Edition, 3rd Printing

Published by
Allied Real Estate Schools
22952 Alcalde Drive
Laguna Hills, California 92653

Printed in the United States of America

ISBN: 978-0-934772-05-1

TABLE OF CONTENTS

PREFACE

This comprehensive textbook is written primarily for real estate students; however, inquiring consumers and investors will also find answers to their real estate law questions.

Each unit in this textbook has been divided into topics. Topic content is reinforced through real-life examples, photographs, illustrations, charts, and tables. Important terms are highlighted in bold type in each unit. Each unit ends with a summary.

Review exercises have been designed for each unit. The quiz exercises features real estate finance terms and multiple choice questions. The multiple choice questions at the end of each unit will help the student prepare for the real estate exam. These questions were designed to test higher-level concepts and will often require the student to combine information they have learned in different units.

After completing a quiz exercise, students can check their answers by reviewing the Answer Key in the Appendix. Students should be encouraged to review their work often to make sure they understand what they have read.

ABOUT THE AUTHORS

FRANK ZOTTER JR.

Frank Zotter Jr. brings a rich background in real estate law to the creation of this textbook. He has over 25 years of experience in public agency law and was a former Chief Deputy County Counsel in Mendocino County, and a District Attorney in San Diego County. Mr. Zotter holds a JD from the University of San Diego School of Law and has extensive litigation experience.

Mr. Zotter is currently an instructor at Mendocino Community College and teaches courses in Business Law and Real Estate Law. He also teaches short-term courses focussing on Landlord-Tenant Issues, Constitutional Law, Wills and Probate, and Land Use Planning.

LEIGH CONWAY

Leigh Conway brings a rich background in real estate to the creation and production of this text. She is a licensed real estate broker in California with experience in commercial brokerage, residential and commercial property management, syndication, and real estate development. With over ten years of experience in real estate education, she has taught various statutory and continuing education courses. In addition, she co-authored a number of real estate textbooks and wrote several continuing education courses for private real estate schools. Ms. Conway has a Bachelor's Degree from the University of California at Los Angeles.

ACKNOWLEDGMENTS

The author would like to thank the following reviewers for their feedback and suggestions. Their experience and expertise assisted in the creation of this textbook.

Rick Boone – Santa Ana, California
Licensed California Real Estate Salesperson
Adjunct Real Estate Instructor, Orange Coast Community College

Hal Bouley – Tustin, California
Licensed California Real Estate Broker
Instructor, Coastline Community College

Ignacio Gonzalez – Ukiah, California

Licensed California Real Estate Broker
Real Estate Coordinator and Adjunct Real Estate Instructor,
    Mendocino Community College
Instructor for the GRI and serves as a faculty member
Author of *California Rea Estate Economics*

Walter "Fritz" Lauritzen – Fresno, California

Licensed California Real Estate Broker
Professor, Department of Finance & Business Law – California State
    University, Fresno

Overview of Law

INTRODUCTION

The word "law" is derived from the Old Norse word "lag," meaning something laid down or fixed. Without laws, society would be in chaos and anarchy would prevail. For this reason, society has designed a complex set of laws that establish guidelines for personal and business conduct. It is rare for any two individuals to agree on all social issues. For example, one person may believe the right to own an automatic weapon is acceptable, and another may believe it creates a danger to society.

Laws are not always constant. Over the years, certain laws have been proposed, accepted, and then challenged. Fair and equitable laws generally survive the test of time. Laws typically follow the Golden Rule, "Do unto others as you would have them do unto you." The practice of real estate changes as new laws are passed. These laws include lending practices, homesteads, landlords and tenants, estates, community property, and other laws related to the practice of real estate. This unit serves as a general overview of law and its application to the real estate industry.

Learning Objectives

After completing this unit, you should be able to:

1A   recognize a historical event that influenced law.

1B   choose the different sources of law from a list.

1C   identify the broad categories of law.

1D   indicate the highest authority in the court structure of California.

HISTORY OF LAW

Law is the body of rules and principles that every member of society must follow. It is a collection of norms and rules that permit, mandate, or forbid conduct by both people and organizations. The system is designed to promote safety, equity, equality, and the general welfare of all its members.

Some early legal systems were monarchical, with kings dictating behavior and doling out severe punishment for failure to follow royal directives. Pharaohs, kings, and emperors acted as legislature, judge, and jury. They promulgated the laws, decided the merit of disputes brought before them, and carried out the sentences. This system of law created inconsistency. When a successor replaced a ruler, the new ruler could change everything and set the entire region into turmoil with an entirely new set of rules.

Laws eventually became codified. **Codify** means to compile, arrange, systemize, and write the laws of a given region into a code. Laws are codified when they are recorded, uniform, and consistent. The Code of Hammurabi is one of the first examples of codified law. Hammurabi was the sixth king of Babylon and was born in 1810 B.C. What set Hammurabi apart from other monarchs was that he codified a set of laws that he published on a stone monolith for everyone to see. This stone marker, called a **stela**, resides in the Louvre museum in France. The code covered such items as theft, property damage, murder, injury, and punishments. The importance of the Hammurabic Code is that after inscribing the law on the monolith, it became absolute and permanent, giving rise to the phrase written in stone.

Several centuries later, the Roman emperor Justinian codified the Roman civil law into the Justinian Code. The Justinian Code formed the basis for many modern systems of civil law. **Civil law** is the body of law imposed by the state or government for its citizens.

In contrast to the codified systems described above, England followed a system of common law and equity. **Common law** refers to the body of law based on custom and judicial precedent rather than on codified statutes. Because the United States started as an English colony, the American legal system is a mix of common law and civil law.

SOURCES OF LAW

Laws in the United States are a collection of rules that derive from four main sources: (1) constitutional law, (2) statutory law, (3) administrative law, and (4) common law.

Constitutional Law

Constitutional law consists of a body of rules created by federal and state constitutions. The prime example of constitutional law is the **United States Constitution**, which is one of the most respected and honored documents ever written. The Bill of Rights in 1789 ratified the U.S. Constitution with the support of the original thirteen states. The Bill of Rights is the name given to the first ten amendments made to the original Constitution. The Constitution is the supreme law of the land and has experienced many changes over the nation's history. Changes to the Constitution itself take place by an amendment ratified by two-thirds of each house of Congress and then approved by three-fourths of the state legislatures.

The Constitution sets forth the three principal branches of the federal government, outlines its jurisdictions, and expresses the basic rights of U.S. citizens. The powers not delegated to the United States by the Constitution are reserved to the states. The United States Constitution is the standard against which all other laws must be judged.

The Constitution consists of a preamble, seven original articles, and twenty-seven amendments. Some of these amendments are of importance to property ownership.

> **Amendments Pertinent to Real Estate**
>
> The **First Amendment** addresses the freedom of speech and of the press. This guarantees the right to advertise property for sale and place for sale signs on property.
>
> The **Third Amendment** prohibits the government from using private homes as quarters for soldiers without the consent of the owners.
>
> The **Fourth Amendment** prohibits the seizure of property without due process of law.
>
> The **Fifth Amendment** prohibits the government from taking private property for public use without just compensation. It serves as the basis for eminent domain in the United States.
>
> The **Thirteenth Amendment** abolished slavery and makes discrimination on the grounds of race, color, or creed unconstitutional.
>
> The **Fourteenth Amendment** provides for equal protection of the law and is the basis for antidiscrimination laws.

Statutory Law

Statutory law is written law enacted by federal and state legislative bodies. Statutory law is also termed **black letter law**, meaning the words committed to paper that govern. A **statute** is a law passed by a legislature. Congress enacts laws that affect all citizens. The California legislature enacts statutes affecting the entire state, and city councils pass local laws (ordinances) affecting the residents of the city.

Sometimes the federal, state, and local governments have similar laws covering the same subject. When this occurs, the federal law usually governs a particular activity in interstate commerce and the state law governs the same activity within the state.

Federal Laws

A process involving the Congress and the U.S. President generally creates federal statutes. Congressional members draft proposed legislation called a **bill**. It undergoes debate, revision, and discussion before being voted on by both the House of Representatives and the Senate. If both houses of Congress pass the bill, it goes to the White House for the President to review. The President can sign the bill into law, veto it, or ignore it. If vetoed, Congress can vote on it again and if two-thirds of Congress approves the bill, it becomes a law without presidential approval.

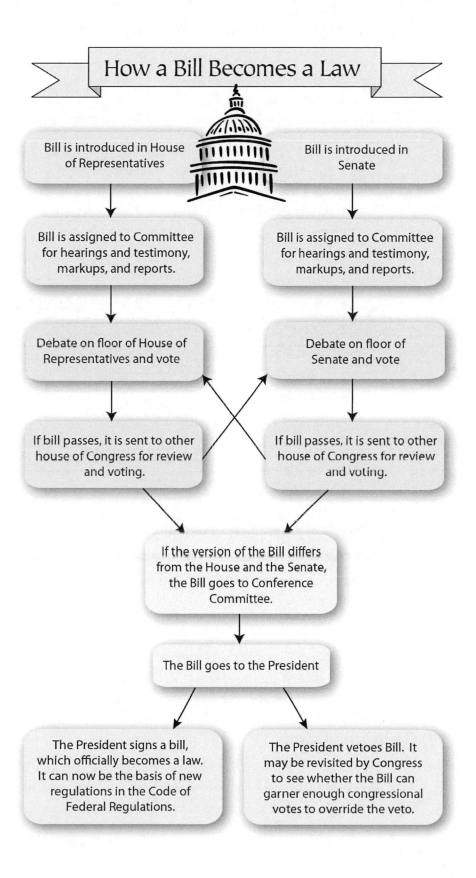

How a Bill Becomes a Law

Bill is introduced in House of Representatives	Bill is introduced in Senate

Bill is assigned to Committee for hearings and testimony, markups, and reports.

Bill is assigned to Committee for hearings and testimony, markups, and reports.

Debate on floor of House of Representatives and vote

Debate on floor of Senate and vote

If bill passes, it is sent to other house of Congress for review and voting.

If bill passes, it is sent to other house of Congress for review and voting.

If the version of the Bill differs from the House and the Senate, the Bill goes to Conference Committee.

The Bill goes to the President

The President signs a bill, which officially becomes a law. It can now be the basis of new regulations in the Code of Federal Regulations.

The President vetoes Bill. It may be revisited by Congress to see whether the Bill can garner enough congressional votes to override the veto.

Federal Laws Affecting the Real Estate Industry

- Americans with Disabilities Act
- CAN-SPAM Act of 2003
- Clean Air Act
- Clean Water Act
- Community Reinvestment Act
- Comprehensive Environmental Response, Compensation, and Liability Act (Superfund)
- Endangered Species Act
- Equal Credit Opportunity Act
- Fair Credit Reporting Act
- Fair Housing Act
- Financial Institutions Reform, Recovery and Enforcement Act
- Foreign Investment in Real Property Tax Act
- Interstate Land Sales Full Disclosure Act
- National Environmental Policy Act of 1969
- Oil Pollution Act
- Real Estate Settlement Procedures Act
- Secure and Fair Enforcement for Mortgage Licensing Act of 2008
- Sherman Antitrust Act
- The Residential Lead-Based Paint Hazard Reduction Act of 1992
- Truth-in-Lending Act

A similar system is in place at the state level. The California legislature consists of the Assembly and the Senate. Drafts of proposed legislation undergoes debate, votes, and revisions before the proposed bill winds up on the desk of the governor. The governor, like the president, may approve or reject the proposed legislation.

California, however, also has provisions for the voting populace to be directly involved in creation of new laws, called initiatives or propositions. This is mostly done at the state level, but cities and counties can also pass initiatives.

California Laws

The state of California has its own constitution. While California attained statehood in 1850, the current constitution was not ratified until 1879. It is similar to the U.S. Constitution in many respects; however, it is one of the nation's longest constitutions, at over 110 pages.

The state constitution is the foundation for all state laws. It grants powers to governing agencies and bodies, and protects individual rights. The state constitution, however, is always subordinate to the federal constitution. If there is a conflict between the two, the federal constitution controls.

The creation of state laws is similar to the process used to enact federal law. A member of the state legislature drafts a bill, which when approved by both the House and the Senate is sent to the governor for signature. Once signed, it becomes a state law. The state laws are implemented by regulations promulgated by various state and local agencies. California passed the first real estate license law in 1917, which was followed by many other regulations that revolutionized the regulation of licensed professionals in the real estate industry.

California Laws Affecting the Real Estate Industry

- California Americans with Disabilities Act
- California Asbestos Health Protection Act
- California Fair Housing Act
- California Hazardous Substances Act
- California Megan's Law
- California Subdivided Lands Law
- California Foreign Investment in Real Property Tax Act
- California Real Property Loan Law

It is important to know the local fair housing laws. These can, and do, vary from city to city. Various cities have enacted fair housing laws to implement the Federal Fair Housing Act, and have even broadened the Fair Housing Act. An example is making it illegal to discriminate in residential real estate sales and leasing based on sexual orientation.

Most state and local laws mirror or interpret federal laws. If there is a conflict between state and local law, state statutes take precedence over city ordinances, the regulations of governmental agencies, and sometimes the common law. However, the more restrictive statute usually takes precedence.

Administrative Law

Most federal and state acts establish broad goals, but not the methods needed to carry out the goals. Different federal and state agencies take on the task of creating regulations to enforce the goals of an act. A **regulation** is a rule issued by a federal or state executive-branch department or administrative agency, generally under authority granted by statute, which enforces or amplifies laws enacted by the legislature and has the force of law.

> Example: Regulation Z issued by the Board of Governors of the Federal Reserve System, implements the federal Truth in Lending Act.

Administrative laws are written rules and regulations adopted by governmental agencies to enable the agencies to carry out regulatory duties. Regulations created by agencies carry the force of law. In California, most of the regulations governing real estate are in the **Business and Professions Code**.

The regulations can cover only the specific activities authorized by the statute. Some of the regulated activities include licensing, housing, financing, building construction and safety, land use and development, health and sanitation, pollution control, development of natural resources, parks and public recreation, liquor control, and industrial safety.

The **Bureau of Real Estate (CalBRE)** is the state agency that administers the Real Estate Law in California, which deals with the licensing of real estate professionals. The regulations it enacts are found in the Business and Professions Code.

Municipal Ordinances

In addition to the statutes passed by the state legislature, **municipal corporations** (incorporated cities) may adopt ordinances. An **ordinance** is a municipal law or regulation. Once a state statute becomes law, an ordinance may be enacted by agencies at the local level.

Local ordinances and regulations are part of the statutory law even though they are subordinate to the state and federal laws. The municipal ordinances only apply within the city limits. Typically, ordinances are concerned with public safety, zoning, building permits, housing, health and sanitation, licensing, and many other matters.

Common Law

Despite the fact that the modern legal system is a codified, civil system, there is still a strong component of common law. Common law is not based on legislative (statutory) law, but on the decisions of judges in previous cases. That is why common law is referred to as **case law** or judge-made law. Because common law is based on years of judicial proceedings and opinions, it helps unify constitutional, statutory, and administrative law.

One of the most important concepts of common law is the theory of *stare decisis*. **Stare decisis** (to stand by things decided) means the court is bound by the precedents set by other courts. **Precedent** is the term used to describe the concept of looking back at cases previously decided and following those decisions for the sake of consistency and fairness.

This expresses the reasoning or rationale that every case has an impact on every other case that follows. It is a defining characteristic of the common law system followed in the United States and Great Britain.

Judges deciding new cases examine similar cases decided previously, and often make their decisions based on the outcome of those cases. Generally, precedent follows a hierarchical structure. Lower courts are bound by the decisions of the courts above them. However, a higher court is not bound to follow the precedents established by a lower court. Courts may use precedents from equal-rank courts or courts from another state as non-binding guidelines.

CATEGORIES OF LAW

The two broad categories of law are civil law and criminal law. **Civil law** deals with private offenses, such as violations of contracts, and failure of professional duty. **Criminal law** concerns wrongs against persons or society.

Civil Law

Civil law attempts to right a wrong, honor an agreement, or settle a dispute. Typical civil law cases include disputes involving contracts, property ownership, and divorce. In civil law, courts apply reason based on general rules and principles of statutory code, often drawing from statutory provisions to fill in any voids in order to achieve understanding and agreement between parties.

Areas of Law

Many areas of the law, such as agency law, property law, and tort law are governed extensively by common law. Others, such as contract law, are covered partly by common law and partly by statutes. Laws may be subcategorized by type—each with its individual rules, regulations, and applications.

Licensing Law. California real estate license holders are regulated by the Bureau of Real Estate (CalBRE) under the Business and Professions Code.

Fair Housing Law. Fair housing laws deal with ending discrimination in housing. The laws include renting, purchasing, financing, and insuring a home. In addition, advertising and zoning is affected by fair housing laws.

Antitrust Law. Antitrust law is a body of law, consisting of statutes and common law that regulate against limiting free choice, competition, and efficient markets.

Agency Law. Agency law is the area of law that governs the fiduciary relationships between brokers and their principals.

Contract Law. Contract law deals with promises between people or companies, and establishes the circumstances in which a contract is binding. Real estate licensees deal with contracts and contract law almost every day in a real estate transaction.

Landlord & Tenant Law. Landlord and tenant law is the law concerning renting and leasing property and the rights of both the owner and the renter or lessee.

Property Law. Property law is the area of law that governs the ownership of real property and personal property.

Water Law. Water law is the body of laws that describe the ownership, control, and use of water as a resource.

Probate Law. Probate law sets out the legal process to prove a will and transfer property upon a person's death.

Lending Law. Consumers are protected through a variety of federal and state lending laws.

Tax Law. Tax law is the body of laws that describes the federal, state, and local government levies on income, real and personal property, capital gains, estates, corporations, LLCs, partnerships, and investments.

Land Use & Environmental Regulations. Land use regulations and environmental laws protect the natural environment, which may be impacted or endangered by human activities. It is a complex body of laws, consisting of treaties, conventions, statutes, common law, policies, and regulations.

Criminal Law

Criminal law is designed to protect society from wrongful actions. Criminal offenses are viewed as offenses against not just individual victims, but the community as well. Criminal law is the body of law dealing with crimes, associated punishment, and involves prosecution by the state for an act that qualifies as a crime. A **crime** is a violation of the federal or state criminal laws.

There are many different kinds of crime—from murder and assault to fraud and theft. Property crime includes arson, trespass, littering, and vandalism. Criminal law in real estate applies when fraud is committed during a transaction involving real estate, or when a person attempts to sell a property that he or she does not actually own. **Fraud** is the intentional misrepresentation or concealment of a material fact made to induce someone to act to his or her detriment. The typical punishment for a crime is imprisonment, fines and/or community service, depending upon the severity of the crime.

COURT STRUCTURE OF CALIFORNIA

Even though the modern legal system in California is civil and codified, common law is still inherent in the system. For the most part, the legal system consists of precedent and stare decisis, but the two are not the only factors that courts use when making decisions. Courts now look to written laws (statutes) and to the drafters' intent for the codified law. California courts, and virtually all other courts in the nation, use precedent in every case they decide, though stare decisis is still an important factor.

Auto Equity Sales, Inc. v. Superior Court

In *Auto Equity Sales, Inc. v. Superior Court* (1962) 57 Cal.2d 450, 455, the California Court of Appeals scolded lower courts for not following precedent.

The case established that, "Decisions of every division of the District Courts of Appeal are binding upon all the justice and municipal courts and upon all the superior courts of this state, and this is so whether or not the superior court is acting as a trial or appellate court. Courts exercising inferior jurisdiction must accept the law declared by courts of superior jurisdiction. It is not the courts' function to attempt to overrule decisions of a higher court".

Generally, precedent follows a hierarchical structure. Lower courts are bound by the decisions of the courts above them. This is true regarding the court structure of California, which consists of three different levels.

Court Structure of California from Highest to Lowest

1. California Supreme Court
2. California Courts of Appeal
3. Superior Courts of California

The Superior Courts of California has 58 courts for each respective county in California. The 58 trial courts have the authority to listen to civil or criminal cases and render decisions based on the evidence supplied by the parties. The California Courts of Appeal consist of six appellate districts found in San Francisco, Los Angeles, Sacramento, San Diego, Fresno, and San Jose. The California Courts of Appeal have the power to review and overturn Superior Court decisions. The California Supreme Court is the highest court level and all courts in California are bound by its decisions.

Parker v. Dunfield

Patricia Parker is the neighbor of Deborah Dunfield. They have a dispute concerning their property line and a fence Deborah built that may encroach on Patricia's property by four inches. The fence is unusual and Dunfield used specially designed wrought iron scrollwork that cost her tens of thousands of dollars. Their dispute escalates to the point of litigation in a California Superior Court because Dunfield refuses to move the extravagant fence

Parker v. Dunfield (continued)

over a trifling four-inch dispute. At trial, evidence showed that Dunfield knew she was encroaching on Parker's property.

The judge looked through prior cases and found one decided 70 years earlier by a higher court. That court held that the party who knowingly built a fence on a neighbor's land had to remove the fence, repair the damage, and pay an additional penalty equal to twice the value of the fence to the injured party. According to stare decisis, the judge in *Parker v. Dunfield* must follow the earlier decision, and order Dunfield to remove the fence, repair the damage to Parker's property, and pay Parker twice what the fence cost to build. Thus, although the fence cost Dunfield $25,000 to build, she will be required to remove it (a $3,000 expense), repair the damage to Parker's lawn (an additional $3,000), and pay Parker $50,000 more, before she places the fence within her own property line at an additional cost.

Even though the trial judge found a clear precedent that would determine the case, he only awarded Parker $10,000, reasoning that following the prior decision would cause a ridiculous financial windfall to Parker for a very minor encroachment. Parker appealed the decision to the California Court of Appeals and that court overturned the decision and ordered the trial court to keep the prior precedent.

California also has courts for handling specific matters of federal jurisdiction and cases involving diversity of citizenship. At the federal level, the courts from lowest to highest in the hierarchy are the **Federal District Courts**, the **Court of Appeals**, and the **United States Supreme Court**.

Settling Disputes

Real estate licensees must be aware of the laws that affect the practice of real estate. Many real estate practitioners erroneously believe they understand the law, because they have not been sued. The result of a consumer complaint could be an expensive lawsuit, and possibly the suspension or revocation of a real estate license.

Real estate licensees protect themselves best by practicing real estate ethically. This often provides a barrier for disciplinary action and lawsuits. Unfortunately, doing everything by the book may not always be enough. A licensee may have caused damage due to negligence, which would be an **unintentional tort**. However, intentional omissions, misrepresentation, or wrongful acts are **intentional torts**. A **tort** is a legal wrong for which civil remedies for injuries or damages are provided.

> Example: Seller Sam knows that his house is in a flood plain, but tells buyer Bob that the property is not in a flood plain. If Bob purchases the property based on these assurances, Sam has committed fraud. Fraud is a tort violation, because it harms another. If the fraud were egregious, it might also be a criminal violation, resulting in fines as well as imprisonment.

If confronted with a potential lawsuit, a real estate salesperson must report the incident immediately to his or her sponsoring broker. Too often, a real estate salesperson believes he or she can handle it alone, which may escalate the situation. One of the best defenses in a lawsuit is good documentation. Documentation provides evidence of things said and done in the course of a transaction. Licensees should always verify information before giving advice, retain copies of all records, and keep the documents involved in each transaction, even when a transaction does not close. Some disputes are settled out of court and some go to litigation to decide a remedy for the harmed party.

Litigation

Litigation is the process of bringing a lawsuit against someone. Most of the lawsuits are civil cases, which involve contract disputes and personal injury matters. There are countless things that can form the basis of a lawsuit, but essentially they all boil down to one party believing another party has caused them some form of harm whether financial or otherwise.

Lawsuits can be very complex and convoluted, depending on the issues and number of parties involved. The description that follows is a broad overview of the litigation process.

The Complaint and Answer

When litigation occurs, a party files a complaint with the court and sends a copy of the filed complaint to the accused party through a summons. The **complaint** summarizes the plaintiff's case against the defendant including the actual harm done and the demand for compensation for damages incurred. A **summons** is a written request that establishes the plaintiff's position in filing a complaint and calls for the defendant to answer or appear in court.

After receiving the complaint, the defendant can respond with an answer. The **answer** explains the position of the defendant and his or her view on the plaintiff's allegations. A **default judgment** occurs when a defendant in a lawsuit fails to respond to a complaint and the court then rules in favor of the plaintiff by default. The plaintiff can issue a response to the answer through a **reply**. Any factual discrepancies between the plaintiff and defendant can be settled through amendments. Once the basis for the complaint, answer, and reply are settled, the case is now at issue and resolutions can now occur.

Settlement Alternatives

Before a case actually goes before a judge and jury, there are multiple attempts to resolve it. The attorneys may try to negotiate a settlement. If that fails, the court system sometimes attempts to get the parties to a compromise through mandatory settlement conferences that all parties and their respective attorneys must attend. The parties usually appear in court before a judge or retired judge, and attempt to work through the issues with an eye toward resolution before trial.

Sometimes, the court recommends that the parties solve the case through alternative dispute resolution. **Alternative Dispute Resolution (ADR)** is gaining in popularity, because it is not only less costly than formal litigation, but it is usually quicker than the long, drawn out legal process of preparing for a trial. Alternative dispute resolution involves mediation or arbitration.

Mediation

Mediation is the process in which a neutral, uninterested third party helps the parties involved in a dispute to negotiate a settlement or other resolution. The mediator talks with each party individually, offers suggestions and his or her opinions as to the viability of the case, and attempts to help the parties come to a mutually agreeable resolution. The mediator has no power to require any party to compromise or settle, and cannot impose a decision.

Arbitration

Arbitration is like a trial, without a jury. **Arbitration** is a process in which the parties (and/or their attorneys) present their cases to an arbitrator, who renders a decision. Parties are usually present with their attorneys, legal briefs are usually prepared, and documentary and other physical evidence is provided. Testimony is often given under oath. Attorneys often make opening and closing remarks.

The arbitrator, instead of a jury, makes a decision based on all the evidence and the arguments of counsel. The rules of evidence are often somewhat relaxed in an arbitration setting, whereas in a formal trial, evidentiary issues can be contested between the parties. This can sometimes result in separate legal proceedings that must be resolved before the current trial can proceed. Arbitration generally saves both time and money. This is beneficial to all the parties involved in the dispute. Arbitration can be binding, meaning that the parties must abide by the decision of the arbitrator and may not request a new trial. Alternatively, a nonbinding arbitration allows the parties to request a new trial should the results prove unfavorable.

Many real estate contracts have arbitration clauses in them. When parties sign a contract that contains an arbitration agreement, they agree to settle all disputes through arbitration.

Case Preparation and Discovery

In the event of an actual trial, preparations are necessary prior to appearing before a judge and jury. To prepare for a trial, the parties are entitled to seek various kinds of information from each other called **discovery**. The parties are soliciting bits of information that may affect the outcome of a trial.

Usually, the first forms of discovery take place through **interrogatories**, which are written questions that must be answered in writing under oath within a specified time period. There are various kinds of interrogatories and the parties initially begin by serving each other with standard, preprinted forms approved by the state. At about the same time, early in the litigation process, the parties involved can request for documents, known as document production, that are pertinent to the case. A party requests that the other party produce verified copies of pertinent documents.

Eventually, after completing sufficient background discovery, the parties may opt to conduct depositions. **Depositions** are live, oral testimonies under oath.

Depositions typically take place in an attorney's office, but they can occur in other places, depending on the particular circumstances. Depositions are usually the most expensive part of the discovery process. If necessary, the parties may request expert witnesses to bolster their case. If that occurs, there is further discovery involving those expert witnesses, their reports, and depositions.

Trial

Most lawsuits never make it to the trial phase and are either settled or dismissed. Those that do go to trial begin with pre-trial **motions**, which are requests for certain rulings on evidence in advance of the trial or other requests.

After the pretrial rulings, the parties proceed with jury selection or sometimes the parties opt to have the judge rule and eliminate the jury. Jury selection can be a long, involved process, or can take a matter of a few hours. After selecting the jury, the trial begins. Lawyers make opening remarks, call their witnesses, present evidence, and cross-examine witnesses.

After presenting all the evidence and witnesses, the lawyers make closing arguments. The judge instructs the jury to base its decision on the law that applies to the particular case. The jury then privately enters into deliberations and when it reaches a decision, the decision is given to the judge. In some cases, the judge may decide to overturn the jury's decision, but in most cases, the judge enters the judgment based on that decision.

Judgment and Appeal

In many instances, a judgment signifies the end of a case. Sometimes, however, a party is dissatisfied with the judgment rendered and files an appeal. As shown above, an appeal is not a re-trial of the lawsuit. Instead, the party challenging the decision of the trial court must show that there was an error of law to get the court of appeal to overturn the trial court's decision. For example, the appellant might argue that the judge incorrectly instructed the jury about the law that applied to the case. The appeals court also does not reconsider the evidence, such as the credibility of witnesses, which is entirely a matter for the jury or the trial judge if there is no jury. The court of appeal can uphold the judgment of the trial court, modify it, or reverse it.

Remedies

A **remedy** refers to compensating the plaintiff for any injuries incurred. Remedies fall into two categories—legal and equitable.

Legal

Essentially, legal remedies are monetary. Although courts are not limited to awarding monetary damages depending on the kind of case involved, they cannot impose equitable remedies unless monetary damages are inadequate to make the plaintiff whole. Monetary damages fall into three general categories.

Three Categories of Monetary Damages

1. **Compensatory damages** are monetary damages designed to compensate the injured party for the injury that was sustained.
2. **Punitive damages** are awarded as a means of punishment, in addition to whatever compensatory damages may be appropriate. Usually, punitive damages are only permissible in cases involving willful, wanton, malicious, or otherwise fraudulent conduct.
3. **Nominal damages** are token monetary figures, usually of one dollar or so. Nominal damages are awarded when the defendant was in the wrong, but no real damage occurred.

Equitable

Equitable remedies are based on fairness and conscience. Sometimes an award of money simply is inappropriate or insufficient. That is when equitable remedies are used. Generally, there are seven different types of equitable relief.

Seven Types of Equitable Relief

1. **Specific Performance** is a highly specialized and seldom-used form of equitable relief. It is generally used in cases involving contracts or property that cannot be otherwise replaced. An order directing specific performance requires that one party go through with a contract as agreed or give actual property to another. This cannot be used to force someone to work for someone else, which would be akin to slavery or indentured servitude.
2. **Reformation** occurs when a court rewrites a contract to state the true intention of the parties, for the sake of clarity, if the contract does not say what it ought.

3. **Recission** is another form of equitable relief that generally applies to contracts. The basic idea is that the court rescinds the contract and puts the parties in the position they were in prior to executing the contract. This might occur because of a mutual mistake on the part of both parties or in situations in which the contract initially was valid when the parties entered into it but subsequently became illegal by operation of law.

4. **Foreclosure** is a form of equitable relief with which everyone in the real estate business is familiar. In a foreclosure action, the court terminates someone's interest in real property. Usually, the lienholder seeks foreclosure after the mortgagor fails to pay on the mortgage of a home.

5. **Injunction** is a means of stopping some activity from occurring or requiring it to occur. It is an order issued by a court that directs someone to do something or, more often, enjoins (stops) someone from doing something.

6. **Quiet Title** is a form of equitable relief specific to real property. It is used to end disputes concerning ownership or to clear up problems with obtaining a clear title.

7. **Declaratory relief** is a kind of equitable action to determine what someone's rights are before a problem comes to fruition.

SUMMARY

Law is a body of rules of conduct established to secure social order for the benefit of the population as a whole. The American legal system is a mix of common law and civil law. Civil law is the body of law imposed by the state or government for its citizens. The common law system is based on custom and judicial precedent.

Laws in the United States are a collection of rules that derive from four main sources: (1) constitutional law, (2) statutory law, (3) administrative law, and (4) common law. Constitutional law consists of a body of rules created by federal and state constitutions. Statutory law is written law enacted by legislative bodies. Administrative laws are written rules and regulations adopted by governmental agencies to enable the agencies to carry out regulatory duties. Common law is based on the decisions of judges in particular cases.

The two broad categories of law are civil law and criminal law. Civil law deals with private offenses, such as violations of contracts, and failure of professional duty. Criminal law is the body of law dealing with crimes, associated punishment, and involves prosecution by the state for an act that qualifies as a crime.

In California, the lowest court, which is the trial level court, is the superior court at the state level. Until recently, there were two levels of trial courts—the municipal and superior courts—now referred to as the limited division and unlimited division of the superior court. Above them are the Courts of Appeal, which consist of six appellate districts found in major cities. The highest court in California is the California Supreme Court. California also has federal courts for handling specific matters of federal jurisdiction and cases involving diversity of citizenship. At the federal level, the lowest courts are the Federal District Courts. Next, the hierarchy is the Court of Appeals, followed by the United States Supreme Court, the highest court in the land.

When a dispute occurs between a real estate licensee and another party, there are legal remedies available to settle the dispute. Litigation is the process of bringing a lawsuit against someone. Mediation is the process in which a neutral, uninterested third party helps the parties involved in a dispute to negotiate a settlement or other resolution. Arbitration is a process in which the parties (and/or their attorneys) present their cases to an arbitrator, who renders a decision.

UNIT 1 REVIEW

Matching Exercise

Instructions: Write the letter of the matching term on the blank line before its definition. Answers are in Appendix A.

Terms

A. answer

B. arbitration

C. black letter law

D. civil law

E. codify

F. common law

G. compensatory damage

H. complaint

I. criminal law

J. defendant

K. default judgment

L. deposition

M. law

N. litigation

O. mediation

P. plaintiff

Q. precedent

R. remedy

S. summons

T. tort

Definitions

1. _____ Body of rules and principles that every member of society must follow

2. _____ Compile, arrange, systemize, and write the laws of a given region into a code

3. _____ Body of law imposed by the state or government for its citizens

4. _____ Body of law based on custom and judicial precedent rather than on codified statutes

5. _____ Words committed to paper that govern

6. _____ Occurs when a defendant in a lawsuit fails to respond to a complaint and the court then rules in favor of the plaintiff by default

7. _____ Concept of looking back at cases previously decided and following those decisions for the sake of consistency and fairness

8. _____ Law that concerns wrongs against persons or society

9. _____ Legal wrong for which civil remedies for injuries or damages are provided

10. _____ Process of bringing a lawsuit against someone

11. _____ Person filing the civil suit in a court of law

12. _____ Person who is being sued

13. _____ Summarizes the plaintiff's case against the defendant including the actual harm done and the demand for compensation for damages incurred

14. _____ Explains the position of the defendant and his or her view on the plaintiff's allegations

15. _____ Written request that establishes the plaintiff's position in filing a complaint and calls for the defendant to answer or appear in court

16. _____ Process in which a neutral, uninterested third party helps the parties involved in a dispute to negotiate a settlement or other resolution

17. _____ Process in which the parties (and/or their attorneys) present their cases to an arbitrator, who renders a decision

18. _____ Live, oral testimony under oath

19. _____ Compensating the plaintiff for any injuries incurred

20. _____ Damages designed to compensate the injured party for the injury that was sustained

Multiple Choice Questions

Instructions: Circle your response and go to Appendix A to read the complete explanation for each question.

1. What is the significance of the Code of Hammurabi?
    a. It established inconsistency in a system of law.
    b. It stressed the ideology that laws are never permanent.
    c. It was an early example of codifying laws.
    d. It was the first real estate law.

2. Our laws are derived from four main sources: (1) constitutional law, (2) statutory law, (3) administrative law, and (4) common law. Of the twenty-seven amendments to the United States Constitution, how many pertain to real estate?

   a. 4
   b. 6
   c. 10
   d. 14

3. Which of the following is a federal law affecting the real estate industry?

   a. Real Estate Settlement Procedures Act
   b. Fair Housing Act
   c. Foreign Investment in Real Property Tax Act
   d. All of the above

4. Which laws are written rules and regulations adopted by governmental agencies to enable the agencies to carry out regulatory duties?

   a. Administrative laws
   b. Common laws
   c. Fair housing laws
   d. Statutory laws

5. The two broad categories of law are _____ law and _____ law.

   a. administrative / civil
   b. civil / criminal
   c. civil / constitutional
   d. common / property

6. A crime is a violation of the federal or state criminal laws. What is the typical punishment for a crime?

   a. Community service
   b. Fines
   c. Imprisonment
   d. All of the above

7. In the court structure of California, which court is ranked as the highest?

   a. California Courts of Appeal
   b. California Supreme Court
   c. Small claims court
   d. Superior Courts of California

8. Of the following, which is a way to settle a dispute?
    a. Arbitration
    b. Litigation
    c. Mediation
    d. All of the above

9. Which of the following statements is true regarding Alternative Dispute Resolution (ADR)?
    a. ADR is more costly than the litigation process.
    b. ADR includes arbitration or litigation.
    c. ADR includes arbitration or mediation.
    d. ADR renders a quicker settlement.

10. Compensating the plaintiff through legal and/or equitable means is called a(n):
    a. appeal.
    b. discovery.
    c. motion.
    d. remedy.

Property & Legal Descriptions

Unit **2**

INTRODUCTION

Anything that may be owned and gained lawfully is known as property. In America, land is owned by the people, except for public property, which is owned by the government to be used for the benefit of its citizens.

The right to own property in the United States is protected under the U.S. Constitution. Property law governs the ownership of real property and personal property. This unit discusses the differences between real property and personal property in detail. Understanding these differences is necessary in order to handle a real estate transaction properly.

The ownership of property includes the location and description of the land itself. Ever since individuals and states took possession of land, there have been inventive ways of describing it in order to claim the rights of ownership. This is accomplished through a legal description, which provides evidence of the location and area of the land involved in the transfer of ownership.

Learning Objectives

After completing this unit, you should be able to:

2A   recognize the rights inherent in the bundle of rights.

2B   select examples of personal property.

2C   identify the characteristics of real property.

2D   recall classifications of water in California.

2E   identify the different methods used for legal descriptions.

BUNDLE OF RIGHTS

In common law, the word property refers more to the rights that the owner has in property than to the fact that the property is owned. Property rights are known as the bundle of rights. The **bundle of rights** consists of all legal rights that are attached to the ownership of physical property.

The bundle of rights includes the right to use, possess, transfer, encumber, and enjoy property. This bundle of rights safeguards the owner's rights to the property. An owner may choose to sell or give away one of the rights and keep the rest. For example, under a lease agreement, an owner may give away the right of use for a certain time to a tenant. However, if one of these rights is affected, control of the property is diminished.

Use. The **right of use** is a right that gives an owner of property the ability to control the use of the property within the boundaries of the law. For example, the right of use allows a person to add an addition to a house, add another structure to the property, or paint the exterior of the house. It allows the owner to put up a fence, tear down a fence, paint a fence pink, or never install a fence at all.

Possession. The **right of possession** gives an owner of property the ability to live on the property and to exclude others from access. Trespassing on private property violates a property owner's right of possession and is a civil violation of law, which has the potential of ending up in court. The right of possession can be sold, usually for a certain period of time. When the right of possession is sold for consideration, the consideration is called **rent** and a leasehold interest is created. Once this right is sold, the owner no longer has the right of possession. The right of possession now belongs to the tenant. The owner retains all other rights.

An owner of property can give away the right of possession as well. If the owner gives the right away, the same circumstances apply as they do when the right is sold. If you let friends stay at your place, while you are taking an extended vacation, you have given them the right of possession. Once the right of possession is sold or given away, it may require legal proceedings to regain it.

Transfer. The **right of transfer** gives an owner of property the right to dispose of the property in any way permitted by law, including transferring ownership of the property by gift, sale, or trade. The easier the right of transfer, the greater value the property will have. If the property cannot be disposed of without the influence of the courts, the value will decline. Without the open right to dispose of a property, those in the real estate profession are out of business.

Encumber. The **right to encumber** property gives a person the right to borrow money in order to purchase or refinance a property and allows the lender to use the property as security for the loan. Lenders do not provide loans without this protection because they would have no recourse if the borrower were to default on the loan.

Enjoyment. The **right of enjoyment** gives an owner of property the right to quiet and peaceful enjoyment of the property that he or she owns or occupies. With any right, there is responsibility. The right of enjoyment for property does not allow a person occupying the property to become a nuisance to surrounding neighbors or to use the property for illegal purposes. Deed restrictions may also affect certain rights of the occupants of a property. For example, a condominium community may limit the number or size of pets that a person is allowed to keep on the property. The right of enjoyment allows you to grow a flower garden, build a fence, and to sit out back and enjoy a nice cool drink, without the prospect of someone telling you that you are not allowed to do so.

PROPERTY

Property is anything that may be owned and gained lawfully. Property can be real or personal and anything that is not real property is personal property. Each type of property has unique features that distinguish one from the other.

Personal Property

Personal property refers to those items that are not permanently attached to land and are usually moveable and portable. Essentially, personal property is everything other than real property and is often referred to as movable property. [C.C. §663] Personal property can also be referred to as **personalty** or **chattel**.

Personal property can be transferred or sold using a bill of sale and may be pledged as security for a loan. Some examples of personal property include cash, negotiable instruments, securities, royalties, goods, emblements, intangible assets, cars, boats, airplanes, bank accounts, wages, furniture, equipment, insurance policies, jewelry, and patents.

Real Property

The components of **real property** include the land, anything permanently attached to the land, anything appurtenant to the land, or anything immovable by law. [C.C. §658]

In addition to the physical real estate, real property includes the legal bundle of rights inherent in the ownership of real property. The terms real property and real estate are often used interchangeably. Real property is immovable and is usually transferred or sold by a deed. When real property is sold, anything that has become attached to it goes to the buyer as part of the sale unless other arrangements have been made.

Land

The physical component of real property is land. Land is three-dimensional because **land** includes the surface, limited quantities of airspace above the surface, and the materials and minerals beneath the surface to the center of the earth (subsurface). [C.C. §659]. A good illustration of this concept is an inverted pyramid with the tip at the center of the earth and its base extending out into the sky above the property to a reasonable height.

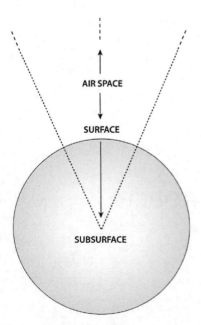

The surface is the topsoil and the rights to the use of the soil. Surface rights include the right to build on the land, grow crops, hunt, fish, and the basic enjoyment of the land. Surface rights also include the right to drill or mine through the surface when subsurface rights are involved.

Attachments

Items permanently attached to the land are real property and belong to the owner. These items include natural attachments, improvements, and fixtures. [C.C. §660].

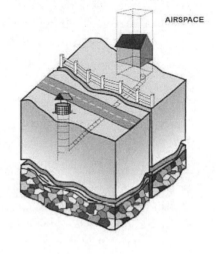

Natural Attachments

Real property includes natural attachments. Natural attachments are growing plants attached by their roots, such as trees, shrubs, and flowers. The two types of natural attachments are *fructus naturales* and *fructus industriales*.

Fructus Naturales

Fructus naturales are naturally occurring plant growth, such as grasses, trees, and shrubs and are considered part of the real property. Therefore, when a home is sold, the planted trees and landscaping are real property and are included in the sale.

Mushrooms growing wild in the fields and the berries on wild raspberry bushes are real property, until picked. When this occurs, the mushrooms and berries become personal property of the person who picked them and they may be sold separate from the land.

Fructus Industriales

Fructus industriales are annual crops produced by human labor, such as fruits, nuts, vegetables, and grains. The main difference between cultivated plants and wild plants is that cultivated plants are considered personal property even before they are harvested.

Example: Pat owns a home on 10 acres. Pat allocated part of the acreage for a small vegetable garden and seven of the acres to a vineyard. Wild blackberry bushes grow on both sides of the creek, which is the boundary to her property. Every year, Pat hires a local crew to harvest her grapes. The vineyard is personal property since the crops are produced by human labor. However, the wild blackberries are real property while on the bushes. If the harvesting crew picks the berries for their personal use or consumption, the blackberries become the personal property of the person who picked them. The blackberries are *fructus naturales* and do not belong to Pat because they are not the result of human cultivation or labor.

Established trees are considered immovable by law and must be sold with the property. For example, a seller may not sell the property and exclude the orange grove from the sale. The seller may have sold the oranges as personal property, but the actual orange trees are real property and may not be excluded from the sale.

Emblements

Emblements are a specific type of *fructus industriales*. **Emblements** are annual crops cultivated by tenant farmers and sharecroppers. Tenant farmers are individuals who lease land for agricultural use. Sharecroppers are individuals who agree with a landowner to grow crops on the land and at harvest time to share with the owner a portion of the harvested crop as payment of rent for the use of the land. The crops are the personal property of the farmer—not the landowner. The tenant farmer has an irrevocable license to enter the land to care for and harvest the crop.

If a large tract of farmland is being sold, it is important to have a written agreement stating who will retain ownership of the crops that are growing in the field. The emblements rule does not apply to ornamental trees, rose bushes, or any other type of perennial growth.

Improvements

Improvements, such as houses, garages, fences, swimming pools, or anything resting on the land to become permanent are owned as a part of the land.

Fixtures

A **fixture** is anything that is permanently attached to real property. It also includes anything permanently attached to the fixture, such as the door to a cabinet. When real property is sold, the buyer may assume that all fixtures will remain with the property, unless there is a written agreement to the contrary.

Tests to Determine Status of a Fixture

If there is a dispute, there are five tests used to determine if property is considered a fixture or personal property. The tests are agreement of the parties, method of attachment, adaptation, intent of the parties, and the relationship of the parties.

Agreement of the Parties

When there has been no clear agreement between the parties in a dispute about fixtures, the courts will apply this test to determine who is in the right.

> Example: Imagine that you are a prospective buyer. You walk into a house and fall in love with the chandelier hanging from the ceiling in the dining room. You make an offer to buy the house, it is accepted, and the escrow goes through smoothly. The sellers get their money and you get the deed to the house.
>
> When you arrive with your moving van, your anticipation turns to hostility when you discover a lonely light bulb hanging where the elegant chandelier had been. The former owners wonder why you are annoyed when you call to arrange the return of your chandelier. They tell you it is not your chandelier; it has been in the family for generations. They never intended it to go with the house.
>
> If you did not know the difference between real and personal property, you might think the sellers had a right to the chandelier.

Part of a real estate agent's job is to make sure all parties involved in a sale know what goes and what stays. In the above case, the listing agent should have asked the sellers if they wanted to keep the chandelier and disclose to prospective buyers that the chandelier is not included in the sale of the house.

Since it was not excluded from the listing, it was reasonable for the buyer to assume it was real property. It had become a fixture and therefore should have gone with the sale.

When a buyer makes an offer on a property, there is a section in the offer-to-purchase contract where he or she may request any item of real or personal property, such as the chandelier, washer and dryer, a refrigerator, or a bedspread that matches the custom drapes. The buyer should always put an intention in writing to make sure the seller is informed and agrees.

Method of Attachment

The next criterion to consider is whether or not a piece of property is attached. Most believe this to be the overruling factor, but the first and primary factor is whether an agreement exists between the parties. If the buyers and sellers have not agreed that a particular item is included in a sale, the next step is to look at the method of attachment. In the law of real property, fixtures are anything that is permanently attached to real property by man or by nature.

An item, such as a painting hung on a wall, is personal property. It is not considered permanently attached to the property. It is only hung on a hook or similar attachment and can be easily lifted away from the wall.

What if a mural is painted by a famous artist on the living room wall? A mural painted directly on a wall, even if it is painted by a famous artist, is considered a fixture because it is attached to the wall. If the painting is worth $50,000 and the house is worth $50,000, it might be worth a try for the seller to remove it. However, the only way it can be taken by the seller is through a fully executed written agreement between the buyer and the seller. If there are any concerns related to the form and content of this type of agreement, the salesperson should tell his or her client to seek legal advice and assistance in creating a clause or addendum to the sales contract.

Adaptation

Was the item made specifically for the property? For example, have the drapes been custom-made for the windows? Was the carpet cut to fit the specific size or shape of the rooms? Is the oven built into the counter? If so, each has become a fixture and is no longer personal property.

The test of adaptation considers whether an item materially affects the use of the property as intended in the contract. In other words, does a particular item substantially adapt to a property for its intended use?

Intention

What does the agreement of the parties include? What did they agree to? Is there a meeting of the minds over the related item? All parties must be in agreement for a contract to exist. When the two parties to a contract agree, it overrules all other criteria for determining if property is real or personal property.

> Example: A house is listed for sale. It is a three bedroom, two-bath house priced at $175,000. There is a wagon wheel light hanging from the ceiling in a modern living room, with modern furniture and white walls. The wagon wheel light fixture seems out of place as a centerpiece in this modern living space. When the listing is taken, the listing agent neglects to ask the sellers if there are any fixtures that they wish to take with them when the house is sold.
>
> The sellers receive an offer on their home in only a week's time. Before the buyers' agent writes the offer, the buyers ask their agent about the wagon wheel light fixture, which seems out of place. The buyers' agent acknowledges the buyers' concern and writes in the offer that the wagon wheel light is to be left with the property. In this case, the sellers reluctantly decide to include the light fixture (even though it is a family heirloom) and accept the offer as written.
>
> Comment: Because the buyers' agent confirmed in the offer that the wagon wheel light fixture was included in the sale of the home, a meeting of the minds occurred when the sellers accepted the offer. The contract is binding. When taking a Listing Agreement, it is important for the agent to ask the sellers if there are any fixtures they wish to exclude from the sale.

Miscommunication may occur in conversation. Suppose the seller is home when a buyer arrives to see it. When the buyer and seller are in the kitchen, the buyer looks at the seller and then points at the refrigerator and asks, "What about the refrigerator?" The seller quickly responds, "It goes."

Problem: What did the buyer hear? The buyer heard that "The refrigerator goes with the house." What did the seller mean? The seller meant, "The refrigerator goes with me to Wyoming."

Solution: Always clarify agreements in writing when conversations like this occur. Miscommunication can occur easily, but when all parties to an agreement read and sign a document, the possibility of a dispute is minimized.

Relationship of the Parties

In a dispute about fixtures, when there is no convincing evidence of the right of one party, courts will look at whether the parties are landlord-tenant, lender-borrower, or buyer-seller. The court then makes a decision based on the relationship of the parties in the case. Usually the court will favor the tenant over the landlord, the lender over the borrower, and the buyer over the seller.

Exception - Trade Fixtures

Trade fixtures are considered personal property not real property. **Trade fixtures** are fixtures that are attached to real estate by a tenant, usually for the purpose of conducting a trade or business from a commercial property. Courts normally rule that tenant-owned trade fixtures do not become the property of the landlord, even when attached to the real estate. However, the tenant must remove the trade fixtures, prior to the end of the lease without significant damage to the building. [C.C. §1013]. Therefore, when selling a commercial building that is currently occupied by businesses, be sure to  include in the contract an inventory list of everything that could possibly be construed as a trade fixture.

Appurtenances

Appurtenant means belonging to. **Appurtenances** are all those rights, privileges, and improvements that belong to and pass with the transfer of the property, but that are not necessarily a part of the actual property. Therefore, an appurtenance does not exist apart from the land to which it belongs.

Appurtenances to real property pass with the real property to which they are appurtenant, unless a contrary intention is written. Typical appurtenances are air rights, water rights, support rights, subsurface rights, easements, rights-of-way, and any property improvements. [C.C. §662].

Air Rights

Air rights are the rights an owner of real property has to the air space above the property to a reasonable height. As real property, air rights can be sold, leased, or encumbered separately from the land.

Air rights can be severed or restricted under certain circumstances. The United States Code §40110 allows reasonable use of the airspace above real property as a public highway for the navigation of airplanes, satellites, and spacecraft. Often the height of telecommunication towers, water tanks, power line poles, and signs is restricted near airports or in areas where there could be over flight of aircraft.

Additionally, there may be restrictions on the placement of trees or other tall structures that would either block a neighbor's view or dramatically impair the amount of sunlight that would otherwise naturally occur on a neighbor's property.

Water Rights

In addition to the rights that someone acquires to use the land, fee simple ownership may have certain appurtenant rights in the waters located on, adjacent to, or beneath one's property. The extent of such rights, and the use that can be made of each kind of water, however, are quite different from one another.

Water in its natural state on the surface of the land or underground is real property. All water within California is the property of the State. Therefore, a water right in California is a property right allowing the use of water, but it does not involve ownership of the water. Because of the many disputes over the use of water, the law is very clear about the rights of owners. California's water law is contained in the California Code of Regulations, Title 23, found at: www.calregs.com. Due to the complex nature of water rights in California, the following is merely a brief overview. For more information go to the State Water Resources Control Board at www.swrcb.ca.gov.

Types of Water

California recognizes two sources of water—surface water and groundwater. It is important to know the types of water because the California water rights system is based on the type of water.

Surface Water

Surface water is the water found on the land in watercourses, such as natural springs, streams, or rivers and in bodies of water, such as ponds or lakes. It also includes drainage water, storm water, and floodwater until it replenishes groundwater by percolating through the soil. Drainage water is typically runoff after rainfall or snowmelt over a tract of land.

Groundwater

Groundwater is the water beneath the surface of the land that fills the spaces and cavities between the rocks and soil. California has three legally recognized classifications of groundwater: subterranean streams, underflow of surface waters, and percolating groundwater. Percolating groundwater has two sub-classifications: overlying land use and surplus groundwater.

Water Rights

California's system of water rights is based on riparian rights, appropriation, percolating groundwater rights, and pueblo rights.

Riparian Rights

The owner of property bordering a surface water source (stream, river, pond, or lakes) has **riparian rights**. Riparian rights apply to surface waters flowing over, adjacent to, or standing on the property (e.g., a lake).

Riparian rights are sometimes referred to as **usufructuary rights**—that is, they are limited to the reasonable and beneficial use of the surface water for beneficial purposes on the riparian lands. The surface water cannot be owned, nor can it be channeled or dammed for the benefit of one landowner to the detriment of other property owners.

The riparian right is not a personal right; it is part of the land. Therefore, when riparian land is sold, the riparian right remains with the land. If riparian lands are subdivided and sold, any parcels that are no longer adjacent to the water source lose their riparian rights, unless the rights are reserved. A riparian landowner does not have to use his or her riparian rights. Therefore, a riparian right cannot be lost through non-use. Because riparian rights are part of the land, riparian landowners do not have to apply for a permit to use their water.

Appropriative Water Rights

An **appropriative water right** is the right to take riparian surface water for a beneficial use on non-adjacent property. For purposes of appropriation, subterranean streams and underflow of surface waters are treated like surface water. California policy is that the use of water for domestic purposes is the highest use of water and that the next highest use is for irrigation. Other beneficial uses include fire protection, mining, watering stock, sprinkling to protect crops from heat or frost damage, recreation, industrial, wildlife protection, and power generation.

Prior to 1914, appropriative water rights could be claimed simply by diverting the water, posting a notice, and recording a copy of the notice with the County Recorder. Since 1914, an appropriative water right can only be obtained through application to the State of California Water Resources Control Board (SCWRCB). In California, any legal entity—individuals, trusts, corporations, agencies, etc.—can hold appropriative water rights.

In practice, given the length of time that California has been settled and subject to American law, many watercourses have had their appropriative rights applied for and awarded many years ago. Someone who is interested in asserting an appropriative right should therefore investigate whether a given watercourse is "fully appropriated" before filing for such rights.

Appropriative water rights are considered real property. They can be owned together or separately from the land on which the water is used or diverted. These water rights can be transferred temporarily or permanently from one owner to another.

Appropriative water rights can be lost by five or more years of continuous non-use or by abandonment. The rights to waters lost through abandonment or non-use revert to the public.

Percolating Groundwater Rights

In many areas of California (as, indeed, through the United States), the development of rural properties depend on underground sources of water from wells. This percolating groundwater is treated differently from surface waters. When the Water Commission Act defined the allocation of surface water rights in 1914, it did not address allocation of the percolating groundwater resource. Therefore, percolating groundwater has few regulations.

Under the **doctrine of correlative rights**, landowners overlying percolating groundwater, such as an aquifer, may use the water on an equal and correlative basis. Each owner is treated as having an equal right to groundwater regardless of when first use was initiated. **Overlying rights** are similar to riparian rights and the landowners do not have to obtain a permit to use their percolating groundwater.

Pueblo Rights

California recognizes pueblo rights, which are derived from Spanish law, giving pueblos the right to claim surface water and groundwater under the town. Today, water use under a pueblo right is limited to ordinary municipal purposes that occur within city limits.

Support Rights

A property owner has the right to have his or her property naturally upheld by the soil beneath and by the adjoining properties. Neighboring property owners not only have the obligation to avoid trespasses onto their neighbor's land. They also owe an affirmative duty to provide surrounding properties (or, in some cases, different estates on the surface if the ownership in question is underground) support from landslides and cave-ins. There are two primary kinds of support that neighboring property owners owe to one another. One is known as lateral support; the other is subjacent support.

Lateral Support

Lateral support is a landowner's legally enforceable right to have his or her land in its natural condition held in place from the sides (laterally) by adjoining land so that it will not fall away. Natural condition of the land means it is free from structures or buildings. The owner of the adjoining land cannot change the land in such a way that it weakens or causes the support to collapse causing slippage, cave-in, or landslide.

Adjoining landowners who excavate near their boundary landowner will be liable for damages to the natural condition of the land that results from the removal of the lateral support of a neighbor's property. Therefore, an adjoining owner who excavates into the soil, e.g. foundation, basement, landscaping, etc. must construct a retaining wall (or take other protective measures) to prevent a collapse.

An adjacent property owner downhill from another property owes the neighboring property support to prevent land subsidence. This means that the owner of the lower portion of the land cannot undertake excavation or make a road-cut into a hillside if doing so would undermine the uphill property and cause a landslide or subsidence of structures on the uphill portion.

Astoria, Oregon – Soil Slippage

Example: During the construction of a supermarket parking lot in Astoria, Oregon, the toe of the slope of a hillside was cut off to make more room for parking. A retaining wall was built to keep the slope from moving, but it proved inadequate. In this instance, soil located five city blocks away moved toward this removed slope toe.

As a result, the streets showed a tremendous amount of cracking. There were sewer system pipes that failed and utility service was disrupted. Although city experts announced that the soil was stabilized, it continued to creep at a slower rate.

Victorian home damaged by soil movement. Note the house was tilting to the left.

Many historic houses, such as the Victorian home shown in the photograph, suffered damage due to the soil movement. In fact, a few houses were condemned because the damage was so extensive.

Astoria, Oregon – Soil Slippage (continued)

A Lutheran Church was located very close to the site of the removed hillside. The church had damage in the main sanctuary and huge cracks in the church basement that compromised the structure's integrity. The cost to repair the improvements on the church property was estimated to exceed $1,100,000.

In this case, a well-known community leader, the city of Astoria, and others were plaintiffs. The case was settled during the trial when all parties realized that it was in their best interest to come to a compromise rather than to continue paying the price of litigation.

Subjacent Support

Subjacent support is the absolute right of the property owner to have his or her land supported from beneath its surface. The owner of the land below the surface has a duty to retain the natural condition of the land and cannot alter it in a way that weakens the subjacent support of the adjoining property. Someone excavating below ground or removing minerals, oil, or gas owes the surface owner subjacent support.

The construction of buildings on the surface of the land does not lessen a person's right to subjacent support. The surface owner may sue the subsurface when the land actually subsides, not when the excavation is made.

> ### Hollywood Blvd. Subsidence and Sinkhole
>
> The Los Angeles Metropolitan Transit Authority (MTA) was constructing a subway tunnel along Hollywood Boulevard for the Red Line subway project. During construction in August 1994, the subway tunnel roof partially collapsed resulting in the subsidence of a several-block-long section of Hollywood Boulevard. Because the subsidence was nearly 12 inches, transit officials were forced to shut down the street for nearly five months.
>
> Ten months later, in June 1995, a massive sinkhole developed on Hollywood Boulevard west of Vermont Avenue. Three blocks of Hollywood Boulevard were closed, a gas pipe was broken, and local residents were evacuated.
>
> The cause was attributed to a variety of factors, including water content in the soil and the alleged use of improper materials in the support shield of the tunnel.
>
> In an effort to mitigate the damage, the MTA helped businesses offset their losses by subsidizing rents, granting interest free loans, and other monetary compensation.

Subsurface Rights

Subsurface rights are the rights to the natural resources, such as minerals, oil, and gas below the surface. The rights to the minerals, oil, and gas can be sold or leased separately. Oil and gas are considered migratory minerals and may not be owned until taken from the ground, at which time they become the personal property of whoever removed them.

Easements

An **easement** is a right, privilege, or interest limited to a specific purpose which one party has in the land of another. Common examples include easements for the purposes of access to adjoining land and access to public utility equipment and services.

Rights of Way

A **right of way** is a legal right to pass over another person's land. A public right of way is a designated area, such as a sidewalk, footpath, bridleway, bike path, or any alley street, or road that is dedicated to public use.

LEGAL DESCRIPTIONS

Along with understanding the rights inherent in owning property, the identification of the property itself is necessary through a legal description. A **legal description** is a written description of a particular parcel of land that identifies it as precisely as possible. A street address is an informal reference and is not sufficient for a legal description. It only tells you how to find a property, but does not tell you the boundaries of the property. A legal description should be written in such a way that any person in the future would be able to understand the description and determine the property location, with reasonable certainty.

The sales contract should have a legal description of the property to be conveyed. A real estate licensee needs to be careful when writing the legal description in a contract. An inaccuracy in the legal description written in a contract or described in a deed can create serious problems for the owner and possible financial liability on the part of the broker.

> Example: A salesperson inadvertently writes the wrong legal description on a purchase contract that is completed for a buyer purchasing a small lot on which the buyer intends to build a home. After the transaction closes, the buyer begins the construction of the home. At that point, the error in the legal description is discovered. Fortunately, the lot that was purchased was small. In this case, it may only cost the broker a few thousand dollars to correct the error.

> Note: There could be other situations like this that would be much more costly to a broker, depending on the price and size of the property that is purchased and the resulting problems that an error in the legal description creates for the buyer.

> Solution: To ensure accuracy, if the legal description is complicated, it is good practice to photocopy and attach the copy to the contract.

In today's world, legal descriptions of property result from land surveys that are completed by qualified surveyors. Legal descriptions and surveys are important to a real estate transaction. They provide evidence of the location and area of the land that is involved in the transfer of ownership.

Surveys

Surveyors complete surveys by measuring angles and distances in accordance with specific procedures. A **survey** is the professional measurement of a tract of land with its boundaries, contents, and location relative to other property. A survey includes the total area of the land with its mapped boundaries and elevation.

When measuring land, a surveyor uses datum. A **datum** is a point, line, or surface against which measurements are made. Horizontal datums use longitude and latitude. Vertical datums are used to measure height as in a condominium unit or depth, such as subsurface mineral rights. The most common datum used in the United States is mean sea level. Starting at a datum, government survey teams establish benchmarks to act as reference points for surveying. A **benchmark** is a survey reference mark made on a monument indicating a known location and elevation.

In addition, surveyors use bearings, distances, and courses. **Bearings** are compass directions of a survey line, **distances** are linear measurements, and **courses** are directions of a line as it varies from north or south. If a boundary is a navigable river or lake, this boundary is called a **meander line**.

The surveyor begins with a benchmark from which a point of beginning (POB) can be determined. From the POB, the surveyor takes bearings and courses to describe the direction of travel and delineate the perimeter of the property. Directions are measured and described in degrees. There are 360 degrees in a circle, 60 minutes in each degree, and 60 seconds in each minute. A second of a minute of a degree may seem small, but a measurement that is off by a second could equate to several miles on a map. A surveyor may use rods, poles, and perches, all of which are the same length. 320 rods, poles, or perches make up a linear mile.

The two basic elements of a survey are actual and improvement. The **actual survey** describes the land with its exact boundaries and provides the legal description of the property. After the actual survey is performed, a **survey sketch** is completed, which is a drawing that shows the location and dimensions of the property. An **improvement survey** shows the location, size, and dimensions of buildings on the tract of land.

Land surveys have many uses in real estate transactions. For example, a physical survey is made to determine the boundaries and building locations of a property that will be conveyed. Lenders require surveys to show that there are no structures encroaching on a property and that the improvements are within code requirements. Surveys are made to prepare subdivision maps.

Methods of Description

The three common ways to describe property are metes and bounds, Public Land Survey System, and the recorded plat system. The Public Land Survey System describes more land (in surface area) in the United States than any other method. However, when based on the number of properties, the recorded plat method is the most frequently used method to describe land.

Metes and Bounds

The **metes and bounds** description is the oldest method used to describe real property. **Metes** mean measurements in length (measured in feet) from one monument to another. **Bounds** refer to the direction. The direction of the boundary lines are given in degrees (°), minutes ('), and seconds (").

A metes and bounds description measures the dimensions of the property using direction and distance between landmarks and monuments. A **landmark** is a geographic feature, such as a large rock, an old tree, a fork in a creek, or the intersection of two roads. A landmark may also refer to a monument (Washington Monument), prominent building (the White House), or structure (Statue of Liberty). **Monuments** used by surveyors are man-made objects, such as stakes or iron posts. Both landmarks and monuments are used as a point of reference to establish the boundaries of the property, locate its corners, or identify the point at which the boundary changes direction.

Land that is irregular in shape or cannot be described using other methods may have a metes and bounds description. In a metes and bounds description almost every tract of land has a different shape and size. Some are simply box or rectangle-shaped. Other lots are called **chair lots**, because they resemble the shape of a chair. Because of the irregular shapes, surveyors must be able to draw a tract with extreme accuracy. A metes and bounds description is often lengthy, because it must identify each line and angle.

When beginning a metes and bounds description, the surveyor first identifies the benchmark and determines the point of beginning. The **point of beginning (POB)** is the point from which a metes and bounds survey begins. The point of beginning is also called point of commencement or place of beginning. The description continues by following the boundaries of the land, measuring the distances between landmarks, and returning to the beginning of the survey. Sometimes this is referred to as the **terminus**. A metes and bounds land description always ends at the POB, so that the boundary of the survey produces a closed area.

Example: Description of an uneven, hilly parcel of land with an avocado grove in Vista, California:

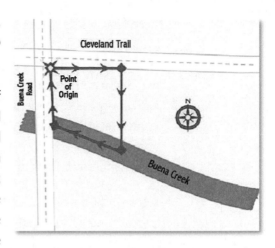

Beginning at the intersection of the east line of Buena Creek Road and the south line of Cleveland Trail; thence east along the south line of Cleveland Trail 300 feet; thence south 657.5 feet to the center line of Buena Creek; thence northwesterly along the center line of Buena Creek to its intersection with the east line of Buena Creek Road; thence north 325 feet along the east line of Buena Creek road to the place of beginning.

When reading a metes and bounds description in a deed, the survey lines will state distance and direction. The direction is always based upon compass readings, but the distance can be described in varying units. In old deeds, the length of boundaries may be stated in rods or poles instead of feet or meters. Names of adjacent property, landmarks, roads, or streams are a part of the legal description in a metes and bounds survey. If there is a creek, stream, or river along one boundary of the property, the term *meanders* will be used in the land description, which will read something like "...*thence along the meanders of said river to the first fork.*" There is usually no distance shown in this part of the land description. The directive in the deed or survey is simply to "follow the river" from one given point to another given point.

Review – Metes and Bounds Survey System
- Boundary of the survey must produce a closed area
- Bearing of the courses must be continuous from the POB around the area of the tract of land until the final course ends at the terminus
- Bearings must be given the same basis of true direction

Interpreting Metes and Bounds Descriptions

It may be difficult to interpret a metes and bounds description. For example, a landmark, such as the large oak tree, may have died or been cut down. Creeks and streams may have dried up or changed course. Roads, walls, fences, posts, markers, or stakes may have been used to determine the real boundaries, but these features sometimes move, change, or disappear over time. Canals and drainage ditches may be filled in and streets may be closed, widened, or have their names changed. When the time comes to survey the land again, for instance when property is sold, subdivided, or built on, it may be difficult or nearly impossible to identify the exact location of its boundaries, based on the original land description. With tracts of land that have been in the same family for generations, tradition and actual use can help to determine boundaries that have lost certain identifiable landmarks.

If conflicts do occur, there are rules to follow that can be helpful when determining which legal description will control.

Priorities in Metes and Bounds Descriptions

1. Natural or permanent monuments are used over less permanent ones.
2. Lot and block descriptions are more widely accepted than metes and bounds descriptions.
3. Map references generally control a metes and bounds description.
4. If the call (description) for a monument refers to one having width, the boundary line generally extends to the center of such monument. For example, land adjoining highways and streets vests title to the center of the street.

Public Land Survey System

By the late 19th century, the U.S. government had established a system of land description for new territories, states, and other public lands. It was known as the U.S. Government Section and Township Survey or the rectangular survey system. Currently, it is known as the **Public Land Survey System (PLSS)**.

When a survey is done using the PLSS, all its distances and bearings are measured from two imaginary lines that are at right angles to each other. These two lines, from which the measurements are made, are the **principal meridians**, which run north and south, and the **base lines** that run east and west. Both are located by reference to degrees of longitude and latitude. The intersection of principal meridian and base lines creates grids, which form the basis for surveying and measuring all the lands within the territory that they control.

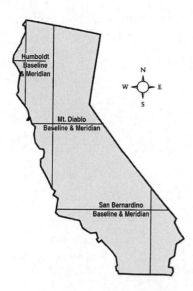

In California there are three such starting points: the Humboldt Baseline and Meridian (Northwestern California), the Mt. Diablo Baseline and Meridian (Northeastern and Central California), and the San Bernardino Baseline and Meridian (Southern California).

After establishing a starting point at the intersection of a chosen principal meridian and baseline, the government surveyors drew imaginary vertical lines called **range lines** every six miles east and west of the meridian to form columns called **ranges**. Each range was numbered either east or west of the principal meridian. For example, the first range east of the meridian was called Range 1 East (R1E), and the first range west of the meridian was called Range 1 West (R1W).

Imaginary **township lines** were drawn every six miles north and south of the baseline to form a horizontal row or **tier of townships**. These rows were numbered according to their distance from the baseline. For example, the first row of **townships** north of the baseline was called Township 1 North (T1N) and the first row of townships south of the baseline was called Township 1 South (T1S).

Thus, a grid of squares, called **townships**—each six miles by six miles (36 square miles)—appears. Townships run east and west in ranges and north and south in tiers. Each township is described by its location, relative to the intersection of the baseline and meridian we have just discussed. A particular township in the fourth tier north of the baseline and in the third range west of the meridian—with "T" for township and "R" for range—would be described as follows: T4N, R3W, San Bernardino Baseline and Meridian.

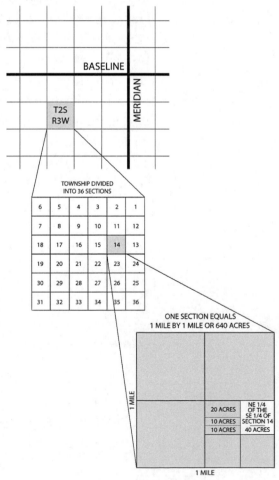

The way to locate T4N, R3W is to start at the intersection of the baseline and meridian and count up (or north) four rows and then count to the left (or west) three rows.

Each township is six miles square and contains 36 square miles. Each township is divided into 36 squares, which are called **sections**. Sections are one mile square and contain 640 acres.

The sections are numbered, starting with section 1 in the northeast corner and continuing in a snake-like manner to section 36 in the southeast corner. A section may then be divided further into quarter sections containing 160 acres each and then divided into smaller and smaller parcels.

Using the PLSS, a particular piece of property could be described as the Northeast quarter of the Southeast quarter of section 14, Township 2 South, Range 3 West. It is normally expressed as a legal description in abbreviated form: NE ¼ of the SE ¼ of the section 14, T2S, R3W. The quickest way to calculate the acreage contained within this description is to multiply the fractions by 640 acres (acres within a section). ¼ x ¼ x 640 = 40 acres.

Recorded Plat

The **recorded plat system** describes property by identifying the registered lot and the block on a recorded subdivision plat or survey. The recorded plat system is also called the lot and block system or subdivision map system. It is one of the easiest and most widely used methods of describing land. A **plat** is a subdivision map filed with the county recorder's office that shows the location and boundaries (lot and block number) of individual parcels of land (lots), street right-of-way, subdivision name, and easements. Lots and blocks are assigned numbers or letters. A **lot** is a single parcel of land that will be sold within a subdivision to a buyer. A **block** is a contiguous group of lots, which are generally bounded by man-made features, such as streets or natural features, such as creeks.

When developers divide parcels of land into lots, they are required by the California Subdivision Map Act to prepare and record a subdivision map or plat map. The subdivision map shows the location and boundaries of each separate new lot in the subdivision and the map must be recorded in the county recorder's office. Each

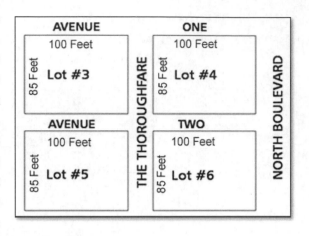

lot in a subdivision is identified by number, as is the block in which it is located; each lot and block is in a referenced tract. The platting process ensures that all lots comply with the local city's standards for development. Plats are reviewed for compliance with regulations regarding minimum lot size, street access and width, setback distance, utility provisions, building codes, open space provisions, and drainage regulations.

After the **subdivision map** has been filed or recorded, it is public knowledge and is available to anyone. When a parcel of land lies within an existing platted subdivision, the legal description is usually short and straightforward. This is because the dimensions and boundaries of the parcel have already been described in detail in the subdivision plat at the time it was recorded in the public records of the county. Therefore, the legal description of a parcel is written in simple terms.

> Example: Lots 3 and 4, Block 3, Lakeside Acres, Any County, State of California.
>
> The subject parcels of land are depicted on the subdivision plat as two particular lots lying within a particular block of the subdivision plat. This short description is sufficient because the legal description of this parcel has already been described in detail in the subdivision plat recorded under the name of Lakeside Acres in Any County, California.

Each subdivision plat accepted by the public agency having jurisdiction over the development of the subdivision will be given a unique name. Subdivision names are not duplicated.

Subdivisions are commonplace in urban and suburban areas. As cities are developed, the recorded plat system is extremely useful in simplifying the process of describing the land to be developed, sold, and recorded.

SUMMARY

In common law, the word property refers more to the rights that the owner has in property than to the fact that the property is owned. Property rights are known as the bundle of rights. The bundle of rights consists of all legal rights that are attached to the ownership of property, which include the right to possess, use, enjoy, and dispose of property.

Anything that may be owned and gained lawfully is known as property. Property can be real or personal. Personal property refers to those items that are not permanently attached to land and are usually moveable and portable. Real property is the land and the bundle of rights inherent with its ownership. Land includes both the land and anything attached to it by nature from the center of the earth into the sky above the property. The components of land include air rights, surface rights, subsurface rights, water rights, and support rights.

Items permanently attached to the land are real property and belong to the owner. Improvements, such as houses, garages, fences, swimming pools, or anything resting on the land to become permanent are owned as a part of the property. A fixture is anything that is permanently attached to real property. It also includes anything permanently attached to the fixture, such as the door to a cabinet.

Along with understanding the rights inherent in owning property, the identification of the property itself is necessary through surveys and land descriptions. A survey is a professional analysis of a property and its location relative to other property. A survey includes the total area of the land with its mapped boundaries and elevation. A benchmark is a survey reference point from which a metes and bounds survey will begin and is a permanent object or location that is easily found.

Legal descriptions are important to a real estate transaction. A legal description is a written description of a particular parcel of land in a way that identifies it as clearly and precisely as possible. A street address is not sufficient for a legal description. The three common legal descriptions currently used in the United States are recorded plat, the Public Land Survey System, and metes and bounds.

UNIT 2 REVIEW

Matching Exercise

Instructions: Write the letter of the matching term on the blank line before its definition. Answers are in Appendix A.

Terms

A. air rights

B. appropriative water rights

C. appurtenances

D. benchmark

E. block

F. bundle of rights

G. emblements

H. fixture

I. fructus industriales

J. fructus naturales

K. groundwater

L. lateral support

M. legal description

N. lot

O. metes and bounds

P. personal property

Q. plat

R. point of beginning

S. real property

T. riparian rights

U. subjacent support

V. subsurface rights

W. survey

X. township

Y. usufructuary rights

Definitions

1. _____ All legal rights attached to the ownership of property

2. _____ Moveable items not permanently attached to land

3. _____ Land, anything permanently attached to the land, anything appurtenant to the land, or anything immovable by law

4. _____ Naturally occurring plant growth, such as grasses, trees, and shrubs as part of the real property

5. _____ Annual crops produced by human labor, such as fruits, nuts, vegetables, and grains

6. _____ Annual crops cultivated by tenant farmers and sharecroppers

7. _____ Anything permanently attached to real property

8. _____ Rights to the air space above the property

9. _____ All rights, privileges, and improvements that belong to and pass with the transfer of the property, but that are not necessarily a part of the actual property

10. _____ Water beneath the surface of the land filling the spaces and cavities between the rocks and soil

11. _____ Right of an owner of property bordering a surface water source to use the water

12. _____ Rights limited to reasonable and beneficial use

13. _____ Right to take riparian surface water for a beneficial use on non-adjacent property

14. _____ Landowners' right to have their land in its natural condition held in place from the sides by adjoining land so that it will not fall away

15. _____ Absolute right of the property owner to have his or her land supported from beneath its surface

16. _____ Rights to the natural resources, such as minerals, oil, and gas below the surface

17. _____ Written description of a particular parcel of land identifying it as precisely as possible

18. _____ Professional measurement of a tract of land with its boundaries, contents, and location relative to other property

19. _____ Survey reference mark made on a monument indicating a known location and elevation

20. _____ Oldest method used to describe real property

21. _____ Point from which a metes and bounds survey begins

22. _____ Grid of square, each six miles by six miles (36 square miles)

23. _____ Subdivision map showing the location and boundaries of lots, street rights-of-way, project name, and easements

24. _____ Single parcel of land within a subdivision

25. _____ Contiguous group of lots generally bounded by man-made features, such as streets or natural features, such as creeks

Multiple Choice Questions

Instructions: Circle your response and go to Appendix A to read the complete explanation for each question.

1. Tom and Sarah have decided to sell their home. Which of the bundle of rights gives them the right to sell their property?
   a. Right of enjoyment
   b. Right of possession
   c. Right to transfer
   d. Right to use

2. What is the commonality of air rights, surface rights, and subsurface rights?
   a. Bundle of rights
   b. Contracts
   c. Land
   d. Personal property

3. Of the following, which would not be considered permanently attached and therefore is not real property?
   a. Ranch style, 3-bedroom, 2-bath home
   b. A crop of wheat ready to be harvested
   c. Wild red raspberry bushes
   d. A recently installed skylight on the roof of a cottage

4. Which of the following statements is correct when determining whether property is personal or real?
   a. If no agreement exists between the parties, the next step is to look at the method of attachment.
   b. The adaptation of the property is the first and primary factor.
   c. The intention of the parties is only a qualifier to distinguish real or personal property.
   d. The method of attachment should be the first and primary factor.

5. Mike leased commercial space from Jim, for his pizza business. Mike bought and attached a restaurant-sized pizza oven. He plans to take it to a new location upon expiration of the lease. What is the status of the oven at the end of the lease?

    a. As an attached fixture, the oven is real property belonging to Jim.

    b. The oven is a trade fixture belonging to Jim, so he can leave it for the next tenant or remove it.

    c. The oven is Mike's personal property, and he must remove the oven even if it means damaging the unit.

    d. Since the oven is a trade fixture, Mike may remove it as long as he does not damage the space.

6. What is the commonality of "subterranean", "percolating", and "overlying land use"?

    a. Appropriation

    b. Groundwater

    c. Riparian rights

    d. Surface water

7. Which doctrine allows landowners overlying percolating groundwater, such as an aquifer, to use the water on an equal basis?

    a. Correlative rights

    b. Laches

    c. Precedent

    d. Relation back

8. Which of the following is true of a legal description?

    a. It is a written description of a particular parcel of land that identifies it as precisely as possible.

    b. A street address is not sufficient to be a legal description.

    c. It should be able to be valid indefinitely.

    d. All of the above are true about legal descriptions.

9. Which of the following would not be a type of legal description?

    a. The NW ¼ of the SW ¼ of the section

    b. Beginning at a point on the north side of King Street 40 feet East from the corner formed by the intersection of the East boundary of Rose Road and the north boundary of King Street; thence East 80 degrees 100 feet; thence north 200 feet; thence West 100 feet; thence direct to the POB

    c. 1375 Rose Road, Any City, County of Sutton, State of California

    d. Lot 9, Block 4, Riverview, County of Sutton, State of California

10. What type of legal description uses grids to determine the location of a specific tract of land?
    a. Recorded map
    b. Metes and bounds
    c. Lot and block
    d. Public Land Survey System

Real Property Interests

Unit 3

INTRODUCTION

In 1066, William of Normandy crossed the English Channel and defeated a Saxon army in the Battle of Hastings; thereafter, he became known as William the Conqueror. As King William I of England, he introduced a land-holding system, commonly known as the feudal system, which is the basis for real property law in both England and the United States today.

When considering the various legal relationships to land that are based on this English heritage, it is helpful to define some terms at the outset. The broadest term, an **interest**, includes any of the various rights, privileges, powers, and immunities with respect to any kind of property, including real property. The totality of all rights, privileges, powers, and immunities with respect to a particular item of property is "complete ownership" or "complete property."

Learning Objectives

After completing this unit, you should be able to:

3A classify freehold estates.

3B recall leasehold estates.

3C differentiate voluntary liens from involuntary liens.

3D categorize non-financial encumbrances.

3E identify homestead exemptions.

INTERESTS IN REAL PROPERTY

Real property interests can be categorized in a number of different ways. One way to divide them is into possessory and non-possessory interests. A **possessory interest** means the present right to physically occupy land and to exclude others from that same land. A **non-possessory interest** is one that cannot presently be exercised today but which may or will become possessory in the future or under appropriate circumstances.

Another way to categorize the interests that someone can own in land is into present interests and future interests. A **present interest** in land, as the term implies, is one that can be exercised by the owner today. A **future interest** is one that cannot be exercised today, but which might be exercised in the future. Present interests are usually possessory and are often called present possessory interests. While future interests, because they cannot be exercised today, are non-possessory interests. However, they can be bought, sold, and transferred as if they were possessory.

POSSESSORY INTERESTS

An **estate** is the quantity, quality, degree, and nature of a person's interest in real property that may become possessory. Ownership of the estate is measured by its duration—indefinite or definite. An estate with indefinite duration or that is measured by the length of someone's life is classified as a **freehold estate**. Whereas, an estate with a fixed or determinable duration is classified as a **nonfreehold estate**.

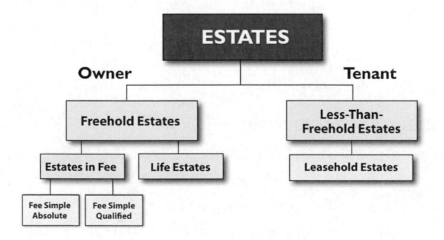

Freehold Estates

A freehold estate is an estate of indefinite duration. In California, there are three types of freehold estates: fee simple absolute, fee simple defeasible, and life estates.

Fee Simple Absolute Estate

A **fee simple absolute estate**, also referred to as a fee simple, a fee interest, estate in fee, or a fee, is the most complete form of ownership of land under the Anglo-American concept of real property ownership. This is the most common type of estate that is transferred in a normal real estate transaction. It is known as an estate of inheritance or a **perpetual estate** because a fee simple estate can be left to one's heirs via will or other testamentary disposition.

A fee simple absolute is a **present possessory freehold estate** that includes all the rights to sell, exclude others, finance, and do any other thing with real property that the law allows. If the deed by which someone acquires property shows no restrictions on ownership and none can be found in past transactions, then the title is an unencumbered fee simple absolute.

> Example: Paul buys a parcel of land from Sally. The deed by which he acquires the property from her has no restrictions on his use of the land. The title search performed by the title company before he pays her for the land shows no restrictions imposed by any previous owners. Therefore, at the conclusion of his transaction with Sally, Paul has a fee simple absolute.

Under the English notion of land ownership, a fee simple absolute could be divided into various "pieces," both physically and, especially, temporally. That is, someone could convey land today but split apart the present possessory interest from a future, non-possessory interest, with the present interest being conveyed to one person and the future interest to another—and the person making the conveyance could create both interests at the same time in the same deed.

These other freeholds, although they are freeholds (i.e., ownership interests) are each something less than a fee simple absolute. All of these other freehold estates and interests must eventually add up to a fee simple interest, as will be shown in the other examples of freehold estates below.

Fee Simple Defeasible Estates

Several freehold estates are known collectively by the term **fee simple defeasible** or simply as **defeasible fees**. Each of these, like a life estate, is less than a fee simple. Unlike a life estate, they can be conveyed by will or other testamentary instrument; but, as long as the estate lasts, it is subject to a conditional restriction that makes it worth less than a life estate. If the condition specified in the deed or will that creates the defeasible fee takes place, then the fee interest may be set aside.

Fee Simple Determinable

A **fee simple determinable** vested a present possessory interest in a grantee with a reversionary interest in the grantor. Depending on the condition included in the grant, the reversionary interest might (or might not) be exercised. The language used phrases, such as "so long as" or "while" the grantee complied with the condition. If the grantee failed to comply with the condition, the estate automatically terminated and reverted to the grantor.

Walton v. City of Red Bluff

In *Walton* v. *City of Red Bluff* (1992) 2 Cal.App.4th 117 a woman and her son conveyed land to Red Bluff in 1908 and 1916 for the city to use as a library. They also left funds for the support of the library. The instruments that conveyed the land stated, "If the property herein conveyed shall at any time, be abandoned by the said Town of Red Bluff, . . . or if the said property shall cease to be used, for library purposes, by said Town, . . . or shall be put to [any] use other [than] the uses and purposes herein specifically referred to, . . . then the grant and conveyance herein made shall cease and terminate . . ."

In 1986, the city removed the books from the building because of a lack of space, lack of access for handicapped and elderly patrons, and lack of parking. It intended to continue to use the building for public, educational, and entertainment purposes (although not as a library). Walton, a descendant of the original grantors, sued for the reconveyance of the land. The trial court agreed with the city that passage of time had nullified the conditions in the grant, although it did hold that the city had to use the property for some public purpose.

Walton appealed and the appellate court reversed. It construed the language of the original grant as a fee simple determinable and held that, because the city had discontinued the use of the land "for library purposes," Walton had the right to exercise his possibility of reverter.

As the *Walton* case shows, if the grantee ceases to comply with the condition imposed in the grant, then the grantor (or as in *Walton* itself, the grantor's heir) can challenge the original grantee's continuing enjoyment of the determinable fee.

In 1982, the Legislature passed a statute that tried to limit the effect of some of these holdover estates from the common law. The **Marketable Record Title Act**, also known as just the Marketable Title Act, is a comprehensive statute designed "to simplify and facilitate real property title transactions in furtherance of public policy by enabling persons to rely on record title." [C.C. §880.020, (b)].

The public policy declared by the Legislature is that land is a basic resource that should be freely alienable [C.C. §880.020, (a)(1)] and that "interests in real property and defects in titles created at remote times, whether or not of record, often constitute unreasonable restraints on alienation and marketability. . . ." [C.C. §880.020, (a)(2)]. The Legislature also found that these remote interests foment litigation to quiet title and accurate title that "should be determinable to the extent practicable from an examination of recent records only." [C.C. §880.020,(a)(4)].

The Marketable Title Act had a significant impact on defeasible estates. It abolished the fee simple determinable estate, the possibility of reverter, and the right of entry following a fee simple on condition subsequent. Any estate that would have been created with any combination of those interests is now **a fee simple subject to condition subsequent** coupled with a **power of termination**. [C.C. §885.020].

The Marketable Title Act also requires that owners of some of these future interests, including powers of termination, record a notice of their intent to preserve their interest. Failure to record the notice within a given period of time (typically 30 years from the creation of the interest, or 5 years after the adoption of the Act if the 30 years had already expired) normally terminates the interest.

Ironically, in the *Walton* v. *City of Red Bluff* case, the court acknowledged that the plaintiff, Walton, had indeed waited too long after the Act was passed to record a notice of his intention to enforce his ancestor's possibility of reverter. Nevertheless, it ruled in his favor (finding, among other things, that the City held only a fee simple determinable) merely because the City failed to raise the Act as a defense during the trial court proceedings! Had the City been aware of and raised the Act as a defense early in the case, it is doubtful that Walton would have won.

Fee Simple Subject to Condition Subsequent

Since 1983, a **fee simple subject to condition subsequent** is any fee estate containing a condition that if violated, could lead to the termination of the estate and give the grantor a right of entry. Language in a fee simple subject to condition subsequent will describe some condition and, if that condition occurs, the grantor can exercise a right of entry. These conditions typically have words like "until," "unless," "but if" in the condition, so that its occurrence is more clearly a specific event that triggers the right of entry. Before 1983, the future interest was sometimes called a right of reentry.

> Example: Tom conveys land to a City "for the use as a park." The grant states, "If the land is ever not used for a park for a period of two consecutive years, then this grant is abolished and reverts to the grantor." Because the grant contains a reversion to the grantor and has a condition which, if it occurs (in this case, the land not being used for a park for two years) it will cut off the City's interest. Therefore, the City has a fee simple on condition subsequent and Tom (or his heirs) will have a right of entry.

Life Estates

A **life estate** is a present possessory interest that gives the grantee a possessory interest for the length of a measuring life. The **measuring life** is usually the grantee's life—but it does not have to be. It can even be created on the life of a designated person who has no interest in the property as the measuring life—known as **pur autre vie**.

The person to whom a life estate is conveyed is known as the **life tenant**. Since a life estate is a type of freehold, or fee estate, the life tenant has all the rights that go with fee ownership except disposing of the estate by will. Remember, the life estate is tied to a designated life and when that party dies, the estate goes to either the person in reversion or the person in remainder or their heirs.

Life tenants must pay the taxes and maintain the property. They may collect all rents and keep all profits for the duration of the life estate. They may encumber the property or dispose of it in any way except by will. Any interest the life tenants may create in the property—extending beyond the life of the person used to measure the estate—will become invalid when that designated person dies.

Estate in Reversion

If no one is identified as having the ownership of the property after the life tenant's death, then the conveyance automatically reserves a **reversionary interest** in the grantor.

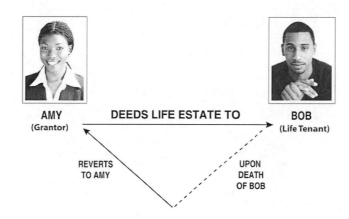

AMY
(Grantor)

DEEDS LIFE ESTATE TO

BOB
(Life Tenant)

REVERTS
TO AMY

UPON
DEATH
OF BOB

Example: Amy conveys a property to her friend Bob. The language in the deed states, "I convey my property at 125 Main Street, Susanville, California, to Bob Smith for life." Following this transaction, Bob is the life tenant and has the right to live at 125 Main Street for as long as he lives. Bob is obligated to pay taxes on the property and is responsible for its condition. If someone is injured on the property, Bob will be named if a lawsuit is filed, because he has the control of the property. Because Amy did not identify anyone to receive the property when Bob dies, the property will revert to Amy upon Bob's death. If Amy dies before Bob, Amy's heirs will inherit the property. However, Bob cannot leave the property to anyone by will upon his death, because Amy has retained this right as part of the conveyance. It in essence is something that Amy did not give to Bob.

Reserving a Life Estate

An elderly couple sells their property to a developer reserving the right to live on the property until their death when the developer will be able to take possession of the property. This is called reserving a life estate.

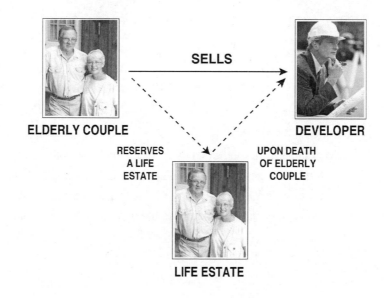

ELDERLY COUPLE

SELLS

DEVELOPER

RESERVES
A LIFE
ESTATE

UPON DEATH
OF ELDERLY
COUPLE

LIFE ESTATE

Pur Autre Vie

Tom grants a life estate to Susan for the life of Elizabeth, with the provision that it goes to Laura when Elizabeth dies. Susan may enjoy the benefits of the life estate as long as Elizabeth is alive. Upon Elizabeth's death, the estate goes to Laura or her heirs.

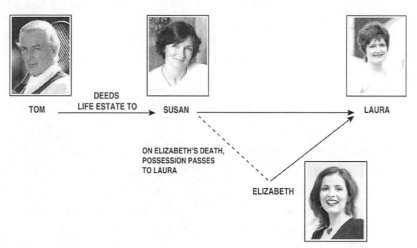

Estate in Remainder

Instead of keeping a reversionary interest, the grantor can instead identify someone to receive the property when the life tenant dies. That interest is known as a remainder and the person identified in the instrument creating the interest is known as the **remainderman**. A **remainder** is a future interest that takes effect upon the expiration of a life estate when the life tenant dies.

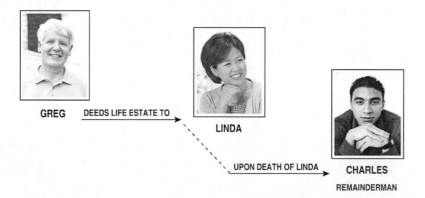

Example: Greg conveys a parcel of land to his friend Linda and the language in the deed states, "I convey my property at 125 Main Street, Susanville, California, to Linda Smith for life, with a remainder to Charles Baker." Following this transaction, Linda is the life tenant and has the right to live at 125 Main Street for as long as she lives. She will have the obligation to pay taxes on the property and will be responsible for its condition because she has a present possessory interest.

Charles has a remainder interest, but has no present right to enter the property or to use it. If he attempts to do anything with the property (e.g., to cut firewood), Linda can have him arrested as a trespasser. If someone is injured on the property, Charles is unlikely to be named if a lawsuit is filed, because he has no present right to control the condition of the property; that belongs exclusively to Linda as long as Linda is alive.

Once Linda dies, the remainder interest and the life estate are merged. Charles's remainder interest exists only while Linda is alive. Immediately upon Linda's death, Charles or his heirs will once again own the complete fee simple interest that Greg "divided" into a life estate and a remainder in the original transaction.

Although, in the example given, Linda has the present possessory interest and Charles has only a future interest that he cannot take advantage of until some unknown time in the future, Linda does have certain obligations to Charles. Just as someone cannot tear down a house that he or she is leasing without the permission of the owner, Linda cannot commit waste. To **commit waste** would be to commit any act that will damage the property in a way that will impair Charles's eventual right to possession of the property. [C.C. §818].

For example, Linda probably cannot tear down a house on the property unless she has a good reason (for example that it is badly damaged by termites and she intends to build a replacement structure). She also must pay the taxes and, if she does not, she might be liable to Charles (or Charles's heirs) if they must step forward and do so in order to protect their future interest.

Although the life estate that Greg created will only last as long as Linda is alive, Linda can "sell" it during her lifetime. That is, she can sell the right to occupy the property as if she owned the full fee simple estate. The "buyer" of the life estate can only buy what Linda has to begin with—namely, the right to use and occupy the property during Linda's lifetime. Once Linda dies, the property will belong to Charles or his heirs just as if Linda had left it to them in a will. How much Linda can obtain for the life estate will probably depend on the buyer's assessment of Linda's health and life expectancy. The buyer would also have the same obligation not to commit waste that Linda herself would have.

In the same way, Charles or his heirs can sell the remainder interest while Linda is alive. The value of that interest is inversely proportional to the value of Linda's life estate—that is, the healthier and likely Linda is to have many more years of life, the less the remainder interest is worth and vice versa.

Nonfreehold Estates

A **nonfreehold estate** is also known as a **leasehold**, which is a tenant's possessory estate in land or premises. As with freehold estates, both the law and much of the terminology for such property relationships are still rooted in medieval concepts today. The most obvious example is a person who owns land and rents it to someone else is commonly referred to as a **landlord** or as a **landlady**—two terms that expressly conjure up images of feudalism and allegiance to vassals. The modern term for this person (male or female) is **lessor**. The holder of a leasehold estate was historically known as a **tenant**. The modern term for the person who rents land and pays for that use is a **lessee**.

Whether referred to as a tenant or a lessee, the person who hires land usually pays some form of monetary consideration, commonly known as **rent**. Although rent is usually money, rent can take the form of some kind of non-monetary compensation, such as the tenant making repairs in exchange for the right to live on the property. Although the relationship between the lessor and lessee is a leasehold, it is commonly referred to as a **tenancy**. During any leasehold, the lessor has a **reversionary interest** because at the end of the lessee's term, the property reverts to the lessor.

There are four basic tenancies recognized by the law today. They differ in how they are initiated, how they are terminated, and in the relationship between the lessor and lessee during the term of each tenancy.

> **Four Types of Leasehold Interests**
> - Periodic tenancy
> - Tenancy for years
> - Tenancy at sufferance
> - Tenancy at will

Periodic Tenancy

A **periodic tenancy** (estate from period-to-period) refers to a leasehold interest that is for an indefinite period of time. The duration of the estate is determined by the term or frequency of rent payment. The most common version of a periodic tenancy is the month-to-month tenancy. California law presumes that renting real property, unless the parties have agreed otherwise, is for a period of 30 days. [C.C. §1944].

> Example: Linda took a consulting job for an accounting firm for six months in a city distant from where she normally lives. She found an apartment, moved

in, and paid rent to the landlord every 30 days. If the rental agreement does not specify a certain end date, she will be able to move out at the end of any 30-day period by giving a 30-day notice of her intention to do so. Linda has a periodic tenancy.

A periodic tenancy automatically renews at the end of each period unless one party, either the lessor or the lessee, gives notice of termination to the other. Notice equal to the length of the period of tenancy must be given to terminate the tenancy. In the absence of such a notice, the lessee is entitled to remain and the lessor to receive rent for the ensuing time period merely by not giving notice of the termination of the tenancy. If a tenancy for years is fulfilled, the tenancy converts to a periodic tenancy after 30 days if the lessor accepts rent.

Tenancy for Years

A **tenancy for years** lease has a fixed term and definite end date. It is sometimes called an estate for years and is what most people in everyday usage mean when they refer to having a lease. An estate for years does not actually have to be for a term of years, but refers to any rental of property with a specific beginning and ending date.

> Example: Linda decided to sign an apartment lease with specific dates when she moved to the city to start her 6-month consulting job for an accounting firm. The lease begins on August 1 and ends on January 31 of the following year. Even though the rental agreement allows her to pay the rent on a monthly basis, she has a tenancy for years.

> Linda would have no legal right to continue on the premises on or after February 1. If she remains at the end of the lease and the parties have not made any other arrangements, the lessor would have the right to initiate a lawsuit for eviction immediately without further notice to her.

Since the end date is mutually agreed upon, notice to terminate is not required. The tenancy terminates automatically at the end of the specified rental period. During the term of a lease, the owner cannot end the tenancy without cause, such as the tenant not paying rent on time.

Tenancy at Sufferance

A **tenancy at sufferance** is often referred to as a **holdover tenancy**. It occurs when the tenant originally obtained possession lawfully, but the tenant's right to remain has expired (as when a lease ends and there is no agreement for an extension or the conversion of that lease to a month-to-month tenancy). If the tenant does not leave, the owner must commence eviction proceedings to remove the tenant.

> Example: Ted had a lease for premises owned by Larry that ran from January 1 through June 30. On July 1, the term of the lease expired and there was no provision for extension of the lease. Ted has not moved out and Larry has not asked him to leave. There have been no discussions about what happens next. Ted has an estate at sufferance because, although he took possession of the premises lawfully, his continued presence on the premises is not covered by the expired rental agreement and there is no other agreement, including compensation of Larry with non-cash remuneration.

A property owner who does not want a tenant to remain past the expiration of a lease is well-advised to initiate eviction proceedings during the first 30 days after the lease ends—otherwise, new tenancy rights might well ripen that require additional notice to the former tenant before a court process can begin. [C.C.P. §1161.1].

Avoiding Risk

In a holdover situation following the expiration of a lease, the first 30 days are critical. During that time, it truly is an "estate at sufferance" because the tenant's rights expired upon the end of the lease and the owner has an absolute right to go to court to retake possession of the premises. Once the tenant stays more than thirty days, even without the permission of the owner, a court might well require that the owner give 30 days' notice of the termination of the tenancy, perhaps finding that the owner's failure to take steps promptly has caused additional tenancy rights to ripen.

If a tenant holds over on an expired lease, it is important for the owner to take one of three steps: 1) to seek the tenant's voluntary surrender of the premises; 2) to enter into a new rental agreement; or 3) to exercise his or her legal rights to initiate an eviction promptly.

Tenancy at Will

A **tenancy at will** is created when a tenant obtains possession of the property with the owner's permission, but without a rental agreement. A tenancy at will has no specified term and no regular time period. Usually no rent is paid or else the rent is paid in some form that has no reference to a specific period of time.

> Example: Laura allows her friend Tim to live in a house that she owns in exchange for his maintaining the property and making certain repairs. He does not sign a lease or pay rent on a monthly basis. Tim has an estate at will because he moved onto the premises with the permission of the lessor, his tenancy is for an indefinite time, and he is not required to pay Laura rent on a periodic basis.

Apart from the example given, an estate at will can arise when a tenant moves onto the leased premises while the rental agreement is still under negotiation with the permission of the owner, but before an agreement for the payment of rent has been fully negotiated. Since there is no agreement regarding the amount of rent, it is not a periodic tenancy; rather, it is a tenancy at will.

A tenancy at will endures as long as both parties are willing, but may be ended by the unilateral decision of either party. To terminate a tenancy at will, the landlord must give the tenant a 30-day notice. [C.C. §789]. A tenancy at will automatically terminates upon the death or incapacity of the landlord or the tenant and is not transferable or assignable.

NONFREEHOLD ESTATES				
	Periodic Tenancy	**Tenancy for Years**	**Tenancy at Will**	**Tenancy at Sufferance**
Creation	Agreement or by accepting rent at end of lease term	Oral or written agreement	Take possession while negotiating lease	Remain in possession at end of term
Duration	Indefinite	Definite	No duration	None
Term	Indefinite	Fixed term	No specified term	None
Termination	30-day notice or per lease terms	Automatic termination at end of lease	30-day notice	No notice

NON-POSSESSORY INTERESTS

Non-possessory interests in real estate are encumbrances. An **encumbrance** is an interest in real property that is held by someone who is not the owner. Anything that burdens or affects the use or the title of the property is an encumbrance. Real estate licensees must make inquiries regarding any encumbrances on the property, such as easements, because they can inhibit use or transferability. Because encumbrances are so commonplace, most buyers purchase encumbered property, i.e. burdened with some type of easement or lien. Encumbrances fall into two categories—financial encumbrances and non-financial encumbrances.

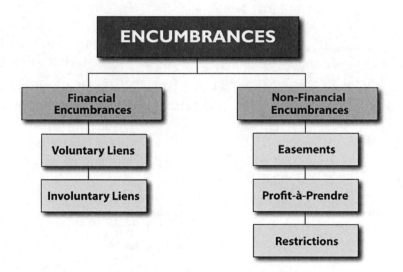

Financial Encumbrances

Having discussed easements, which affect the use of property, we direct our attention to **financial encumbrances**, which affect the title to property. The financial encumbrances that create a legal obligation to pay are known as liens. A **lien** is an interest in real property owned by someone else that secures the payment of a debt or financial obligation. A lien uses real property as security for the payment of a debt.

Liens may be specific or general. A **specific lien** is one that is placed against a certain property, such as a mechanic's lien, deed of trust, and property tax lien. A **general lien** affects all property of the owner, such as a judgment lien or federal or state income tax liens. Additionally, liens are classified as voluntary or involuntary.

Voluntary Liens

An owner may choose to borrow money, using the property as security for the loan, creating a **voluntary lien**. A voluntary lien does not have to be recorded, but if it is not recorded, then other parties (such as purchasers and lenders) may not be bound by it.

The rights and duties of lenders and borrowers are described in a document called a security instrument. A **security instrument** is a legal document that is given by the borrower to hypothecate (pledge) the property to the lender as collateral for the loan. **Hypothecation** is a legal arrangement that allows a borrower to remain in possession of a property secured by a loan. **Collateral** is something of value given as security for a debt. Although the lender retains a security interest in the property, the borrower retains right of possession as long as payments are made according to the loan agreement. If the borrower does not make payments per the agreement, he or she loses the rights of possession and ownership. The lender or subsequent noteholder holds the security instrument and the note until the loan is repaid. Deeds of trust and mortgages are the most common types of security instruments used in real estate finance.

Deeds of Trust

Most real estate transactions in California are financed with the lender's interest protected by a voluntary lien known as a deed of trust. A **deed of trust** (trust deed) is a security instrument that secures a loan on real property. When a promissory note is secured by a deed of trust, three parties are involved: the borrower (**trustor**), the lender (**beneficiary**), and a neutral third party (**trustee**).

The trustor (borrower) signs the promissory note and the deed of trust and gives them to the beneficiary (lender), who records the deed of trust in the local property records and holds them for the term of the loan. Recording creates a lien against the property and gives public notice of the existence of a debt owed on the property. The deed of trust does not have to be recorded to be valid. It legally secures the loan whether it is recorded or not. In the case of foreclosure, the recording date establishes the order of lien priority for the deed of trust against other liens placed on the property.

Title

In the deed of trust, the trustor (borrower) holds equitable title while paying off the loan. **Equitable title** is the right to obtain absolute ownership to property when legal title is held in another's name. As equitable owner, the borrower has all the usual rights that go with ownership, such as the right to possess, will, encumber, and transfer.

The borrower conveys bare legal title to the trustee, to be held in trust until the note is paid in full. **Bare legal title** is title that lacks the usual rights and privileges of ownership. The bare legal title held by the trustee allows the trustee to do only two things: reconvey the property to the borrower upon final payment of the debt or foreclose if the borrower defaults on the loan.

Reconveyance

Under a deed of trust, when the loan is paid off, the lender (beneficiary) sends the note and deed of trust to the trustee along with a request for reconveyance. The trustee cancels the note, signs a deed of reconveyance, and sends it to the borrower. The **deed of reconveyance** conveys title to the property from the trustee to the borrower (trustor). The deed of reconveyance should be recorded to give public notice that the lien has been paid in full, which removes the lien from the property.

Remedy for Default

Under a deed of trust, the lender has a choice of two types of foreclosure—trustee's sale or judicial foreclosure. The common remedy for default of a trust deed is a trustee's sale (non-judicial foreclosure). This is because a deed of trust has a power-of-sale clause. The power-of-sale clause gives the trustee the right to foreclose, sell, and convey ownership to a purchaser of the property if the borrower defaults on the loan. The trustee can start the sale without a court foreclosure order because the borrower has already given bare legal title to the trustee in the deed of trust. Additionally, the power-of-sale clause in the deed of trust gives the trustee the authority to sell the property.

Under a deed of trust with a power of sale, there is no statutory redemption period after the trustee's sale. The sale is final.

In most cases, when a loan is secured by a deed of trust and the lender forecloses under a power of sale (trustee's sale), no deficiency judgment is available. In states in which deeds of trust are used to secure loans, the only security for a beneficiary is the property itself. Any other personal or real assets of the borrower are protected from judgment under the deed of trust.

The rights of the lender (beneficiary) under a deed of trust do not end when the statute of limitations has run out on the note. The trustee is given both bare legal title and power of sale in the deed of trust. The power of sale in a deed of trust never expires.

Mortgages

The deed of trust virtually replaced the use of mortgages when financing real estate in California. A **mortgage** is a financing arrangement that is still common in many other states. In a mortgage, there are two parties—the **mortgagor** (borrower) and the **mortgagee** (lender). The promissory note is proof of the obligation of the debt and the mortgage is a lien against the described property until the debt is repaid.

Involuntary Liens

Other kinds of liens are involuntary—they are used to collect money from debtors who have real property among their assets. If an owner fails to pay taxes, assessments, or other debts, a lien may be placed against his or her property without permission, creating an **involuntary lien**. Typical involuntary liens include judgment liens, tax liens, and mechanic's liens.

Judgment Liens

A **judgment lien** is a lien acquired by a judgment creditor, usually the plaintiff, against the judgment debtor. The **judgment creditor** is the person prevailing in a lawsuit who was awarded money damages. The **judgment debtor** is the person against whom damages were awarded.

Abstract of Judgment. Once a court judgment for money damages becomes final, the judgment creditor can obtain an abstract of judgment from the court that awarded the damages. The **abstract of judgment** is a one-page document that contains information about the court judgment. It can be recorded with each county recorder where the judgment debtor owns real property. Once recorded, the abstract of judgment creates a general lien— that applies to all parcels of real property owned by the judgment debtor in that county. [C.C.P. §687.310]. The county recorder will send the judgment debtor a notice of this involuntary lien. In fact, the judgment creditor may record the abstract of judgment in counties where the judgment debtor owns no property.

The judgment lien only applies to non-exempt real personal property—not a homestead or personal property. If the judgment lien has not expired, it automatically will attach to any non-exempt after-acquired real property.

All judgments earn simple interest at 10% per annum, on the principal amount of the judgment until it is paid. [C.C.P. §685.010].

Duration of Liens. An initial judgment lien is good for as long as the underlying judgment is valid, namely, 10 years. However, a judgment can be renewed twice. Therefore, a judgment lien could be enforceable for maximum of 30 total years.

Validity of Liens. A judgment for an unsecured debt is wiped out by a Chapter 7 (liquidation) bankruptcy. However, it is questionable whether the judgment liens themselves are affected by bankruptcy. Although the underlying debt is gone, by recording an abstract of judgment, the judgment creditor has in effect converted the debt into a form of an ownership interest, which should survive the bankruptcy.

If the judgment debtor pays off the lien or reaches an agreement with the judgment creditor, the judgment creditor will record a document known as a **notice of satisfaction of judgment** acknowledging payment of the judgment. This is a document resembling the abstract of judgment and expunges the lien against the debtor's real property. A notice of satisfaction of judgment can be full or partial—full if the entire judgment has been paid, partial if only part of the judgment has been satisfied.

Writ of Execution. While the judgment creditor *can* simply sit back and allow the judgment lien to collect interest, he or she can also **foreclose** the lien in much the same way that the trustee under a deed of trust or the holder of a mortgage forecloses against a borrower if the loan goes into default. The judgment creditor obtains a document from the court called a **writ of execution** and pays the county sheriff a fee to start the foreclosure process.

The sheriff records a **notice of levy** with the county recorder, provides various notices to the judgment debtor of the pendency of the sale of the real property, and publishes a notice of sale pursuant to Section 6063 of the Government Code. The notice of levy allows any concurrent owner (who has an interest in the property, but is not a judgment debtor) to seek a hearing on that claim of ownership. Although technically a third party's co-ownership interest cannot be sold via a judgment sale, preserving such an interest after a sale is complicated. This procedure allows for a quick determination of the third party's rights before the property is sold so that the third party owner's interest is not impaired.

Execution Sale. If no one raises a third-party right of ownership and the judgment debtor does not pay the debt or make other arrangements with the judgment creditor sale (e.g., by paying what is owed or working out a different arrangement), the sheriff then advertises an auction of the property. The judgment creditor and interested parties, such as junior lienholders, can bid at the auction. Since an execution sale extinguishes all subordinate liens, the junior lienholders often bid at auction.

The minimum acceptable bid is the amount to satisfy the judgment debtor's lien. If the property is homesteaded, the sale cannot go forward unless there is sufficient equity in the property to satisfy both the debt and the judgment debtor's homestead. If there are excess proceeds, they belong to the judgment debtor, since the only purpose of the sale is to make the judgment creditor whole.

At the end of the process, the sheriff's office issues the successful bidder a **sheriff's deed** for the former owner's interest in the property. [C.C.P. §701.660]. However, if there are other owners of the property, the successful bidder may find himself or herself a tenant in common with the other co-owners, because such interests are unaffected by an execution sale. All sales are final with no right of redemption. [C.C.P. §701.680].

Pre-judgment Writ of Attachment

A somewhat rarely used process available to creditors to use to prevent the debtor from transferring property to protect it from a lawsuit is known as a **pre-judgment writ of attachment**. The pre-judgment form of attachment is simply used to tie up property pending a trial on the merits of the creditor's claim. The creditor may have to post a bond in order to convince the court to order the attachment. [C.C.P. §487.010]

Lis Pendens

If title to real property is disputed in a lawsuit, either party can record a *lis pendens* to put third parties on notice that there is a lawsuit pending. The term *lis pendens* means, "Lawsuit pending," and does not give either party any foreclosure rights. Instead, it is a "buyers beware" notice to prospective lenders or buyers that title to the property is disputed. It also does not actually prevent anyone from buying the property, but it warns parties that they could be involved in a lawsuit if they do. Public entities can also file a special kind of *lis pendens* when they file lawsuits seeking to correct a code violation on a particular property.

Tax Liens

A **tax lien** is an involuntary, financial encumbrance placed upon property as a claim for payment of a tax liability. Tax liens are levied by local, state, and federal government agencies. Tax liens can attach to any property owned by the taxpayer or acquired after the lien is placed. They continue until the tax liability is satisfied or becomes unenforceable.

Although tax liens may be imposed for failure to pay city, county, estate, income, payroll, property, sales, or school taxes, the most common tax lien is for delinquent property taxes and special assessments. Property taxes and special assessments are specific liens, whereas other government taxes, such as unpaid income taxes, are general liens. This means that if the property owner fails to pay a specific tax lien, it only affects the parcel of land subject to the tax or special assessment; the tax or assessment cannot be collected from any other property owned by the taxpayer.

Property Tax Liens

When a property tax is assessed against a property, a property tax lien for that amount is placed on the property. This type of lien is superior to all other liens and cannot be cleared by a foreclosure. Since tax liens are superior to any other lien, the property can be sold at a public auction, which in turn, dissolves all other liens, except for property tax liens and special assessments.

Assessment of Property Taxes

Real property in California is taxed at the local level through *ad valorem* property taxes and special assessments set by local tax authorities. **Ad valorem** means "according to value." These taxes are imposed on real property as a percentage of the fair market value based on the most recent sale or improvement of the property to raise money so local public entities can carry out their duties. *Ad valorem* taxes are collected annually.

Real property, interests in real property, and taxable possessory interests are taxable in the county where they are located, regardless of where the owner lives. If a parcel of real property spans more than one revenue district, the portion lying within each district is taxable in that district. All property will be taxed unless specifically exempt.

> **Exempt Property**
>
> > **Homeowners' Exemption.** $7,000 reduction of taxable value for qualifying owner-occupied homes. The homeowner must make a simple one-time filing with the county assessor for the exemption.
> >
> > **Veterans' Exemption.** $4,000 tax exemption applied to the assessed value of property owned by a veteran. This exemption claim must be filed every year.
> >
> > **Other Exemptions.** Other tax exemptions are available for a variety of property owners. Churches, nonprofit organizations, and owners of timberlands, young orchards, or grapevines less than three years old may also qualify for tax exemptions. Certain senior citizens may qualify for tax relief.

Since 1978, the California Constitution has limited how much property tax can be imposed. Commonly known as **Proposition 13** (found in Article 13A of the California Constitution), it limits *ad valorem* taxes to 1% of the full cash value of a given parcel. The **full cash value** is based on the fair market value—not necessarily, the actual sales price of the property and a new base year appraisal is established. Commonly, local taxes are added to the 1% assessment.

The county assessor can also increase the assessed value of each property if property values in the community have generally been increasing. However, regardless of how much other properties may have gone up in value, Proposition 13 limits this annual increase to 2% above the previous year's value.

Transfer of Ownership

When a parcel changes hands, the increase in taxes over the previous year's *ad valorem* tax can therefore be dramatic if the property has not been sold for many years. In addition, any person buying real property is required to file a change-in-ownership statement with the county recorder or assessor. The change-in-ownership statement must be filed within 45 days of the change date. Failure to report a change results in a $100 penalty. A supplementary tax bill will be sent to the new owner, reflecting the change in taxes as of the date of transfer.

> Example: Frank and Helen purchased their three-bedroom house in San Diego in 1979 for $70,000. For the first year that they lived in the house, their property taxes were $700 per year (1% of $70,000). The following year, because property values in San Diego were increasing, the assessor re-assessed their property to $71,400 ($70,000 plus $1,400, which is 2% of $70,000). That second year

their taxes were therefore $714. The third year that they lived there, property values were again on the increase, so the assessor set their property's value at $72,828 ($71,400 plus $1,428, which is 2% of $71,400).

When Frank and Helen sold their house in 1982, property values increased much more than the 2% annual increases. They were able to sell their home for $125,000, so the new owner's taxes started at $1,250 and would increase from there as long as the market was on the rise.

Some transfers of ownership, such as those between spouses, may be excluded from reappraisal. **Proposition 58** and **Proposition 193** provide property tax relief for real property transfers between parents and children (Prop 58) and from grandparents to grandchildren (Prop 193). These propositions make it easier to keep property in the family. [Revenue & Taxation Code §63.1].

The Senior Citizen's Replacement Dwelling Benefit (**Propositions 60** and **Proposition 90**) allows senior citizens to transfer the trended base value from their current home to a replacement property if certain requirements are met. Proposition 60 relates to transfers within the same county (intra-county). Proposition 90 relates to transfers of base value from one county to another county in California (inter-county). [R & T Code §69.5].

Eligibility Requirements
- Homeowner must be at least 55 years of age when the original property is sold.
- Original property was eligible for the Homeowners' or Disabled Veterans' Exemption.
- Replacement property must be the principal residence and must be eligible for the Homeowners' Exemption or Disabled Veterans' Exemption.
- Replacement property must be of equal or lesser current market value than the original property.
- Replacement property must be purchased or built within two years (before or after) of the sale of the original property.

Property owners can also request a reduction in their assessed value if property values have been declining. Unlike increases, these are not limited to 2% of the previous year's assessment, but once property begins to increase, the assessor can "recapture" the difference between the earlier, higher assessment and the temporary reduction based on lowered property values. [R & T Code §51].

Collection of Property Taxes

In California, property taxes (even for property within cities and special districts) are imposed by each county's assessor and collected by the county tax collector. (In some counties, the two offices are combined.) The county assessor assesses the value of all taxable property in the county yearly to establish the tax base. The county tax collector decides how much tax is to be paid by each property owner, depending on the assessments and then mails out the tax bills. The tax bill identifies a property by an assessor's parcel number, which is not a legal description but is used for taxation purposes only.

California follows a fiscal tax year from July 1 through June 30. On January 1, preceding the fiscal tax year, property taxes become a lien on real property. July 1 the fiscal tax year begins. Each tax year, the tax rate is determined on or before September 1st. Taxes may be paid in two installments or in one payment on or before November 1. The first installment is due November 1, but no later than December 10. The second installment is due February 1, but no later than April 10.

Taxation Time Line

Jan. I	July I	Nov. I	Dec. 10	Feb. I	April 10	June 30
Taxes become a lien	Tax year starts	1st installment due	1st installment delinquent	2nd installment due	2nd installment delinquent	Tax year ends

Tax Default Status and Tax Sale

If a property owner does not pay property taxes when due, the property is declared in **tax default status**. The default opens a 5 years waiting period for residential property and 3 years for non-residential commercial property during which the delinquent taxes, interest, and penalties accumulate until redeemed. While the property is in a tax-defaulted status, the owner does not actually lose title and keeps possession for five years. The owner who owes the back taxes has five years to redeem the property by paying the back taxes and penalties. The property may be redeemed by bringing the taxes current or by paying installments of 20% or more per year.

At the end of the 5 years for residential property (3 years for commercial property), if the tax remains unredeemed, the county tax collector has the power to sell the property. The county tax collector sends the property owner a notice of impending sale followed by a Notice of Auction. Once all of the statutory requirements are met, the property may be sold at public auction, by a sealed bid sale, or at a negotiated sale to a public agency or qualified non-profit organization. Public auctions are the most common way of selling tax-defaulted property. The auction is conducted by the county tax collector and the property is sold to the highest bidder. The county transfers title to the new owner with a **tax deed**.

After paying the delinquent taxes, penalties, and costs, any excess money is paid to the original owner. Even if the proceeds of the sale are insufficient to satisfy the delinquent taxes and costs, the original owner's tax liability is extinguished.

Special Assessments

Special assessments are levied against property owners to pay for local improvements, such as underground utilities, street repair, or water projects. Payment for the projects is obtained through a special form of borrowing called **bonds**. The money borrowed through the bond is secured by the special assessment, which becomes a lien against real property. Assessments are collected annually in the same way as property taxes until all of the borrowed funds have been repaid.

Like taxes, special assessments in California are now governed by a state initiative, this one known as Proposition 218. **Proposition 218** requires that before an assessment can be imposed, the entity that wants to borrow the money must hire an engineer who will calculate how much each parcel of land that will be subject to the special assessment will benefit from the new public improvement. Those property owners must then be sent a ballot with which to vote for or against the assessment. Their ballots are "weighted" according to how much the engineer's study calculates that each parcel will have to pay. Only property owners are entitled to vote on an assessment; neither tenants nor residents who will not have to pay the assessment are entitled to vote on them.

Finally, the local entity that wants to construct the improvement holds a public hearing and opens the ballots. If more than half the weighted ballots favor the special assessment, it goes into effect; if not, the special assessment fails and the local entity must either abandon the planned improvement or find a different way to finance it.

Mechanic's Liens

A **mechanic's lien** is a statutory lien that secures payment for labor or materials supplied in improving, repairing, or maintaining real property. Mechanics include contractors, subcontractors, laborers, materialmen, architects, and other parties who improve a specific parcel of real property.

Because this is a remedy for the improvement of a certain parcel, it is a specific lien much like a tax lien, but it has priority only based on the time of recordation, relating back to the date the work actually commenced. A mechanic's lien must be verified and recorded. The law is very time specific about the recording. The statutory procedure must be followed exactly if the mechanic's lien is to be valid.

Four Essential Steps for a Mechanic's Lien

1. **Preliminary Notice:** A preliminary notice is a written notice that must be given to the owner within 20 days of first furnishing labor or materials for a job by anyone eligible to file a mechanic's lien. This document gives owners notice that their property may have a lien placed on it if they do not pay for work completed. [C.C. §3097].

2. **Notice of Completion:** If the owner records a notice of completion within 10 days after the project is finished, the original contractors have 60 days after the notice is filed and all others have 30 days after the notice is filed, to record a mechanic's lien. [C.C. §3086].

3. **No Notice of Completion:** If the owner does not record a notice of completion when work is finished, all claimants have a maximum of 90 days from the day work was finished to record a mechanic's lien.

4. **Foreclosure Action:** After a mechanic's lien is recorded, the claimant has 90 days to bring foreclosure action to enforce the lien. If he or she does not bring action, the lien will be terminated and the claimant loses the right to foreclose.

The owner can take two steps to protect himself or herself from assertion of a mechanic's lien. First, if the owner discovers *unauthorized* work, he or she can post the property with a prominent **notice of non-responsibility** within 10 days of obtaining knowledge of the unauthorized work. [C.C. §3094]. This notice must be recorded and posted on the property to be valid, stating the owner is not responsible for work being done. [C.C. §3129]. This notice releases the owner from the liability for work done without permission.

For work that is *authorized*, the owner can also record a **notice of completion** indicating that the work has been completed. This shortens the time for mechanic's liens to 30 days; otherwise, mechanic's liens can be recorded for up to 90 days after actual completion of work. [C.C. §3086].

Determining the starting date for a mechanic's lien is very important. Mechanic's liens have priority as of the date work began or materials were first furnished for the job. A mechanic's lien has priority over any other liens filed after the commencement of labor or delivery of materials with the exception of tax and special assessment liens. That means if there is a foreclosure action, the mechanic's lien would be paid before any other liens that were recorded after work started on the job.

Mechanic's Lien Time Line

Here are the major events to be followed, in a timely manner, whenever improvement of real property is done.

1. Work Commences
2. Preliminary 20-Day Notice
3. Work Completed
4. Notice of Completion Recorded
5. Lien Recorded
6. Foreclosure Action and Lis Pendens Recorded
7. Service of Process
8. Court Decision
   a) Judgment
   b) Release of Lien
   c) Dismissed
   d) Foreclosure

That includes trust deeds or mortgages recorded prior to the filing of the mechanic's lien, but after the start of the work. Lenders will make a physical inspection of the property to determine that no materials have been delivered and no work has been done before recording a construction loan to assure the priority of their trust deed or mortgage.

Example: Work started on a project on June 15 and a deed of trust was recorded on June 18. A mechanic's lien was recorded on September 28, but a notice of completion was recorded on Sept 1. Between the deed of trust and the mechanic's lien, the mechanic's lien has the priority over the trust deed, because work started on June 15. A mechanic's lien has priority over any other liens filed after the commencement of labor or delivery of materials with the exception of tax and special assessment liens.

Non-Financial Encumbrances

A **non-financial encumbrance** is one that affects the physical use or condition of the property, such as easements, profit-à-prendres, and restrictions.

Easements

An **easement** is an interest owned by one person in the land of another person. An easement allows its owner to use or, in some cases, to prevent the use of, the land burdened by the easement. Easement rights are often created for the benefit of the owner of adjoining land. Easements are  created for the benefit of at least one party, at the expense of the property owner. The land benefiting from the creation of the easement is the **dominant tenement**; the land that is subject to the easement is the **servient tenement**. [C.C. §803]. Unless the easement is specifically described to be "exclusive," its creation does not prevent the owner of the land from using the land and the portion covered by the easement in a way that does not interfere with the use of the easement. Unless agreed otherwise, the owner of the dominant tenement has the responsibility to maintain a right-of-way easement.

Easements are characterized as affirmative or negative. An **affirmative easement** gives the owner of the dominant tenement the right to do something, such as allowing another access to or across a certain piece of property. Most easements fall into this category. A **negative easement** gives the owner of the dominant tenement the right to prohibit the servient tenement owner from doing something with a certain piece of property, such as building height restrictions. There are not many negative residential easements today because these types of restrictions are usually covered in zoning regulations and private restrictions, such as CC&Rs.

Easements can be created with the approval of the servient tenement or in rare cases, against the wishes and desires of the servient tenement. Such an easement is called an **adverse easement** and is created by continuous use against the wishes of the servient tenement. An example of this type of easement would be a path used by pedestrians to the beach over private property. This can become an easement by prescription after all the requirements are met.

Differentiating Easements from Licenses

A **license** is a permissive use of land, differing from all other rights to use the land of someone else. It is freely revocable by the grantor. A license coupled with an interest of some kind (e.g., consideration) is in essence an easement, not a license. If it is an easement, it can no longer be revoked. The limited right that one acquires, for example, to park in a space in a parking garage, to sit in a seat in a movie theater, or to enter and stroll around a museum are all licenses.

Because a license is freely revocable, the person to whom the license is granted (known as the licensee) can be removed by the landowner if the licensee does not abide by the rules under which it was granted. Thus, for example, if a person misbehaves in a theater, the theater operators would be entitled to evict that person or to call the police for assistance if the person refuses to leave.

Classification of Easements

There are two kinds of easements—appurtenant easements and easements in gross.

Appurtenant Easements

An **appurtenant easement**, as the name implies, is a right attached to one parcel of land that comes along with the normal rights that a buyer acquires in taking title to that property. An appurtenant easement has a dominant and a servient tenement. It is sometimes said to "run with the land," because the right passes from one owner to the next and is not held personally by anyone except the owner of the dominant tenement.

The owner of a parcel who can exercise an appurtenant easement does so at the expense of the otherwise unfettered rights another property owner would otherwise have over his or her property.

> Example: Donna acquires a parcel of land from Fred. Her deed includes both a legal description of the parcel that she is acquiring and also a legal description of a 10-foot wide strip of land over another parcel "for ingress and egress." The land that the 10-foot strip is located on is owned by Sam. Sam's parcel is located directly adjoining the county road nearest to both parcels.

> Without the 10-foot strip of land across Sam's parcel, Donna's land would be **landlocked**—that is, she would be unable to get to her property without crossing someone else's land. Donna's property has an appurtenant easement, which is

the dominant tenement. Sam owns the servient tenement because Donna will be allowed to cross his property in order to reach the public road whenever she wants to get access to or from her parcel.

In the situation described above, Sam still owns the underlying fee interest in the land across which Donna's easement lies. He can still make reasonable use of the property when Donna is not exiting or entering her parcel. For example, if Sam is gardening, he can park the wheelbarrow in which he carries potting soil, tools, or other implements on the 10-foot strip while he is working. If Donna should happen to drive up and need to get through, he can move the wheelbarrow, just as someone would move his or her shopping cart in the aisle of a grocery store to let another shopper pass by.

On the other hand, his right to use the 10-foot strip is more limited than the other land that makes up his fee interest. He can plant grass on this strip, but he cannot build a permanent fence across it unless he puts in a gate and gives Donna a key. He also cannot build any permanent structures in such a way that they intrude into this area; if he did, Donna could sue him to remove such a permanent obstruction.

Donna still must use the 10-foot strip within the strict limitations of the language in the deed—that is, "for ingress and egress" only, i.e., to get to or from her land. If, for example, she decides to build an addition to her house, she will not be allowed to store building materials on the 10-foot strip even for a short time unless she gets permission from Sam. If she ignored Sam and stored her building materials on the 10-foot strip anyway, she would be committing a trespass. Donna's only right to use this strip of land is for ingress and egress.

Finally, because easements are, by definition, an interest in the land of another, if Donna acquires Sam's parcel or he acquires hers, the easement that Donna's parcel formerly enjoyed is extinguished by **merger**. In effect, the easement over the one parcel and the encumbered title of the other parcel are "merged" when both parcels come under a single ownership.

Easements in Gross

An **easement in gross** is a personal right of one person to use land owned by another. In this case, the easement benefits an individual or organization, not a particular parcel of real estate. Unlike an appurtenant easement, there is still a servient tenement burdened by the easement, but no dominant tenement. In that sense, it is the opposite of an appurtenant easement. It does not "run with the land" and is only a personal right.

Example: Ed has owned a parcel of land for many years. The land is heavily forested and during the autumn and winter, he often cuts down a few trees to make one or two cords of firewood.

Ed decides to sell the property and he intends to buy a parcel that does not have any trees suitable to cut for firewood. Before he sells his original parcel of land, therefore, he tells the buyer that he wants to include a clause in the deed reserving the right to come onto the property between October 1 of every year and April 1 of the following year in order to cut firewood.

The buyer insists that the clause also provide that Ed give the new owner at least 48 hours' notice of his intention to exercise his right; that Ed's right be limited to no more than four times during the October-April span; and that the right be limited to Ed's lifetime only. Ed agrees to these conditions in order to close the sale and once the sale is complete, he has an **easement in gross** to cut firewood on his former parcel that he will hold until his death.

Utility easements are examples of easements in gross. They are created to allow employees of the utility company to gain access to the property for the installation and maintenance of utility equipment. In many cases, the utility company has an easement for the equipment and an easement in gross to allow access to that equipment.

Creation of Easements

Easements may be created in various ways, such as by express agreement, implication, prescription, or estoppel.

Easement by Express Agreement

The most common way to create an easement is by express grant or reservation in a grant deed or by a written agreement between owners of adjoining land. An easement always should be recorded to assure its continued existence. It is recorded by the party benefiting from the easement as the dominant tenement.

An **easement by grant** is the most straightforward way that an easement is created: one parcel or person acquires an easement by the express terms of a deed or other document. An easement by grant can be conveyed separately by the owner of the servient tenement (usually for a price, although it can be given as a gift); or, it can be reserved from a conveyance at the time of transfer.

Any easement created by deed must comply with the usual requirements of any deed and may arise either by express grant to another or by express reservation to oneself.

An **easement by reservation** is created when an owner sells property but retains an easement for personal use. The common law rule was that if an easement was created by reservation, it could not be vested in a "stranger to the title." In 1972, the California Supreme Court abolished this rule.

Willard v. First Church of Christ, Scientist

In *Willard* v. *First Church of Christ, Scientist* (1972) 7 Cal.3d 473, Genevieve McGuigan owned two abutting lots in Pacifica. There was a building on one and the other was vacant. McGuigan was a member of the Christian Science Church located across the street from her lots, and she allowed the church to use the vacant lot for parking during services.

She sold the improved lot to a man named Petersen, who used the building as an office. He later wanted to sell it, so he listed it with Donald Willard, a real estate broker. Willard himself expressed an interest in purchasing both lots and he and Petersen signed an agreement to that effect.

However, when Petersen agreed to sell the vacant lot to Willard he did not yet own it, so he approached Ms. McGuigan with an offer to buy it. She was willing to sell the lot provided the church could continue to use it for parking, so she referred the matter to the church's attorney. He drew up a provision for her deed to Petersen that stated the conveyance was "subject to an easement for automobile parking during church hours for the benefit of the church, ... such easement to run with the land only so long as the property ... is used for church purposes." Once this clause was inserted in the deed, McGuigan sold the property to Petersen and he in turn conveyed the lot to Willard.

While Petersen did mention to Willard that the church "would want to use the vacant lot for parking," he did not tell Willard of the easement clause in the deed he had received from Ms. McGuigan. Petersen also did not include the easement in his

Willard v. First Church of Christ, Scientist (continued)

deed to Willard—and Willard, despite being a real estate broker, apparently had no title search run by a title insurance company before he closed escrow on his purchase.

When he learned of the easement provision, Willard sued the church, arguing that under the common law, a "stranger to the title," such as the church could not have an easement reserved in a deed from McGuigan to Petersen. Ms. McGuigan either would have had to transfer the easement to the church in a different instrument or in a more complicated "straw man" transaction, would first have had to transfer the property to the church, which then could have immediately transferred it back to her while reserving the easement.

The Supreme Court decided that the common law rule was outmoded and that there was no reason that Ms. McGuigan could not "reserve" an easement to the church in the same instrument by which she had transferred the land to Petersen. The court found that the common law rule conflicted with the modern approach to construing deeds and also produced inequitable results because the grantee has presumably paid a reduced price to reflect the easement property. The Supreme Court overturned a lower court ruling in favor of Willard, upholding the church's easement.

Easement by Implication

Easements may arise by implication of law or by virtue of long use. Typically, these are implied easements or easements by necessity.

Implied Easement

An **implied easement** is an easement created by law when an owner severs property into two parcels in such a way that an already existing, obvious, and continuous use of one parcel is necessary for the reasonable enjoyment of the other parcel. An implied easement is based on prior use that was so obvious and of such duration as to be entitled to recognition today even if it does not amount to a prescriptive use. Civil Code §1104 provides for the recognition of implied easements.

Example: Scott has a parcel that is located some distance from a public road. He has an appurtenant easement across Betty's property that allows him to get to and from the public roadway. Because he and Betty are on good terms and the winter weather in their area is rainy, she agrees to let Scott pave the area covered by the easement so that he does not create a muddy track in the wintertime.

Scott later buys Betty's property. Because he now owns the parcel subject to the easement, the easement is extinguished by being merged into his complete fee ownership of both parcels. Two years later, in order to raise money, he decides to sell his former parcel to Heather. However, he forgets to reserve an easement in Heather's favor in the parcel he sells to her, even though she will need it to get to and from the public road just as he once did.

Nevertheless, Heather can assert an implied easement across Scott's (formerly Betty's) parcel. First, the parcel she purchased from Scott will be useless without an easement allowing access to a public road. Second, there was an easement there at one time that both Scott and Betty acknowledged. Indeed, Scott was even allowed to pave it when he was the one who used it. Scott's former use of the easement before he owned both parcels and the paving of the area used to access, support Heather's implied easement even if it is not specifically mentioned in her deed.

Easement by Necessity

An **easement by necessity** is an easement created by operation of law because the easement is essential to the reasonable use of the property. An easement by necessity is subject to a fairly strict rule that it can only be recognized when one parcel has been created out of another and the resulting parcel would be completely inaccessible without access across the "parent" parcel from which it was created. If a parcel has legal access to a public roadway, even if it is circuitous and inconvenient (e.g., crossing an unpaved hill when a public road could be reached across a shorter path), then an easement by necessity cannot be created because it is not, in fact, a necessity.

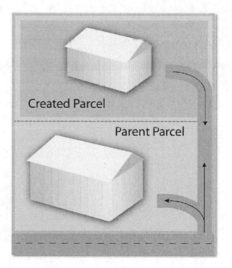

Created Parcel

Parent Parcel

Because modern requirements for the creation of parcels through the Subdivision Map Act require that every new parcel have legal access to a public road, easements by necessity will usually be a problem only with parcels created many years ago or created when someone subdivides land illegally by deed. (Subdivision by deed has been illegal since 1972.) In practice, because a parcel that is truly inaccessible is rare, easements by necessity are rarely the only way to make a parcel accessible.

Easement by Prescription

An **easement by prescription** is an easement that is created when one person or parcel (in the case of an appurtenant easement) acquires an involuntary easement in the land of another. An easement by prescription is obtained when one property owner uses the land of another in what amounts to a trespass. The use must be done in a way that would put a diligent property owner on notice that someone is using his or her property without permission. There are five elements needed in the creation of an easement by prescription.

Elements Required to Create a Prescriptive Easement
- Open use (i.e., some assertion of control, such as crossing the other land);
- Notorious use (i.e., use that a reasonable person would recognize);
- Hostile use (i.e., without the other owner's permission);
- Adverse to a claim of right (i.e., adverse to the other property owner's title); and
- Continuous use for a five-year time period.

If the use is done with the other owner's permission, then it is not adverse or hostile and does not ripen into a prescriptive easement.

The law allows prescriptive rights because if the landowner subjected to what amounts to a trespass does nothing to enforce those property rights, the person making the prescriptive use will eventually come to rely on that use. It is also based on the notion that if someone is using someone else's land productively, even without permission, land is too valuable to allow someone to restrict that use if the owner has failed to object to the use for a certain period of time.

A prescriptive easement is merely an interest in a certain property—not ownership. Although the method used for acquiring property rights through prescription is similar to adverse possession, adverse possession requires the payment of taxes for five continuous years, while prescription does not. Also, remember one acquires title to property through adverse possession, but only a specified interest in property through prescription.

Easement by Estoppel

An **easement by estoppel** is an easement that is created when the conduct of the owner of land leads another reasonably to believe that he or she has an interest in the land so that he or she acts or does not act in reliance on that belief.

Termination of Easements

Easements may be terminated (extinguished) in a similar manner as they are created—express agreement, implication, prescription, and estoppel. [C.C. §811].

Termination by Express Agreement

The owner of the property benefiting from the easement (dominant tenement) is the only one who can release an easement. The usual way would be for the owner of the property with the dominant tenement to sign a grant deed or a quitclaim deed in favor of the owner of the property with the servient tenement. The owner of the property with the servient tenement cannot revoke or terminate the easement.

Termination by Implication

The actions of the property owners, rather than an express agreement, can terminate an easement.

Merger. An easement is an interest in the property of another person. Therefore, an easement is terminated when one person obtains fee ownership of both the benefited property (dominant tenement) and burdened property (servient tenement).

Destruction of the servient tenement. If the easement is for the use of a structure, such as a building or bridge and the structure is destroyed, the easement terminates. Rebuilding the structure does not automatically create a new easement.

Necessity for or purpose of the easement ends. An easement created for a specific purpose or need ends when the purpose ends.

> Example: Parcel B is landlocked and an easement by necessity is created over Parcel A for ingress and egress. Four years later, the county extends a road that gives access to Parcel B so that it is no longer landlocked. Therefore, the easement created by necessity is no longer relevant.

Most likely, the owner of the servient tenement would bring an action to quiet title against the owner of the dominant tenement in order to terminate the easement. A lawsuit to establish or settle title to real property is called a **quiet title action** or an action to quiet title.

Abandonment: Abandonment is the obvious and intentional surrender of the easement. When determining if an easement is abandoned, mere non-use is not sufficient—certain criteria must be met. According to California C.C. §887.050, an easement is abandoned if ALL of the following conditions are satisfied for a period of 20 years.

1. The easement is not used at any time.
2. No separate property tax assessment is made of the easement or, if made, no taxes are paid on the assessment.
3. No instrument creating, reserving, transferring, or otherwise evidencing the easement is recorded.

Owners can protect themselves from losing their easement rights by recording a notice of intent to preserve the easement. [C.C. §887.060].

Termination by Prescription

The owner of the servient tenement, by his or her own use, may prevent the dominant tenement owner from using the easement for a period of five years, thus terminating the easement. Just as with creating an easement by prescription, terminating an easement by prescription requires the interference to be open, adverse, notorious, hostile, and continuous.

Termination by Estoppel

The conduct of the owner of the easement may lead the property owner burdened by the servient tenement to believe that he or she has no further use of the easement. If the property owner takes an action in reliance on the conduct of the owner of the easement, the easement may be terminated in accordance with the doctrine of estoppel.

> Example: John owned several acres of land. He sold two acres to Donna, reserving an easement across the west side of her property so Bob, his son would have a shorter walk to the high school. Upon graduation, Bob left for

college and John fenced his field and built a large barn, which blocked access to the shortcut. Donna, seeing the fence and barn, assumed that John had no more use for the shortcut, so she had a small barn built for her horse. John knew that Donna had built the barn. In fact, John's wife, Kate, and Donna frequently went riding together. Eighteen months later, John removed the fence and told Donna he planned to use the easement.

John is estopped from using the easement because Donna reasonably relied on John's action (fencing the field and building a barn) when she had her small barn built; thus, terminating the easement.

Types of Easements

An easement can be under, over, or on the property of another. An easement can be underground (for example, a pipeline easement enjoyed by a utility company) or it can be overhead (for example, a power line easement enjoyed by a private electric company). Alternatively, it can be on the surface (a road easement held by one person over land owned by another). In some instances, an easement can encompass the entire property but only remove one right, as in a conservation easement.

Underground Easements

Underground easements lie below the surface of the ground. They include pipeline easements of all types, such as storm drainage, sewer, water, and underground conduits for electrical cable. Underground easements often do not unduly restrict the use of the surface for residential purposes.

> Example: A subdivider or developer grants most underground utility easements along the rear or sideline of a residential lot, so that the utility company may provide service to that and other lots. These easements, usually only 5 feet wide on each lot, do not unduly restrict the use of the lot, since most residential lots have setback lines that preclude the building of any structure within a certain distance of the property line. The owner can usually grow small trees and shrubs and enjoy such easement-encumbered land in a normal manner.

However, some underground easements would restrict the use of the surface for residential purposes. For example, the existence of an underground easement for a pipeline running diagonally across a backyard would restrict the building of a swimming pool.

Overhead Easements

The most common type of overhead easement is the power line easement. Depending on the placement of the overhead easement, use of the surface property could be restricted. For example, an easement for a power line that diagonally crossed the backyard of a home possibly could restrict planting trees or constructing a swimming pool.

Although it might seem unusually restrictive to prohibit construction of a swimming pool because of an overhead power line, people have been electrocuted when the extended handle of a vacuum cleaner they were using to clean a pool contacted a high-voltage line. In addition, there could be occasional interference with radio and television reception.

Surface Easements

The most common type of **surface easement** is the road easement. Easements for roads or for any other purpose that uses the land surface—flood control channels, drainage ditches, and so on—are generally valued at 100 percent of fee value of the area occupied by the easement. The land surface is usually the most usable portion of the property.

Conservation Easement

A relatively new type of surface easement is the conservation easement. A **conservation easement** is an interest in real property voluntarily conveyed by the owner of the property to qualified nonprofit organizations. Its purpose is

to preserve land in its natural, scenic, agricultural, historical, forested, or open-space condition. [C.C. §815]. Typically, the government agencies and environmental groups acquire these rights, because it costs less to purchase the easement than a 100% fee simple ownership of the land.

Conservation easements are perpetual in duration and limit the future use of a property to preservation, conservation, or wildlife habitat. [C.C. §815.2]. Since the conservation easement creates open space, the underlying property owner is left with limited uses.

Profit-à-Prendre

The right to enter another's land to remove soil or substances of the soil (water, minerals, timber, fruit, game, or other resource) is known as **profit-à-prendre**. An example would be the right to harvest timber on land owned by someone else.

It is created by the owner granting the profit-à-prendre to the profit-à-prendre holder in writing. It differs from an easement because an easement only gives the right to use the land, whereas, a profit-à-prendre gives the right to remove the soil or products of the soil. A profit-à-prendre can last indefinitely. If an owner grants a profit-à-prendre to someone and then sells the property, the new owner will still have to abide by the terms of the profit-à-prendre. The profit holder can sell, lease, give away, or bequeath the profit-à-prendre to someone else.

Private Restrictions

The use of property is limited by restrictions. Restrictions may be placed on property to assure that land use is consistent and uniform within a certain area. They may be placed by a private owner, a developer, or the government. Public restrictions are used primarily to promote the general public welfare. Private restrictions placed by a present or past owner affect only a specific property or development.

Private restrictions are deemed to be voluntarily accepted by the purchaser of property subject to these restrictions, because, unlike governmental restrictions, the purchaser can choose to avoid them by buying elsewhere. Of course, in some cases, this may be more a theoretical than a realistic choice if the property is desirable for other reasons or if most property in a certain area is subject to some kind of private restrictions.

Creation of Restrictions

Occasionally, private restrictions can be created by a separate contract between property owners. Sometimes, private restrictions are included in a deed as a condition of the grant. An example of a deed restriction is the reservation of mineral rights by a previous owner. This type of restriction must be carefully reviewed because it can include the right of surface entry. The holder of the mineral rights can mine for those minerals at any time without regard to any improvements on the property. That situation would make building on the property extremely difficult. However, the most common way to create private restrictions is to include them as part of the general plan of a subdivision.

Covenants, Conditions, and Restrictions

As many homeowners who have purchased property in newer subdivisions have discovered, the new property often comes with a lengthy packet of limitations on what they can do with their property. These "pre-packaged" limitations often are referred to by the shorthand of "CC&Rs," which stands for "**conditions, covenants, and restrictions**." **CC&Rs** are the rules and regulations established for a parcel of land and accepted by the owner when the property is purchased or transferred. The CC&Rs for a new subdivision are listed in a recorded **Declaration of Restrictions**, which gives each owner the right to enforce the CC&Rs.

Although they are commonly referred to by the collective phrase, the three terms actually have distinct meanings and origins.

Covenants

A **covenant** is a term in a deed—in effect, a promise—that a certain act will, or will not, be performed. A covenant in a deed may resemble a condition, but it is enforced differently. If a court deems a limitation in a deed to be a covenant, then it is enforced by a **lawsuit for injunctive relief**. The party seeking enforcement has the right to have the covenant performed according to its terms. However, the defendant does not lose title even if the court finds that a covenant has been violated.

Conditions

A **condition** is a limitation imposed by a grantor in a deed that can cause the ownership of the property to revert to the grantor who imposes the condition if the condition is not satisfied. Conditions actually lessen or diminish the estate that a purchaser obtains in acquiring title to property. Whereas the normal real property estate is an unrestricted fee simple absolute, an estate truly subject to a condition is a fee simple subject to condition subsequent. In effect, the seller imposes a contingency upon the fee and retains a reversionary interest if a condition in a deed happens, the buyer will lose title, and the fee reverts to the seller.

Conditions are generally disfavored under modern law because the penalty— loss of title—is so harsh. Often, courts will try to interpret a condition as a covenant or a restriction so that it can be enforced or damages are awarded for breach, but without resulting in divestiture of title. Nevertheless, conditions occasionally are upheld by a court.

> Example: In *Walton* v. *City of Red Bluff* (1992) 2 Cal.App.4th 117, the court of appeal reviewed whether a charitable conveyance was enforceable as a condition. In 1908 and 1916, respectively, a woman and her son conveyed two parcels of land to the City of Red Bluff in Tehama County "for the uses and purposes of a public library." The library was constructed and used by the city for many years, even after the city library system was merged with the county system. In 1986, however, the city moved the books to a new building, citing a lack of space in the old building, lack of access for handicapped and elderly patrons, and a lack of parking.
>
> The trial court ruled in favor of the city, but the court of appeal held that the city's discontinuation of the building's use as a library amounted to a violation of the condition in the grants. It directed the trial court to quiet title in favor of the descendants of the two donors of the land from 1908 and 1916.

Restrictions

A **restriction**, except when used in the phrase "conditions, covenants, and restrictions," does not have a special legal meaning in the same way that "condition" and "covenant" do. Rather, as already noted, CC&Rs are a blanket term for what is normally a comprehensive series of mutual promises that bind the owners of all parcels in a subdivision that was developed at the same time.

Frequently, restrictions are required by the local city or county where the subdivision is created, especially if there is any common area in the subdivision— that is, property owned jointly by all owners of parcels within that development (such as a community clubhouse, pool, or private park area). However, CC&Rs are often more restrictive than municipal zoning or restrictions. The CC&Rs may have a lengthy list of requirements detailing how each parcel in the subdivision can be used and must be maintained. The justification for such requirements is that they give the development a common "look" and that they prevent activities (e.g., junkyards) that lower the value of surrounding properties.

Kinds of Restrictions often Imposed by CC&Rs

- Every owner in the subdivision to pay annual dues that support insurance and maintenance of the common areas
- List of approved exterior colors for houses within the subdivision
- Prohibition against outdoor antennas or satellite dishes
- Maintenance standards for outdoor landscaping
- Prohibiting the parking of motor homes on the subdivision's streets or driveways or restricting how long (e.g., 72 hours) such vehicles can be parked
- Garage doors not be left open for lengthy periods of time
- Prohibiting auto repairs on the subdivision's streets or driveways
- Requiring that backyards be surrounded by a six-foot solid fence

Enforcing CC&Rs

CC&Rs are not enforced by municipalities, but are privately enforced by a homeowners' association (often abbreviated HOA) elected from among the owners of the parcels within the subdivision. Because of the breadth of their activities, HOAs are sometimes referred to as a "second municipal government." Occasionally, they overreach in their efforts to control how owners maintain their property.

Cunningham v. Superior Court

In *Cunningham v. Superior Court* (1998) 67 Cal.App.4th 743, the court of appeal reviewed a superior court decision absolving a homeowners' association of liability for negligence, invasion of privacy, trespass, and breach of contract. The property in question was an attached home similar to a condominium. The association's representatives visited the property to respond to complaints of "debris" on Mr. Cunningham's outdoor patio that blocked a contractor hired by the association from doing work on a roof on the building.

In response to a threat of litigation about an alleged fire hazard, Cunningham also allowed the HOA's representatives inside his dwelling. Although local fire officials had already concluded that there was no fire hazard, the HOA's attorneys wrote Cunningham a letter telling him, among other things, to clear his bed of all papers and books, not use his downstairs bathroom for storage,

> ### *Cunningham v. Superior Court* (continued)
>
> and to donate unused clothing to the Salvation Army. The letter did tell him he could keep the books on his bookshelf "which are considered standard reading material."
>
> The court of appeal's opinion began by stating that, "like Shel Silverstein's Sarah Cynthia Sylvia Stout . . . Cunningham would not take the garbage out." Nevertheless, the court found the association's directives to Cunningham unreasonable and "particularly galling" was "the presumptuous attempt to lecture Cunningham about getting rid of his old clothes, the way he kept his own bedroom, and the kind of 'reading material' he could have." The court of appeal reversed the trial judge's decision and sent the case back for trial.

Despite the result in *Cunningham*, homeowners' associations are generally within their authority to enforce almost any restriction about the exterior condition of a homeowner's property so long as the restrictions are enforced evenhandedly among all properties within a subdivision.

> ### *Laguna Audubon II Master Association v. Henderson*
>
> The Laguna Audubon II Master Association prohibits parking commercial vehicles on common streets or driveways in the community. Members must park personal vehicles inside garages.
>
> The Hendersons, an elderly couple living in the community, continued to park their white van in the driveway, because the vehicle was used to transport Mr. Henderson, who is in a wheelchair. It was easier to access the van if it was parked in the driveway.
>
> The homeowners' association gave the Hendersons multiple parking tickets totaling $1,400 because the van, which displayed handicap plates, looked more like a commercial vehicle than a residential vehicle. The Hendersons refused to pay the $1,400 amount.
>
> The homeowners' association then placed a $5,500 lien on the Hendersons' home. The president of the homeowner's board stated that the homeowners' association was not trying to profit

> *Laguna Audubon II Master Association v. Henderson*
> (continued)
>
> at the expense of the Hendersons, but was simply trying to raise awareness of the rules among the owners in the community.
>
> During a court hearing, the Hendersons were ordered to pay the $5,500 fees because their lawyer did not appear in court. The Hendersons stated that they would probably file a countersuit, but the disagreement between the Hendersons and the homeowners' association was settled out of court using a mediation program before the Hendersons took legal action. The association agreed to waive their legal right to all of the fees levied against the Hendersons and gave the Hendersons the right to park their vehicle in the driveway. In return, the Hendersons must abide by the community's rules for a period of one year or move out before the one-year period expires. The Hendersons agreed to the settlement. They plan to move out of the community.

HOMESTEADS

California and many other states have homestead laws to protect families. There are two homestead statutes in California: Articles 4 and 5 of Chapter 4, Division 2, Title 9, and Part 2 of the California Code of Civil Procedure (Sections 704.710-704.995). **Homestead** property is the home (primary residence) occupied by a family that is exempt from the claims of, or eviction by, unsecured creditors.

A **homestead exemption** is in effect a lien that protects a certain amount of equity in a person's home by limiting the amount of liability for certain debts against which a home can be used to satisfy a judgment. The amount protected varies depending on the age, marital status, and income of the property owner. A homestead exemption does not stop the sale of the property. Its purpose is to ensure that the homeowner receives the amount of the exemption before the creditors are paid from the sale proceeds.

Homestead property can be sold if the sale proceeds are sufficient to:
- pay all existing liens on the property.
- pay off all mortgages and loans secured by the equity in the home.
- pay the costs of selling the home.
- allow the homeowner to keep equity in the amount protected by the homestead exemption.

Because they are subject to the general rule regarding liens that "first in time is first in right," homestead exemptions are not effective against prior liens, such as a purchase money deed of trust or mortgage. They are also not effective against tax liens, mechanic's liens, or judgment liens for child, family, or spousal support.

Types of Homestead Exemptions

California law provides for two types of homestead exemption—automatic and declared.

Automatic Homestead

The **automatic homestead** is just that—automatic. Anyone living in his or her home has an automatic homestead exemption protecting the equity. A declaration of homestead does not need to be filed. The automatic, or **statutory homestead exemption**, only applies on the forced sale of the property. The homeowner must live continuously on the property from the date the judgment creditor's lien attaches until the date the court determines that the dwelling is a homestead. [C.C.P. §704.710(a)]. A **dwelling** is the place where a person resides.

Dwellings Protected by Automatic Homestead Exemption
- House together with the outbuildings and the land upon which they are situated
- CID (condominium, planned development, stock cooperative, or community apartment project)
- Mobile home
- Boat or other waterborne vessel

Declared Homestead

A **declared homestead** is the dwelling described in a homestead declaration. A **declaration of homestead** is a recorded notice a property owner files to protect the equity in his or her real property. The declaration of homestead only protects real estate dwellings—not dwellings that are personal property, such as mobile homes on leased land, houseboats, or other waterborne vessels. [C.C.P. §704.710(c)].

Requirements for a Declaration of Homestead

- Name of the declared homestead owner
- Description of the declared homestead
- Statement that the declared homestead is the principal dwelling of the declared homestead owner. [C.C.P. §704.930(a)].
- Individuals Allowed to Sign and Record a Declaration of Homestead
- Declared homestead owner
- Spouse of the declared homestead owner
- Guardian, conservator, attorney in fact or any of the person otherwise authorized to act for the declared homestead owner or the owner's spouse

The declaration of homestead must be signed, acknowledged, and recorded to take effect. Once the declaration of homestead is recorded, the property becomes a homestead. A homestead can be terminated by recording a **notice of abandonment**, by conveying the property, or through an execution and forced sale. An owner must file an **Abandonment of Homestead** form in order to obtain a homestead on a new property. If the owner moves from the homesteaded property and does not wish to file a new declaration of homestead, the original homestead remains valid. Sale of the property automatically causes the homestead to terminate. However, neither death of the homesteader nor destruction of the property terminates the homestead.

A homestead declaration does not restrict or limit any right to convey or encumber the declared homestead. [C.C.P. §704.940]. If a property owner records a declaration of homestead against their primary residence, it in effect drains the property of its equity up to the statutory limit of the homestead. Subsequently, if the owner seeks to borrow against the property, a lender may want the property owner to **subordinate** the homestead to a new loan's security instrument before the lender will give a new extension of credit.

A properly recorded declaration of homestead allows exempt funds received from the voluntary sale of the property to remain exempt from debt collection attempts for six months. In addition, they can be used to purchase another residence.

RECORDING REQUESTED BY

WHEN RECORDED MAIL TO

NAME

ADDRESS

CITY

STATE&ZIP

Title Order No.   Escrow No.

SPACE **ABOVE** THIS LINE FOR RECORDER'S USE

HOMESTEAD DECLARATION

I,_____

(Full Name of Declarant)

do hereby certify and declare as follows:

(1) I hereby claim as a declared homestead the premises located in the City of _____,
County of _____, State of California, commonly known as _____
_____

(Street Address)

and more particularly described as follows: [Give complete legal description]

(2) I am the declared homestead owner of the above declared homestead.

(3) I own the following interest in the above declared homestead:

(4) The above declared homestead is: [] my principal dwelling, or, [] the principal dwelling of my spouse, and

I am, or,   my spouse is currently residing on that declared homestead.

(5) The facts stated in this Declaration are true as of my personal knowledge.

Dated: _____, 20___   _____

(Signature of Declarant)

STATE OF CALIFORNIA
COUNTY OF _____   } SS

On _____, before me, the
undersigned, _____, a Notary Public in and for
said State, personally appeared _____
_____

personally known to me (or proved to me on the basis of satisfactory
evidence) to be the person whose name (s) is/are subscribed to the
within instrument and acknowledged to me that he/she/they executed
the same in his/her/their authorized capacity(ies), and that by his/her/
their signature(s) on the instrument the person(s), or the entity upon
behalf of which the person(s) acted, executed the instrument.

WITNESS my hand and official seal

_____
Notary Public in and for said State.

Amount of the Homestead Exemption

The amount of the homestead exemption varies depending on the age, marital status, and income level of the property owner. [C.C.P. §§704.720 - 704.730].

Homestead Exemptions

- $75,000 for an individual
- $100,000 if the homeowner lives with at least one family member who has no interest in the house
- $175,000 if the homeowner is 65 years of age or older or is physically or mentally disabled
- $175,000 if the homeowner is 55 years of age or older and single with an annual income of $15,000 or less
- $175,000 for a married couple with a combined annual income of $20,000 or less

A creditor with a recorded abstract of judgment can force the sale of a homestead property to satisfy a money judgment, but only if the equity exceeds the homestead exemption. [C.C.P. §704.740(a)].

Example: Mr. Baker, who owns a single-family home that he shares with his mother, filed a declaration of homestead on the property. The home currently is worth $300,000 and has a $225,000 deed of trust. An unsecured creditor was successful in a lawsuit against Mr. Baker and an abstract of judgment for $30,000 was recorded, attaching a lien against the property.

In this instance, the unsecured creditor could not force a sale of the property, because there is not enough equity in the property to satisfy his judgment. The equity in the home is $75,000 ($300,000 - $225,000). Since, the homestead exemption for Mr. Baker is $75,000, there is not enough to cover the $30,000 debt. The property would have to be worth at least $330,000 in order for the unsecured creditor to force a sale.

SUMMARY

Interests in real property can be either possessory or nonpossessory. Those that are possessory are usually present interests meaning that they can be exercised today. Nonpossessory interests are those that cannot be exercised today, but normally can be exercised in the future. Therefore, they usually are known as future interests.

Another term for an ownership interest is a freehold estate. The largest freehold estate that one can own in California is the fee simple absolute, which includes all the rights to sell, exclude others, finance, and do any other thing with real property that the law allows. Other freehold estates include the fee simple subject to condition subsequent and the life estate.

Nonfreehold estates are known as leaseholds. A leasehold consists of an interest held by the tenant (or lessee) to reside on the property or to use it and a reversionary interest held by the property owner or lessor.

Non-possessory interests include financial encumbrances, such as liens and non-financial encumbrances, such as easements, profit-à-prendre, and restrictions. A lien is a financial interest in the property of another. Easements may be either appurtenant or in gross.

A property owner can protect his or her property against judgment liens by recording a declaration of homestead before the judgment lien takes effect.

UNIT 3 REVIEW

Matching Exercise

Instructions: Write the letter of the matching term on the blank line before its definition. Answers are in Appendix A.

Terms

A. abstract of judgment

B. appurtenant easement

C. CC&Rs

D. condition

E. covenant

F. Declaration of Homestead

G. dominant tenement

H. easement

I. easement in gross

J. encumbrance

K. estate

L. fee simple absolute

M. fee simple determinable

N. financial encumbrances

O. freehold estate

P. future interest

Q. homestead property

R. interest

S. judgment creditor

T. license

U. life estate

V. non-financial encumbrance

W. nonfreehold estate

X. periodic tenancy

Y. possessory interest

Z. present interest

AA. profit-à-prendre

BB. servient tenement

CC. tenancy for years

DD. writ of execution

Definitions

1. _____ Various rights, privileges, powers, and immunities with respect to real property

2. _____ Present right to physically occupy land and to exclude others from that same land

3. _____ Interest in land that can be exercised by the owner today

4. _____ Interest that cannot be exercised today, but which might be exercised in the future

5. _____ The quantity, quality, degree, and nature of a person's interest in real property that may become possessory

6. _____ Estate with indefinite duration or that is measured by the length of someone's life

7. _____ Estate with a fixed or determinable duration

8. _____ Freehold estate that includes all rights to sell, exclude others, finance, and do any other thing with real property allowed by law

9. _____ Freehold estate with present possessory interest in a grantee with a reversionary interest in the grantor

10. _____ Freehold interest that allows the owner to live on a parcel until death, but that cannot be bequeathed via a will

11. _____ Leasehold interest for an indefinite period of time

12. _____ Leasehold interest with a fixed term and definite end date

13. _____ Interest in real property that is held by someone who is not the owner

14. _____ Encumbrance that affects title to property

15. _____ Party to a lawsuit who obtains a money judgment against the other party

16. _____ One-page, recordable document that contains information about a court judgment

17. _____ Document directing the sheriff to commence a lien-sale of a parcel of real property

18. _____ Encumbrance that affects the physical use or condition of the property

19. _____ Interest for use owned by one person in the land of another person

20. _____ Land benefiting from an easement

21. _____ Land burdened by an easement

22. _____ Permissive use of land that is freely revocable by the grantor

23. _____ Easement that "runs with the land"

24. _____ Easement that is a personal right of one person to use land owned by another

25. _____ Right to enter another's land to remove soil, substances of the soil, or other resource

26. _____ Rules and regulations established for a parcel of land and accepted by the owner when the property is purchased or transferred

27. _____ Promise that a certain act will, or will not, be performed

28. _____ Limitation imposed by a grantor in a deed that can cause the ownership of the property to revert to the grantor who imposes the condition if the condition is not satisfied

29. _____ Home, occupied by a family, exempt from the claims of unsecured creditors

30. _____ Recorded notice to protect the equity in a home from forced sale by unsecured creditors

Multiple Choice Questions

Instructions: Circle your response and go to Appendix A to read the complete explanation for each question.

1. Real property interests can be categorized in a number of different ways. An estate with indefinite duration is classified as a freehold estate and one with a fixed or determinable duration is classified as a nonfreehold estate. Which pair is correct?
   a. Freehold estate – Free simple absolute
   b. Freehold estate – Perpetual estate
   c. Nonfreehold estate – Tenancy in common
   d. Nonfreehold estate – Pur Autre Vie

2. Which of the following is correct about the real property concept of a leasehold?
   a. A leasehold is an ownership interest, but it is not an estate in land.
   b. A leasehold is not an ownership interest, but it is an estate in land.
   c. A leasehold is neither an ownership interest nor an estate in land.
   d. A leasehold is both an ownership interest and an estate in land.

3. Of the four types of leasehold estates, which one indicates that the tenant is considered a holdover tenant?

    a. Periodic tenancy
    b. Tenancy at sufferance
    c. Tenancy at will
    d. Tenancy for years

4. As defined most broadly, a lien is:

    a. a way to tie up property for several generations.
    b. the most common way of enforcing a money judgment.
    c. a financial interest in the real property of another.
    d. a possessory interest in the real property of another.

5. What is the commonality of trustor, trustee, and beneficiary?

    a. Involuntary lien
    b. Lis pendens
    c. Voluntary lien
    d. Writ of attachment

6. In California, ad valorem taxes differ from special assessments in which of the following ways?

    a. Ad valorem taxes are a percentage of the fair market value of real property based on its most recent sale or improvement and are collected annually.
    b. Special assessments are a percentage of the fair market value of real property based on its most recent sale or improvement and are collected annually.
    c. Ad valorem taxes are levied against property owners to pay for local improvements, such as underground utilities, street repair, or water projects.
    d. Ad valorem taxes are levied against real property, but special assessments are not.

7. An easement appurtenant differs from an easement in gross in that:

    a. with an easement in gross, there is a dominant tenement, but no servient tenement.
    b. with an easement appurtenant, there is a dominant tenement, but no servient tenement.
    c. with an easement in gross, there is a servient tenement, but no dominant tenement.
    d. there is little practical difference between the two kinds of easements today.

8. The right to enter another's land to harvest timber is known as:
    a. adverse possession.
    b. a license.
    c. an easement.
    d. profit-à-prendre.

9. Which of the following could lead to loss of title, if not satisfied?
    a. Condition
    b. Covenant
    c. License
    d. Life estate

10. Which of the following is protected by an automatic homestead exemption, but not by a declared homestead?
    a. Condominium
    b. Mobilehome and the land upon which it is situated
    c. Mobilehome on leased land
    d. Single-family home

Public Restrictions on Land Use

Unit 4

INTRODUCTION

All land in the United States is subject to various obligations and public restrictions imposed by federal, state, and local governments. **Public restrictions** on use of real property are those associated with government intervention.

Within any region, federal and state environmental regulations affect the way in which it is developed. County and city agencies regulate and enforce building codes, health codes, and safety codes. They provide water, recreation, libraries, public housing, transportation, and other services that affect a local community. Local zoning ordinances control the areas in which housing and businesses are located. Businesses must seek approval for the size, style, and location of signage from the local government. Homeowners who want to add a pool in their yard must secure a permit for the pool addition and for most remodeling projects. Builders must apply for building permits from the local government and business owners must acquire business licenses before they open their doors to the public.

Learning Objectives

After completing this unit, you should be able to:

4A   recognize the powers of government that affect private ownership of real estate.

4B   classify planning and zoning techniques used in California.

4C   recall how the takings law affects land use.

4D   name federal and state environmental protection laws.

GOVERNMENT CONTROL OF LAND USE

All private ownership of real estate is subject to the legitimate powers of government, which includes eminent domain, taxation, escheat, and police power. Three of the four powers deal with specific situations while the fourth, police power, is used by government to support the enactment of laws and regulations and the enforcement of these for the benefit and protection of the public health, safety, and welfare.

Eminent domain is the power given to government agencies to take private property for public use or purpose. The payment of just compensation is required and an appraisal is usually necessary. The owner has nothing to say as to the *taking*, only the amount of compensation that may be considered just. **Taxation** is the right of the government to tax the owners of private property to raise revenue for both general purposes and special assessments, which have a defined purpose. Most property taxes are based on value and are known as **ad valorem taxes. Escheat** is the process by which private property reverts to the government when the owner dies without heirs and without a will (intestate).

Police power is the most important of the four powers of the government and the one under which most governmental regulation and restrictions are promulgated. The **police power** is a government's authority to regulate the health, safety, welfare, and morals of its citizens. This power allows the government to make and enforce laws and regulations for the safety, health, and welfare of the public. Zoning regulations, building codes, and fire codes are all enacted under the government's police power.

The California Constitution, Article XI, Section 7 gives cities and counties the same police power authority within their boundaries as the State Legislature exercises for the entire state, subject only to restrictions set by the Legislature itself. Even when there is no state law allowing them to do so, both cities and counties can pass laws regulating the use of land.

PLANNING AND ZONING REGULATIONS

When the underground highway project known as "the Big Dig" was being constructed beneath the City of Boston, the project's architects and construction workers were confronted with more than 300 years of accumulated infrastructure—including sewers, water pipes, electrical cables, old tunnels, and basements, both in the path of the project and in the surrounding area. The project had to be designed and built so that everything that pre-existed the project was either moved or consolidated so that the new tunnel could be constructed in its place.

City, suburban, and even rural planners confront a similar problem. Their most basic task is to keep different uses of land that might be incompatible, such as residential and industrial, away from one another, even though each has a place in the life of a given community. This would be easier if the existing world could be re-designed or things moved around to create a more orderly plan from the dirt up. Of course, this is not possible, except when new communities are built. Therefore, local governments use the planning process to take into account what is already there while trying to be systematic and creative about new development that is proposed.

Although local governments in California have the power to establish local land use regulations, the California Legislature also requires them to exercise that power to establish various controls on the use of real property within their respective jurisdictions. In the **Planning and Zoning Law** [Govt. Code §§65000-66403], the Legislature declared that California's land is an exhaustible resource, not just a commodity, and accordingly, lists a variety of actions that every city and county must undertake to protect that resource.

General Plan

Since 1971, the Planning and Zoning Law has required all cities and counties to have a general plan. The **general plan** is the *constitution* for land use within that city or county. General plans are required to have separate chapters, known as **elements**, that discuss the city's or county's overall goals with respect to certain topics.

Seven Mandatory Elements in a General Plan	
1. Land use	5. Noise
2. Circulation	6. Public safety
3. Conservation	7. Open space
4. Housing	

Cities or counties located on the coast must also address coastal development and protection of natural resources and wetlands. In addition, general plans can and often do have other elements, such as seismic safety or water conservation.

The land use element lists land use classifications, such as agricultural, commercial, industrial, or residential. The general plan must be internally consistent and contain a diagram or diagrams—usually a map or several maps. Each land use element is tied to a map that shows how every parcel in the city or county is designated with one of these categories. Broad areas of a given community might have the same general plan classifications, but different parcels within the same general plan classification might have different zoning.

In addition, a given parcel's zoning must be consistent with the general plan category for that parcel. Thus, if two parcels each had a general plan classification of residential, one of those parcels could be zoned for apartment buildings and the other for single-family homes, but neither could be zoned for industrial use.

Subject to the requirements for the seven mandatory elements and other standards set forth in state law, the precise structure and organization of the plan is left largely to each jurisdiction. The typical format for each element, though, is to begin with a narrative, followed by a series of goals; the goals, in turn, are supported by several policies intended to help achieve those goals. Courts usually give wide latitude to a city council or county board of supervisors in how it interprets its general plan.

> Example: Ted has proposed a housing project in his city. The project is inconsistent with some goals or policies of the open space and circulation elements of the city's general plan because it will use up former agricultural land and cause more traffic. On the other hand, the project will help the city meet the goals and policies in its housing element because it will provide badly needed housing. If the city council decides to approve the development because it furthers the goals and policies of the housing element, the project generally is upheld by a court despite the inconsistencies with the open space and circulation elements.

Zoning

Zoning was the earliest of all modern land-use tools—the "granddaddy" of contemporary planning. It was developed mainly in urban areas in the early twentieth century to try to prevent conflicts between incompatible land uses in close proximity to large cities, such as a factory belching smoke near a row of tenement buildings.

As municipalities around the United States began to experiment with zoning schemes during the first quarter of the twentieth century, developers and property owners began to test them on constitutional grounds. Lower state and federal courts disagreed about their validity. Finally, the United States Supreme Court reviewed a lower court decision that had struck down the zoning ordinance of Euclid, Ohio (a relatively modest ordinance by current standards).

U.S. Supreme Court Case *Euclid v. Ambler Realty Co.*

In *Euclid v. Ambler Realty Co.*, 272 U.S. 365 (1926), the court reversed the lower court decision and upheld Euclid's zoning ordinance as a valid exercise of the police power. In doing so, the Supreme Court stated,

"Regulations, the wisdom, necessity, and validity of which, as applied to existing conditions, are so apparent that they are now uniformly sustained, a century ago, or even half a century ago, probably would have been rejected as arbitrary and oppressive. Such regulations are sustained, under the complex conditions of our day, for reasons analogous to those which justify traffic regulations, which, before the advent of automobiles and rapid transit street railways, would have been condemned as fatally arbitrary and unreasonable."

The *Euclid* decision laid the foundation for modern land use regulation, because local and state governments knew that, as a general principle, these regulations did not violate the Constitution.

In the absence of zoning, the only restriction that can be placed on the use someone can make of his or her land is the common law of nuisance.

Example: Paul lives in a rural area. His neighbor, Linda, owns the neighboring parcel. Linda has created an animal rescue operation on her property. Her property is large enough to build many outdoor pens where she brings abandoned dogs that she obtains from animal shelters in a nearby city. She advertises for people interested in adopting rescued dogs to visit her property, which many people do.

Because the dogs do not stay on Linda's property long enough to become acclimated, dozens of them bark when visitors come to the property. The dogs will also bark when they are left in the pens for long periods of time as the dogs compete with one another, sometimes into the late hours of the night.

Paul's home is located only a few hundred feet from the nearest dog pens. The dog waste attracts flies. The barking and vehicle noise and dust from the unpaved road force him to keep his windows closed even on summer days when he would like to enjoy the breeze. He has complained to Linda, but she is committed to her rescue activities. Local officials have explained that the local zoning code permits owners of large parcels, such as Linda, to conduct this kind of activity.

Paul decides to sue Linda. He seeks a court order that she either ceases the activity or at least reduces the number of animals. He also seeks damages for her interference with the use of his property. Because Linda's operation is allowed by the zoning for her parcel, Paul relies on the legal theory that Linda's rescue operation constitutes a nuisance.

While there are some places where there is still un-zoned land (e.g., Houston, Texas), in California all land under the jurisdiction of a city or county must be zoned. Even land over which the local government does not have direct control, such as federal land or property under the control of a native American tribe, will be given a zoning designation such as public facility so that if the land ever becomes subject to local control, it will be under some regulation.

Basic Principles of Zoning

Zoning works much the same as the general plan classifications, except on a smaller scale. In fact, the way that general plans currently work in California is based on zoning codes that pre-dated them—zoning codes that are now subordinate to the general plans. Like the general plan, a zoning ordinance divides a city or county into different geographic **zones**, identifying what uses can and cannot be made on each parcel.

A typical zoning code will first contain a list of different **zoning districts**, which are all of the possible classifications that might be given to any particular parcel of land. For ease of reference, these are identified by a one-, two-, or three-letter designation (or sometimes a combination of letters and numbers).

Example: In a certain city, a zoning district that allows manufacturing and other kinds of light industrial use to take place is designated MF under the local zoning code. Businesses with large plants and warehouses that have large vehicles coming and going frequently to unload raw materials and to pick up merchandise are permitted in this zone, which normally is not located next to residential property.

Another district, typically found in another part of the city, allows suburban residential development, such as single-family homes and duplexes and is designated SR. In areas of the city between these two kinds of districts are a number of parcels falling under one of two different kinds of commercial zoning districts. One of them allows large commercial activities like shopping centers and is designated C-1 for general commercial activity. A second designation allows only limited commercial activity, such as doctor's offices and small neighborhood grocery stores, and is designated C-2. These are only four of eighteen different zoning designations within that city.

Typical Zoning Symbols

A – Agriculture

C – Commercial

R1 – Single-Family Home

R2 – Duplex

R3 – Multiple Residential Units

PD – Planned Development

M – Manufacturing

P – Public Uses

On rare occasions, a parcel might be split-zoned, with a line running through the parcel with different zoning classifications on different parts of the parcel. The uses that are permitted on one side of the line will be different, as if there were two separate legal parcels.

Avoiding Risk

Although many zoning codes use similar terminology, no two jurisdictions in California use exactly the same zoning restrictions even if the terms they use are identical. Do not assume, therefore, that a parcel with the designation SR in one city or county has the same meaning as the same classification in another city or county. Many cities and counties now have their entire local codes online. Sometimes they are linked to the land use maps or to a list by the assessor's parcel number for that community, so that the general zoning definitions and, even the zoning for individual parcels, can be obtained.

Contents of Zoning Ordinances

Each zoning district lists various kinds of allowances and limitations for each parcel that has been given that zoning designation. Some ordinances begin with a general **statement of intent**. For example, an industrial zoning district in a given city may state that it is intended to create and preserve areas where a full range of industrial uses can be located, even those with moderate to high nuisance characteristics, in order to allow such businesses to locate in the city.

Allowed Uses

Following a statement of intent is usually a list of those **allowed uses** that are permitted as a matter of right in that district. Some codes also refer to these as **permitted uses**. These are activities that a property owner can undertake without first having to get special permission from a local planning commission, zoning administrator, or some other local official or planning body.

> Example: Alexandra is interested in buying a parcel in a city that has designated the parcel as suburban residential (SR). She checks the city's code and finds that the allowed uses within the SR district are single-family dwellings, cemeteries, police and fire stations, religious assemblies, and duplexes. Because Alexandra wants to construct a single-family home on the property, she decides to buy it.
>
> This does not mean, however, that Alexandra can begin building as soon as she takes title to the property at the close of escrow. She will still have to apply for

a building permit and pay a fee to obtain it. The permit application must have drawings to scale showing features, such as the internal construction, the type of materials used, and the placement of the structure on the lot in relation to the property lines.

Nevertheless, once all of these features meet the city's building code, the city will have to issue her a permit and she will be able to begin construction as soon as her building permit application has been reviewed and approved. The city cannot refuse to allow her to build some kind of a single-family dwelling.

Conditional Uses

The second list that usually appears in a zoning district are those uses that are not allowed as a matter of right, but that might be allowed if the owner gets a special permit, also known as a **conditional use permit** (CUP). A local planning commission, zoning administrator, or other local official or body grants these permits. The city or county normally has wide discretion to approve the request, to approve it subject to conditions, or to deny it.

If the request is denied, there is sometimes the opportunity to appeal the decision to the city council or board of supervisors upon payment of a fee. If the permit is denied on appeal, the owner has the option of challenging the denial in superior court.

> Example: Alexandra is a doctor and wants to open a community medical clinic in an SR district. The city's code lists apartment houses, medical clinics, parks, schools, business offices, and mobile home parks as conditional uses. When compared with the list of allowed uses, these are usually more intensive uses for the same property (e.g. apartment buildings) or commercial activities (e.g. shopping centers) that generally are compatible with residential uses.
>
> Alexandra will have to go before the city planning commission to obtain a use permit before she can use the property for her clinic. Alexandra files an application for the permit and pays a fee. The city planning department will review her application and write a report discussing the application. Eventually, the city staff concludes that the neighborhood where Alexandra wants to establish her new clinic is an appropriate location to do so.
>
> Next, a date will be scheduled when Alexandra's application will come before the city planning commission. Neighboring property owners will receive a notice when the meeting will be held. A notice is also published in the local newspaper. On the day of the meeting, the planning commission reviews the staff's report and

allows Alexandra to explain why she thinks this is a good place to locate a clinic. Neighbors who live nearby will also testify, as will any other interested citizens. Some of the neighbors express concerns about the increased traffic the clinic will bring and that more cars will be parked on local streets. Others say that they support Alexandra's proposal and want a clinic nearby.

The commission members consider such factors as how many homes are located near the proposed clinic, how much traffic it is likely to generate, and whether there are similar uses in the neighborhood. At the conclusion of the hearing, the commission decides to approve her application for a permit. Even though it grants the permit, the commission imposes conditions to address issues raised by the city and the neighbors. Alexandra will only be allowed to operate the clinic on weekdays from 7:00 a.m. to 6:00 p.m. She will have to provide five parking spaces on her parcel (which will limit the size of the clinic). The commission also sets a five-year term on the permit, which means she must renew it, allowing the commission to review whether the clinic has been a good neighbor to surrounding properties.

Once a use permit is granted, it ordinarily runs with the land. The permit in effect is issued to the property, not to the applicant, so that if Alexandra sells the property to another doctor, he or she will be able to operate a clinic on the same terms that she did.

Prohibited Uses

Any uses that are not listed as either allowed or conditional are presumptively **prohibited uses** by the zoning code.

Example: Mike wants to establish a mortuary on a parcel that is zoned SR. Mortuaries are not listed as either allowed or conditional uses in the SR district. If Mike wants to establish a mortuary on this particular parcel, therefore, he will have to apply to the city to change the zoning on the property to C-1, general commercial, where mortuaries are an allowed use.

The fee to apply for a zoning change is $1,000, will take more than six months, and there is no guarantee that the city council will agree to make the change to one parcel of SR property just to allow Mike's plans to go forward. Mike decides to abandon his purchase of this parcel and instead looks for property that is already zoned C-1 where he can establish a mortuary as an allowed use.

In fact, if Mike were able to convince the city to change his one parcel from SR to C-1, it might also constitute spot zoning. **Spot zoning** occurs when a public entity makes the decision to change the zoning for a single parcel without considering the larger planning context. A single parcel of C-1 surrounded by a sea of parcels zoned SR is at least some evidence that the city has engaged in spot zoning; and if it has acted just to benefit the applicant without considering the surrounding land uses, it may be subject to invalidation by a court as arbitrary—and illegal—spot zoning.

Size Restrictions

Zoning ordinances often list size restrictions applicable to each parcel with a given zoning district. Examples of those restrictions include height limits, setbacks, and the minimum lot size. **Height limits** state how tall the buildings can be above the average grade. **Setbacks** limit how close a structure can be built to neighboring property lines. The **minimum lot size** limits how small the parcels can be if the property were subdivided. If the minimum lot size in the SR zone in the example above were a half-acre, a two-acre parcel could be subdivided into no more than four resulting lots.

Legally Nonconforming Uses

If a city or county changes the zoning of a parcel so that the existing uses are no longer allowed by the new zoning, those existing activities are known as **legally nonconforming uses**. Nonconforming uses that existed prior to the adoption of the current zoning that were lawful when established are normally allowed to continue indefinitely.

Example: Dave operates a medical clinic in a different part of the same city where Alexandra wanted to establish her clinic. His parcel is also zoned SR, but the clinic was already on the parcel when the city's zoning code was adopted. Because the clinic was opened before the establishment of the code, it did not have to obtain a use permit to operate.

Even though he would have to get a use permit today, Dave's clinic is legally nonconforming. He can continue to operate his clinic without a use permit indefinitely as long as he does not abandon the use for more than six months. Even though the neighborhood where his clinic is located is similar to the one where Alexandra's new clinic will be built, he does not have to allow any parking on his property, he can operate during any hours he sees fit, and he can stay open on the weekends if he chooses.

Nonconforming uses cannot be continued if they constitute nuisances. Furthermore, because they in effect create a favored class not subject to the current law, a nonconforming use normally cannot be expanded (such as by conducting it on a larger area than before). The one exception that the California Supreme Court has recognized, in *Hansen Brothers Enterprises, Inc. v. Board of Supervisors of Nevada County* (1995) 12 Cal.4th 533, is for mining operations. Because mining uses up the land itself, mining operations have a limited right to expand even if they are legally nonconforming.

However, public entities can get rid of legally nonconforming uses in two ways. First, they can ban them immediately and pay the owner compensation for a "taking" under the Fifth Amendment to the U.S. Constitution. Second, they can **amortize the use**, giving the landowner a period of time to continue the use in order to recapture the owner's investment. At the end of that time, the activity must cease without compensation.

> Example: Mike operates a rock quarry on a parcel where the zoning no longer allows rock quarries, even with a use permit. Because he has a legal nonconforming use, he can continue to operate the quarry indefinitely.
>
> Over the years, houses have been built closer to the quarry and the neighbors complain about the noise, dust, and traffic Mike's quarry generates. The neighbors could bring a nuisance lawsuit, but instead they approach the county board of supervisors, seeking a new ordinance that requires quarries to cease operation when they are no longer permitted by the zoning.
>
> The board passes the ordinance, but it includes a provision that it does not affect existing quarries until five years after its effective date. Even though Mike will have to discontinue his operation after five years, he probably cannot get compensation from the county, because five years gives him a reasonable time to continue mining before his use becomes illegal.

Abatement

Public entities do not have to pay compensation for the abatement of a nuisance or a violation of the local code. **Abatement** is the legal process by which a public entity removes nuisances and code violations.

> Example: Dan has been quarrying rock on his property and selling it without a use permit. However, the zoning for the parcel where he operates his quarry requires a conditional use permit to do any mining. The county goes to court and obtains a court order prohibiting any mining unless Dan obtains a permit. The county will not have to pay Dan any compensation for the time he is unable to operate a quarry because his operation was never legal to begin with.

Variances

A **variance** is a local land use decision allowing a use that is not strictly in compliance with local zoning or building regulations. California has a strict rule for variances. The city or county must find that, because of unique conditions of the property in question (its size, topography, shape, location, or surroundings), the strict application of the zoning ordinance deprives the owner of privileges enjoyed by other property owners in the vicinity.

> Example: Donna owns a parcel that is unusually long and thin. She wants to build a house on the property, but the local zoning code requires a ten-foot setback between the exterior of a structure and any property line. The only house that Donna could build on her parcel given those restrictions would be exceedingly long and thin.
>
> Because her parcel is so narrow, Donna applies for a variance from the conditions of the zoning code. She asks the city planning commission to allow her to construct her house with only a five-foot setback from each of the two property lines. Her house will still be relatively long compared to its depth, but it will at least allow her to have more interior space. The commission agrees, finding that the strict application of the code to Donna's parcel would be unfair because she cannot build a conventionally sized house on the property as the owners of most other nearby parcels could.

Subdivision Restrictions

The creation of new lots out of old ones is actually regulated by different, but interrelated sets of statutory controls—the Subdivision Map Act and the Subdivided Lands Law. The former is concerned with the physical aspects of a subdivision, while the latter regulates land divisions creating the kind of lots that one finds in suburban residential developments.

Subdivision Map Act

Today, cities and counties throughout California have complete control of the subdivision process under the **Subdivision Map Act** (Map Act), which is found at Government Code §66410 et seq. The Map Act defines a **subdivision** as any division of land for the purpose of sale, lease, or financing. The Act regulates all physical aspects of subdividing land—laying out lines for utilities, establishing monumentation, designing a realistic layout for the new parcels given existing buildings, and locating roads, easements, and other infrastructure.

Since 1972, the law now provides that the city or county where the land is located will decide whether the land that the applicant wants to subdivide, in fact, can be subdivided at all, even to create just one new parcel.

The Map Act exempts certain transactions from its regulation. Among the more important is a lot line adjustment. With a **lot line adjustment**, a part of one lot is transferred from one owner to another (making, e.g., one lot bigger and another smaller) but without creating a new lot. Since 2001, only four or fewer lots may be adjusted in this way without having a new subdivision map recorded. Cities and counties still review these transfers to ensure that the resulting parcels meet zoning standards (such as minimum lot sizes) and building standards, such as setbacks from existing buildings to the new property lines.

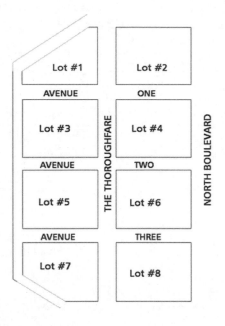

Relationship to Zoning

Although subdivisions are regulated primarily under the Map Act, there is still some interrelationship between zoning—the backbone of most other land use regulations—and the subdivision of parcels. The **minimum parcel size** is one standard set in the zoning ordinances of every city or county. That is, in addition to listing what can and cannot be done on each parcel in each kind of zoning district, the zoning districts will also list the smallest-size parcel that a parcel in that district can legally be subdivided.

> Example: Sam is the owner of a 26-acre parcel zoned Rural Residential with five-acre minimum lot sizes. In the city where his land is located, it is abbreviated RR-5, which refers to the district and the minimum size parcels. If Sam wanted to subdivide this parcel, he could theoretically create four new five-acre parcels, leaving a six-acre remainder parcel.
>
> Although the remainder parcel has enough land to create one more five-acre parcel out of the remaining six-acre piece, the one-acre parcel that would be left over would be too small to meet the minimum set by the RR-5 zoning district. Therefore, after creating four new parcels, Sam would have to leave at least one parcel of six acres.

He could choose several alternative configurations depending on the topography of the parcel and other factors. Instead of creating five parcels (four fives plus the six-acre piece), Sam could create 3 seven-acre parcels plus one five-acre parcel; or he could create only two ten-acre parcels and one six-acre parcel. The possibilities are quite large as long as no one parcel is smaller than the five acres allowed.

Objectives of the Map Act

The first objective is to coordinate the subdivision plans and planning, including lot design, water supply, street patterns, right-of-way for drainage and sewers, etc., with the community pattern and plan as laid out by the local planning authorities.

The second objective is to ensure initial proper improvement of areas dedicated for public purposes by having the subdivider file subdivision maps, including public streets and other public areas, so that these necessities will not become an undue burden in the future for taxpayers in the community.

Subdivisions that create five or more new parcels are referred to as **major subdivisions**. The Map Act requires that when an applicant wants to process a major subdivision, the subdivider must prepare two different maps of the subdivision, a tentative map and a final map. [Govt. Code §66426]. The **tentative map** means what it sounds like. It is a map that shows the conceptual design of the proposed subdivision and the improvements that will go along with it, such as streetlights, roads, and the drainage system. Any changes required by the planning commission are indicated in a **final map**, which is recorded in the county where the property is located. Final maps are governed by an extensive series of requirements found at Government Code §§66434-66443. Section 66434 requires, at the outset, that the map be prepared "by or under the direction of a registered civil engineer or licensed land surveyor, shall be based upon a survey," and must conform to a lengthy set of detailed requirements that even specify the kind of ink and the size of the paper on which the map is prepared.

Generally, a **parcel map** must be recorded for any subdivision for which a final map is not specifically required by the Map Act, unless the parcel map requirement is waived by the city or county. [Govt. Code §§66426 and 66428]. Because final maps are normally required for subdivisions creating five or more new parcels, a parcel map is required for most other subdivisions, including those creating four or fewer parcels and condominium projects. **Minor subdivisions** are those in which the developer creates four or fewer new parcels and the division qualifies for a waiver of the parcel map requirement. Public entities are required by Government Code §66428 to establish an alternative procedure for processing subdivisions creating four or fewer new lots so that, in most cases, a parcel map does not have to be prepared to complete such a subdivision.

Intentional violations of the Map Act can be treated as a criminal violation and they carry both misdemeanor and felony penalties, punishable by jail time and by a fine of up to $10,000. [Govt. Code §66499.31].

The Subdivided Lands Law

The **Subdivided Lands Law** (Lands Law) is found in the Business and Professions Code §§11000 et seq. and is administered by the Bureau of Real Estate (CalBRE). Unlike the Map Act (which is concerned with the physical process of dividing a larger lot into smaller ones—how the lots will be laid out, where roads will go, and so forth), the Lands Law is essentially a consumer protection law. It is intended to prevent members of the public who purchase lots or homes in subdivisions from being defrauded by unscrupulous developers.

The Lands Law regulates the sale of new parcels created by the major subdivision process. It does not apply to subdivisions that create four or fewer new parcels nor to subdivisions creating parcels of 160 acres or larger.

Under the Lands Law, a **subdivision** (or subdivided lands) refers to improved or unimproved land or lands, wherever situated within California, divided or proposed to be divided for the purpose of sale or lease or financing, whether immediate or future, into five or more lots or parcels. [B&P §11000(a)]. A subdivision also includes improved or unimproved land in which five or more UNDIVIDED INTERESTS are created for the purpose of sale, lease, or financing. [B&P §11000.1(a)].

Exceptions to Subdivided Lands under the Lands Law
- Divisions of land into four or fewer new parcels
- Subdivisions creating parcels of 160 acres or larger in size
- Subdivisions located entirely outside California

The Lands Law requires the preparation of a **public report** for all major subdivisions. This report must show that the developer has completed (or provided sufficient security, such as a bond, to ensure completion) all of the subdivision's improvements and has complied with the other conditions that the local government required for the subdivision.

CalBRE's regulations require that the subdivider give a copy of the public report to each prospective buyer for review. The buyer must sign a receipt acknowledging that the buyer has read the report and the developer must keep a copy of that receipt for three years. By requiring that the public report be given to prospective purchasers, CalBRE ensures that the standards for the creation of new lots have been followed and that all relevant information about the subdivision is available to the buying public.

RECEIPT FOR PUBLIC REPORT

The Laws and Regulations of the Real Estate Commissioner require that you as a prospective purchaser or lessee be afforded an opportunity to read the public report for this subdivision before you make any written offer to purchase or lease a subdivision interest or before any money or other consideration toward purchase or lease of a subdivision interest is accepted from you.

In the case of a preliminary subdivision public report you must be afforded an opportunity to read the report before a written reservation or any deposit in connection therewith is accepted from you.

In the case of a conditional subdivision public report, delivery of legal title or other interest contracted for will not take place until issuance of a final subdivision public report. Provision is made in the sales agreement and escrow instructions for the return to you of the entire sum of money paid or advanced by you if you are dissatisfied with the final public report because of a material change. (See Business and Professions Code §11012.)

DO NOT SIGN THIS RECEIPT UNTIL YOU HAVE RECEIVED A COPY OF THE REPORT AND HAVE READ IT.

I read the Commissioner's public report on _____

_____ [File Number]

_____

[Tract Number or Name]

I understand the report is not a recommendation or endorsement of the subdivision, but is for information only.

The issue date of the public report which I received and read is:

_____   _____

Signature   Date

_____

Address

Once the developer submits the information about the subdivision to the Commissioner's office, there may be a lengthy period of time until the report is issued. However, the developer can apply for a **preliminary public report**. Once the developer obtains this document, it cannot legally sell any of the lots or accept any non-refundable deposits; but it can accept reservations from prospective purchasers pending the completion of the report.

Ministerial vs. Discretionary Projects

There are two other paired concepts that someone may encounter in weaving through the thicket of regulations that surround land use.

Ministerial Projects

Ministerial projects are those permits or entitlements an applicant has an absolute right to receive. Examples of these kinds of projects are building permits, certificates of occupancy, or a permit to drill a well. (Non-planning examples would include a dog license, a passport application, or a marriage license.)

Ministerial projects do not require any form of public notice, a public meeting, or a public hearing. The local agency of the city or county reviews such applications to verify that the plans or other activity meets the safety and health standards (building code, plumbing code, etc.) that allow the issuance of the permit in the first place. Once the agency decides that the permit meets those standards and the necessary permit fee has been paid, it can issue the permit over the counter without further notice to anyone else. Indeed, it cannot refuse to issue a permit for a structure that meets the zoning standards (height, setbacks, etc.) and that is designed in compliance with the building code.

Discretionary Projects

On the other hand, **discretionary projects** are those that a decision-maker has the authority to approve, to approve with conditions, or to deny. General plan amendments, zoning changes, subdivisions, use permits, and variances are all discretionary and a public agency can choose to approve or to turn down such projects.

Discretionary projects usually require some form of public notice and most discretionary projects will require at least a public meeting. For example, Alexandra's medical clinic was a discretionary use and could have been turned down by the planning commission instead of being approved subject to conditions.

Quasi-Legislative vs. Quasi-Judicial

Discretionary projects can be further divided into **legislative projects** and **adjudicative projects** (sometimes referred to as **quasi-legislative** and **quasi-judicial**). General plan changes and amendments to zoning ordinances are quasi-legislative. The decision to approve a new subdivision, a use permit, or a variance is quasi-judicial. One way to think of this distinction is that a city council or board of supervisors is acting at a POLICY LEVEL when making a quasi-legislative decision, while it or another decision-maker is acting at a PERMIT LEVEL when making a quasi-judicial decision.

HOW THE "TAKINGS" LAW AFFECTS LAND USE

No discussion of land use law today would be complete without mentioning some of the principles of the "takings" law derived from the Fifth Amendment of the U.S. Constitution. While the literal language of the Amendment seems to refer just to the government "taking" private property to build a jail, a road, or a school, there are three distinct applications of the takings principles to land-use planning decisions: physical takings, regulatory takings, and conditions on development.

Physical Takings

A **physical taking** occurs when the government actually takes and occupies private land for what is indisputably a public purpose, such as building a public building or establishing a public road or utility easement. When the government physically takes real property, the landowner is entitled to just compensation. If the government appropriates land without payment, a landowner can seek compensation under a parallel legal theory known as inverse condemnation.

Regulatory Takings

Less intrusive (in theory) are regulatory takings. A **regulatory taking** occurs when the government does not physically take private real property, but places an excessive amount of restrictions on the use that can be made of land. The concept is derived from a 1922 Supreme Court decision, *Pennsylvania Coal Co. v. Mahon* (1922) 260 U. S. 393, which held that all regulation affects the value of property to some extent. However, "if regulation goes too far, it will be recognized as a taking."

 Lucas v. South Carolina Coastal Council

One kind of regulatory taking occurs if a law eliminates ALL economically viable use of a parcel. In *Lucas v. South Carolina Coastal Council* (1992) 505 U.S. 1003, the U.S. Supreme Court decided that Mr. Lucas was entitled to compensation for the value of two lots he owned on a barrier island. The basis for the decision was that South Carolina had imposed so many restrictions on developing its barrier islands that Mr. Lucas could make no use of them. This has come to be known as a **Lucas Wipeout**.

A regulatory takings can also occur if a landowner can make certain uses of real property but the government limits the uses of a parcel (and hence its value). This concept was articulated by the Supreme Court in *Penn Central Transp. Co. v. New York City* (1978) 438 U. S. 104. However, the *Penn Central* case did not fix any set formula for determining when the government must bear the burden of a given regulation. A court will consider a variety of factors, especially how much the regulation has interfered with "reasonable investment-backed expectations" and the purposes served by a particular regulation. In practice, government regulation that falls short of a **Lucas Wipeout**, even if extensive, usually defeats a regulatory takings claim.

Conditions on Development

Public agencies place conditions on development of specific projects regarding dedications of land in return for the permit. If the purpose of the dedication is not sufficiently related to the project being developed, the dedication may actually be a taking.

In some recent cases, property owners challenged the conditions imposed by the public agency. In many ways, these cases have been the most successful challenges to land use regulations, because while property owners rarely get monetary compensation, courts frequently strike down permit conditions that they find go "too far."

Nollan v. California Coastal Commission

The first case to recognize this principle was *Nollan v. California Coastal Commission* (1987) 483 U. S. 825. The Nollans obtained a permit to tear down their beachfront house to build a larger one. They were told that they would have to dedicate a strip of land along the beach to the state because the new house would be a "psychological barrier" to public awareness of a nearby public beach.

The Supreme Court held that there was no logical connection (nexus) between the size of the new house and the need for the Nollans to give up a part of their property. Even though the Coastal Commission could have turned down the Nollans' permit entirely, the court said that it could not approve it subject to a condition without any connection between the harm supposedly being mitigated and the condition imposed.

Dolan v. City of Tigard

> The second case was *Dolan* v. *City of Tigard* (1994) 512 U.S. 374. Mrs. Dolan wanted to build a larger plumbing store on her property and the city approved her permit to do so. However, like the Nollans, she was told that she would have to dedicate a strip of land to the city to help construct part of a pedestrian/bicycle pathway that the city wanted to build along a creek that ran beside her property.
>
> The court found that while the proposed pathway met the nexus test under *Nollan*—because it would help reduce vehicle traffic to the new store—the city had not done its homework. It had not provided enough evidence to show how many vehicle trips the path would really have saved to justify making Mrs. Dolan give up her land. The city also failed to show why outright dedication of title, rather than an easement, was necessary.

ENVIRONMENTAL CONTROLS

The system of regulating land through zoning and, later, general plans, went along with only moderate change during the first 40 or 50 years that such tools were in use. During the 1960s, the public became increasingly concerned about the escalating harm to the natural environment, such as the Santa Barbara oil spill in 1969 or when the Cuyahoga River near Cleveland, Ohio caught fire due to its high concentration of industrial wastes.

In response to public outcry, both the federal and the state governments adopted a series of new laws that required governmental decision to take the environmental consequences of human activity into account before a particular decision was made. This had significant consequences for landowners in California, because many decisions that were once made with only political or economic consequences in mind became subject to strict environmental analysis.

Federal Laws

Federal laws affecting use of all public and private lands include the National Environmental Policy Act, the NEPA process, the Clean Air Act, the Clean Water Act, the Coastal Zone Management Act, and the Comprehensive Environmental Response, Compensation, and Liability Act (CERCLA).

National Environmental Policy Act

The first law to require that the environmental effects of public decisions be considered was the **National Environmental Policy Act** (NEPA) signed by President Richard Nixon on January 1, 1970. It requires that federal agencies and other entities undertaking activities on federal property conduct an environmental analysis of the proposed project. It is sometimes referred to as a **procedural statute**, because unlike such laws as the Clean Air Act or the Clean Water Act that protect specific resources, NEPA changed only HOW federal agencies make decisions.

The NEPA Process

The NEPA process provides for a three-tiered approach to its application: categorical exclusion, environmental assessment, and environmental impact statement.

Some projects are entitled to a **categorical exclusion**. Projects in this category are generally smaller or have no impact on the environment. They are given a statutory exemption from further evaluation under the NEPA process.

At the second level, a federal agency prepares a written **environmental assessment** (EA) to see whether a federal project may significantly affect the environment. If not, the agency issues a **finding of no significant impact** (FONSI). The FONSI may spell out measures that the agency will take to mitigate (reduce) potentially significant impacts.

Finally, the largest and potentially most environmentally far-reaching projects can require an environmental impact statement (EIS) to be prepared. An **environmental impact statement** is a more detailed evaluation of the proposed action and alternatives. The public, other federal agencies, and outside parties may provide input into the preparation of an EIS and then comment during the process before the agency adopts the EIS and decides whether to go forward with the project.

Nevertheless, NEPA is still somewhat limited in its impacts. It applies mainly to projects undertaken by federal agencies or on federal land (including Native American lands). There is also a requirement for NEPA compliance for certain projects, such as some low-income housing projects that receive federal funds. Receiving federal funds does not automatically require that the recipient follow the NEPA process.

Clean Air Act

The **Clean Air Act**, passed in 1970, requires the EPA to establish national standards for clean air. The EPA designates how many particles of each pollutant can be present in the air. The EPA publishes guidelines called the National Emission Standards for Hazardous Air Pollutants (NESHAP), a must-read for managers of industrial property.

Clean Water Act

The **Clean Water Act** of 1972 is comprised of amendments to the original Clean Water Act of 1948. The goal is to prohibit the discharge of pollutants in natural waters and to create bodies of water that are clean enough for recreational swimming and fishing.

Coastal Zone Management Act

The **Coastal Zone Management Act** (CZMA) passed in 1972 provides for management of the nation's coastal resources, including the Great Lakes, and balances economic development with environmental conservation. The CZMA outlines two national programs, the National Coastal Zone Management Program and the National Estuarine Research Reserve System. The 34 coastal programs aim to balance competing land and water issues in the coastal zone, while estuarine reserves serve as field laboratories to provide a greater understanding of estuaries and how humans impact them.

CERCLA

The **Comprehensive Environmental Response, Compensation, and Liability Act (CERCLA)** of 1980 is known as Superfund. It is called **Superfund** because it has established two trust funds to help finance the cleanup of properties that are impacted by the release of hazardous wastes and substances. The Superfund Amendments and Reauthorization Act of 1986 (SARA) enables the federal government to place a lien on property subject to cleanup action. Unlike most government liens, the Superfund lien is subordinate to established senior liens.

State Laws

The California legislature enacted several laws to protect the environment. Some of these laws include the California Environmental Quality Act, the CEQA process, and the California Coastal Act.

California Environmental Quality Act

Because NEPA only applies to federal agencies or federal property, some states also adopted their own versions of NEPA in the years after NEPA was enacted. The **California Environmental Quality Act** (CEQA) [Public Resources Code §§21000 et seq.] was also enacted in 1970. It has become one of the most far-reaching pieces of legislation adopted by the California Legislature in the last fifty years. CEQA applies to virtually every decision made by the state or by local agencies (e.g. cities and counties) and requires that those entities conduct an environmental review of most public and private projects.

The CEQA Process

Like NEPA, CEQA provides for a three-tiered environmental analysis of all projects subject to its application. Because it was modeled after NEPA, much of its terminology is clearly derived from NEPA.

A small number of projects are entitled to a **categorical exemption**, which means that these projects are entitled to an exemption by law at an early stage (again, usually because such projects are small and will have little if any impact on the environment). All that the agency must do for exempt projects is to note that it has reviewed the project briefly and found it to be exempt.

At the second level, a state or local agency prepares a written negative declaration that usually is not much longer than a dozen pages or so. A **negative declaration** analyzes a proposed project's anticipated environmental impacts in some detail and explains why the project, as proposed or with changes, will not have the potential to cause significant impacts to the environment. (The "negative" in "negative declaration" does not refer to anything about the project itself; rather, it is an explanation by the agency that there will not be impacts to the environment—hence, a negative declaration.) Like a FONSI, the negative declaration may still list conditions with which the party undertaking the project must comply in order to mitigate potential environmental impacts.

Again, following the model from NEPA, those projects that might potentially have significant environmental impacts require an **environmental impact report** (EIR) before a public agency can decide whether to approve or disapprove those projects. Like an EIS, an EIR is a detailed evaluation of the proposed action and alternatives, sometimes running to several hundred pages. The public, other federal agencies, and outside parties can comment on the draft version of an EIR. The EIR is then re-written in response to the comments before the agency can adopt the EIR and use it to decide whether to approve the project.

As compared to NEPA, where CEQA differs in its implications for real property developers is that it applies not only to projects undertaken by public agencies themselves (as NEPA does), but also to any private project that a public agency has discretion to approve or to deny. When it was originally enacted, many people assumed that CEQA only applied to public works projects and not to such private development activities as use permits and subdivisions.

However, two years later in *Friends of Mammoth* v. *Board of Supervisors* (1972) 8 Cal.3d 247, the California Supreme Court agreed with a citizens' group that because these kinds of activities required approval from a public agency, they also required CEQA review and analysis—even to the level of the preparation of an EIR. Because an EIR can cost tens, if not hundreds of thousands of dollars, merely requiring an EIR can end many projects at an early stage in their planning. CEQA has thus become an important tool in the hands of neighbors, environmental organizations, and others interested in slowing the pace of development, either in a particular community or statewide.

> Example: Bob has a parcel that is zoned SR, which in the city where the land is located allows small, suburban-style lots. His parcel is large enough that he can subdivide it into 50 new lots. He files an application that will go before the city's planning commission to create the maximum number of lots allowed by the zoning.
>
> However, when the commission hears his application, the city staff is recommending that the application be denied unless Bob pays for an EIR. The staff points out that there will be an increase in new traffic, much greater demand on the city's water and sewer systems from the new houses, and a greater burden placed on the city's fire and police agencies. There will also be as many as 100 new children who will have to be accommodated in the city's schools.
>
> Bob opposes the requirement for an EIR, arguing that the impact of only an additional 50 houses will not be large enough to warrant an EIR. However, the testimony of other neighboring property owners tips the balance and the commission directs that Bob's application not go forward until an EIR has been prepared. His project will now be on hold until an outside firm has been hired to write the EIR, which will cost about $75,000. Because he is the applicant, Bob will have to pay those costs to the city.

Once the EIR has been completed (and if the project is approved), Bob can recover that cost by spreading it among the sales price of the new parcels. But until that time, the project will be in limbo and depending on the information developed by the EIR, the city may turn the project down or approve a subdivision of fewer than the 50 lots Bob has requested.

After more than 35 years, many developers have come to accept CEQA as part of the cost of doing business in California. Perceptive developers therefore simply factor the potential delays and expense of the CEQA process into the cost of proposed development—while still trying to keep such costs to the possible minimum.

A developer will obviously want to avoid having to prepare an EIR for a project that only requires a negative declaration. On the other hand, some projects are so large or are so likely to have potentially significant impacts that, realistically, an opponent of the project will be able to persuade a court that the project requires an EIR. In such cases, some developers will simply opt to prepare an EIR for such a project to avoid the delay (and wasted time) if a public entity or a court eventually decides that one should have been prepared in the first place.

California Coastal Act

Under the **California Coastal Act**, [Public resources Code, Division 20 §§ 30000-30900] 15 coastal counties and 58 cities, along with the state of California, have stewardship of the 1,100 miles of coast that stretches from Oregon to the border with Mexico. The **coastal zone** contains over 1.5 million acres of land and reaches from three miles at sea to an inland boundary that varies from a few

blocks in urban areas to about five miles in less-developed areas.

Each city and county in the coastal zone must prepare Local Coastal Programs (LCPs), which adhere to the California Coastal Commission's strict standards for coastal development and protection. The **Local Coastal Programs** are the basic planning tools used to review and decide permits for new development in coastal areas. Additionally, they protect the shoreline and environmentally sensitive habitats, determine ways to improve and expand existing ports, improve public access to the shoreline, and establish urban-rural boundaries to direct new development into areas with existing services to avoid wasteful urban sprawl and leapfrog development.

If property is located in the coastal zone, the owner or developer must apply for a **coastal development permit** (CDP) before any new construction can begin. Permits are routinely approved provided the projects comply with the Coastal Act policies and standards. In many areas, the California Coastal Commission retains permit authority over the coastal zone, and many local actions can be appealed to the Coastal Commission.

SUMMARY

Despite the ancient legal maxim that "a man's house is his castle," in a complex modern society, private property rights are frequently limited by the countervailing principle that one person's rights go only as far as the next person's property. Local governments in California impose a detailed list of restrictions on what use can be made of every parcel in the state. The general plan sets forth the constitution for development within each city and county. The goals and policies of their general plans are enforced through zoning ordinances that list allowed uses and conditional uses that can be undertaken on a given parcel. Any uses not listed in a zoning district are prohibited in that district.

Zoning ordinances also impose other restrictions on the way that property can be developed, such as height limits, setbacks, and minimum parcel sizes for the subdivision of land. Despite this, parcels that were developed when the laws regulating the property in question were less restrictive or not in force are deemed to be legally nonconforming and uses established before more restrictive zoning laws were in place can be continued. Public entities can phase out nonconforming uses, but only by paying compensation or allowing a property owner a reasonable period of time to continue the use before it is abolished.

New development is subject to detailed environmental analysis through the CEQA process. Relatively modest projects can be approved using a less expensive and less time-consuming negative declaration (or a categorical exemption), but major projects require an environmental impact report. In some cases, the environmental review process can be used to prevent new development by delaying a project or by driving up the costs to prohibitive levels. On the other hand, wise developers will factor the time and expense of environmental analysis into the development process from the outset.

UNIT 4 REVIEW

Matching Exercise

Instructions: Write the letter of the matching term on the blank line before its definition. Answers are in Appendix A.

Terms

A. abatement

B. allowed uses

C. categorical exclusion

D. CEQA

E. coastal zone

F. conditional uses

G. discretionary projects

H. eminent domain

I. environmental impact report

J. environmental impact statement

K. final map

L. general plan

M. height limits

N. legally nonconforming use

O. ministerial projects

P. negative declaration

Q. NEPA

R. police power

S. prohibited uses

T. public restrictions

U. setbacks

V. spot zoning

W. tentative map

X. variance

Y. zoning

Z. zoning districts

Definitions

1. _____ Limitations on use of real property associated with government intervention

2. _____ Power given government agencies to take private property for public use or purpose

3. _____ Government's authority to regulate the health, safety, welfare, and morals of its citizens

4. _____ The *constitution* for land use in each city and county in California

5. _____ Ordinance dividing a city or county into different districts, identifying what uses can and cannot be made on each parcel

6. _____ Areas showing all of the possible classifications that might be given to any particular parcel of land

7. _____ Activities permitted within a zoning district as a matter of right

8. _____ Activities not allowed in a zoning district as a matter of right, but that can be allowed if the owner gets a special permit

9. _____ Any uses not listed as either allowed or conditional

10. _____ Zoning changed for a single parcel without considering the larger planning context

11. _____ How tall buildings can be above the average grade

12. _____ Limit on how close a structure can be built to neighboring property lines

13. _____ An existing activity allowed to continue despite a change in the zoning of a parcel

14. _____ Legal process used to remove nuisances and code violations

15. _____ Allowing a use not strictly in compliance with local zoning or building regulations

16. _____ Map showing the conceptual design of the proposed subdivision and the improvements that will go along with it

17. _____ Map recorded in the county where the property is located

18. _____ Permits or entitlements an applicant has an absolute right to receive

19. _____ Projects a decision-maker has the authority to approve, to approve with conditions, or to deny

20. _____ Federal law requiring federal agencies to consider the environmental effects of their decisions

21. _____ Statutory exemption under the NEPA process given to small projects having no impact on the environment

22. _____ Detailed evaluation required by NEPA regarding the environmental impact of a proposed development

23. _____ A finding by state or local agency that a proposed project will not have the potential to cause significant impacts to the environment

24. _____ California law providing a three-tiered environmental analysis of all projects subject to its application

25. _____ Report required by CEQA regarding projects potentially having significant environmental impacts

26. _____ Area of land that reaches from three miles at sea to an inland boundary varying from a few blocks in urban areas to about five miles in less-developed areas

Multiple Choice Questions

Instructions: Circle your response and go to Appendix A to read the complete explanation for each question.

1. Which power of government is the basis for county and city zoning regulations and building codes?
    a. Eminent domain
    b. Escheat
    c. Police power
    d. Taxation

2. In the *Euclid v. Ambler Realty Co.* decision, the U.S. Supreme Court:
    a. found that zoning was a valid exercise of the police power.
    b. determined that the states, but not local governments, had the power to zone.
    c. concluded that the zoning of property violated the Takings Clause of the Fifth Amendment.
    d. concluded that zoning of property was only valid to get rid of nuisances.

3. Which of the following is true regarding zoning?
    a. Zoning has been a part of the legal tradition of the United States since it was first settled by Europeans.
    b. All cities and counties in California use exactly the same terms for the zoning districts in their boundaries.
    c. Zoning was developed in rural areas to prevent different farming operations from interfering with one another.
    d. A zoning ordinance divides a city or county into different geographic zones.

4. Jeff wants to open a restaurant on a parcel he owns in the city where he lives. The zoning for his parcel states that the allowed uses are single-family residences, cemeteries, police and fire stations, religious assemblies, and duplexes. The conditional uses are apartment houses, medical clinics, parks, schools, business offices, and mobile home parks. Jeff:

    a. cannot open a restaurant on this parcel unless he gets it re-zoned.

    b. needs a variance to open his restaurant.

    c. can open a restaurant at any time because zoning ordinances that interfere with a proposed business violate the Fifth Amendment.

    d. can open a restaurant but only if he obtains a conditional use permit.

5. Kate has conducted farming on her property for more than 20 years. Because of the encroachment of new, smaller lots, the County changes the zoning on her parcel. The new zoning will not allow farming operations, but has a clause that existing farming operations can continue for 10 years. The county's action is probably:

    a. permissible if the county pays Kate compensation for the value of her land immediately.

    b. lawful without the payment of any monetary compensation.

    c. unlawful and Kate can have the new zoning ordinance set aside by a court.

    d. unlawful unless Kate can continue the farming operation for as long as she wants, not just 10 years.

6. The commonality of tentative, final, and parcel is that they are types of:

    a. allowed uses in zoning districts.

    b. maps in the Subdivision Map Act.

    c. regulations in the Subdivision Map Act.

    d. zoning classifications in the general plan

7. Which of the following subdivisions would be regulated by the Subdivided Lands Law?

    a. Subdivision with 4 or fewer new parcels

    b. Subdivision with 5 or more new parcels

    c. Subdivision with parcels of 160 acres or larger

    d. Subdivision located outside of California and not sold to California residents

8. Which type of "taking" is referred to as a *Lucas Wipeout*?

    a. Inverse condemnation

    b. Physical taking

    c. Regulatory taking

    d. Unconstitutional taking

9. A categorical exemption under CEQA:

    a. is a detailed evaluation of the proposed action and alternatives, sometimes running to several hundred pages.

    b. is a provision entitling a project to an exemption by law at an early stage in the environmental review process.

    c. analyzes a proposed project's anticipated environmental impacts in some detail, usually about a dozen pages, and explains why the project, as mitigated, will not have the potential to cause significant impacts to the environment.

    d. is a lengthy and detailed explanation why a proposed project can have no possible impact on the environment.

10. A real estate developer is planning to build luxury condominiums next to a natural lake. Which law requires the developer to prepare an environmental impact report?

    a. Clean Water Act

    b. National Environmental Policy Act

    c. Clean Air Act

    d. California Environmental Quality Act

Adjacent Owner Issues

Unit 5

INTRODUCTION

At some point, all land adjoins other land owned by someone else. As with most other legal relationships involving real property, being adjacent to another person's land carries with it both rights and duties. It also may create circumstances when one person has a need to use another person's land—and along with those circumstances, the potential for conflicts and the need to resolve potentially conflicting claims.

Learning Objectives

After completing this unit, you should be able to:

5A recognize landmarks and common boundary improvements.

5B designate nuisance, trespass, and encroachment.

5C recall types of boundary disputes.

BOUNDARY LINES

A **boundary line**, or property line, is an artificial or natural perimeter of a parcel of land, separating it from adjacent parcels of land. Usually, the boundary of a property is described in its deed or by a survey. Often the boundary lines are indicated on the property by monuments (man-made objects, such as stakes or iron posts), by landmarks, or by common boundary improvements.

Landmarks

Landmarks include geographic features such as an old tree, an intersection of two roads, rivers, lakes, or other natural breaks, such as an arroyo. If the boundary is a road, the boundary line usually is the center of the road.

When determining boundaries adjacent to waterways, it is important to know whether the waterway is navigable or non-navigable. The property line of two parcels separated by a **non-navigable waterway** will be to the center or thread of the waterway (just as they would be to the center of an adjoining street). If the property boundaries are adjacent to or are separated from an adjacent parcel by a **navigable non-tidal river**, the private property ownerships will extend only to the **mean low-water mark** of the stream. Navigable waters are owned by the state of California. Therefore, adjacent landowners cannot block access to the watercourse or obstruct those within the watercourse itself any more than they could block a public street. Finally, if the boundaries are adjacent to or are separated from an adjacent parcel by a **tidal body of water**, the private property ownerships will extend only to the **mean high-tide line**. When the boundary line adjoining a watercourse or shoreline is changed gradually by accretion, reliction, or erosion, the shoreline remains the boundary line of adjoining land. The owner of the adjoining land acquires title to all additions and extension to his or her land by means of accretion and reliction.

Common Boundary Improvements

Common boundary improvements that indicate the property boundary line include party walls, division fences, and line trees.

Party Walls

A **party wall** is a partition erected on a property boundary, partly on the land of one owner and partly on the land of another, to provide common support to the structures on both sides of the boundary. In general, party walls are support walls for units in common interest developments. As such, an

adjoining owner cannot remove or destroy a party wall without the consent of the other owner.

Division Fences

A **division fence** is a fence that lies exactly on the boundary line separating two properties. Ownership and responsibility for maintenance of division fences belong to adjoining owners, unless one of them wants to leave his or her land unfenced. **Adjoining landowners** are those persons, such as next-door and backyard neighbors, who own lands that share common boundaries and therefore have mutual rights, duties, and liabilities. Sometimes adjoining landowners are called coterminous owners.

Since adjoining landowners both benefit from any fence dividing their properties, and unless otherwise agreed in writing, they are presumed to be equally responsible for the reasonable costs of construction, maintenance, or necessary replacement of the fence. A landowner must give each affected adjoining landowner a 30-day prior written notice of any intent to incur costs for a division fence. [C.C. §841]. The owner who initially paid for the division fence may sue to recover the proportionate share of the fence's value. [*Reusche v. Milhorn* (1933) 218 Cal.696, 24 P.2d 792]. Neither owner may remove or alter the division fence without first obtaining permission from the other owner. [Penal Code §602(i)].

However, if a fence is located entirely on the property of one owner, it is not a division fence. It is the sole property of the person on whose land it lies. The adjoining neighbor is not responsible for the cost to build it or for its maintenance.

The height restriction imposed by most cities for fences is 6 feet tall. In fact, any fence or other structure (trees) that exceed 10 feet in height is a private nuisance. If the fence was erected to annoy the neighbor, it is called a **spite fence**. [C.C. §841.4]. Through an injunction, the neighbor can force the owner to reduce the height of the fence or remove it altogether.

Line Trees

Line trees are trees (or hedges) whose trunks grow on the boundary line. Since the adjoining landowners own these trees in common, both landowners are responsible for the maintenance of the line trees. Either owner may prune or trim a line tree, providing that it is not injurious to the tree. However, if a line tree becomes  dangerous to the one or both of the property owners, it may be declared a nuisance. As such, it may be pruned or removed. [C.C. §3479]. If either landowner destroys line trees, he or she will be liable for damages to the other party for his or her destruction.

Agreed Boundary Doctrine

Under the **agreed boundary doctrine**, if there is uncertainty regarding an actual boundary line, and there is no reasonable way to determine it, the parties may agree to set a new boundary line, called an **agreed boundary line**. The elements of the agreed-boundary doctrine require uncertainty as to the boundary line, is an agreement between the owners as to the boundary line, and five years acceptance of the agreed boundary line. [C.C.P. §318].

Initially, the agreed boundary doctrine was used to settle boundary disputes because surveys were inaccurate or landmarks had disappeared over the years. Today, with accurate surveys, precise legal descriptions, and property boundaries delineated on recorded county maps, the agreed-boundary doctrine to settle boundary disputes is used as a last resort.

NUISANCE, TRESPASS, & ENCROACHMENT

Nuisance, trespass, and encroachment all interfere with another person's rights in real property.

Nuisance

Property owners are expected to use their property reasonably without creating a nuisance or interfering with their neighbors' right to use and enjoy their land. A **nuisance** is conduct or an activity remaining outside the property that substantially interferes with another's right to the reasonable use and enjoyment of his or her property.

> Section 3479 of the Civil Code defines nuisance as "Anything which is injurious to health, including, but not limited to, the illegal sale of controlled substances, or is indecent or offensive to the senses, or an obstruction to the free use of property, so as to interfere with the comfortable enjoyment of life or property, or unlawfully obstructs the free passage or use, in the customary manner, of any navigable lake, or river, bay, stream, canal, or basin, or any public park, square, street, or highway, is a nuisance."

Classifying Nuisances

Nuisances are classified as public or private nuisances. A **private nuisance** affects only a few people; whereas, a **public nuisance** annoys the whole community in general, and not just a particular person. [C.C. §3480].

In addition, nuisances are considered as a nuisance per se or a nuisance per incident. A **nuisance per se** is a nuisance by statute or based on case law. An example would be a spite fence. [C.C. §841.4]. All other nuisances are **nuisances per incident**, which must be settled on a case-by-case basis.

It is difficult to define what degree of annoyance is necessary to constitute a nuisance. An activity may be considered a nuisance in one place, but not in another. Therefore, the situation or locality of the nuisance must be considered.

Example: As residential development sprawls into previously zoned agricultural farmlands, conflicts often arise between the new owners and the farmers regarding the noise and smell inherent in farming activities. A rooster crowing at dawn may be a nuisance to neighbors in a residential housing tract, but would be considered commonplace in a rural, agricultural area. The new residents may deem the agricultural activity a nuisance.

However, if a commercial agricultural activity, operation, or facility has been in operation for more than three years it cannot become a private or public nuisance due to any changed condition in or about the locality, if it was not a nuisance at the time it began. [C.C. §3482.5 (a)(1)]. However, prospective purchasers may be notified that a dwelling is in close proximity to an agricultural activity. [C.C. §3482.5 (d)].

In practice, most neighbor complaints of nuisance relate to excessive noise, parking, obstruction of views, nauseating odors, and unkempt property. Many of these nuisances violate local ordinances, health code, zoning restrictions, or CC&Rs.

For example, local laws control excessive noise. An isolated instance is taken care of by the police under disturbance of the peace laws. However, a person cannot file civil action unless it is a continuing nuisance.

Remedying Nuisances

The first step in remedying a nuisance is to discuss the problem with the neighbor in an attempt to arrive at an amicable solution to the problem. However, if the property owners cannot come to an agreement, the legal remedies to obtain relief from a private or public nuisance include abatement or a civil action. [C.C. §3491]. Local government officials—not private individuals—are responsible to stop public nuisances. [C.C. §3493, §3494].

Abatement. An owner may abate a private nuisance by removing, or, if necessary, destroying the nuisance if it can be done without disturbing the peace or causing injury. [C.C. §3502]. An example would be for a property owner to remove roots of a neighbor's tree that are damaging walkways and hardscape on his or her property.

Civil Action. An owner may bring a civil action against the person creating the nuisance in the form of an injunction, money damages, or both. An **injunction** is a court order forcing the person to stop the activity or condition creating the nuisance. **Money damages** could be recovered for actual money losses due to damage to real estate or for personal injury.

Trespass

Trespass is an intentional and unauthorized entry upon another's real property. Every unlawful entry onto another's property is trespass, even if no harm is done to the property, is a misdemeanor. [Penal Code §602]. A **continuing trespass** is a permanent invasion on another's rights, such as a fence

encroaching on an adjacent property, a sign overhanging another's property, or even a foundation that crosses under a property boundary line. To prevent trespass from maturing into adverse possession, the owner frequently should inspect his or her real property, fence it, and post "No Trespassing" signs every 200 feet along the perimeter.

A person does not have to physically enter another's real property to be trespassing. For example, an **indirect trespass** can occur by one person dumping refuse on another person's property, or by neighbors allowing their animals to wander across another person's property. Other examples of indirect trespass include leaving personal property or household hazardous waste on real property belonging to another person.

An owner may be awarded money damages by bringing an **action for trespass** against the trespasser. Nominal money damages will be awarded if no actual injury occurred. However, the owner may be awarded actual money damages if there was personal injury, injury to the real or personal property, or loss of use of the property caused by the trespass. In addition, to money damages, an owner can file suit and obtain an injunction to stop the trespass.

Encroachment

An **encroachment** is the intrusion into, under, or over the property of another without that person's permission. [C.C. §1013]. No one legally may build a structure that extends beyond that person's property line and intrudes upon adjoining lands. Any part that extends into the property of an adjoining landowner is an encroachment.

All encroachments qualify as a nuisance as well as a trespass. Therefore, an owner may use the legal remedies available to obtain relief for a nuisance—abatement or civil action or for money damages under a trespass.

> Example: Steve built a storage building on his property. He did not have the property line surveyed before he constructed the shed, and because of the size and intended use of the shed, he was not required to have the structure inspected by local building officials. A few weeks after the shed was completed, his neighbor Barney suspected that Steve built the structure too close to his property. Barney hired a surveyor, who confirmed that Steve's shed was two feet beyond the property line onto Barney's parcel. Steve's shed was an encroachment on Barney's land. Barney showed Steve the survey and asked Steve to relocate the shed onto his own property.
>
> If Steve refused, Barney probably would file a lawsuit and obtain an injunction to force the removal of the shed.

The statute of limitations to remove an encroachment is three years of the encroachment, or the improvements will be allowed to remain. Sometimes, the court allows the encroachment to stay, requiring the encroacher to pay the owner money damages for the lost use of his or her property. This is called **balancing the equities** or balancing the hardship. The conditions considered when balancing the equities are: (1) the encroacher acted innocently and in good faith, (2) the owner of the property will suffer an irreparable injury from the continued encroachment, and (3) the cost of removing the encroachment must greatly exceed the damage done to the owner.

> Example: An owner constructed a new home using plans drawn by an architect and approved by the city building department. A year after the owner had moved in, it was discovered that inadvertently, the foundation was two inches over the boundary line onto the adjoining owner's property. Because the owner acted innocently and in good faith and the expense to remove the home far exceeded the damage done to the adjoining owner, the encroachment was allowed to remain, and the homeowner paid damages to the adjoining owner.

When property is transferred in California, a survey is not required. Therefore, disputes regarding boundary encroachments are common. Typically, encroachment disputes involve buildings, fences, driveways, hardscaping, landscaping, signs, or other improvements that have been constructed on an adjacent owner's property.

The property owner will protect his or her property rights by claiming trespass, encroachment, and nuisance. The encroacher will try to defend his or her position with the doctrines of adverse possession, prescriptive easement, or agreed-upon boundaries. **Adverse possession** is a claim of full ownership of the land; whereas, a claim for a **prescriptive easement** is the right to use—not to own or possess—the adjoining land. As you read earlier, the agreed-upon boundary is only effective if the actual boundary is uncertain.

Today, most California courts side with the property owner and the encroaching landowner loses the legal dispute.

Raab v. Casper

In *Raab v. Casper* (1975) 51 Cal. App.3rd 866, Casper built a roadway, utility lines, hardscaping, and landscaping onto the Raab's land. Partway through construction, Raab warned Casper that the improvements were encroaching onto his land, so Casper's encroachment was not innocent or in good faith. Ultimately, Casper's improvements excluded Raab from using that part of his property. Although, the trial court held that Casper was entitled to a prescriptive easement for the encroachment, the appellate court reversed the judgment in favor of Raab.

Harrison v. Welch

In *Harrison v. Welch* (2004) 116 Cal. App. 4th 1084, Harrison sued to stop the encroachment by adjoining owner, Welch. Welch cross complained for a prescriptive easement to maintain a woodshed and landscaping. The Court of Appeals found that this use effectively prevented Harrison from any use of the property and, therefore, concluded that the right being sought was not prescriptive easement, but rather full title to the land by adverse possession. The appeals court denied adverse possession due to Harrison's non-payment of real property tax on the disputed portion.

Armitage v. Decker

In the case of *Armitage v. Decker* (1990) 218 Cal App 3rd 887, 267 Cal Rptr 399, Armitage purchased property in reliance upon the seller's representation that the picket fence was a true boundary. However, as proved by the legal description in deeds of his and the adjoining property owners and multiple surveys, the fence was not the boundary of the property. Armitage claimed ownership of the property lying between the true deed line and the old picket fence under the doctrine of agreed boundaries, even though there was no evidence to prove that the fence had been built to resolve any uncertainty in the boundary location. The appellate court upheld the trial court's decision in favor of Decker. It stated the doctrine of agreed boundaries should not supersede an ascertainable and accurate boundary contained in the legal description.

Mehdizadeh v. Mincer

The case of *Mehdizadeh v. Mincer* (1996) 46 Cal App 4th 1296, 54 Cal Rptr 2d 284 involved a 10-foot encroachment onto Mincer's property. Mehdizadeh fenced, landscaped, and irrigated the ten-foot strip using it for a dog run. He filed a claim for the property based on theory of agreed boundary or prescriptive easement. The trial court held for a prescriptive easement in favor of Mehdizadeh. The appellate court reversed the trial court judgment stating that an exclusive prescriptive easement divested the owners of nearly all rights that owners customarily have in residential property.

BOUNDARY DISPUTES

Most boundary disputes involve backyard fences or encroachments by structures, hardscape, or landscape. Other neighbor disputes deal with trees, views, or a neighbor's incompatible use of the property, such as excessive number of pets, noise, or illegal activities. What are the rights and responsibilities of adjoining owners regarding these issues?

Trees

Owners should not permit trees and other landscaping on their property to intrude onto the land of adjoining owners. Falling leaves, pine needles, and sap can be annoying to rake or clean out of gutters, but they do not constitute a trespass, nuisance, or encroachment. Most of the problems with trees are about overhanging branches, intrusive roots, or trees that block sunlight and views.

A person with a "hazard tree" on his or her property has an obligation to eliminate the danger. A **hazard tree** is an unsound, unstable, or decaying tree with a target, such as a house, sidewalk, driveway, or other improvement. An owner is responsible only if he or she is negligent—not for damage caused by an act of God. For example, if a well-maintained tree is knocked down onto the neighbor's roof during a storm, the owner is not responsible. However, if a tree limb appeared precarious and the owner failed to maintain the tree after warnings, the owner would be responsible for any damage if the limb fell during a storm.

An adjoining owner does not have the absolute right to cut encroaching roots and branches so that they end at his or her property line. The owner may prune tree limbs and remove roots from a neighbor's tree where they cross over the property line, but only if it will not damage the continued viability of the tree.

Booska v. Patel

In *Booska v. Patel* (1994) 24 C.A.4th 1786, Patel mistakenly believed that he had the absolute right to sever the roots of his neighbor's encroaching tree so that they end at his property line.

Booska owned property adjacent to Patel's property upon which a mature Monterey pine tree was situated. The roots of the pine tree encroached into Patel's yard cracking Patel's walkway. Therefore, Patel hired a contractor to repair the walkway. At the same time, the contractor excavated along the length of Patel's yard severing the roots of Booska's tree to prevent them from destroying the new walkway.

Booska v. Patel (continued)

Patel's action caused the tree to become unsafe, so Booska removed the tree at his own expense and filed a lawsuit against Patel. Patel argued that a landowner has the right to prune encroaching roots and branches back to his or her property line any way he or she chooses. The Court agreed with Patel and the case was dismissed. Booska filed an appeal.

The appellate court held for Booska and concluded that "a neighbor must act reasonably when pruning encroaching roots and branches." Patel could have protected his own property interest by taking less severe action.

Before attempting to self-abate a nuisance tree, a person should contact an arborist because some trees require specific maintenance. For example, oak trees, which are prevalent in California, have specific maintenance requirements. The area extending six feet from the trunk should be left undisturbed and uncovered and mature oaks should only be trimmed in June or July. In addition, many cities, such as Los Angeles, have ordinances protecting oak trees 8" or more in diameter, from being cut, destroyed, removed, relocated, damaged, or the tree's dripline being encroached. A prudent homeowner should check city tree ordinances before pruning or cutting trees, because the City of Ojai, for example, not only protects oaks, but also sycamores, heritage trees, and mature trees.

Example: A homeowner was unaware that a permit was needed to trim or prune an indigenous oak in Calabasas. The neighbor's large oak tree had branches overhanging the roof of her new home. Thinking to self-abate the nuisance, the homeowner cut off the offending branches without a permit or permission from the neighbor. The homeowner was fined $10,000 by the Calabasas City Tree Board for the unpermitted tree trimming. If the tree dies, the fine could increase to $40,000 and the homeowner may face a lawsuit from the adjoining owner.

Fruit and nut trees can be a point of contention. If the trunk of a fruit tree is entirely on the land of one owner, but the branches (laden with fruit) extend into an adjoining owner's yard, who owns the fruit? Logic might state that the fruit on the encroaching branch belongs to the person upon whose land the branch encroached. However, the location of the trunk of the tree determines ownership of the tree and therefore its fruit or nuts. Simply because the fruit belongs to an owner, he or she does not have the right to trespass onto the adjoining owner's property to harvest the fruit. The same is true for any fruit that falls from the tree into the adjoining owner's yard. Rather than litigate, most adjoining owners reach agreements about fruit and nuts on encroaching branches.

Sunlight, Air, and View

Many people buy a home, in part, for the view it offers. In fact, part of the home's value may be related to its panoramic view of natural beauty or city lights.

However, in California, no landowner has an absolute right to sunlight and air circulation or to a view over adjoining lands. Local zoning ordinances, building restrictions, easements, or CC&Rs of common interest developments may address these issues. Providing an owner complies with zoning ordinances, restrictions, or easements, he or she may construct a building and plant landscaping without regard to the fact that the neighbor may be deprived of the sunlight, air, or view that was enjoyed before the building was constructed.

Light, Air, and View Easement

A **light, air, and view easement** is a negative easement created by grant that prevents an adjacent landowner from building a structure or planting trees that would prevent sunlight or air from reaching the dominant estate. [C.C. §801]

Ekstrom v. Marquesa at Monarch Beach Homeowners Association

In the case of *Ekstrom v. Marquesa at Monarch Beach Homeowners Association* (2008) 168 Cal.App.4th 1111, Ekstrom sued to force the Homeowners' Association to trim or remove palm trees that interfered with his views. The CC&Rs stated that no tree could be taller than the height of the house on the lot where the tree was situated. Trees growing taller than the limit must be trimmed.

Ekstrom paid a premium for his home when he purchased it in 1999, because it had a full ocean view. At that time, no palm trees in the community exceeded the height of the rooftops. Ekstrom's downhill neighbor had about 20 palm trees  growing on his property. Ekstrom reviewed the CC&Rs before his purchase and was satisfied that the CC&Rs would require the trees to be trimmed or removed if they grew above the roofline

> ### *Ekstrom v. Marquesa at Monarch Beach Homeowners Association* (continued)
>
> and blocked Ekstrom's view. Unfortunately, this rule was enforced by the board of directors for all trees except palm trees, because trimming a palm tree would effectively require its removal.
>
> In 2002, other homeowners, including Ekstrom, were losing their views to obstructing palm trees and demanded that the board enforce the CC&Rs to remove the palm trees. The board refused.
>
> The court upheld the clear language in the CC&Rs forcing the board to remove or top all trees, including palm trees that blocked an owner's view.

Solar Easement

Homeowners are installing solar energy systems on rooftops, building exteriors, and even on the ground. In order for these systems to produce electricity, they need access to the sun. California law follows the "first in time" rule. Whichever is first in time—the tree or the solar energy system—can remain. If the tree is already on the adjacent property, then the owner planning to install a solar energy system must take the tree (and its future growth) into account when planning the system's location. Likewise, if the solar energy system is installed first and an adjacent owner wants to plant a new tree, the tree owner must consider its proposed location in relation to his or her neighbor's system and be prepared to trim or prune the tree so as not to block the sun. A tree owner must keep his or her trees from casting a shadow "greater than 10% of the collector absorption area" at any time between the hours of 10:00 a.m. and 2:00 p.m. [California Public Resources Code §25982].

California Civil Code provides for **solar easements**, which is an easement for the purpose of receiving sunlight across real property of another for any solar energy system. [C.C. §801.5]. All solar easements cannot be implied, but must be written.

Required Items for a Written Solar Easement

1. Description of the easement expressed in measurable terms, such as vertical or horizontal angles by which sunlight must pass, or the hours of the day during which the easement is effective

2. Restrictions placed upon vegetation, structures, and other objects that would impair or obstruct the passage of sunlight through the easement

3. Terms or conditions for revising or terminating the easement

Zipperer v. County of Santa Clara

In *Zipperer v. County of Santa Clara*, [133 Cal. App. 4th 1013 (2005)], the Zipperer family built a home with a "solar home central heating and cooling systems" in the mid-1980s. The County of Santa Clara purchased the adjacent property in 1991, which had a small grove of trees on it. The County designated this land as a park reserve. The existing trees grew significantly after the County acquired the land and began to shade the Zipperer home, limiting their system's performance. In 1997, the homeowners requested that the County trim or remove the offending trees. The County did not respond.

In 2004, the homeowners sued the County under several causes of action, including breach of contract stemming from an implicit right to a solar easement. The Zipperers complained that the County had implicitly entered into a contract to provide a solar easement by allowing them to construct a solar home according to County requirements. The family also contended that the County violated this solar easement by allowing the trees on the neighboring lot to grow to a height that shaded the family's solar energy system.

The court ruled that written documentation is needed to create a solar easement in California, citing Section 801.5 of the California Civil Code as the "governing provision, which specifically requires a written agreement in order to create a solar easement." Further, Section 801.5 requires a "description" of the easement, which implies it must be in writing.

SUMMARY

Adjoining landowners (coterminous owners) are next-door and backyard neighbors who own lands that share common boundaries and therefore have mutual rights, duties, and liabilities. A boundary line is an artificial or natural perimeter of a parcel of land, separating it from adjacent parcels of land, usually indicated by monuments, landmarks, or by common boundary improvements. Monuments are man-made objects, such as stakes or iron posts. Landmarks include geographic features such as an old tree, an intersection of two roads, rivers, lakes, or other natural breaks, such as an arroyo. If the boundary is a road, the boundary line usually is the center of the road. Common boundary improvements that indicate the property boundary line include party walls, division fences, and line trees. A party wall is a partition erected on a property boundary, partly on the land of one owner and partly on the land of another, to provide common support to the structures on both sides of the boundary. A division fence is a fence that lies exactly on the boundary line separating two properties. Line trees are trees (or hedges) whose trunks grow on the boundary line.

Nuisance, trespass, and encroachment all interfere with another person's rights in real property. A nuisance is conduct or an activity remaining outside the property that substantially interferes with another's right to the reasonable use and enjoyment of his or her property. Nuisances are classified as public or private nuisances. The legal remedies to obtain relief from a private or public nuisance include abatement or a civil action. Trespass is an intentional and unauthorized entry upon another's real property and is a misdemeanor. Any part that extends into the property of an adjoining owner is an encroachment.

Owners should not permit trees and other landscaping on their property to intrude onto the land of adjoining owners. A hazard tree is an unsound, unstable, or decaying tree with a target, such as a house, sidewalk, driveway, or other improvement.

In California, no landowner has an absolute right to light and air circulation or to a view over adjoining lands. Local zoning ordinances, building restrictions, easements, or CC&Rs of common interest developments may address these issues.

California Civil Code provides for solar easements, which is an easement for the purpose of receiving sunlight across real property of another for any solar energy system. All solar easements cannot be implied, but must be written.

UNIT 5 REVIEW

◻ Matching Exercise

Instructions: Write the letter of the matching term on the blank line before its definition. Answers are in Appendix A.

Terms

A. adjoining landowners

B. agreed boundary line

C. boundary line

D. continuing trespass

E. division fence

F. light, air, and view easement

G. line trees

H. nuisance

I. nuisance per se

J. party wall

K. private nuisance

L. public nuisance

M. solar easement

N. spite fence

O. trespass

Definitions

1. _____   Artificial or natural perimeter of a parcel of land, separating it from adjacent parcels of land

2. _____   Partition erected on a property boundary providing common support to the structures on both sides of the boundary

3. _____   Fence lying exactly on the boundary line separating two properties

4. _____   Persons owning lands that share common boundaries and therefore have mutual rights, duties, and liabilities

5. _____   Fence exceeding 10 feet in height erected for the purpose of annoying a neighbor

6. _____   Trees or hedges whose trunks grow on the boundary line

7. _____   Adjoining owners of property with an uncertain boundary set a new boundary line

8. _____   Activity remaining outside the property that substantially interferes with a person's reasonable use and enjoyment of his or her property

9. _____ Nuisance affecting only a few people

10. _____ Nuisance annoying the whole community in general

11. _____ Nuisance by statute or based on case law

12. _____ Intentional and unauthorized entry upon another's real property

13. _____ Permanent invasion on another's rights

14. _____ Negative easement created by grant preventing servient landowner from building a structure or planting trees that would prevent sunlight or air from reaching the dominant estate

15. _____ Easement for the purpose of receiving sunlight across real property of another for any solar energy system

Multiple Choice Questions

Instructions: Circle your response and go to Appendix A to read the complete explanation for each question.

1. What is the commonality of stakes, iron posts, and landmarks?
    a. Adjoining owners
    b. Boundary lines
    c. Line trees
    d. Trespass

2. If the boundary is a non-navigable waterway, where is the boundary line situated?
    a. Bank of the waterway
    b. Center of the road
    c. Thread of the waterway
    d. Road or path on the bank of the waterway

3. Since party walls are support walls for units in common interest developments, an adjoining owner:
    a. can destroy a party wall without the consent of the other owner.
    b. can remove a party wall without the consent of the other owner.
    c. cannot paint a party wall without the consent of the other owner.
    d. cannot remove a party wall without the consent of the other owner.

4. What is the name for trees whose trunks grow on a boundary line and are owned by the adjoining landowners?
    a. Agreed-upon trees
    b. Alignment trees
    c. Line trees
    d. Spite trees

5. A house is situated on a corner lot in a very well-kept tract of homes. The owner never maintains the landscaping and throws refuse in the backyard that attracts flies. Legally, this home would be considered a(n):
    a. encroachment.
    b. eyesore.
    c. nuisance.
    d. trespass.

6. Bob frequently crosses Pat's property unlawfully when going to the Town Center. Based on this information, Bob:
    a. has a license.
    b. is a nuisance.
    c. is encroaching.
    d. is trespassing.

7. Who may stop a public nuisance?
    a. Both private individuals and local government officials
    b. Local government officials
    c. Private individuals
    d. The public

8. Does an adjoining owner have the absolute right to cut encroaching roots and branches so that they end at his or her property line?
    a. No, only the owner of the tree has the right to prune or remove it.
    b. No, the encroaching roots and branches may be removed only if it will not damage the continued viability of the tree.
    c. Yes, the adjoining owner is a co-owner of the tree because its roots and branches are on his or her side of the boundary line.
    d. Yes, this is the remedy of self-abatement.

9. David has a large avocado tree planted in the corner of his backyard. It is planted five feet from the lot line and several branches extend into Donna's backyard. In addition, one branch extends only 18 inches into Ted's sideyard. Who is legally entitled to harvest the avocados?

   a. David only
   b. David and Donna
   c. Donna and Ted
   d. Everyone

10. Sarah wants to install solar panels on her roof. There are several small redwoods planted in her neighbor's yard, which may block sunlight from the solar panels when they grow. Which statement is correct?

   a. Sarah cannot install a solar system.
   b. Sarah should design the solar system with the neighbor's trees in mind because they were planted first.
   c. The neighbor should remove the trees while they are small.
   d. The neighbor will have to trim the trees when they start to block sunlight from Sarah's solar panels.

How Ownership is Held

Unit 6

INTRODUCTION

All property has an owner, either the government, a private institution, or an individual. Tenancy refers to a mode or method of ownership or holding title to property. Title vesting is the evidence that the owner of land is in lawful possession; it is the proof of ownership.

Ownership of property in California began with Spanish explorers who claimed it for the king of Spain in the early 16th century. Since the king technically owned everything, all land was granted to private parties. This continued until 1822, when Mexico began colonizing California and took over governing the territory. Under Spanish and Mexican rule, ownership of real property followed the Roman Civil Law. In 1848, the Treaty of Guadalupe Hidalgo ended the war with Mexico, and California became a possession of the United States. When California became a state in 1850, England's Common Law principles governed title and ownership of real property.

Today, in the United States, real property can be owned in a variety of ways. Specifically, someone can own property alone or in concert with others. Ownership in severalty and ownership of an undivided interest are two ways a person or other entity can take title to or own real estate.

Learning Objectives

After completing this unit, you should be able to:

6A   differentiate ownership in severalty from undivided ownership.

6B   recall the types of concurrent ownership.

6C   recognize the business entities that can own real property.

6D   designate types of CID ownership.

OWNERSHIP IN SEVERALTY

The easiest form of ownership is probably ownership by one person. When property is owned by one person or a single corporation (which, legally, has the status of a person) whose rights to the property are not shared with any other person, this form of ownership is legally known as **ownership in severalty**. The property owned by one person is itself sometimes referred to as a "severalty," although this terminology is less common.

The phrase "ownership in severalty" might strike some people as an odd term to describe this status. The first impression that some people may have is that the expression appears to be describing ownership by more than one—i.e., "several" people. The root of the word, however, is not "several" (as in "many") but "sever," as in "detached from (others)." When a person obtains title to property in severalty, the description of that person's status on the deed is often "an unmarried man" or "an unmarried woman," as the case may be.

UNDIVIDED OWNERSHIP INTERESTS

An **undivided interest** is an interest held under the same title by two or more people, whether their rights are equal or unequal in value or quantity. Undivided interests include fractional ownership interests, common interest developments, and timeshares.

Fractional Ownership Interests

When two or more persons or entities own property at the same time with undivided use, **fractional ownership interests** are created because each owner has a fraction of the whole. The owner of a fractional interest has less control over a property than if he or she owned the entire property and cannot unilaterally make decisions regarding the property. Fractional interest ownership includes concurrent ownership and business ownership. Tenancy in common, joint tenancy, and community property are examples of concurrent ownership. Business ownership includes partnerships, corporations, and LLCs.

Concurrent Ownership

Probably, the most common instance of fractional interests occurs with a married couple who shares ownership in the family home as community property. Another common fractional interest is property owned by joint tenants or tenants in common. With multiple owners, it is easy to see how disagreements may occur. One owner may want to sell or renovate, while another owner may not. When disagreements cannot be resolved, the property may be sold or partitioned. Property owned as tenancy in common or joint tenancy can be sold or partitioned under a court-ordered **partition action**. Marital property interests (community property or tenancy by the entirety) are severed as part of divorce proceedings, not by partition.

The situation that is more likely to create potential for conflict—and hence, legal difficulties—is concurrent ownership. **Concurrent ownership** is a blanket term for the ownership of real property by more than one person.

> **Types of Concurrent Ownership in California**
> 1. Tenancy in common
> 2. Joint tenancy
> 3. Community property

Note that, once again, as with a life estate, the parties are often referred to as "tenants" even though they in fact have ownership, not leasehold, interests.

Tenancy in Common

When two or more persons, whose interests are not necessarily equal, are owners of undivided interests in a single estate, a **tenancy in common** (TIC) exists. [C.C. §685]. Each cotenant of a tenancy in common has a defined interest in the undivided ownership of the property, which consists of a single common title. None of the owners may exclude any cotenant from the property, nor claim any portion of the property for exclusive use. The only requirement of **unity** (equality) for tenants in common is the equal right of possession or undivided interest, as it is called.

The "default" method of holding co-owned title in California is the tenancy in common. When more than one person takes title to real property and no other form of concurrent ownership is specified on the deed, then they hold title as tenants in common.

> Example: Arthur, Ben, and Charles purchase a parcel of land. The deed conveying the property to them from Greg, the seller, states that he is conveying, "To Arthur, Ben, and Charles." Because no other form of concurrent ownership is specified, they hold title as tenants in common. Each of the three cotenants has an undivided one-third interest in the property.

The deed also could have stated explicitly that the cotenants were tenants in common or it could have stated that each owner would hold a different percentage interest in the property. This is because the undivided shares of a tenancy in common do not have to be equal. The cotenants might decide to hold title this way if, for example, each contributed different amounts to the down payment or because each cotenant will be responsible for a different share of the monthly payment.

> Example: Arthur, Ben, and Charles purchase a parcel of land. The deed conveying the property to them from the seller states that it is conveying, "To Arthur a 35% share, to Ben a 40% share and to Charles a 25% share of the property located at 118 Green Street, Modesto, California, as tenants in common."

In this case, the use of the term "tenants in common" was unnecessary, because they hold unequal shares. If two or more persons have unequal shares of a parcel of real property, then by definition it must be as tenants in common; tenancy in common is the only form of concurrent ownership that allows for unequal interests in the property.

Rights and Responsibilities

Despite potentially unequal shares in the property, each of the cotenants is entitled to the full use of the co-owned property, subject only to the full use of the property by his or her cotenants. No cotenant can exclude another cotenant from any portion of the property and this is so even if the shares of the undivided ownership are unequal.

As a practical matter, if several tenants in common purchase a single-family home, they may decide that, despite their general rights to the co-owned property, each will select a private bedroom and share the remaining parts of the property, such as the kitchen, bathrooms, and living area.

Obligation for Share of Expenses. Each cotenant is obligated to pay a proportionate share of the expenses of the property (including taxes, maintenance, and insurance). A cotenant who pays a disproportionate share of the expenses (e.g., "fronting" the annual taxes for the benefit of the cotenants) is entitled to recover those costs from the other cotenants.

Improvements to the Property. At the same time, a cotenant is not obligated to contribute to improvements to the property. If a cotenant becomes aware of contributions that improve the property, upon learning of the improvements, the cotenant either can contribute a proportionate share in order to be entitled to share in the enhanced value or must elect to waive the increased value (including an increased share of the rental value, if the improvement will increase that value).

Example: Evelyn, Pat, and Pam own an apartment building in common, each owning an undivided one-third of the property. The building has two apartments. Because one of the units is dilapidated, they decide to upgrade that unit when it becomes vacant. Evelyn and Pam pay the entire cost of the upgrade and add a third unit on some vacant land next to the empty unit, advancing the cost of the city permits and the construction.

Pat decides not to participate in paying for the cost of the addition. Although she is obligated to pay a third of the cost of rehabilitating the second apartment that was part of the property, she is not obligated to pay the cost of adding the third unit. On the other hand, she will not be entitled to any of the rental value of this new unit once it is completed and has a tenant living in it.

Leasing the Entire Property. If the entire co-owned property is leased to a third party, then the cotenants have a right to a share of the rents in proportion to their ownership interests. This would not be true, however, if the cotenant "rents out" only that owner's "share" because the remaining cotenant(s) would have not leased their portion of the concurrent ownership, those cotenants would not be entitled to a share of the rental payments.

Cotenant Leasing His or Her Share. Each cotenant is entitled to lease his or her share without the consent of the other cotenants. However, the cotenants who do not participate in such a lease with a third party lessee, are not bound by its terms as to that lessee; that relationship would then be only between the cotenant entering into a lease with a lessee. Each of the non-leasing cotenants must treat the lessee in all respects as if he or she were the cotenant who leased out the share of the ownership; in effect, the new lessee has the same rights as if he or she were the other tenant in common.

> Example: Tim, Gary, and Jason hold land as tenants in common each holding a one-third undivided interest. Without Tim's or Gary's permission, Jason leases his "share" of the property to Kevin. Jason and Kevin have various rights and responsibilities as between each other as lessor and lessee (for example, Kevin must pay Jason monthly rent for his use of the property), and Tim and Gary are not bound by the terms of that agreement.

> On the other hand, Tim and Gary must treat Kevin as if he were Jason as part of the original tenancy in common among the three owners. So long as Kevin is a lawful tenant of Jason's, he has the same entitlement to use the common areas of the property as if he were Jason. He cannot be excluded from any area of the property to which Jason would have had a right of access before he rented out his "share" to Kevin.

Transferring Ownership

Any cotenant in common may voluntarily sell or will his or her interest. The heirs simply become a tenant in common among the others.

Sale. Each cotenant is entitled to sell his or her share without the consent of the other cotenants.

> Example: Kate, Pat, and Donna hold land as tenants in common, each holding a one-third undivided interest. Without Kate's or Pat's knowledge or permission, Donna sells her share of the concurrent ownership to Sarah. Donna now no longer has any rights to the concurrent ownership, and Sarah is in all respects entitled to the same rights to, and use of, the property to which Donna was entitled before the sale.

Neither Kate nor Pat are entitled to a share of the proceeds realized from the sale of the portion of the property formerly owned by Donna unless one or both of them were owed money by Donna for common expenses (e.g., taxes) that they advanced before the sale. Even then, about the best that they could do would be to pursue Donna in court if she were unwilling to pay those previous obligations out of escrow at the close of the sale to Sarah.

Although tenancy in common may provide a means for some people to purchase property that they could not afford alone, it has some disadvantages. As seen in some of the foregoing examples, anyone who buys into or rents a cotenant's share of co-owned property in effect becomes a "land partner" with the seller's or lessor's cotenants former cotenants—and because those pre-existing owners are already there, the new tenant or owner may find that having these involuntary roommates (or business partners) an uncomfortable arrangement.

Will. Upon the death of a cotenant, the situation is much like a sale—the surviving cotenants continue to maintain their undivided interest and the deceased member of the concurrent ownership can bequeath his or her share through a will. The heirs of the deceased cotenant inherit only that share. In effect, they "stand in the shoes" of the deceased cotenant.

Partition Action. When tenants in common do not agree on matters pertaining to the property, any of the cotenants may file a partition action asking the court to decide the fate of the investment. **Partition action** is a court proceeding to settle a dispute between co-owners (joint tenants or tenants in common) about dividing their interests in real property. Often, the result is a forced sale of the property with the proceeds divided according to ownership interests as the court has ordered.

Joint Tenancy

Another form of concurrent ownership is **joint tenancy**, also known as **joint tenancy with right of survivorship**, sometimes abbreviated as **JTWROS**. Probably the most important difference between joint tenancies and tenancies in common is the **right of survivorship**—which, as shown above, is sometimes included in the phrase on the deed creating the concurrent ownership. (Even if it is not used, every joint tenancy automatically carries with it the right to survivorship.)

As with the tenancy in common, in a joint tenancy each cotenant has an undivided interest in the ownership of the property and as with a tenancy in common, even though there are the multiple owners of a given piece of property, their common ownership is the single "owner" of the property.

Here, however, the similarities between the two forms of concurrent ownership end. Unlike tenancies in common, in which the various shares can be unequal and can be acquired at different times, joint tenancy has inflexible rules that govern whether a joint tenancy exists or not. Joint tenancy is characterized by what are sometimes called the four unities. [C.C. §683(a)]

Four Unities of Joint Tenancy
1. **Unity of time** (created among all owners at the same time)
2. **Unity of title** (acquired on the same deed)
3. **Unity of interest** (equal as between or among all joint tenants)
4. **Unity possession** (rights of use are co-equal)

The only one of the four "unities" that joint tenancy and tenancy in common share is unity of possession. In either co-tenancy, the cotenants have the same right to the full use of the property, subject only to their cotenant(s)' right to the full use of the property. Because most of the rights and responsibilities regarding the management of the property relate to the rights of possession (access to the entire property, payment of taxes and other expenses, proportionate shares of income), most rights and responsibilities of a joint tenancy are also the same as a tenancy in common.

> Example: Bob, Chuck, and Ed own land together. They acquired the land from Alex. The deed from Alex states that the conveyance is from Alex "To Bob, Chuck, and Ed, as joint tenants with right of survivorship." Their interests were acquired at the same time and on the same deed. Because the deed specifies "joint tenancy," each of the three automatically has an undivided one-third share. Therefore, Bob, Chuck, and Ed have ownership in joint tenancy of this property.

When one of the joint tenants dies, the share of the deceased does not go to his or her estate or heirs, but becomes the property of the cotenant without becoming involved in probate. The surviving joint tenant or tenants immediately become the remaining "owner" of the property, with their proportionate share of the total interest adjusted to reflect the resulting smaller ownership following the death of the other joint tenant. Additionally, the surviving joint tenants are not liable to creditors of the deceased who hold liens on the joint tenancy property.

Example: Dan, Gail, and Sam own a parcel together in joint tenancy. As a result, each one owns a one-third undivided share. One day, Gail dies. At the moment of Gail's death, Dan and Sam succeed to the ownership of her share. Dan and Sam are now the owners of a one-half undivided share as joint tenants. Their interests still share the four unities, except that, with Gail's death, the two now are the only remaining members of the original joint tenancy.

Rights and Responsibilities

Joint tenants may sell their interest, give it away, or borrow money against it, without consent of the other co-owners. A joint tenant may sever his or her interest in the joint tenancy by selling it. The new co-owner would become a tenant in common with the remaining joint tenants. The joint tenancy is not severed (broken) if a lien is put against the interest of one of the co-owners. However, a foreclosure on the lien would sever that interest from the joint tenancy.

Due to the right of survivorship, a joint tenant may not will his or her share. Joint tenancy is terminated when any one of the four unities ends, such as by sale, gift, or by mutual agreement.

Avoiding Risk

Many cotenants opt for taking title as joint tenants without considering the consequences. The advantage of joint tenancy is that it avoids probate. The transfer of title under a joint tenancy happens by operation of law—that is, it happens instantly at the moment of death. All that the surviving joint tenant(s) needs to do is record a notice with the county recorder that the joint tenant has died and the change to the title of the property that took place upon the death of the joint tenant is reflected immediately.

The disadvantage of joint tenancy is that the property passes automatically outside of a will, even if the testator's wishes may have changed. This will defeat the decedent's expectations for the disposition of his or her property on death if the deceased joint tenant did not want the property to pass to his or her cotenant(s), regardless of what that person's will might say.

Property held as joint tenants can be an easy and simple way of passing title from one surviving spouse to another, but particularly for those who re-marry later in life, it can have the effect of disinheriting children of a prior marriage even if that is not the cotenant's intent.

Example: Fred and Kendra are both in their fifties. Each was married before and both have adult children from their prior relationships. Although they are unmarried and live together, they purchased a home. They each contributed half of the down payment for their respective share of the purchase. This payment represents a significant portion of each of their personal assets.

Kendra wants her half of the property to go to her adult daughter if she dies. She makes a provision to this effect in her will and assumes that, if she dies before Fred, her daughter will inherit her share of the property. Unfortunately, when she and Fred bought the property, they put it into joint tenancy without paying attention to that phrase.

Kendra is killed unexpectedly in a car accident. Because of the form of title on the deed, there is no house for her will to transfer during the probate process. Instead, Fred has already become the owner of the property immediately upon her death. Kendra's daughter cannot legally force him to give up "her" half of the property despite Kendra's wishes and will have to engage in lengthy and expensive litigation if she wants to challenge the consequences of the survivorship built into the joint tenancy.

If Kendra had wanted her one-half of the property to pass to her daughter upon her death via a will, she should have held title with Fred as a tenancy in common. As a tenant in common, Kendra could have willed her half of the property to anyone. Alternatively, if she had recognized this before she died; she could have converted the joint tenancy to a tenancy in common by making a "straw person" conveyance to herself. That is, Kendra should have executed and recorded a deed from herself to herself. She and Fred would have continued as cotenants, except that thereafter they would have been tenants in common, not joint tenants.

Of course, if both Fred and Kendra wanted the property to pass to the other upon either's death, then the simplest and most expeditious way to do so would indeed be to hold the property in joint tenancy. Once a joint tenant dies, the surviving joint tenant or tenants only have to record a single document—an "affidavit of the death of joint tenant"—with the county recorder's office. This is not strictly necessary to complete the transfer of title; rather, it simply confirms for the world at large that there is one less owner of the property. Neither a will nor a court proceeding is necessary.

Transferring Ownership

As with a tenancy in common, one joint tenant can convey his or her interest to a third party without the knowledge or permission of the remaining joint tenant or tenants. The portion of the property conveyed "out" of the joint tenancy destroys the joint tenancy as to that part of the concurrent ownership—thereafter, that share is held as an undivided interest in common with the remaining owner or owners. [C.C. §683.2(a)]

If there are multiple joint tenants (i.e., more than two) as part of a joint tenancy, the conveyance by one joint tenant to a third party does not affect the status of the remaining joint tenants. Their relationship to one another goes on as before, except that they thereafter hold as joint tenants as to each other and tenants in common as to the party who "broke" the joint tenancy.

> Example: Karen, Peter, and Monica buy a parcel together. At the time of acquisition, title is held among the three as joint tenants.
>
> Two years later, Monica sells her one-third interest to Nate. Karen and Peter still have a joint tenancy as to each other. If either of them dies, the survivor will own a two-thirds share of the entire property.
>
> Nate, on the other hand, is a tenant in common as to the joint tenancy between Karen and Peter. If he dies, his undivided one-third share will be conveyed either by will or by the law of **intestacy** (the law that disposes of property when someone dies without a will). The only way that either of them would be able to obtain a portion of Nate's share when he dies is if he chooses to leave all or part of his one-third interest to either or both via his will.

Community Property

The third form of concurrent ownership in California is community property. **Community property** is a unique form of concurrent ownership that can exist only between spouses. The concept of community property is inherited primarily from the Spanish legal tradition and is used only in fewer than a dozen states, mostly in the southwestern part of the country (e.g., Texas, New Mexico, Nevada, or Arizona) that was controlled by Spain and, later, Mexico. Most other states also have special laws for concurrent ownership by married couples, but use a form known as tenancy by the entirety.

Because California law does not provide for tenancy by the entirety, its subtleties are not directly pertinent to someone working with California real estate. It is, however, important to recognize that community property is more the exception than the rule and that outside California the law still accords married couples a unique form of concurrent ownership, but with differences from California's version.

A married couple in California has three choices when it comes to how they may take title. However, unless otherwise stated, title is presumed community property.

1. The first is joint tenancy, which includes the right of survivorship if one of the spouses dies, which may also include a tax liability for the surviving spouse.

2. The second is community property, which does not include the right of survivorship, but also includes probate after a spouse dies and all the costs involved in that process.

3. The third type of vesting is **community property with the right of survivorship**, which includes the better of the first two types of vesting. There is no particular tax liability because of the death of a spouse and there is no probate with its seemingly endless costs.

   In 2001, California enacted a law allowing spouses to hold title to their property as community property with right of survivorship. Holding title as community property provides a stepped-up tax basis for both halves of the property upon the death of the first spouse. Holding title as joint tenants provides for the immediate and automatic transfer of title to the surviving spouse upon the death of the first spouse. This form of holding title combines the desirable tax features of community property with the right of survivorship of joint tenancy. The words "community property with right of survivorship" must be included in the deed. Additionally, the grantees must sign the deed to indicate that they accept this type of title. [C.C. §682.1(a)].

Basic Principles

Community property is based on the notion that, when a man and woman marry, they implicitly agree to use their efforts jointly for the betterment of the whole—i.e., the "community" created by their marriage—for one another and, eventually, any children born as a result of the marriage. Consequently, property acquired by either of the married parties as a result of the skill, labor, or talents of, or through the expenditure of community funds, is owned as community property. Community property is similar to joint tenancy in how it is acquired or created, but it is similar to tenancy in common in how it is disposed of upon death (or upon dissolution of the marriage).

While the parties are domiciled in California, all property acquired by either one from earnings, profits, or other income is presumed to be community property. [C.C. §687]. Property acquired outside of California that would have been community property if acquired in California is known as **quasi-community property.**

Both spouses have equal rights to the use and disposition of community property during the marriage. [C.C. §§5125, 5127]. Either party can use community assets for his or her support, education, or other expenses, even though theoretically every penny of income is owned 50-50 by each spouse. However, both spouses must sign on any transfer or encumbrance on real property.

Property Excluded from Community Property Treatment

Certain categories of property are treated as the separate property of one spouse instead of as community property.

Excluded Property

- Property owned by either party before marriage [C.C. §5107].
- Property acquired by either partner during marriage as a gift or an inheritance [C.C. §5108].
- Income or the appreciation of value of property that started out as separate property and which has not been converted to community property (e.g., by putting both names on the title).

Example: Dan and Donna are husband and wife. Prior to their marriage, Donna owned a parcel of land that she owned without debt and to which she held title in her name. She also had a bank account that was only in her name. After their marriage, she kept both the parcel of land and the bank account in her name alone. The maintenance of and taxes owed on the land are made by Donna from the funds in her separate bank account, and she never deposits any of her earnings into that account. If Donna dies or if she and Dan divorce, a court will treat the land (and the bank account) as Donna's separate property, because she has not commingled any community funds with either of these two items of separate property.

Spouses can modify the normal rule through a written agreement, either one entered into before or during marriage. They could agree, for example, that despite the normal rule, the earnings of either spouse will continue to be separate property instead of community property. Or the spouses can agree, after the fact, that a specific item of property that would have been community property (because there was no pre-marital agreement) will be treated as separate property instead.

Requirement for a Valid Marriage

In order for a couple to have community property rights, there must be a valid marriage. One exception is if the parties believe, in good faith, that they are validly married, but in fact they are not (e.g., not enough witnesses solemnized the marriage or one of the parties was under age at the time of the marriage). In those cases, the spouse or spouses who believe that the marriage was valid are termed "putative spouses," and they are entitled to the benefits of the law as if they had been married.

By contrast, if a man and woman knowingly cohabit without becoming married (referred to by some courts as a "meretricious relationship"), they do not gain the benefits of California's community property law. In 1976, a noteworthy decision arose from such a relationship.

Marvin v. Marvin

In *Marvin v. Marvin* (1976) 18 Cal.3d 660, well-known actor Lee Marvin, who had appeared in such motion pictures as *The Dirty Dozen*, lived with a woman named Michelle Triola for nearly seven years without being married. She alleged that she gave up a singing career to become the functional equivalent of his wife, devoting herself to being a companion, homemaker, housekeeper, and cook. During this time, Marvin earned several million dollars and acquired valuable properties, such as their residence. When they separated, she sought the equivalent of her share of the community assets that would have been acquired during a marriage of the same duration. (Triola legally changed her name to Michelle Marvin even though the two were never married.)

> ### *Marvin v. Marvin* (continued)
>
> The California Supreme Court concluded that the parties to such a relationship could not rely on family law principles regarding the entitlement to the financial benefits of their relationship. However, the parties could rely on the existence of an express contract short of a marriage between non-marital partners. It also stated that in the absence of an express contract, a court could rely on other legal principles, such as implied contracts, a joint venture, or some other principles rooted in contract law.

Transferring Ownership

Community property is more like tenancy in common than joint tenancy for purposes of the disposition of the property (except that neither party can transfer community property for no consideration without the consent of the other spouse). Since the use and control of marital property is intermingled while both spouses are married and alive, the law effects a division of the property upon dissolution of the couple's marriage or the death of one of the marital partners.

Dissolution of Marriage

When the parties are going through dissolution of the marriage, if they cannot agree upon a division of their property, the court will first determine the character of each item of property as either separate or community.

First, there is a presumption that property acquired during marriage by either spouse is community property. (Family Code §760.) This presumption can be overcome by, e.g., evidence that the property was actually acquired through one of the means that would make it separate property, such as a gift or inheritance.

There is also a presumption that property to which one party takes title in his or her name alone is separate property. As with the presumption that property acquired during marriage is community, this presumption can be overcome with evidence that the parties' actions in fact made it community.

Stitt v. Stitt

In the *Marriage of Stitt* (1983) 147 Cal.App.3d 579 Ida Mae and Richard Stitt bought a parcel of land before they were married while they were living together. Each paid half of the cost of the unimproved lot. The husband then conveyed title to Ida Mae in her name alone and she obtained a construction loan for the house. They later married and except for a few payments from Ida Mae's separate property, they paid for all of the payments on the loan out of earnings that were held in a joint account.

The court of appeal held that the property was community property. Although the wife had held title to the property in her name alone from the time she obtained the construction loan until she filed for dissolution, the court noted that Richard had contributed half of the cost of the lot, and they had made almost all payments from community funds. He also had relied on her assurances that they would own the property equally, despite the way that title was held.

Property acquired with community funds or from the sale of a community asset also retains its character as community property regardless of how title is held. A written agreement is required to overcome this presumption and in the absence of such an agreement, the court will find that it is a community, not a separate property, asset.

The parties have a duty during dissolution to reveal the existence of any community assets to the other party. Failure to do so results in a penalty, under Family Code §1101, subd. (h), equal to the non-disclosing party's entire half of the concealed marital asset.

Rossi v. Rossi

In the *Marriage of Rossi* (2001) 90 Cal.App.4th 34, Denise and Thomas were married in 1971. In 1996, a co-worker of Denise's organized a "lottery pool" to which each member would contribute $5 per week to play the state lottery. Denise claimed that she contributed at the outset, but then stopped some time later. In December 1996, her coworkers won a jackpot of over $6,500,000. Denise claimed that even though she had withdrawn from the pool, her coworkers insisted that she accept a 20% share of the

---

Rossi v. Rossi (continued)

jackpot worth approximately $1,335,000. Her share was to be paid in equal annual installments of $66,800, less taxes.

Shortly thereafter, Denise went to the Lottery Commission and told them that she was contemplating divorce and wanted to conceal the lottery winnings from her (soon to be ex-) husband. They agreed, even mailing the winnings to her mother's house for a time. Denise and Thomas divorced and she continued to receive the proceeds for several years, but did not disclose the lottery winnings in her divorce case. In 1999, Thomas learned that she had won the lottery in 1996. He asked the court to re-open their property settlement based on what he alleged was Denise's deliberate concealment of a possible marital asset.

The trial court found that Denise's testimony that her share of the lottery winnings was a "gift" from her coworkers was not credible and ruled that the lottery winnings were community property. Denise was required to forfeit the entire remaining lottery payments to Thomas. Had she admitted during the dissolution that she had won the lottery, she would have been entitled to at least half the proceeds and possibly could have convinced the court that they really had been a "gift." Instead, she lost her entire share.

Death of One of the Parties

Upon death of the spouse, the court determines the status of property—either community property or separate property. Then the property is distributed according to the terms of the will or by intestate succession if there is no will. When title is taken as community property, either party may will one-half of the community property. The person can leave half of the community property to his or her spouse or the community property can be transferred by will to whomever he or she chooses.

Distributing Community Property. With community property, upon death, the surviving spouse is entitled to one-half of any community assets. If there is a will, the community property is transferred according to the will. However, if there is no will, the surviving spouse inherits all community property by intestate succession.

This is important to know, particularly with multiple marriages, for estate planning. Property may be owned with the intention that it go to one's children, only to learn after the parent's death that children of the first marriage are no longer natural heirs. If there is a subsequent spouse and no will has been made, the new spouse will become the natural heir to any property owned or community property.

Distributing Separate Property. Regarding separate property, if there is no will, the surviving spouse gets one-half and one child gets one-half. If there is more than one child, the surviving spouse gets one-third and the remaining two-thirds interest is apportioned equally among the children.

Business Ownership

A business entity can own real property in many different ways. We will look at several of them and the way each type of entity affects the rights, actions, and liabilities of the owner or owners of a business. Real estate professionals must be aware of the different types of entities, especially if a party in the transaction involves a business. The most common types of business entities include the sole proprietorship, partnership, corporation, and limited-liability company.

The California Corporations Code governs the formation, operation, and dissolution of corporations, limited liability companies (LLCs), partnerships, limited partnerships (LPs), and limited liability partnerships (LLPs) in the State of California.

Sole Proprietorship

A **sole proprietorship** exists when a single individual files with the state and then operates a business with no other owners. This single owner owns all assets and assumes all liabilities. The business can be sold or terminated at the owner's will. The owner is personally liable for all debts without separation. The owner files one tax return, receives profits as income, and avoids double taxation. **Double taxation** occurs when the business entity is taxed along with the owner of the business.

Quite frequently, the business is conducted under the name of the owner, such as Brittany's Brokerage. If the owner decides to operate under a different type of name, such as Best Choice Realty, then the owner would have to file an Assumed Name Certificate or a DBA—**doing business as** certificate with the county clerk. The advantage to the owner of a DBA is that the transfer of ownership during a sale is easier and the new owner can take over without changing the name.

Partnership

A **partnership** is one form of business organization. Partnerships are normally created among natural persons, but other entities, such as unincorporated associations or corporations can also be parties to a partnership. Like any enterprise conducting business under a fictitious name, a partnership must register its partnership name in the county where its principal place of business is located, showing the full names and residences of all of the partners.

Unlike a corporation, which is legally deemed a "person" for various purposes, a partnership does not reflect a different legal "personality" from the partners. Partnerships file an annual information tax return. All partnership income, expenses, gains, and losses pass through to the individual partners and are reported on their personal income tax returns. Typically, partnerships are formed as general partnerships or limited partnerships.

General Partnership

A **general partnership** exists when two or more individuals or businesses join to operate a business for profit. [Corp. C. §15006]. Typically, the partners own the business assets together, share in the profits, and become personally liable for any losses and business debts. Under a general partnership, a separate business entity exists, but creditors  can use the personal assets of each partner for satisfaction of debts. A general partnership usually operates in accordance with a partnership agreement.

Because each partner is considered an agent of the partnership, each partner has the right to make decisions for the other partners and obligate them to certain contracts. If the partnership goes sour and becomes bankrupt, the creditors can pursue each partner **jointly and severally**, which means the creditors can go after any one partner separately or all of them together. The liability issue also takes into account the actions of the partners. If one partner is fraudulent, the entire partnership is held to be fraudulent.

The partnership will terminate upon the withdrawal of any one of the partners. The withdrawal can be voluntary, by death, or severe disability. Most partnerships include a clause in the agreement stating that the partner who leaves the business will have his or her interest bought out by the remaining partners to avoid disruption of business activity.

In a partnership, at least two people known as **general partners** have equal management and control over the business' day-to-day affairs, according to the terms of a **partnership agreement**.

Limited Partnership

Another way that a partnership can be organized is as a **limited partnership** with at least one general partner and one or more limited partners. Limited partners contribute funds into the partnership, but have no additional liability beyond the contribution. Unlike general partners, limited partners

have no right to control the daily affairs of the company. [Corp. C. §15501]. On the other hand, if the business becomes insolvent, the personal assets of the general partners are liable for all debts and liabilities of the business, but a limited partner is liable only for the money invested in the business.

Partnership Property

California follows the **Uniform Partnership Act** of 1994 (UPA), codified at Corporations Code §§ 16100 et seq. Although the law allows partners to hold property in joint tenancy or tenancy in common, under the UPA, "Property acquired by a partnership is property of the partnership and not of the partners individually." [Corp. Code § 16023]. Section 16024 goes on to provide that property is "partnership property" if it is acquired in the name of the partnership or by one or more partners "with an indication in the instrument transferring title . . . of the person's capacity as a partner or of the existence of a partnership" but without doing so in the name of the partnership.

Corporations Code § 16024 also provides that property is "partnership property" if it is transferred to "[t]he partnership in its name," or to one or more partners "in their capacity as partners in the partnership, if the name of the partnership is indicated in the instrument transferring title to the property." Property that is acquired with partnership assets is also presumed to be partnership property, even if it is not acquired in the name of the partnership. Property that is acquired by the members of the partnership that falls outside of these acquisitions is referred to, like community property, as "separate property"—i.e., the separate property of the partners as individuals and not as "partnership property."

Partnership property, whether real or personal, is treated by the partners in a similar manner as other commonly owned property. This is because each partner has an equal right to the management and control over the business' daily affairs (subject to any limitations in the partnership agreement) and each partner likewise has an equal right of access to and use of the partnership property (subject to the other partners' same rights).

By acquiring partnership property, the partners also obtain some protection from the debts and liabilities incurred by the individual partners in their private lives. While the private ("separate") property of the partners is liable for debts and liabilities incurred in the business, partnership property cannot be levied upon by a creditor of the individual partners for their private debts or liabilities.

> Example: Jan, Ken, and Linda operate a business known as JKL Manufacturing Company as general partners. They acquire a building where they manufacture items that they sell wholesale to retail businesses and where they maintain their offices and shipping facilities. Title to the building is held in the name of JKL Manufacturing.
>
> Ken becomes involved in a serious automobile accident while he is on vacation. He is sued by the persons who were injured and ends up with a judgment against him of more than $1 million. Although his home, personal bank accounts, and other investments are subject to levy by the plaintiffs from the lawsuit, they cannot obtain a lien or otherwise satisfy the judgment against Ken by pursuing his interest in the property where JKL Manufacturing is located. Even though, as a partner, Ken retains a one-third ownership interest in the property, the plaintiffs are powerless to get any of the equity in the business property because it is held in the name of the partnership.

Likewise, if a partner dies, his or her rights in partnership property become the property of the surviving partners of the business. Neither the personal survivors of the deceased partner nor that partner's estate acquires an interest in the partnership property. All that the deceased partner's survivors are entitled to is an accounting of the profits and surplus of the business. However, real property held in the name of the partnership would itself not be part of the decedent's estate.

Corporation

A **corporation** is a legal entity, which has a separate legal identity from its owners or members. A corporation is viewed as a legal person (has rights) and not a natural person (has body). Because a corporation is viewed as a legal person, a corporation can buy and sell real property, bind itself to a contract, and pay taxes. The corporation structure offers protection to the business owners' (stockholders) personal assets from debts and liabilities relating to the operation of the corporation. As a legal entity, the corporation has inherent rights and obligations.

Legal Rights of a Corporation

1. **The ability to sue and be sued.** An aggrieved person can use the courts to sue a corporation, but rarely has the right to sue an employee of the corporation.

2. **The right to a common treasury.** The corporation can buy, sell, own, and hold assets.

3. **The right to hire agents.** The corporation has the right to hire employees and others to represent the corporation.

4. **The right to a common seal.** The corporation has the right to obligate the corporation through contracts.

5. **The right to make by-laws.** The corporation has the right to govern itself as long as that power does not violate the law.

6. **The right to issue transferable shares.** The corporation can sell ownership of the company by offering shares that can be bought and sold in the open market.

7. **The right to ensure perpetual succession.** The corporation can continue with or without any of its shareholders or employees. However, if the corporation terminates its existence, the shareholders are the last to receive any benefits.

8. **The right to vote for shareholders.** The shareholders have the right to vote on the corporation's operating staff. The elected corporate officers will manage the affairs of the corporation on a day-to-day basis.

9. **The right of limited liability for its shareholders.** The corporation is held responsible for any liabilities of the corporation unless the ownership has committed fraud.

S-corporations and limited liability companies are other variations of a corporation. An **S-corporation** is a business entity that operates as a corporation, has the tax advantages of a partnership, and passes along any profits or losses through to shareholders. A **limited liability company (LLC)** is a business entity that combines the tax advantages of a partnership and the limited liability of a corporation, but does not require any advanced financial reporting or the complicated structuring that a corporation normally requires. [Corp. C. §17000 et seq.].

Common Interest Developments

A **common interest development (CID)** is defined in the California Civil Code Section 1351(c) as any of the following projects: planned development, condominium project, cooperative, or community apartment project. Each of these projects is similar because they combine the individual ownership of private dwellings with an interest in common with other owners. The interest in common may be through membership in an association. In CIDs, the common areas are owned either in common by the owners as in condominiums or by an association as in planned developments. Condominiums and other commonly owned residential property are governed by the Davis-Stirling Common Interest Development Act, found in Civil Code §§ 1350 et seq.

All CIDs are similar in that they allow individual owners the use of common property and facilities and provide for a system of self-governance through some type of homeowners' association. Membership in the association is automatic. When a person buys a lot, home, or condominium in a CID, he or she automatically becomes a member of the association.

The most important difference in CIDs is their legal structure, e.g. planned developments, condominiums, cooperatives, and community apartment projects. Each type confers specific ownership rights—from fee ownership of the unit including the underlying lot to ownership of stock with a proprietary lease giving its owner an exclusive right to occupy an apartment.

Planned Developments

Planned developments, or PDs, are another form of common ownership. A PD is a community of clustered single-family detached residences, townhouses, garden apartments, and other types of residences, with ample open space, community recreational facilities, and sometimes local shopping and employment centers.

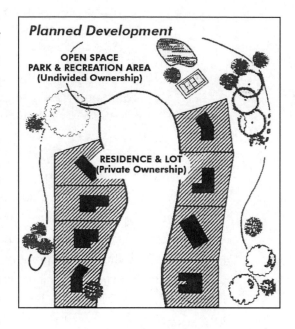

Planned development owners have fee title to their separately owned dwelling along with the lot underneath it. They do not directly own the common areas. The common areas are owned and managed by a homeowners' association to which the owner belongs.

Condominium

A condominium is a form of CID ownership in a housing development that combines a separate interest in an individual unit with co-ownership of common areas. Civil Code §1351(f) defines a **condominium** as "an undivided interest in common in a portion of real property coupled with a separate interest in space called a unit, the boundaries of which are described on a recorded final map, parcel map, or condominium plan in sufficient detail to locate all boundaries thereof." It further explains that, "The area within these boundaries may be filled with air, earth, or water, or any combination thereof and need not be physically attached to land except by easements for access and, if necessary, support." Of course, because a property may be developed with single-story condominium units, the description can, but does not have to, include the elevation of the units as part of the description.

The underlying land and virtually all of the rest of the structure that houses the condominium unit, along with any common ground, lawns, recreational facilities, and the like are owned in tenancy in common with other owners in the development.

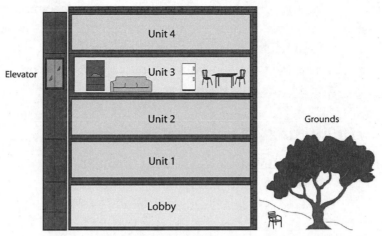

Residential Condominium

In order to manage the common areas, purchasing a unit in a condominium project carries with it membership in a homeowners' association to which the owners of each individual unit also must contribute regular dues for the maintenance of the common areas.

Each person who owns a unit in a given development has a proportionate share in the responsibilities for maintenance fees paid for the common area, as well as a vote in the selection of a homeowners' association board of directors. The board acts somewhat like a "government" of the association, using the fees paid by the owners for the upkeep of the common area. This board typically hires a property management company to take care of such needs as landscaping and building maintenance.

Cooperative

A cooperative (stock cooperative) is another method of providing for common ownership in a housing development. A **cooperative** is different from most other ways of owning real property because a corporation holds title to all of the real property of the cooperative. Co-op owners do not have fee ownership in their unit and do not receive a deed. Instead, they purchase stock in the corporation that owns the property. [C.C. §1351(m)]. The shares of stock give the co-op owners the exclusive right to occupy a particular unit under a **proprietary lease**. When a unit is sold, the proprietary lease is assigned to the buyer along with the seller's stock certificate. Physically, the cooperative apartment might resemble any other apartment building or even a condominium.

The cooperative in effect differs from a condominium in that any charges or debts attached to any units can become the obligation of the other units or shareholders. Another difference is that approval must be received from the other shareholders before a unit can be sold, rented, gifted, or leased or any other similar action can be taken.

Community Apartment Projects

A **community apartment project** is a development in which an undivided interest in land is coupled with the right of exclusive occupancy of any apartment located in the project. [C.C. §1351(d)]. Purchasers generally receive a leasehold interest for a specific unit in the community apartment. Community apartment projects are typically operated, maintained, and controlled by a governing board elected by the owners of the fractional interests.

Timeshares

A **timeshare** is the common ownership of a single piece of property by an association of people with each owner having the exclusive right to occupy a unit for a specified period each year. Timeshare ownerships, which are also known as **interval ownerships**, are usually for specific blocks of time per year. The blocks of time in each timeshare sell for different amounts. Purchasers may pay a premium for certain times of the year, view, exposure, or other amenities. For example, if the timeshare is located in a ski resort, time blocks will sell for a premium during the winter months and possibly at a discount during the summer months. The time blocks are usually for one or two weeks, which can be a fixed week or floating.

Some timeshares are structured more like tenancies in common, but subject to additional restrictions that the buyer agrees to as a condition of purchase, such as the division of use into discrete time periods and a requirement that, except during those times, the timeshare "owner" has no right of control or access to the property. This avoids potential conflicts about right of access that might otherwise arise under a conventional tenancy in common.

Despite these restrictions, such timeshares are as much an interest in real property as any other and can be sold, loaned, given away, traded on a one-time basis with other time-share owners or bequeathed to one's heirs by will (in each case, subject to the same restrictions that were accepted by the original owner).

Other timeshares are structured more like cooperatives with the "ownership" being more of a contractual right and the ultimate property ownership remaining with the developer of the timeshare property. In those cases, the purchaser acquires contractual rights of use to the property but not any ownership interest in the land. This form of a timeshare can also be more in the nature of a short-term lease that automatically renews annually for the same period of time. In California, the sale of timeshares requires a real estate license.

SUMMARY

Property ownership can be held in severalty or as undivided ownership interests. Undivided ownership interests include fractional ownership interests, common interest developments, and timeshares. Fractional ownership interests include concurrent ownership and business ownership. Concurrent ownership is a blanket term for the ownership of real property by more than one person.

Types of Concurrent Ownership in California

1. Tenancy in common
2. Joint tenancy
3. Community property

Business ownership includes partnerships, corporations, and LLCs.

There are also ways that common interest developments can include multiple ownerships. A common interest development (CID) is a project that combines the individual ownership of private dwellings with an interest in common with other owners. Common CIDs are planned developments, condominiums, cooperatives, and community apartment projects.

Finally, a timeshare is the common ownership of a single piece of property by an association of people with each owner having the exclusive right to occupy a unit for a specified period each year.

UNIT 6 REVIEW

Matching Exercise

Instructions: Write the letter of the matching term on the blank line before its definition. Answers are in Appendix A.

Terms

A. CID

B. community property

C. condominium

D. cooperative

E. corporation

F. general partnership

G. interval ownership

H. joint tenancy

I. PD

J. quasi-community property

K. severalty

L. tenancy

M. tenancy in common

N. title vesting

O. undivided interest

Definitions

1. _____ Mode or method of ownership or holding title to property

2. _____ Evidence that the owner of land is in lawful possession; it is the proof of ownership

3. _____ Ownership of a parcel of real property by only one person or entity

4. _____ Interest held under the same title by two or more people or entities, whether their rights are equal or unequal in value or quantity

5. _____ Ownership by two or more persons, whose interests are not necessarily equal, in a single estate

6. _____ Form of concurrent ownership providing for automatic survivorship to the other cotenants upon death

7. _____ Form of concurrent property ownership that exists only between spouses

8. _____ Property acquired outside of California that would be community property if acquired in California

9. _____ Business entity established by two or more individuals or businesses, which join to operate a business for profit

10. _____ Legal entity viewed as a legal person (has rights) but not a natural person (has body)

11. _____ Project combining individual ownership of private dwellings with an interest in common with other owners

12. _____ Community of clustered single-family detached residences, townhouses, garden apartments, and other types of residences, with ample open space, community recreational facilities, and sometimes local shopping and employment centers

13. _____ Undivided interest in common in a portion of real property coupled with a separate interest in space called a unit

14. _____ Form of CID in which a corporation holds title to all of the real property and owners purchase shares of stock in that corporation

15. _____ Timeshare ownerships

Multiple Choice Questions

Instructions: Circle your response and go to Appendix A to read the complete explanation for each question.

1. Which of the following describes a person's status on the deed, if the person obtains title to property in severalty?
   a. A married woman
   b. An unmarried man
   c. As husband and wife
   d. As separate property

2. Which one of the following statements is true?
   a. Any time two or more persons own the same parcel, a joint tenancy is created.
   b. Community property is not a recognized means of co-ownership in California.
   c. Joint tenancy is the default method of co-ownership in California.
   d. Tenancy in common is the default method of co-ownership in California.

3. Bob, Fred, and Jack own equal interests in a parcel of land as tenants in common. Without the consent of the others, Jack leased his 1/3 share to Tom. Which statement is correct?
    a. Bob, Fred, and Jack will share equally in the rent collected from Tom.
    b. Jack is entitled to all of the rent collected from Tom.
    c. Jack must designate the area that would be for Tom's exclusive use.
    d. Tom may use only 1/3 of the property.

4. Henry and Wanda own property in joint tenancy. Unbeknownst to Wanda, Henry leaves "all my property" to Sheryl in his will. Once Henry dies, what happens to the property?
    a. Wanda and Sheryl will each own a ½ interest as tenants in common.
    b. Sheryl will own all of the property.
    c. Wanda will own all of the property.
    d. Sheryl and Wanda will become joint tenants.

5. Kris, Pat, and Donna took title to a property as joint tenants. Kris sold her share to Sally, and then Pat died. Who owns the property now?
    a. Donna owns 2/3 and Sally owns 1/3 as tenants in common.
    b. Donna, Sally, and Pat's heirs own the property 1/3 each as joint tenants.
    c. Donna owns 2/3 and Sally owns 1/3 as joint tenants.
    d. Donna, Sally, and Pat's heirs own the property 1/3 each as tenants in common.

6. How are a joint tenancy interest and a community property interest alike?
    a. Ownership interests are equal
    b. Only spouses are involved
    c. Both owners must join in any conveyance
    d. Both provide the right of survivorship

7. What is required for a couple to have community property rights?
    a. Intestacy
    b. Right of survivorship
    c. Time, title, interest, and possession
    d. Valid marriage

8. Which of the following business entities avoids double taxation and is operated by a single owner?

    a. Corporation
    b. General Partnership
    c. Limited Partnership
    d. Sole Proprietorship

9. Which type of CID is characterized by fee ownership of the dwelling along with the lot underneath it?

    a. Condominium
    b. Community apartment project
    c. Cooperative
    d. Planned development

10. Which type of undivided interest ownership is usually for a set portion of time each year?

    a. Corporate ownership
    b. Fractional ownership
    c. Severalty ownership
    d. Timeshare ownership

How Ownership is Acquired & Conveyed

Unit 7

INTRODUCTION

Ultimately, all real property that is owned by one person eventually will be owned by someone else. Most commonly, of course, someone who owns property will some day decide to sell it. Residential real property, on average, is sold once every seven years. In addition, even if someone holds onto a parcel of land for an entire lifetime, all of us will eventually die and the law provides for an orderly way to pass on property once that happens. It also provides for the satisfaction of money judgments or the government's need for land to build a public building or road.

The Civil Code states that there are five ways to acquire property: transfer, will, succession, occupancy, and by accession. [C.C. §1000].

Real property is most commonly transferred from one person or entity to another by a **voluntary transfer**. That is, the party who owns the property decides to transfer ownership to someone else or perhaps to a corporation, usually (though not always) in exchange for some kind of compensation. The common methods to transfer property voluntarily are by deeds and wills.

Involuntary alienation is the transfer of property against the wishes of the owner. Title may be transferred involuntarily by operation of law, government action, adverse possession, or even by physical changes in the land itself.

Learning Objectives

After completing this unit, you should be able to:

7A   differentiate voluntary and involuntary transfers of real property.

7B   classify testamentary instruments.

7C   recall intestate succession.

7D   identify the steps to obtain land through adverse possession.

7E   recognize methods on enlarging or reducing land by natural forces.

7F   recall the importance and effect of recording.

TRANSFER

Property is acquired by **transfer** when, by an act of the parties or law, title is **conveyed**, or transferred, from one person to another by means of a written document. [C.C. §1053]. The transfer may be voluntary, such as the sale of a home, or involuntary by act of law, such as a foreclosure sale. The act of transferring or conveying property to another—voluntarily or involuntarily—is called **alienation.**

Deeds

The most common method of transferring real property is with a deed. A **deed** is a written instrument that is used to transfer title to real property from one person to another. (Deeds, of course, can also be used to transfer real property from or to non-living but legally recognized entities, such as a corporation or governmental body, but for simplicity, the discussion that follows will refer to transfers between human beings.) A deed must satisfy certain requirements in order to be legally binding.

Requirements for a Valid Deed

- Writing
- Competent grantor
- Property description
- Granting clause
- Execution
- Delivery and acceptance

Writing

A deed must meet certain basic requirements to accomplish the transfer of title. First, as anything else involved in the transfer of real property, it must be in writing so that it complies with the statute of frauds. [C.C. §1624].

Competent Grantor

A deed must identify the parties involved in the transaction. The person conveying the property is referred to as the **grantor** and the person to whom it is conveyed is the **grantee**. Like a contract, a deed must be conveyed from someone who is competent. That is, the grantor must be able to understand the nature of the act of signing the deed and consequences of doing so, as well as harbor the intent to convey the property.

However, a deed can be given to a minor or to an incompetent person, such as someone who is under conservatorship; the legal guardian of the minor or conservator of an incompetent grantee can accept the deed on behalf of the grantee named in the deed.

Property Description

The real property must be adequately described so that it is clear which parcel of land is being conveyed. Although it is not necessary to use a legal description, as a practical matter it is better to use a description that identifies the parcel more specifically, such as a metes and bounds description or by reference to a recorded plat map.

A grantor could legally transfer title to a parcel of land with language as vague as "The property I own on Peach Street in Visalia, California" if that grantor only owns one parcel of land in Visalia on that street. Because such a deed would require **extrinsic evidence** to identify the parcel—that is, evidence outside the deed itself—such a description would create problems in recording the document and in obtaining title insurance.

Granting Clause

A deed must have a granting clause, which was once referred to as "words of purchase." The **granting clause** must contain words that demonstrate intent on the part of the grantor to transfer a present interest from the grantor to the grantee, although no specific words are required. Words stating that the grantor "grants," "conveys," "transfers," or "sells" the interest set forth in the deed to the grantee would be deemed sufficient if the issue were challenged in court.

The granting clause can transfer the entire fee simple estate or it can limit the scope of the estate that is being granted. In the absence of some restriction—such as conveying the property only for life—the deed will be presumed to convey a fee simple absolute. [C.C. §1105].

Execution

The grantor must sign the deed—that is, execute it. The form of the grantor's name must be in the same form that the grantor received title to the property or provide an explanation for using a different name. [C.C. §1096]. Thus, if a woman obtained title when single but has since married, she could execute the deed using her married name only if she also refers to her former name in the deed.

> Example: Jane purchased a parcel of land five years ago when she was unmarried. The deed she received at that time referred to her as "Jane Morrison." She married three years ago and now uses the name "Jane Harris." If she wanted to convey the land to a buyer today, she could execute the deed, "Jane Harris, formerly known as Jane Morrison." This will allow a title examiner to match the title she received under her former name with her deed to the new buyer today, in order to confirm that the new buyer has clear title.

Delivery and Acceptance

A deed must be both delivered by the grantor and accepted by the grantee. Execution of a properly drafted deed, followed by delivery and acceptance, is all that is necessary to convey title. **Delivery** involves more than physically handing the deed to the grantee. In doing so, the grantor must intend to part irrevocably with title to the property as that title is described in the deed. [C.C. §1054]. The language spoken by the grantor and the grantor's actions when handing over the deed will be considered by a court if that is necessary to determine whether title has been transferred.

> Example: Fred intends to transfer his home to his niece, Ann, but only wants this to take place upon his death. He executes a deed and hands it to Ann, telling her that he only wants her to take title until after he has died. Fred likewise instructs Ann not to record the deed until after his death. If Fred later changed his mind and asked Ann for the deed back, a court would probably find that Fred's delivery of the deed to Ann was ineffective to transfer title to her, because the instructions he gave to her showed that he had no present intent to convey title to her at that time. (Obviously, all of this would be easier to prove if there were a witness besides just Ann and Fred available to testify if a dispute arose later.)

A grantee must accept a deed before it is considered effective. Just like the act of handing over the deed, a grantee must show some intent to accept the deed at the time of delivery for title to pass. Acceptance is automatic if the grantee is an infant or incompetent person. The failure to return the deed, coupled with any exercise of control (such as taking possession) would demonstrate that a deed has been accepted. In addition, acceptance may be shown by the acts of the grantee, such as moving onto the property.

> Example: Assume that in the above example when Fred handed the deed to Ann, he did not make any statements about only wanting her to wait until his death to take title. Also, assume that Fred and Ann have recently quarreled and when Fred hands her the deed, she crumples up the paper and throws it back at him. Even if she later thinks better of his gesture and retrieved the crumpled piece of paper, a court might well find that her refusal to accept the deed when it was delivered voided the transfer at the time of delivery.

Despite the lengthy list of requirements needed to create a valid deed, there are a number of things not necessary for title to be conveyed. Although these items are not necessary for a deed to be valid, some of them should not be dispensed with capriciously. A deed that is not acknowledged before a notary, for example, cannot be recorded; and a deed that cannot be recorded opens the door to fraud—because one person can then sell property to more than one person.

Things a Valid Deed Does Not Require
- Signature of the Grantee
- Date
- Consideration
- Habendum Clause
- Recordation

Signature of the Grantee

The grantee does not need to sign the deed.

Date

Although not required, dating the deed helps show intent of delivery.

Consideration

Property may be given as a gift or by will, with no consideration required. However, if a deed has no consideration, a grantee is not considered a bona fide purchaser. A **bona fide purchaser** is one who in good faith paid valuable consideration for property without notice of prior adverse claims.

Habendum Clause

In California, deeds no longer require language known as the **habendum clause**. This language was sometimes nicknamed the "marriage clause" because it invariably began with the words, "To have and to hold . . . ." The habendum clause was a throwback to a time when most landowners were illiterate and land was transferred not by a deed or other written document but by a medieval process known as "livery of seisin." This was a ceremony in which a physical object, such as a clod of earth, was handed from the grantor to the grantee before a number of witnesses—much as a marriage is still conducted by a ceremony in the presence of family and friends. Real estate practitioners should be aware of it because it will be found in many older deeds and it is still required for a valid deed in some states.

Recordation

Since a deed does not have to be recorded to be valid, it does not need an **acknowledgment**. Recording a deed is not necessary for title to pass. However, **recordation** of a deed creates a presumption that a deed was delivered and accepted. A presumption is a legal substitute for formal proof of fact. Most real property transactions, in fact, do not involve the grantor physically handing the deed to the grantee; rather, the grantor delivers the deed to the escrow officer (or executes a deed prepared by the escrow company), which is later recorded at the conclusion of the transaction.

Of course, if someone receives a deed and takes possession of the property, that in itself is strong evidence that the person, in fact, has title. However, if someone intends to rent out property, to sell it to someone else, or to obtain a loan against the property, an unrecorded deed creates problems with doing all three. The best practice, therefore, is to have a deed acknowledged and to record it as soon as possible afterwards—or better yet, to allow professionals who handle such transactions routinely to assist in that process.

Types of Deeds

The kinds of deeds commonly used for private grants include grant deed, quitclaim deed, gift deed, and warranty deed.

Grant Deed

The most commonly used deed to transfer real property in California is the **grant deed**. A grant deed has two **implied warranties** of title. [C.C. §1113]. The grantor of a grant deed impliedly promises that he or she has not conveyed the property to anyone other than the grantee under that deed and that the estate shown on the deed is free from any encumbrances, other than those identified by the grantor at the time of the conveyance.

A grant deed conveys both whatever title the grantor has at the time of the conveyance and **after-acquired title**. This means that if the grantor later obtains title to the property—even if he or she did not have it at the time of the conveyance—then it will be conveyed to the grantee should the grantor later obtain it.

> Example: George's grandmother has told him that she intends to leave him her stately Victorian home in her will. He has seen what he believes to be the most recent version of her will and it confirms this.
>
> However, George is in need of money right away to pay some gambling debts. He approaches Sam, a real estate speculator and presents Sam with a variety of documents showing that George's grandmother owns this valuable property, as well as a copy of his grandmother's will, showing that George is likely to inherit the property someday.
>
> George offers to sell Sam his "expectancy"—that is, his title in this property that he has not received yet. The selling price will be heavily discounted compared to the fair market value of the property because Sam does not know when—or even if—George will receive title. If George's grandmother decides to change her will, for example, or if the property must be sold during the probate process to pay expenses before George ever obtains title, Sam will get nothing. Sam also must take into account the relative health and age of George's grandmother in setting a selling price; the older or poorer her health, then the likelier and sooner he may realize a profit from his (somewhat ghoulish) bargain.
>
> Once they reach a price for the transaction, George executes a grant deed to Sam. Sam can record this deed at any time if George does in fact obtain title to his grandmother's property. Although George had no interest in the property when he executed the deed, his deed to Sam means that Sam will automatically receive title instead.

Quitclaim Deed

Unlike a grant deed, a **quitclaim deed** has no warranties. The grantor of a quitclaim makes no representation about the grantor's interest or title. The grantor simply gives up (quits) all interest that the grantor *may* have in the property—if any. They are commonly used to eliminate possible clouds on title, particularly by spouses (or former spouses), distant relatives of former owners, or neighbors when there is a title dispute. Unlike a grant deed, a quitclaim does not convey after-acquired title because it only gives up any *present* interest that the grantor may have.

Gift Deed

A **gift deed** is used to make a gift of property to a grantee, usually a close friend or relative. The consideration in a gift deed is called **love and affection**.

Warranty Deed

Because almost all land transactions in California are covered by title insurance, warranty deeds are rarely used here. A **warranty deed** is a document containing six **express covenants** of title. Unlike a grant deed, a general warranty deed is in effect a guarantee that title to the property is good.

Contract for Deed

A **contract for deed** (also referred to as a land contract or installment land contract) is a conditional sales contract for the sale of real property. In a land contract, as the name implies, the seller and the buyer enter into an agreement to sell the property. However, in this transaction, the seller (**vendor**) finances the purchase by carrying back a loan from the buyer (**vendee**). A seller is said to **carry back** when the seller extends credit to a buyer by taking a promissory note executed by the buyer for the property purchased. The vendee pays the vendor in installments over several years.

A land contract differs from a deed of trust or a mortgage in that the buyer/ vendee does not obtain title to the property during the time that the contract is being paid off. The vendee is allowed to take possession of the property immediately and begins to make payments to the vendor.

Because the vendor will not receive the full purchase price for a long time (usually many years), the vendor retains legal title to the property and the vendee has **equitable title**. When all the terms of the contract are met, the vendor will pass title to the vendee.

Operation of Law

Sometimes property is transferred by the **operation of law** or **court action**. It is usually an involuntary transfer involving foreclosure or is the result of a judgment or some other lien against the title. Frequently, courts establish legal title regardless of the desires of the record owners.

Foreclosure

Foreclosure is the legal procedure lenders use to terminate the trustor or mortgagor's rights, title, and interest in real property by selling the property and using the sale proceeds to satisfy the liens of creditors. Deeds of trust or mortgages that contain a **power-of-sale clause** allow the lender to initiate the foreclosure process.

In California, there are two ways to foreclose—non-judicial foreclosure or judicial foreclosure. Any deed of trust or mortgage with a power-of-sale clause may be foreclosed non-judicially by a trustee's sale or judicially by a court procedure. Without the power-of-sale clause, the only remedy a lender has is a judicial foreclosure by a court proceeding. Most deeds of trust in California include the power-of-sale clause, so the lender may choose either type of foreclosure method.

Methods of Foreclosure
1. Non-judicial foreclosure—requires power of sale
2. Judicial foreclosure—requires court-ordered sale

Non-Judicial Foreclosure

A **non-judicial foreclosure** (or trustee's sale) is the procedure a lender uses to sell a property without the involvement of a court. A **trustee's sale** is the quickest and easiest method taking approximately four months. First, the beneficiary (lender) notifies the trustor (borrower) of default and requests the trustee to record a  **Notice of Default**. Anyone who has recorded a **Request for Notice** must be notified of the default. The trustee must wait at least three months after recording the Notice of Default before advertising the trustee sale. Then the trustee advertises a Notice of Sale once a week for three weeks (21 days) and posts a Notice of Sale on the property.

As you can see, the minimum time between recording the Notice of Default and the trustee sale is three months and 21 days. During this time the trustor may **reinstate** (bring current) the loan up to five business days prior to the trustee's sale.

The trustee holds a public auction, collects the winning bid price from the successful bidder and issues a **trustee's deed** to the highest bidder. A trustor has no right of redemption after the trustee sale.

Order Proceeds from Sale of the Property are Paid
1. Trustee's fees, costs, and expenses of the sale
2. Any tax and assessment liens that are due and owing
3. Deeds of trust, mortgages, and mechanic's liens in their order of priority
4. Defaulting borrower

The sale is subject to certain liens of record that are not eliminated by a foreclosure sale. These include federal tax liens and real property assessments and taxes. That means the new owner is responsible for payment of those liens. The non-judicial foreclosure process eliminates any junior liens.

Judicial Foreclosure

A lender may choose a judicial foreclosure instead of a trustee sale under a deed of trust. A **judicial foreclosure** is the procedure a lender uses to sell a mortgaged property with the involvement of a court. The process of judicial foreclosure is commonly used when foreclosing mortgages rather than deeds of trust. The reason a lender may decide to choose a judicial foreclosure under a deed of trust is that a deficiency judgment is allowable.

To foreclose in accordance with judicial procedure, a lender must prove that the borrower is in default. Once the lender has exhausted its attempts to resolve the default with the homeowner, the next step is to contact an attorney to pursue court action.

The lender goes to court to start the foreclosure. The court issues a decree of foreclosure and an order of sale. After publication and posting of the sale notice, the court-appointed commissioner sells the property to the highest bidder and gives the buyer a Certification of Sale. After a court foreclosure sale on a mortgage, the borrower gets to keep possession of the property and has one year to redeem the property by satisfying the loan in full including court costs and any interest. This is called **statutory redemption**. If after one year, the mortgagor does not redeem the property, a **sheriff's deed** is issued to the new buyer.

If a deed of trust is foreclosed in court, it is treated like a mortgage and the trustor (borrower) may keep possession during the redemption period. Sometimes a lender with a deed of trust may elect to foreclose by a court foreclosure. This may be the only way the lender can obtain a deficiency judgment against the borrower.

Sue on Promissory Note

For a lender, sometimes the proceeds of the sale are not sufficient to satisfy the foreclosed debt. In addition, the expenses incurred while pursuing a foreclosure can be costly and the lender may want to recover those expenses as well. If that happens, the lender may try to sue on the promissory note and obtain a deficiency judgment against the borrower to recover the money owed on the defaulting balance of the loan.

A **deficiency judgment** is a personal judgment against a borrower for the balance of a debt owed when the security for the loan is not sufficient to pay the debt. In a deed of trust, the lender must decide whether to sue on the promissory note or pursue foreclosure. Once the lender decides to pursue foreclosure in a deed of trust, the lender cannot obtain a deficiency judgment against the trustor after the trustee sale.

If a lender (beneficiary or mortgagee) chooses to foreclose a deed of trust or mortgage with a power of sale using a trustee sale, no deficiency judgment is allowed if the proceeds do not satisfy the debt and all costs. Since deeds of trust are used almost exclusively in California to secure loans, the only security for a beneficiary is the property itself. Any other personal assets of the borrower in default are protected from judgment under a deed of trust.

Additionally, a lender cannot get a deficiency judgment against a borrower if the loan is a purchase money loan secured by either a deed of trust or a mortgage. Any loan made at the time of a sale, as part of that sale, is known as a **purchase-money loan**. This includes first deeds of trust, junior loans used to purchase the property, and seller carry-back financing.

A deficiency judgment is allowed on hard money loans. A **hard money loan** is one made in exchange for cash, as opposed to a loan made to finance the purchase of a home. Typically, a hard money loan refers to junior loans used to take money out for consumer purchases, home equity loans, debt consolidation, and even a refinance.

Partition Action

A **partition action** is a court proceeding to settle a dispute between co-owners (joint tenants or tenants in common) about dividing their interests in real property. [C.C.P. §872.210]. A partition action may be available to terminate the interest of one co-owner (a partial interest) or to terminate the entire ownership through physical division or sale.

To initiate a partition action, a complaint is filed in the county where the property is located. Once the complaint is filed, a Notice of Pendency is recorded with the county recorder's office to notify anyone interested in the property that a legal action is in process. The judge will make a determination on the merits of the partition request. If the request is upheld, the court will appoint a referee to physically divide the property or sell it and divide the money derived from its sale.

Quiet Title Action

Quiet title action is a court proceeding to establish an individual's right to ownership of real property against one or more adverse claimants. It is used to clear a cloud on the title of real property, such as titles based on adverse possession or the seller's title under a forfeited, recorded land contract. An action for quiet title requires a description of the property to be quieted, the names of anyone who might have an interest (including descendants known or unknown of prior owners), and the legal basis for the claim of title. Notice must be given to all potentially interested parties by publication. The court may grant a quiet title judgment, which can be recorded to remove the cloud on title and thus provide good legal title.

Tax Sale

A **tax sale** is the forced sale of real property (usually via an auction) by a taxing authority (usually the county) to satisfy delinquent taxes along with any penalties and costs. Persons who buy such property receive a **tax deed**.

Execution Sale

An **execution sale** is a forced sale of property under a **writ of execution** with the proceeds used to satisfy a money judgment. A sheriff's deed is given to a buyer when property is sold through court action in order to satisfy a judgment for money or foreclosure of a mortgage. A **sheriff's deed**, as the name implies, is issued by the sheriff of the county where real property is located when the property goes through a sheriff's sale to satisfy a civil court judgment against the property owner.

Eminent Domain

The power of **eminent domain** is the power of the government to take private property for public use. Eminent domain is mentioned in one of the amendments to the U.S. Constitution. The Fifth Amendment ends with the words, "Nor shall private property be taken for public use without just compensation." The "Takings Clause" as it is known actually imposes two requirements on the government: first that the "taking" be for a "public use"; and second, that the public entity pay "just" (fair) compensation to the owner of the property for the land that has been taken. **Just compensation** is fair and reasonable payment due to a private property owner when his or her property is condemned under eminent domain.

Condemnation

Condemnation is the process by which the government acquires private property for public use, under its right of eminent domain. The traditional understanding of a "public use" was that the government could condemn land for such things as roads, schools, hospitals, or military bases because the needs of the larger community outweighed the desire of one property owner to hold onto a specific parcel of land. Over time, however, the notion of what is a "public" use expanded to include such things as elimination of "blighted" areas through urban redevelopment. Local governments would use the condemnation power to acquire dilapidated buildings in city centers to construct public housing. Over time, this expanded to include the idea of using condemnation to acquire even unblighted land merely to provide economic stimulus.

Kelo v. City of New London

In a controversial recent case, *Kelo v. City of New London, Connecticut,* 545 U.S. 469 (2005), the city wanted to obtain 115 homes in an established, older neighborhood as part of a comprehensive plan to generate more tax revenue by turning these residences into a commercial development.

Fifteen property owners object, but when the case ultimately reached the U.S. Supreme Court, the court held, 5-4, that the acquisition of the property over the objection of the property owners as part of a comprehensive plan of redevelopment was lawful. Even though the property might eventually be transferred to a private developer, this was not an unlawful use of the power of eminent domain, so long as the public entity paid lawful compensation to the (former) owner, and the purpose of the transfer was not to benefit the eventual new owner *per se,* but to benefit the public entity by increasing the local tax base and creating jobs. The *Kelo* court did not actually create a new rule, but simply applied cases going back to the 1950s that had upheld similar "redevelopment" or "revitalization" plans for urban areas.

Inverse Condemnation

A related concept is **inverse condemnation**, in which a private party can argue that activity by a public entity has effectively caused a "taking." Public entities do not always go through a public process to obtain title to land, even if it can be shown later that governmental activity has taken or damaged land.

Example: If a public improvement affects the natural drainage in an area, water might collect on a portion of a nearby private parcel where it never had accumulated previously. The landowner could argue that the flooding of his land due to the public improvement is in effect a "taking" without just compensation.

WILLS & TRUSTS

The person who has died, known as the decedent, can leave written instructions or a **testamentary instrument** (usually in the form of a will or a trust) explaining how that person wanted his or her property (estate) to be disposed. If those documents are properly prepared, the law requires that the decedent's wishes expressed in those instructions to be carried out. A person who prepares such documents is known as the **testator** and is said to have died **testate**—that is, having left proper instructions for the disposition of the decedent's estate.

Wills

California Probate Code §88 defines a **will**, somewhat cryptically, as including a "codicil and any testamentary instrument which merely appoints an executor or revokes or revises another will." This definition is apparently intended to make sure that these other documents will also be treated by a court as a "will."

A will or other testamentary instrument is revocable because it does not take effect until the testator dies. Until that time, it can be revoked or amended as the testator may choose. Once the testator has become the decedent, of course, the terms of the will become irrevocable. A will can also make provisions for the care of the person's minor children if no other person (such as a surviving spouse) is available for their care. The person who drafts and signs a will is known as the testator.

A will normally consists of one or more pages that are physically bound together (e.g., stapled at one corner or the top). The writing can be on one or both sides of the paper, in which case (if on more than one side), the testator's intent to include the writing on the back to be part of the will should be included, either by reference or, e.g., numbering that refers to the whole as a will.

Types of Wills

California recognizes three types of wills: witnessed wills, statutory form wills, and holographic wills.

Witnessed Will

A **witnessed will**, usually prepared by an attorney, is signed by the maker (testator) and is witnessed by at least two persons. A witnessed will is valid in California if its execution complies with the law of California; or with the law of the place of its execution if it was executed outside of California; or the law of the place where the testator was domiciled at the time of the testator's death. [Prob. Code §6113]. According to Prob. Code §6110, in order for a witnessed will to be valid, it must have certain required elements.

Requirements for a Witnessed Will

- In writing
- Signed by the testator or signed by someone else in the testator's presence, and at the testator's direction
- Witnessed by at least two persons each of whom:
  - was present at the same time, witnessed either the signing of the will or the testator's acknowledgment of the signature or of the will, and
  - understand that the instrument they sign is the testator's will.

Section 6110 relaxed a number of provisions under the former law, including that the will be signed "at the end," that the testator "declare" to the witnesses that the document is his or her will and that the witnesses sign the will in the testator's presence.

Testator's Signature on a Will. The testator's signature on the will is sometimes referred to as the testator's **authentication** of the will. [Prob. Code §6110]. Section 6110 does not refer to making a **signature by "mark"** when the testator does not know how to read or write. However, cases decided under earlier versions of the Probate Code held that the earlier statutes, when read together with Code of Civil Procedure §17 (which defines a signature as including a "mark") meant that a will could be signed in that way. Today, §6110 allows someone other than the testator to sign the will (physically) if, e.g., the testator is blind, too infirm, etc. This provision requires that the person acting for the testator sign the will in the testator's presence and at the testator's direction.

Witnesses' Signatures. Most of the cases dealing with the witness requirement were decided under former law. Section 6110 continues the requirement that the will be authenticated in the presence of two witnesses who are present at the same time and that the witnesses sign the will.

Statutory Form Will

Probate Code § 6240 provides for a statutory form will. Any person over the age of 18 and of sound mind may execute a **statutory form will**. The form of the statutory will is set forth in an appendix to §6240. Many commercial versions are available and it can also be obtained from the California State Bar's website at: www.calbar.ca.gov. A statutory will still requires two witnesses and can be amended by codicil or revoked in the same manner as other wills.

Holographic Wills

A **holographic will** is a will entirely in the handwriting of the testator. Under Probate Code §6111, a will that does not comply with the requirements of §6110 may still be valid if the signature and the material provisions of the will are in the handwriting of the testator. Unlike a regular will, a holographic will does not require witnesses. Under former law, a holographic will had to be dated. Now, the law does not require this directly. The new law also allows some information in a holographic will to be in something other than handwriting (such as filling in blanks in a form). Section 6111 allows a holographic will to be a combination of "the testator's own handwriting [and] part of a commercially printed form will."

Codicils

A **codicil** is a later testamentary instrument that supplements or affects the validity or dispositions of an earlier will. A codicil can be used to accomplish such purposes as adding to a prior will, revoking or partially revoking a prior will, reviving a previously revoked will, or validating an invalid will.

A codicil can be done in any format as long as it complies with the formal requirements for a complete will. Thus, a handwritten codicil may be made to a witnessed will. A codicil normally "republishes" the earlier will, so that if the codicil only changes one provision (such as substituting a new executor in place of the former executor), then the remaining provisions of the original will are unaffected as if the codicil had never been executed.

Disinheriting a Relative

A testator is free to disinherit any relative, including a child. However, the law does provide for a child accidentally omitted from a will or for a child born after a will was executed but not updated to reflect that child's birth. Therefore, if someone genuinely wants to disinherit a child, the will should leave either a small bequest or state that it is the testator's intent not to leave that child an inheritance. Otherwise, an omitted child is entitled to the equivalent of an intestate share that would have been awarded if the decedent had died without a will.

Revocation of a Will

Probate Code §6120 provides for a number of different ways in which a will can be revoked. The most common ways are to include language in a later will revoking prior wills or to mutilate or destroy a prior will with the intent to revoke it. Merely damaging a will, such as by tearing a corner when separating the pages, will not affect its validity. In addition, California law prohibits someone convicted of murdering the testator from benefiting under his or her will.

California follows the **doctrine of dependent revocation**. If a person revokes a prior, valid will on the assumption that a subsequent will is valid but it later turns out to be invalid for some reason, the law presumes that the testator would rather have had the prior, valid will take effect instead of having the property pass by the law of intestacy. In other words, a person is assumed to revoke a prior will only if a later will is valid; the revocation of the earlier will is therefore dependent on the validity of the later will. Some attorneys therefore counsel that, even if a prior will has been revoked, some record of it should be retained (e.g., a photocopy or the pieces of a will that has been torn up) in case a later will turns out to be invalid for some reason.

Probate

Probate is the legal process to prove that a will is valid. Probate proceedings are held in the superior court to determine creditors' claims and beneficiaries' interests in an estate upon the owner's death. A probate court's jurisdiction is jurisdiction **in rem**. That is, it is jurisdiction over a thing, or, in Latin, *rem*. In probate, the *rem* is the decedent's estate that is to be administered and distributed with regard to the rights of creditors, devisees, and all other persons.

A hearing is held to appoint a representative to handle the estate of the deceased. If that person is named in a will, he or she is referred to as an **executor** or **executrix**. If there is no will or someone named in a will to administer the estate, the court will appoint an **administrator** or **administratrix**.

By giving the notice prescribed by statute, the whole world is (theoretically) called before the court and the court acquires jurisdiction over all persons to determine their rights to any portion of the estate, whether or not they appear in the proceeding. Parties who believe that the decedent died owing them funds are entitled to put a claim against the estate and those claims, if valid, will be paid out of the estate before the heirs receive any of the estate.

A will controls the disposition of the testator's personal property according to the law of the place where the testator was domiciled at the time of the testator's death. Real property is governed by the law of the place where the real property is located regardless of where the testator is domiciled when the testator dies. The executor or the administrator of the decedent's estate must open a separate "mini-probate" in every state where there is real property belonging to the estate.

Estate property may be sold during the probate period at a public or private auction. An executor or administrator may list the property for up to 90 days with court permission. The court confirms the final sale and sets the broker's commission. The first offer must be for at least 90% of the appraised value and a subsequent offer at least 10% of the first $10,000 original bid, plus 5% of the remainder.

Sample Probate Bid

Appraised value	$100,000
1. First bid: at least 90% of appraised value	$90,000
2. Second bid: at least 10% of first $10,000	$1,000
Plus 5% of the remainder ($80,000)	$4,000
Total minimum second bid required	$95,000

Trusts

A trust is an alternative way of voluntarily transferring property. A **trust** is a three-party relationship in which one party, known as the **trustor** or **settlor**, places property into the possession and control of another party, known as a **trustee**, for the benefit of a third party, known as a **beneficiary**. The settlor establishes a trust with a document known as a **trust instrument**, which designates the property to be held in trust, names the trustee, and sets forth the terms under which the property is to be managed.

> Example: If the property placed into a trust generates income (such as an apartment building), the settlor could direct that income. Upon the settlor's death, the trustee will continue to manage the apartment building (with title remaining in the name of the trust), with the income to be paid to the beneficiary on a regular basis. Or the settlor could direct that title to the property is to pass to the beneficiary in fee, much as would happen if the settlor left the property to the beneficiary in a will.

Advantages of a Trust

There are several reasons why someone might choose a trust instead of a will to dispose of property after death. Unlike a will, the validity of which must be approved by a court through the probate process, a trust can be established while the settlor is alive. The property that would constitute the decedent's estate can be placed into the trust before the settlor dies, which can then be administered when the settlor dies just as it was before death. A settlor can even designate himself or herself as the trustee to manage the property before death and then designate another person or institution as a **successor trustee** to manage the property after the settlor's death.

A trust, even though it is intended to dispose of a person's property upon death, does not have to be witnessed according to the formalities of a will. It does have to be acknowledged before a notary public. However, this provides evidence of the settlor's identity and, if the person owns real estate, allows the trust instrument itself to be recorded.

Because the trust instrument does not have to go through probate, this saves on fees that the law otherwise requires to be paid to the executor at the conclusion of the probate process. Furthermore, during the probate process, the decedent's property in larger estates must be accounted for to the court. Because the court file is a public document, persons who want to keep their financial information away from public view may therefore also find a trust attractive.

Finally, at least in the days when estate taxes were higher than they have been in recent years, there was more favorable estate tax treatment of property that passed from parents to children using a trust. Although, in recent years, the exemptions from estate taxes have risen to the point where only people with estates worth several million dollars have to worry about estate taxes. For anyone with large estates, estate planning with a trust should be considered.

Disadvantages of a Trust

Despite these considerations, there are some reasons why someone might choose not to use a trust in their estate planning. A will is simpler and easier to prepare and many people, especially those with a smaller estate or fewer heirs, manage to get by with just a holographic or statutory form will. A trust is a complicated legal document that almost certainly should be prepared by an attorney, perhaps one specializing in estate planning. The up-front cost of preparing a trust is therefore likely to be higher than for a will.

In addition, while a trust avoids the "prying eyes" of strangers when all transactions for an estate take place in court, the probate process ensures that the court carries out the decedent's wishes. Despite its high-sounding name, a trust is only as good as the integrity of the person selected to administer it. If the settlor makes a charitable gift in a trust, for example, there is no court supervision to ensure that the trustee does not ignore the settlor's wishes.

Such problems can be avoided by naming an **institutional trustee**, such as a bank, because such entities are subject to routine audits even though the trust is not overseen by a judge. But banks and similar entities normally only manage larger trusts (i.e., in the hundreds of thousands of dollars) and will charge high fees to administer a trust. Using an institutional trustee, therefore, is realistically only an option for wealthier individuals whose trusts will be both large enough to meet these requirements and also have sufficient assets to justify the trustee fees.

Types of Trusts

Generally speaking, there are two kinds of trusts—inter vivos and testamentary. *Inter vivos* **trusts** (i.e., "between living persons") are established while the settlor is still alive and can be managed by the settlor himself or herself until he or she dies. **Testamentary trusts** are established by will. This avoids any possible concern that the trustee will fail to carry out the decedent's wishes, because a testamentary trust, like the probate of a will, is overseen by the court and can have a non-institutional trustee. However, testamentary trusts share the same disadvantages with probating the estate directly via will—the lack of financial privacy and probate costs.

SUCCESSION

Not everyone is prudent enough to prepare a will or other such documents before his or her death. Such a person is said to have died **intestate**—that is, without having prepared a testamentary instrument, such as a will or a trust.

Even when someone dies without a will or other written instrument, the law provides an alternative way to distribute the decedent's estate, called succession. **Succession** is the legal transfer of a person's interests in real and personal property under the **laws of descent and distribution**. The decedent is referred to as **"an intestate"** and is said to **"die intestate."** The law of **intestate succession** is what governs the transfer of property from a decedent to an heir when the decedent fails to dispose of the property by will. Probate Code §6400 provides that "any part of the estate of a decedent not effectively disposed of by will passes to the decedent's heirs as prescribed in this part."

Succession is largely governed in California by the Probate Code. It was extensively revised in 1991. (Some of the discussion that follows refers to the procedure under the former code and the Probate Code as it is today, because many of the court decisions that dealt with the issues surrounding the disposition of property when someone dies were decided under the old version of the Code.)

If there is a surviving spouse, that spouse is entitled to a one-half share of the community property, which is discussed in more detail below. The decedent's separate property (i.e., non-community property) is governed by a series of either-or provisions, depending upon whether the intestate decedent left a surviving spouse only or a surviving spouse and children—and if neither of those, other relatives according to degree. The following chart shows these possibilities with regard to the separate property.

Distribution	
Surviving spouse (only)	All separate property
Surviving spouse and one child	One-half to surviving spouse/one-half to child
Surviving spouse and a parent (or parents)	One-half to surviving spouse/ one-half to parent(s)
Surviving spouse and two or more children or one child and the "issue" (descendants) of any deceased child or children	One-third to surviving spouse/ two-thirds to children

If there is no surviving spouse, Probate Code §240 provides that "the property shall be divided into as many equal shares as there are living members of the nearest generation of issue." **Issue** means descendants of the testator.

California distributes property to the decedent's descendants according to *per stirpes* ("by roots") distribution. Some states follow a different process, known as *per capita* ("by head"). Under *per stirpes*, the issue of a later generation (such as grandchildren) are entitled to receive a share of an estate by "right of representation" when a member of an intervening generation (such as the parent of those grandchildren) dies before a member of the older generation whose property is being distributed. The following example illustrates how *per stirpes* distribution works and how it differs from *per capita*.

> Example: Fred, who has recently died without leaving a will, had three children, Allan, Brenda, and Cathy. Both Fred's wife and his daughter Brenda died before Fred, but Brenda had two children of her own, David and Eric. Neither Allan nor Cathy has any children. Fred leaves an estate, after expenses, of $600,000.
>
> The state where Fred lived at the time of his death follows the same rule for intestate succession as California, *per stirpes*. The court divides Fred's estate into thirds, and awards $200,000 (one-third) to Allan, $200,000 to Cathy, and $200,000 to David and Eric by "right of representation" for their late mother, Brenda (so that each of them receives $100,000).
>
> However, if the state where their grandfather lived were a *per capita* state, David and Eric would have received nothing and Allan and Cathy would each have received $300,000 (one-half of Fred's estate). Under the *per capita* rule, the children of his deceased daughter, Brenda, would be ineligible to receive anything from his estate if he died without a will unless Allan, Brenda, and Cathy all had died before Fred, making David and Eric (and any children of Fred's other children) his nearest living descendants. Of course, Fred could have disposed of his property in any way he chose (such as giving it all to only one of his children, or all to his grandchildren, or even all to a charity) if he had simply prepared a will before his death.

Probate Code §6402 also sets forth the order of inheritance among any surviving relatives—from parents through nieces and nephews. If there are still no surviving relatives, then the property can pass to the next of kin—nearest blood relatives of the decedent who do not fall into one of the earlier categories. If no one meets those requirements, it can then be distributed to the parents or other close relatives of a predeceased spouse.

Finally, if no one can be identified once all the possibilities have been exhausted, the property escheats to the State of California. **Escheat** is a legal process in which property reverts to the state because the deceased owner left no will and has no legal heirs. The State theoretically holds the property in trust indefinitely, waiting for a time when someone may come forward who can prove that he or she is entitled to the estate.

ADVERSE POSSESSION

Adverse possession is the ability to obtain title by occupying land for a statutory time period without the permission of the owner. [C.C. 81007]. Somewhat ironically, adverse possession converts what would legally be a trespass into ownership of the land that the adverse possessor occupies.

The concept of adverse possession is based on the notion that land is too valuable to allow one person to own land without putting it to productive use. Someone who occupies the land and makes a productive use of it will penalize the party who "slumbers on his or her rights" by not investigating the state of his ownership. Viewed in this way, adverse possession not only rewards the occupier who makes use of the land, but also gives the property owner an incentive to manage his or her ownership.

Requirements for Adverse Possession

In order for a non-owner to oust the ownership of another through adverse possession, the adverse possessor must meet six requirements. [C.C. §1007 and C.C.P. §325]. Paying the property taxes is often the most difficult requirement to meet, because in many counties the tax collector will return a second payment on the same piece of property.

Requirements to Acquire Ownership through Adverse Possession

- Open possession (some assertion of control, such as fencing or use)
- Notorious possession (i.e., such as a reasonable owner of the property would otherwise recognize)
- Continuous for a five-year time period
- Pay property taxes on the disputed property for the entire five years of the disputed claim
- Hostile (not with the original owner's permission)
- Adverse to a claim of right (adverse possessor must claim the title)

Merely because someone has met all of the steps for successful adverse possession claim, does not mean that everyone will recognize the "new" owner's claim to the property. The adverse possessor will have to file a lawsuit to **quiet title** against the person who, until that point, had valid title to the property.

Defeating Adverse Possession

An owner with lawful possession of land can take steps to prevent a person from asserting a claim through adverse possession. A person who is an "absentee owner" should, at a minimum, visit the property regularly, at least once a year or every other year, which will allow an investigation whether anyone else is living on or using the property. Checking the county tax records periodically to confirm that the correct person is listed and that the owner, and not an adverse user, is receiving the tax bill for the correct parcel is also a prudent step.

Unoccupied property should be fenced and any gates should be locked so that someone who wants to make adverse use will not have ready access to the property. At each entrance to the property and at 200-foot intervals along the boundary, the owner should post signs stating, "Right to pass by permission and subject to control, of owner." [C.C. §1008]."

Another method of protecting one's title if it is discovered that someone has made adverse use of property is to send the person a notice in writing that states that his or her use of the property constitutes a permissive use by the owner under a **license**, which is a freely-revocable right of use granted by a landowner to another person. Because one of the conditions of obtaining adverse possession is that the use be hostile, putting the adverse user on notice that the owner is 1) aware of the use and 2) granting the user permission to use the land should be sufficient to defeat an adverse possession claim.

Finally, if a property owner discovers that someone has begun "squatting" on the true owner's property, the owner can bring a lawsuit for injunctive relief to obtain a court order barring the user from making such use in the future. Although this can be the most expensive remedy, the cost, even when represented by an attorney, is usually minor compared to the cost of defending a quiet title action or—even worse—losing title in the end.

ACCESSION

Accession is a process by which there is an addition to property by the efforts of man or natural forces. The land itself can be enlarged or reduced by natural forces—gradually through accretion and reliction or quickly through avulsion.

Gradual Changes. **Accretion** is the gradual and imperceptible addition of land to a parcel by the natural deposition and accumulation of **alluvium** (or **alluvion**) upon the bank of a stream or river. Another gradual change is **reliction**, which is the process of land adjacent to a watercourse covered by water becoming uncovered because of receding water. It is a slow and imperceptible recession and the recession must be permanent. In both instances, the landowner acquires title to the newly formed or exposed land on the bank. [C.C. §1014].

A riparian owner will lose title to land that gradually becomes eroded or permanently inundated with water. **Erosion** is the gradual wearing away of land by the natural processes of water, wind, or glacial ice. In this context, erosion is the opposite of accretion. It is the owner's responsibility to improve and protect his or her shoreline from erosion. If this is not possible, over time, the entire parcel may be lost to erosion.

Sudden Changes. **Avulsion** is the process by which the action of water causes a sudden, perceptible loss of or addition to land. A large quantity of land is suddenly removed from the land of one person and added to the shore of another person— usually caused by flood or a change in the stream.

Ownership of the land does not change due to avulsive changes, such as a river breaking through the narrow part of an oxbow in a stream or river. If the land can be identified on the opposite bank, avulsion has occurred; otherwise, the courts may presume that accretion has occurred. To establish title to lands lost by avulsion, the original landowner has one year to reclaim the part that was carried away by avulsion. If unclaimed, the original land-owner will lose title and it will become part of the new land to which it has attached. [C.C. §1015].

IMPORTANCE OF RECORDING

Recording permits, rather than requires, documents that affect title to real property to be filed. Whenever an interest in real property is transferred voluntarily or involuntarily, the new owner should record the transfer instrument to protect his or her legal interests.

Recording Process

The Recording Act of California provides that, after acknowledgment, any instrument affecting the title to—or possession of—real property may be recorded. In fact, a deed must be acknowledged before it can be recorded. **Acknowledgment** is a formal declaration before a notary public or certain public officials, by the person (grantor) who signed (executed) the instrument (deed) that he or she in fact did execute (sign) the document. [C.C. §1185]. A **notary public** (notary) is a licensed public officer who takes or witnesses the acknowledgment. Acknowledgment acts as a safeguard against forgery and once acknowledged, a document is accepted as prima facie (on its face) evidence in court.

To be valid, documents must be recorded by the county recorder in the county within which the property is located. [C.C. §1169]. When the recorder receives a document to be filed, he or she marks the original document as "filed for record," stamps it with the proper time and date of recording, and returns to the person who requested the recording. The instrument to be recorded is copied into the proper index, and filed in alphabetical order, under the names of the parties. [C.C. §1171].

Effect of Recording

Recording serves the function of protecting subsequent bona fide purchasers (BFP) and lien creditors against prior unrecorded interests. A **bona fide purchaser** (bona fide purchaser for value) is a person who in good faith pays valuable consideration for property without notice of prior claims.

Recording any conveyance pertaining to real property (deed or lien) gives constructive notice of its contents to subsequent purchasers and mortgagees. [C.C. §1213]. **Constructive notice** is imputed by law, which means that everyone is presumed to have knowledge about a particular recorded document, because it can be looked up in the public records. Conversely, if a person has direct, express information about the ownership interest of a property, it is called **actual notice**. Actual notice is a fact, such as seeing the grant deed or knowing that a person inherited a property by will. Actual notice deals with facts a person actually knows; whereas, constructive notice deals with things a reasonably prudent person should know or investigate and discover.

That is why a buyer should always check that no one is living on or using the property who might have a prior claim. It is the buyer's duty to conduct proper inquiry before purchasing any property. Failure to do so does not relieve the buyer of that responsibility.

> Example: Ann bought a property through her broker, sight unseen. The escrow closed and the deed was recorded. However, when Ann tried to move into her new home she found George living there. He told her that he bought the property one year ago but had not bothered to record the deed. He then moved in and considered it his home. When she consulted her attorney, Ann found that indeed George—because he was in possession of the property—had given notice to anyone who might inquire. One remedy for the situation would be legal action against the grantor who sold the property to both George and Ann. At the moment, George does have legal title because of his possession of the property. To protect his title, George should record his deed.

Priorities in Recording

As we have seen, recording laws are meant to protect citizens against fraud and to give others notification of property ownership. Whether it is a grant deed, deed of trust, or some other evidence of a lien or encumbrance, the priority is determined by the date stamped in the upper right-hand corner of the document by the county recorder. [C.C. §1214]. **Priority** means the order in which deeds are recorded. To obtain priority through recording, a buyer must be a bona fide purchaser, for a valuable consideration, and record the deed first. California follows a **race-notice recording statute**, which means that the first valid deed that is recorded determines the owner, unless that person, prior to recording, had either actual or constructive notice of the rights of others.

If several grant deeds are recorded against the property, the one recorded first is valid. If several deeds of trust are recorded against a property, no mention will be made about which one is the first deed of trust, which is the second and so forth. A person inquiring about the priority of the deeds should look at the time and date the deed was recorded for that information.

There are certain instruments not affected by the priority of recording rule. Certain liens, such as tax liens and mechanic's liens, take priority even though they are recorded after a deed.

SUMMARY

All real property is eventually transferred from one person or entity to another, either voluntarily or involuntarily. Voluntary transfers are made while the owner is alive via deed and, upon the owner's death, with a testamentary instrument, such as a will or a trust.

A deed is a written instrument that is used to transfer title to real property from one person to another. A deed has a number of formal requirements, such as identifying the grantor and the grantee, having an accurate property description, and being signed by the grantor. A deed must be delivered (physically hand over) to the grantee, who must accept it, all in order for title to pass. The grant deed and a quitclaim deed are the two deeds most commonly used in California. Sometimes property is transferred by the operation of law or court action. It is usually an involuntary transfer involving foreclosure or is the result of a judgment or some other lien against the title.

Property is passed from one owner to another upon death by using a testamentary instrument. A will is a document by which the person who signs it, known as the testator, disposes of real and personal property upon the testator's death. California recognizes three types of wills: witnessed wills, statutory form wills, and holographic wills. A trust is a three-party arrangement involving a trustor (or settlor), a trustee, and a beneficiary.

Succession is the legal transfer of a person's interests in real and personal property under the laws of descent and distribution. The decedent is referred to as "an intestate" and is said to "die intestate."

Property can pass from one person to another involuntarily through adverse possession. Adverse possession requires that the property to be adversely possessed be used by the adverse possessor openly, notoriously, continuously, hostile to the original owner, and adversely, all for a period of five years. In addition, an adverse possessor must pay the taxes on the disputed parcel or portion of a parcel for the five years.

Accession is a process by which there is an addition to property by the efforts of man or natural forces. The land itself can be enlarged or reduced by natural forces—gradually through accretion and reliction or quickly through avulsion.

Recording permits, rather than requires, documents that affect title to real property to be filed. Whenever an interest in real property is transferred voluntarily or involuntarily, the new owner should record the transfer instrument to protect his or her legal interests.

UNIT 7 REVIEW

Matching Exercise

Instructions: Write the letter of the matching term on the blank line before its definition. Answers are in Appendix A.

Terms

A.	accretion	P.	holographic will
B.	adverse possession	Q.	*inter vivos*
C.	alienation	R.	intestate
D.	avulsion	S.	involuntary alienation
E.	codicil	T.	issue
F.	constructive notice	U.	judicial foreclosure
G.	deed	V.	partition action
H.	deficiency judgment	W.	*per stirpes*
I.	eminent domain	X.	priority
J.	escheat	Y.	probate
K.	execution sale	Z.	quiet title action
L.	executor	AA.	quitclaim deed
M.	foreclosure	BB.	settlor
N.	gift deed	CC.	tax sale
O.	granting clause	DD.	trustee's sale

Definitions

1. _____ Voluntarily or involuntarily transferring or conveying property to another

2. _____ Written instrument used to immediately transfer title to real property from one person to another

3. _____ Words of purchase, such as grants, conveys, transfers, or sells

4. _____ Deed with no warranties

5. _____ Deed whose consideration is love and affection

6. _____ Transfer of property against the wishes of the owner

7. _____ Legal procedure lenders use to terminate the trustor's or mortgagor's rights in real property to satisfy their liens

8. _____ Foreclosure method taking approximately four months

9. _____ Procedure lender uses to sell a mortgaged property with the involvement of a court

10. _____ Personal judgment against a borrower for the balance of a debt owed when the security for the loan is insufficient to pay the debt

11. _____ Court proceeding to settle a dispute between co-owners by dividing their interests in real property

12. _____ Court proceeding to establish an individual's right to ownership of real property against one or more adverse claimants

13. _____ Forced sale of real property by the county to satisfy delinquent taxes

14. _____ Forced sale of property to satisfy a money judgment

15. _____ Power of the government to take private property for public use

16. _____ Property reverts to the state because the deceased owner left no will and has no legal heirs

17. _____ Will entirely in the handwriting of the testator

18. _____ Later testamentary instrument that supplements validity or disposition of an earlier will

19. _____ Legal process to prove that a will is valid

20. _____ Person named in a will to administer it

21. _____ Person who sets up a trust on behalf of a beneficiary

22. _____ Trust in which the settlor is still alive when the trust is established

23. _____ Term describing a person who dies without leaving a valid will

24. _____ Descendants of the testator

25. _____ Method of dividing property among the descendants of someone who has died intestate

26. _____ Obtaining title by occupying land for a statutory time period without the permission of the owner

27. _____ Gradual enlargement of land through the accumulation of sediment

28. _____ Sudden, perceptible loss of land

29. _____ Notice given by recording a document

30. _____ Order in which deeds are recorded

Multiple Choice Questions

Instructions: Circle your response and go to Appendix A to read the complete explanation for each question.

1. When transferring real property by deed, the correct order of the steps to create a valid deed are:
   a. execution, acceptance, and recording.
   b. delivery, execution, and acceptance.
   c. execution, delivery, and acceptance.
   d. acceptance, delivery, and recording.

2. Which of the following is not required to create a valid deed in California?
   a. Execution by the grantor
   b. Granting clause
   c. Legal description
   d. Writing

3. Each of these instruments is used by a third party to convey an interest in someone else's property, except a:
   a. quitclaim deed.
   b. sheriff's deed.
   c. tax deed.
   d. trust deed.

4. Which court proceeding establishes an individual's right to ownership of real property against one or more adverse claimants?

    a. Adverse possession
    b. Partition action
    c. Pendency action
    d. Quiet title action

5. Carl has a valid will. His financial situation has changed and he decides to have a new will drafted reflecting those changes. Carl is not aware that there are defects in his new will and he tears up the old will because of his mistaken belief that his new will is valid. He does save a copy of his earlier will in his files. Assuming that Carl dies shortly thereafter, what will be the result?

    a. The court will treat Carl as having died without a will, because he destroyed the valid will and his new will is invalid.
    b. Carl's wife will be entitled to "set aside" the provisions of his new will and rely on his earlier will.
    c. The court can give effect to Carl's new will even though it is invalid because his earlier will was valid.
    d. The court can revive Carl's former will under the doctrine of dependent revocation because he destroyed his old will under the mistaken belief that his new will was valid.

6. One important way that a trust differs from a will is that a trust:

    a. does not have to go through the probate process in court.
    b. usually will result in the payment of much higher estate taxes than property passed on by will.
    c. requires the signature of two witnesses, but a will can simply be signed in front of a notary public.
    d. can only be created by a will after the testator has already died.

7. When no relatives can be found to whom a deceased person has left property in a will or when the person has died without a will, which term is used to describe the transfer of the property to the State of California?

    a. Ademption
    b. Codicil
    c. Escheat
    d. Testamentary

8. The notion that land is too valuable to allow one person to own land without putting it to productive use is the rationale behind the concept of:
    a. accretion.
    b. adverse possession.
    c. alienation.
    d. avulsion.

9. With accretion and reliction, the landowner:
    a. acquires title to the newly formed or exposed land.
    b. loses title to the land formed by accretion or reliction.
    c. shares title to the land formed by accretion or reliction.
    d. escheats title to the state.

10. If a deed that is valid is nevertheless not recorded, what are the possible negative consequences for the grantee?
    a. The grantee cannot re-convey the parcel.
    b. An unscrupulous grantor might convey the property to another party.
    c. The property will not be eligible for property or casualty insurance.
    d. The grantee could be liable for a criminal violation of the recording statutes.

California License Law

Unit **8**

INTRODUCTION

Regulating real estate licensees has been around for almost 100 years. Real estate laws and regulations relate to the events that take place in a real estate transaction. The laws enacted by the federal and state governments are constantly changing and adapting to the times to coincide with the interests of its citizens.

In an attempt to create and maintain higher professional standards and to develop greater trust in general from the public, the real estate industry has supported legislation that protects consumer interests. A person must not only acquire a real estate license, but also maintain a good professional reputation to have a successful career in real estate. Once licensed, a licensee is required to practice real estate within the guidelines of state laws.

Ignorance of the law is never an excuse. Therefore, it is important for a licensee to keep abreast of the latest changes in the law. A broker must incorporate any changes in Real Estate Law into office policy and salespeople must implement these changes in their daily activities. A violation of the law may expose the licensee to disciplinary action, as well as financial damages.

Learning Objectives

After completing this unit, you should be able to:

8A   identify the purpose of the Real Estate Law.

8B   recall the acts that require a real estate license.

8C   recognize the different types of real estate licenses.

8D   identify the ways to enforce the Real Estate Law, if violated.

CALIFORNIA REAL ESTATE LAW

California has long been a leader in real estate trends. In fact, the nation's first real estate licensing law passed in California in 1917. As previously mentioned, the body of law for the State of California is comprised of statutory law and regulatory law. The statutes are enacted by the state Legislature and the regulations are promulgated by the regulatory agencies that help carry out the statutory law.

Many of the provisions of California Real Estate Law are covered in the **Business and Professions Code** (B&P Code), which is part of California's codified law that regulates real estate professionals. As its name implies, however, the Business and Professions Code covers more than just the real estate profession—attorneys, doctors, and many other professions are regulated by it. The bulk of the laws concerning licensing of real estate professionals are included in Division 4 – Real Estate, Parts I through IV. Parts I and II are the most important part for real estate licensees.

Part 1 is titled "Licensing of Persons" and is called the Real Estate Law. Part 2 is titled "Regulation of Transactions" and is called the Subdivided Lands Law. Part III (Licensing and Certification of Real Estate Appraisers) and Part IV (Certified Common Interest Development Manager) are not discussed in this text.

The **Real Estate Law**, sometimes referred to as the **License Law**, is designed mainly for the protection of the public in real estate transactions involving a licensee. The term, Real Estate Law, means the law that affects the licensing and conduct of real estate brokers and salespeople. It must be seen separately from what is known as real property law, law of agency, contract law, or other legal aspects of real estate ownership and transfer.

Main Purposes of the Real Estate Law

1. Protect consumers from loss because of dishonest and incompetent agents

2. Uphold the good standing of ethical agents from the adverse publicity caused by unprincipled licensees

ADMINISTERING THE REAL ESTATE LAW

The **Bureau of Real Estate** (CalBRE), which is part of the California Business, Transportation, and Housing Agency, oversees the real estate profession. The **Real Estate Commissioner** (Commissioner) is the head of the Bureau of Real Estate. The Commissioner is appointed by the Governor. To be appointed, the designee must have been a real estate broker for five years and actively engaged in the real estate business in California.

The Business and Professions Code, Article 3, Section 10175 authorizes the Commissioner to determine administrative policy and to enforce the provisions of the Real Estate Law and the Subdivided Lands Law. Therefore, the Commissioner is empowered to adopt regulations to enforce the Real Estate Law. Duly adopted regulations become part of the California Code of Regulations and, in effect, have the force and authority of the law itself. Therefore, all licensees and prospective licensees should be thoroughly familiar with the Real Estate Commissioner's Regulations as contained in the California Code of Regulations, Title 10, Chapter 6.

These Regulations should be considered in conjunction with the law, as they specifically outline procedures directed and authorized by the statutes. This is to ensure that the public is protected when dealing with licensees and purchasing subdivided real property.

Responsibilities of the Real Estate Commissioner

- Screen and qualify applicants for license
- Issue, restrict, suspend, or revoke real estate licenses
- Review and investigate complaints against licensees
- Pursue formal action against licensees, when appropriate
- Monitor real property securities transactions
- Regulate prepaid rental listing services
- Regulate specific aspects of the sale of subdivisions

One of the jobs not assigned to the Commissioner is settling commission disputes. That issue falls under the power of a court of law and must be handled by an attorney if the parties involved cannot settle the matter agreeably.

Real Estate Fund

All fees charged and collected from the licensing of persons or from the regulation of transactions are placed in the **Real Estate Fund**. The money is used by the Commissioner to carry out the provisions of the Real Estate Law. This includes running the Bureau of Real Estate and paying salaries to the Commissioner and his or her deputies, clerks, and assistants. Part of the fees collected in the Real Estate Fund is set aside into two separate accounts for education and for recovery.

Education and Research Account

The Commissioner may credit up to 8% of the fees collected into a separate account called the Education and Research Account. The **Education and Research Account** pays for the advancement of real estate education at California universities, California state colleges, and California community colleges. It also funds real estate research projects conducted by colleges or qualified associations.

Consumer Recovery Account

The **Consumer Recovery Account** is a separate account funded through collection of up to 12% of license fees collected. This fund assures the payment of otherwise non-collectable court judgments against licensees who have committed fraud, misrepresentation, deceit, or conversion of trust funds in a transaction. Under specific conditions of law, the person with a qualifying judgment may seek reimbursement from the Consumer Recovery Account for actual and direct loss to a statutory maximum. Currently the amount paid will be $50,000 per transaction, with a possible total aggregate maximum of $250,000 per licensee.

If the Commissioner pays a judgment on behalf of a broker or salesperson, the license is automatically suspended. A suspended license will only be reinstated after full reimbursement, plus interest, is repaid to the Recovery Fund.

LICENSING

Obtaining a real estate license is a prerequisite for performing real estate work. Specifically, unless someone is involved in the direct sale or purchase of property for him or herself, a real estate license is a prerequisite for performing real estate work. Under section 10131 of the Business and Professions Code, a real estate broker is someone who, for compensation, performs or negotiates to perform one or more of the acts requiring a real estate license. A salesperson, if employed by a real estate broker, may also do any of the following activities.

Acts Requiring a Real Estate License
- Soliciting buyers or sellers
- Soliciting tenants or rentals
- Negotiating sales, leases, or loans
- Negotiating promissory notes secured by real property
- Negotiating exchanges

The failure to possess a valid license while engaging in any of the above activities is a crime, and can result in civil and criminal penalties against the violator. There are also fines against people who utilize the services of an unlicensed person.

A licensed real estate broker may not employ or compensate, directly or indirectly, any person who is not a licensed real estate salesperson or broker. The exception is a broker licensed in another state. In addition, a licensed salesperson may not accept compensation from anyone except his or her employing broker. (*Section 1013*) The broker may be fined $100. (*Section 10138*)

> Example: Tom is a broker whose nephew, Paul, is studying to take his real estate licensing exam. He has been getting on-the-job training from his uncle. Paul helped show a home that Tom ultimately sold, and Tom paid Paul part of the commission he made on the sale. Tom may be fined, because Paul is not licensed, and cannot be paid a commission on a real estate transaction.

Prior to paying a commission, an escrow holder should require a broker to present evidence he or she is a regularly licensed real estate broker at the time of earning the compensation.

It is unlawful for any **unlicensed person** to pose as a real estate broker or salesperson or to advertise that he or she is a real estate broker. The punishment for an individual falsely claiming to be a broker or salesperson is a fine of up to $20,000 or imprisonment in the county jail up to six months, or both. A corporation is subject to a criminal fine not to exceed $60,000. (*Section 10139*)

There are certain exemptions from licensing requirements. The following list shows many, but not all of the people who are exempt from obtaining a real estate license.

Real Estate License Exemptions

- A person who deals only with his or her own property
- A corporation that performs any of the specified activities through one of its regular officers, who must receive no special compensation for doing so
- Anyone holding a duly executed power of attorney from the owner of property
- An attorney-at-law performing services in the regular course of business as an attorney
- Resident managers of apartment buildings and complexes or their employees
- Short-term (vacation) rental agents
- Employees of certain lending institutions
- Clerical employees of real estate brokers for specific, limited functions
- Licensed personal property brokers
- Any film location representative employed to arrange for the use of real property for photographic purposes
- Cemetery authorities
- Certain collectors of payments for lenders or on notes for owners in connection with loans secured directly or collaterally by liens on real property, provided such collectors annually meet exemption criteria

Real Estate License Exemptions (continued)

- Any receiver, trustee in bankruptcy, or person acting under order of any court
- Any trustee selling under a deed of trust
- Lenders making loans guaranteed or insured by an agency of the federal government
- An employee of lending institutions, pension trusts, credit unions, or insurance companies, in connection with loans secured by liens on real property or a business opportunity
- Escrow agents collecting funds in connection with loans secured by liens on real property when the funds are deposited in the escrow agent's trust account

Types of Real Estate Licenses

It is important for brokers and salespeople to understand the obligations and restrictions of the different licenses held. Any person who wants to engage in the real estate business and act as a real estate broker or real estate salesperson within the state of California must obtain a license from the Bureau of Real Estate (CalBRE).

Currently, CalBRE issues real estate broker and salesperson licenses for a four-year period. A license obtained by fraud, misrepresentation, or deceit may undergo suspension by the Commissioner, without a hearing within 90 days after its issuance.

Real Estate Broker

A **real estate broker** is someone who holds a broker license issued by the Bureau of Real Estate. The license legally permits the broker to perform any acts for which a real estate license is required. In a real estate transaction, a broker is the **agent** of his or her principal.

A real estate broker is also an independent businessperson who can employ sales associates—someone who holds a salesperson or a broker license. These sales associates are agents of their employing broker—not the buyer/seller or the lessor/lessee. Therefore, brokers are legally responsible for all the business actions of their employed sales associates.

Individual Broker License

A real estate broker license allows a licensee to run a brokerage business under his or her own name or under a fictitious business name. Any broker who places his or her license with an employing broker is a **broker associate** and must have a written employment agreement.

Licensed real estate brokers may use a **fictitious business name** (DBA) or any name other than their own names. They must submit a copy of a Fictitious Business Name Statement that is filed with the county clerk's office in the county where the principal place of business is located. Each fictitious business name is an addition to the existing license, and it will expire at the same time as the license. The broker's main office license certificate lists the multiple fictitious business names. Any business location other than the main office is designated as a **branch office**. For each additional business location, the broker must obtain a **branch office license**. A broker and his or her sales associates may work under any fictitious business name at any business location maintained by the broker. Filing a Fictitious Business Name Statement is good for five years from December 31st of the year filed.

Corporate Real Estate License

A corporation may be licensed as a real estate broker as long as one officer of the corporation is a qualified real estate broker and acts as the corporation's responsible **designated broker-officer**. Salespeople may be employed by a corporate real estate broker as long as they are supervised by the designated broker-officer.

Partnership

CalBRE does not issue partnership licenses. A real estate business may be run as a partnership as long as every partner through whom the partnership acts is a licensed real estate broker. A salesperson may be employed by a broker who is a member of a partnership formed by written agreement and may work in any branch office managed by any one of the partners.

Broker's Responsibilities

An active broker must maintain an office (home office is acceptable) in California. If a broker has sales associates, their license certificates are kept at the main business office and must be available for inspection by CalBRE.

A broker must have written agreements with his or her sales associates, whether licensed as a salesperson or as a broker associate. The agreement must be dated and signed by the parties and cover the relationship between the parties, including supervision of licensed activities, duties, and compensation. A broker must supervise his or her salespersons (both sales associates and broker associates). Reasonable supervision includes creating and following policies and procedures to review and manage contracts, documents, advertising, trust funds, and other licensed activities.

When a salesperson transfers his or her employment to another broker, the current broker must notify CalBRE immediately in writing and return the license certificate to the salesperson. (*Section 10161.8*). The new employing broker must notify the Commissioner within five days of the transfer.

When any real estate salesperson is discharged by his or her employing broker for a violation of any of the provisions of the Real Estate Law, a certified written statement of the facts with reference thereto shall be filed forthwith with the Commissioner by the employer. If the employer fails to notify the Commissioner as required by this section, the Commissioner may temporarily suspend or permanently revoke the real estate license of the employer, in accordance with the provisions of this part relating to hearings. (*Section 10178*)

Real Estate Salesperson

A **real estate salesperson** is someone who holds a salesperson license issued by the Bureau of Real Estate. The salesperson must be employed by a licensed real estate broker in order to perform any of the activities that require a license. A salesperson is an agent of the employing broker.

Salesperson License

A **salesperson license** is required for people employed as salespeople under the supervision of a licensed broker. A person may obtain a salesperson license even if he or she does not intend to be employed immediately by a broker. However, a salesperson without an employing broker may not perform acts requiring a license. The salesperson license authorizes real estate activity only if the salesperson is in the employ of a licensed broker.

Restricted License

The Commissioner will sometimes issue a restricted license. A **restricted license** is a type of probationary license issued when a license has been suspended, revoked, or denied after a hearing. Typically, restrictions are placed by term (one month, three months, etc.), employment by a particular broker (for a salesperson), limitation to a certain type of activity, requiring detailed reports of each transaction, requiring the filing of a surety bond, or any combination.

If a real estate broker license is revoked or suspended by CalBRE, any salesperson licenses held by that broker are cancelled until the license is transferred to a new employing broker.

> **Review – License Facts**
> - Brokers and salespeople are both licensees
> - Brokers are agents of the principal
> - Salespeople are agents of their broker (not the principal)
> - A salesperson must be employed by a broker to be paid
> - A salesperson can only be paid by his or her employing broker

Licensing Requirements

As we have seen, the purpose of a real estate license is to protect both the consumer and the licensee. With that in mind, the state places strict requirements on those who wish to practice real estate in the form of real estate licensing. The Business and Professions Code specifies all the requirements for obtaining and maintaining a real estate license. Its provisions are too lengthy to be provided here, but we will highlight some of the most important items contained within the statutes, and common pitfalls of which licensees should be aware. Detailed information is found at the CalBRE website.

Before an applicant for a real estate salesperson or broker license may obtain a license, he or she must fulfill certain real estate education requirements and then apply for and pass a real estate examination. After completing the education requirements and passing the examination, additional documentation is necessary when applying for the actual license.

Eligibility Requirements

Before applying for a broker or salesperson license, a prospective licensee must meet certain eligibility requirements.

Eligibility Requirements for Obtaining a License
- Be at least 18 years old
- Provide a social security or tax ID number
- Be honest and truthful
- Complete real estate course(s) as required by law
- Apply for and pass the state qualifying examination
- Apply for the license

Age Requirement

Only persons who have reached the age of majority can become licensees. The reason behind this is that contracts entered into by persons who are minors are voidable contracts under law. Consequently, having someone who has not reached the age of majority negotiate a real estate transaction would be illegal.

Morality Requirement

It is harder to quantify the requirement that a candidate be honest and truthful. In all respects, a licensee must conduct business in a way that demonstrates that he or she has applied the highest standards of ethical behavior.

Required Education

A prospective licensee must submit evidence, in the form of transcripts or certificates, showing that he or she completed the statutory license courses. Prospective licensees may take courses from a CalBRE-approved private vocational real estate school or from a college accredited by the Western Association of Schools and Colleges or a comparable regional accrediting entity. Unless the California Real Estate Commissioner has granted prior approval, no private vocational real estate school outside California may grant credit for the required pre-license courses. The required number of hours for a statutory course is 45 hours if taken from a real estate school. If taken at an accredited college, a course for three-semester units or four-quarter units is acceptable.

Required Courses for Salesperson License

A salesperson must submit proof of completion of three approved real estate courses—Real Estate Principles, Real Estate Practice, and an elective selected from the Required Education Chart. A salesperson must be employed by a licensed broker to perform acts regulated by a salesperson license.

Required Courses for Broker License

A broker candidate must complete eight approved real estate courses. Five of the eight courses are mandatory—Real Estate Appraisal, Real Estate Practice, Real Estate Finance, Legal Aspects of Real Estate, and Real Estate Economics or General Accounting. The remaining three courses are electives, which may be selected from the Education Chart below. If both Real Estate Economics and General Accounting are completed, only two electives are required.

Real Estate Courses	Salesperson	Broker
Real Estate Principles	Required	Elective
Real Estate Practice	Required	Required
Legal Aspects of Real Estate	Elective	Required
Real Estate Appraisal	Elective	Required
Real Estate Finance	Elective	Required
Real Estate Economics	Elective	Required
General Accounting	May waive RE Economics	May waive RE Economics
Business Law	Elective	Elective
Common Interest Developments	Elective	Elective
Computer Applications in RE	Elective	Elective
Escrows	Elective	Elective
Mortgage Loan Brokering/ Lending	Elective	Elective
Property Management	Elective	Elective
Real Estate Office Administration	Elective	Elective
Adv. Legal Aspects of Real Estate	Not allowed	Elective
Adv. Real Estate Appraisal	Not allowed	Elective
Adv. Real Estate Finance	Not allowed	Elective

Additional Requirements: Broker License

In addition to the required real estate education, an applicant for an original real estate broker license must meet experience standards. A broker candidate must have two years of full-time licensed real estate experience within the past five years or the equivalent. An acceptable equivalent is a four-year degree from an accredited college with a major or minor in real estate.

Real Estate Examination

The purpose of the real estate license examination is to ensure that consumers have protection in all transactions that involve representation by an agent. License applicants must have knowledge of the English language, including reading, writing, spelling, and math common to real estate and business opportunity practices.

The exam tests an applicant's general knowledge of real estate, appraisal, finance, forms, and other fundamentals of the industry. The subject matter covered in the examination includes agency law, contract law, financing, general knowledge of real estate, land use controls, mandated disclosures, market analysis, property ownership, transfer of property, and valuation.

License Application

Upon passing the state exam, the applicant may apply for the salesperson or broker license within one year of the examination date. After passing the exam, the applicant must make formal application for a license, pay the appropriate fees, and provide any supporting documentation as requested by CalBRE. The applications and fee schedule are available on the CalBRE website.

Unless a prospective licensee is currently licensed as a salesperson, there are other documents to include with the license application. The applicant will need to submit one set of classifiable fingerprints, a social security or tax ID number, and an irrevocable Consent to Service of Process for out of state applicants.

Fingerprint Requirements

An applicant for an original real estate license must submit one set of classifiable **fingerprints**. The fingerprints must be submitted electronically to the state Department of Justice (DOJ) using the Live Scan Program, which takes and transmits fingerprints to the DOJ and the Federal Bureau of Investigation (FBI). Social Security numbers are now required on examination applications

so fingerprint results can be processed. An original license will not be issued until a report from the DOJ and the FBI is received either stating that there is no criminal history, or disclosing criminal history information, which then must be reviewed and evaluated. More information can be found on the CalBRE website.

Tax Identification Requirement

The Legislature finds that it is in the best interests of the State of California to allow people who are not lawfully present in the United States to obtain real estate licenses. [B&P code 135.5(a)]. Therefore, the California Bureau of Real Estate cannot deny licensure to an applicant based on his or her citizenship status or immigration status.

However, a real estate license applicant must provide his or her social security number, or if the applicant is a partnership, its federal employer identification number. [B&P Code 30(a)].

A licensee failing to provide the federal employer identification number, or the individual taxpayer identification number or social security number shall be reported by CalBRE to the Franchise Tax Board. [B&P Code30 (b)]. CalBRE cannot process an application for an initial license unless the applicant provides its federal employer identification number, or individual taxpayer identification number or social security number where requested on the application. [B&P Code 30(c)].

Out-of-State Applicants

A person does not have to live in California in order to possess a license in the state, but the applicant must take the appropriate written examination in California and meet all other requirements. California has no reciprocity with any other state to allow a waiver of any of the requirements to obtain a license.

Out-of-state residents must file an irrevocable Consent to Service of Process with the California Bureau of Real Estate. Brokers must maintain a California business address if engaging in business in California, and salespeople must be licensed with a California broker if engaging in business in California.

Renewing a Real Estate License

In general, licensees can renew both types of licenses by submitting the appropriate fee and application, along with evidence of completion of CalBRE-approved continuing education courses. Both broker and salesperson licenses are valid for four years and may be renewed at that time upon payment of a fee and evidence that the requirements for continuing education have been met.

Continuing Education

Each time brokers and salespeople renew their licenses—every four years—they must present evidence of completing the required continuing education (CE) courses.

Initial Renewal - Broker and Salesperson

There is a 45-hour CE requirement for the first renewal of a broker or salesperson license. The required courses are 3 hours each of Agency, Ethics, Fair Housing, Management and Supervision, Risk Management, and Trust Fund Handling and 27 more CE hours of which 18 hours must be in the consumer protection category.

Subsequent Renewals - Broker and Salesperson

Subsequent renewals offer two options. The first option is to complete 45 hours of continuing education, broken down as 3 hours each of Agency, Ethics, Fair Housing, Management and Supervision, Risk Management, and Trust Fund Handling and 27 more CE hours of which 18 hours must be in the consumer protection category. The second option is to complete 45 hours of continuing education, broken down as an eight-hour Survey Course and 37 more CE hours of which 18 hours must be in the consumer protection category.

Equivalent Activities in Lieu of Continuing Education

Commissioner's Regulation 3011 describes the criteria used to determine whether a specific activity qualifies as an acceptable alternative to completing an approved continuing education offerings. The licensee must submit a petition for equivalency to CalBRE, which is reviewed to determine if the equivalent activity is sufficient to waive the continuing education requirement.

Examples of Equivalent Activities

- Authorship of published professional articles, periodicals, or books on current real estate procedures and law

- Development of real estate education programs if the program meets the requirements necessary for approval for continuing education credit

- Instructing others in approved continuing education for real estate license renewal

- Presentation of real estate related topics if the petitioner can demonstrate that the material conveyed contained reasonably current information designed to assist real estate licensees in providing a high level of consumer protection or service

- Attendance at courses not approved by the Commissioner

Payment of Child Support

California now requires suspension of any state-issued license if the licensee falls behind on child support payments. Thus, even though maintaining such payments is not directly related to the practice of real estate, failure to make the payments on time can adversely affect the renewal of a license. Therefore, if a licensee has delinquent child support payments, a four-year license will not be renewed or issued. The California Department of Child Support Services prepares a list of people, called **obligors**, who owe child support payments. A child support obligor may receive a 150-day temporary license. During the 150 days, a person must show CalBRE proof of clearing the delinquency and removal from the list, for issuance of a permanent license.

Late Renewal

A real estate license that has expired may be renewed within two years of the expiration date. A **two-year grace period** for renewal is allowed as long as all real estate activity has ceased during that time and a late fee is paid at the time of renewal. There is no provision for an inactive license status. Two years after a license expires, all license rights lapse, and the person will have to go through the state examination process again to get another real estate license.

However, if a broker's license expires, all licensed activities of the broker must stop and all of the broker's salespeople (if any) are immediately placed in a non-working status. Any branch office licenses are cancelled. That means no listing, selling, showing, leasing, or any licensed activity between the date of license expiration and the date of late renewal. A commission may not be claimed without a valid license. Once the broker has renewed his or her license, all the salesperson licenses and branch office licenses must be reactivated.

e-Licensing Transactions

CalBRE now offers **eLicensing**, an interactive online system allowing users to complete license renewal and change transactions via the Internet. The following list includes many of the available transactions.

eLicensing Transactions

- Online Registration with CalBRE
- Mailing Address Changes
- Broker Main Office Address Changes
- Salesperson Requests To Change Employing Broker
- Broker Certification Of Salesperson Employment
- Salesperson/Broker License Renewals
- Duplicate License Requests
- Examination Services

User-friendly features include customized menus, e-mail confirmations, status tracking of online transactions, and clear instructions. eLicensing is available on the CalBRE website.

ENFORCING THE REAL ESTATE LAW

The Real Estate Law is only effective if enforced. The Commissioner can investigate both licensed and non-licensed persons, but can only discipline licensed persons. Persons who violate the licensing law may be subject to a variety of penalties. Some violations may result in civil injunctions, criminal prosecutions, or substantial fines. Licenses may be suspended, revoked, or otherwise restricted. A licensee may face a combination of these penalties and encounter lawsuits from parties adversely affected by the violation.

When the Commissioner investigates a complaint, which may involve criminal activities, it is the duty of the local district attorneys to prosecute all criminals in their respective counties. The Commissioner must follow the established legal procedures found in the Administrative Procedure Act to discipline licensees. Only the Commissioner—not the courts—can restrict, suspend, or revoke a real estate license.

Representatives of the Commissioner also investigate persons or firms who appear to be operating improperly, without a license, or who subdivide land without complying with the subdivision laws enforced by the Commissioner. If sufficient evidence of a violation is obtained, an Order to Desist and Refrain is issued, or a complaint is brought, and the parties are prosecuted in a court of competent jurisdiction. An **Order to Desist and Refrain** is a court-ordered demand that prohibits a business or individual from carrying on a particular activity.

Investigation and Accusation

An investigation of the actions of a licensee is initiated upon receipt of a verified written complaint from someone who believes he or she has been wronged by the real estate licensee. The complaint is investigated by the **Enforcement and Audit Section** of CalBRE. The investigator takes statements, obtains, and verifies documents from witnesses and the licensee. An informal conference may be called to determine the validity and seriousness of the complaint. If it appears that the complaint is of a serious nature and that a violation of law has occurred, an **accusation** is filed. There may be a formal hearing, which could result in suspension or revocation of the license.

Formal Hearings

A **formal hearing** is held according to the Administrative Procedures Act. The accusation or statement of issues is served upon the affected licensee. In the hearing, the Commissioner is the **complainant** and brings the charges against the licensee. The licensee, known as the **respondent**, may appear with or without an attorney. The Commissioner's counsel presents the case to an administrative law judge. An **administrative law judge** will preside over the hearing and make recommendations to the Commissioner for discipline after the hearing.

The Commissioner may accept, reject, or reduce the proposed penalty from the administrative law judge and makes an official decision. Sometimes the charges against the respondent (licensee) are dismissed, but if the charges are sufficiently serious, the license of the respondent is suspended or revoked. Under Section 10175.2(a) of the B&P Code, the Commissioner may permit a real estate licensee to pay a monetary penalty to the department in lieu of an actual license suspension.

A person whose license has been revoked or suspended must wait one year until he or she can apply for reinstatement. As a condition to the reinstatement of a revoked or suspended license, the Commissioner may require the applicant to take and pass a qualifying examination. (*Section 10182*)

Specific Violations

The B&P Code outlines the prohibited conduct for a person acting as an agent or not as an agent in a real estate transaction. Although most violations of Real Estate Law occur under sections 10176 and 10177 of the Business and Professions Code, included are some of the other sections that need discussion and mention. Section 10176 refers to actions committed while conducting business under a real estate license. Section 10177 refers to circumstances when a licensee is not necessarily acting as an agent. (Note: Following each section of text of the law, a fictional case example is provided.)

Section 10176: Acting as an Agent in a Real Estate Transaction

When someone is acting as an agent in a real estate transaction, he or she is prohibited from certain conduct under B&P Code § 10176. Much of the prohibited conduct concerns fraud and misrepresentation in various forms. If a licensee is found guilty of any of the following acts, the Commissioner may temporarily suspend or permanently revoke the person's real estate license.

Misrepresentation

A great majority of the complaints received are about **misrepresentation** (false statement of fact) on the part of the broker or salesperson. The failure of a broker or salesperson to disclose to his or her principal material facts of which the principal should be made aware is included as a cause for discipline under this section. *Section 10176(a)*

> Example: Dan, the buyer's agent, told Pat that the home he was interested in purchasing passed its termite inspection, to push the sale through. In truth, the home was riddled with termites, and was structurally unsound as a result. This was a material fact of which the principal ought to be advised. This kind of misconduct could cost the agent his license.

False Promise

A false promise and a misrepresentation are not the same thing. A misrepresentation is a false statement of fact. A **false promise** is a false statement about what someone is going to do in the future. *Section 10176(b)*

> Example: Kate is a licensee who is eager to make a sale. She tells some prospective buyers of a property that, if they make an offer and close escrow within the month, she will cover the cost of a new exterior paint job after closing. She has no intention of carrying out her offer. This kind of false promise can be the basis of formal discipline.

Continued Misrepresentation

The Commissioner has the right to discipline a licensee for a continued and flagrant course of misrepresentation or making false promises. *Section 10176(c)*

Example: Sarah has been having a dry spell in sales, because the properties for sale in her area are affected by radon gas. To give her business a boost, she tells prospective buyers that the properties she shows have all been issued radon-clean clearances, and produces phony certificates professing that the property has been inspected, and has insignificant radon exposure. Finding that people are willing to accept the phony document as reliable, she continues to sell properties under this ruse. This is cause for severe disciplinary action.

Dual Agency

A licensee must inform all principals if the licensee is acting as agent for more than one party in a transaction. Section 10176(d)

Example: Alex represents the seller in a listing. His best friend, Ted, wants to buy the property. He tells Ted that he will help him with the purchase, but does not disclose to the seller the dual agency relationship he now has in the transaction. This is a violation of Real Estate Law, because Alex is in the position of representing both parties, but has not made full and proper disclosure to both. This lack of full disclosure of a dual agency relationship may cost him his license.

Commingling

Commingling is the mixing of the principal's funds with the broker's own money. Commingling is not the same thing as conversion. **Conversion** is misappropriating and using the principal's funds. *Section 10176(e)*

Example: Joe receives some money from his principal, Fred, in connection with a real estate transaction. Joe has not had time to set up a trust account, so he puts Fred's money into his own savings account for safekeeping. Even if Joe has no intention of misappropriating the money, he has commingled it into his own funds. This constitutes a violation of Real Estate Law and, when discovered would lead to disciplinary action against his license.

Definite Termination Date on Listings

If the broker claims a fee or receives compensation, he or she must have a specified termination date is required on all exclusive listings relating to transactions for which a real estate license is required. *Section 10176(f)*

Example: Don takes an exclusive listing for a highly desirable, multi-million dollar home. He fails to put a termination date on the listing. This is improper and cause for disciplinary action.

Secret Profit

A **secret profit** is the taking of a secret or undisclosed amount of compensation. Secret profit cases usually arise when the broker already has a higher offer from another buyer, but the seller is not aware of it yet. The broker makes a low offer, usually through a dummy purchaser. The broker then sells the property to the interested buyer for the higher price. The difference is the secret profit. *Section 10176(g)*

> Example: Sally knows that Alan is interested in purchasing Tom's home for $500,000. However, Tom does not know this. Sally procures a different buyer, Todd, who purchases Tom's home for only $300,000, on Sally's behalf. Sally then "flips" the property and immediately resells it to Alan for the full $500,000. Sally has made a $200,000 secret profit, to Tom's detriment. This secret profit could lead to the loss of Sally's license and prosecution against Sally for both civil and criminal penalties.

Failing to Disclose Listing-Option Profits

A licensee who has both a listing and an option to buy on a property must inform the principal of the amount of profit the licensee will make, and obtain the written consent of the principal approving the amount of such profit before the licensee may exercise the option. *Section 10176(h)*

> Example: Donna has both a listing and an option to buy on a property. If she does not inform the principal of the amount of profit she stands to make, and does not get the principal's consent in writing before exercising the option, she may be subject to disciplinary proceedings.

Dishonest Dealing

Dishonest dealing is a catchall section similar to Section 10177(f). The difference is that under Section 10176(i) the acts must have been those requiring a license, while there is no such need under Section 10177(f). *Section 10176(i)*

Signatures of Prospective Purchasers

Brokers must obtain a written authorization to sell from a business owner before securing the signature of a prospective purchaser to any such agreement. *Section 10176(j)*

> Example: Tom believes Gary may be interested in selling his business. Tom thinks Teri would be very interested in acquiring that business, and draws up papers for her to sign to buy it. Unfortunately, Gary has not given Tom the authorization to offer

his business for sale. Failure to procure a written authorization to sell the business opportunity would subject Tom to disciplinary action.

Failure to Disburse Funds

Brokers must disburse funds in accordance with a commitment to make a mortgage loan that is accepted by the applicant, if the broker represents that he or she is the lender or is the representative of the lender. *Section 10176(k)*

> Example: Dan is a broker who told Tim, the purchaser, that he represents a lender that could assist with the transaction. Tim relied on Dan and Dan said that the mortgage would be approved. Ultimately, Dan reneged on the deal and did not produce the funds. This is a cause for disciplinary action because there was a failure to disburse funds as promised.

Intentionally Delaying the Closing of a Loan

Licensees cannot intentionally delay the closing of a mortgage loan for the sole purpose of increasing the borrower's interest, costs, or fees. *Section 10176l)*

> Example: Paul was strapped for cash. The closing on the Baker property was just four days away. Knowing that if he could draw out escrow just a few extra days, it would mean he would receive a few extra hundred dollars in loan costs and fees he could charge the buyer, he demanded a new termite inspection, which was not needed. This is actionable.

Real Estate Transfer Disclosure Statement Violations

The Commissioner may suspend or revoke a license if the licensee willfully or repeatedly has violated any of the provisions of the Transfer Disclosure Statement. *(Section 10176.5a and NAR Code of Ethics Article 2)*

Section 11077: Not Acting as Agent in a Real Estate Transaction

In addition to all the foregoing, a licensee may be subject to discipline for a variety of things, even if he or she is not acting in his or her capacity as an agent at the time. These items are specified in Business and Professions Code Section 10177, which is reproduced below with an example following each section of law. (Note that this also applies to corporations, if their officers, directors or a shareholder, with more than ten percent of the stock, perform any of these acts.) Generally, a licensee can be disciplined or denied a license for any of the following acts.

Obtaining a License by Fraud

The Commissioner may proceed against a licensee for misstatements of fact in an application for a license, and in those instances where licenses have been procured by fraud, misrepresentation, or deceit. *Section 10177(a)*

> Example: Alex is collecting public assistance in the form of welfare and unemployment checks. He does not want his application for a real estate license to interfere with receiving those checks. He, therefore, files his application under his father's social security number instead of using his own. He has tried to obtain a license by fraud, which is actionable under the statute.

Convictions

This section permits proceeding against a licensee after a criminal conviction for either a felony or a misdemeanor, which involves moral turpitude and is substantially related to the qualifications, functions, or duties of a real estate licensee. **Moral turpitude** is conduct considered contrary to community standards of justice, honesty, or good morals. *Section 10177(b)*

> Example: Six years ago, Joe was found guilty and sentenced for having sex with an underage youth, which is statutory rape. This crime of moral turpitude may prevent him from obtaining a real estate license.

> Example: Tracy worked at a large law firm as a legal secretary. For years, she was skimming money from the corporate coffers by inflating her boss's expenses and then pocketing that money from his firm's expense account. Over the course of several years, she took in excess of $25,000. When the firm and her boss finally realized there was something wrong, they uncovered the embezzlement, and had Tracy prosecuted. Her felony conviction can be the basis for denial of her license.

False Advertising

Licensees who are parties to bait-and-switch and false advertising are subject to disciplinary action. **Bait-and-switch** is the action of advertising a product with the intention of substituting it with a different product that is inferior or more expensive. *Section 101779(c)*

> Example: Gary advertised that he had 3-bedroom/2-bath, view condominiums for sale for $99,000. When the Winters showed up at Gary's office the next morning, ready, willing, and able to buy, the condominiums were suddenly no longer available. Instead, he offered to sell them similar view condos for $139,000. This is known as "bait and switch," and is a form of false advertising that could subject Gary to disciplinary action.

Violations of Other Sections

This section is the Department's authority to proceed against the licensee for violation of any of the other sections of the Real Estate Law, the Regulations of the Commissioner, and the subdivision laws. *(Section 10177(d)*

Misuse of Trade Name

Only active members of the National Association of REALTORS® may use the term REALTOR®. It is unlawful and unethical to misuse the terms "REALTOR®" and/or "Realist" or any trade name or insignia of which the licensee is not a member. *Section 10177(e)*

> Example: Kris is a real estate salesperson working for a local broker. In her newspaper advertisements, she claims to be a REALTOR®, but she is not an active member of the National Association of REALTORS®. This is unethical and a violation of the registered trademark of REALTOR®.

Conduct Warranting the Denial of Real Estate License

This is a general section of the Real Estate Law. Almost any act involving a crime or dishonesty will fall within this section including the denial or suspension of a license issued by another government agency. *Section 10177(f)*

Negligence or Incompetence

Demonstrated negligence or incompetence while acting as a licensee is cause for disciplinary action. *Section 10177(g)*

> Example: Sarah sold a parcel of land to Don, who intended to build a residential development on the site. Sarah failed to determine whether the parcel was zoned for residential development, and, in fact, later found it was only zoned for industrial use. Unfortunately, Don lost the chance to obtain a more suitable parcel of land because of Sarah's negligence. This may ultimately cost Sarah her license.

Supervision of Salespersons

A broker is subject to disciplinary action if the broker, or the officer designated by a corporate broker licensee, fails to exercise reasonable supervision over the activities of the broker's salespersons. *Section 10177(h)*

> Example: Fred is a broker with several salespeople working for him. Joe is one of them, and he has worked for Fred for five years. Over the course of the five years, though, Joe has been making questionable negotiations with his clients. On fourteen occasions, he told attractive female clients that he would reduce

his commission to two percent, if they would go on a date with him. This "technique" worked for him four times. Fred always marveled at Joe's ability to "land" pretty women, and encouraged his behavior. The last time, though, the female client was so offended by the proposition that she brought a complaint of sexual harassment and misconduct. Fred, as the broker, faces disciplinary action for inadequate supervision of his employee.

Improper Use of Government Records

A licensee may not use government employment to violate the confidential nature of records thereby made available. *Section 10177(i)*

Example: Kelly, who worked for a large brokerage, had an idea for drumming up business that she thought was very clever. She had access to social security numbers from former clients. She used this information to run credit checks, looking for people who might be having financial difficulty. Her search indicated that Mr. and Mrs. Baker had some problem, because it seemed like Mr. Baker was frequently changing jobs, and had been running up credit card debt. Then she looked for people who might be wealthy. She found that Mr. Green seemed very financially secure and owned several pieces of property. She told Mr. Green that the Bakers were in real financial trouble, and, although their house was not yet on the market, they might be motivated to sell because they needed cash. Kelly will likely face disciplinary action for misusing access to confidential records and attempting to use the information for her own personal gain.

Other Dishonest Conduct

Any other conduct that constitutes fraud or dishonest dealing may result in licensee suspension or revocation. This is a general provision that applies to any kind of conduct that might be construed as dishonest dealing, and that may subject a licensee to disciplinary action. *Section 10177(j)*

Violating Terms of Restricted License

Violations of the terms, conditions, restrictions, and limitations contained in any order granting a restricted license are grounds for disciplinary action. *Section 10177(k)*

Example: Ted previously faced disciplinary hearings for commingling assets. The Commissioner restricted his license for a period of time. The restriction limited Ted to showing property only; all other real estate transactions and activities had to be under the direct supervision of the broker for whom he worked.

Ted did not follow those directions; instead, he continued his work as though his license were not restricted. Ted will likely face more severe penalties for violating the terms of his restricted license.

Inducement of Panic Selling

This is also called blockbusting or **panic peddling**. A licensee may not solicit the sale, lease, or the listing of residential property on the grounds of loss of value, increase in crime, or decline in the quality of schools due to the present or prospective entry into the neighborhood of a person or persons of another race, color, religion, ancestry, or national origin. *Section 10177(l)*

> Example: A large parcel of undeveloped land was located in a residential neighborhood. Bob saw a great opportunity. He knew a philanthropist, Paul, who had enough money to purchase the land. He told Paul about the location and the opportunity it presented. Bob told Paul that the property was far enough away from any daycare or local school and would be suitable property to build a halfway house for convicted sexual predators that he had been planning to build. Bob facilitated the sale. During escrow, though, Bob went door-to-door to the local residents, warning them that a halfway house for convicted pedophiles was coming into the neighborhood, and that he could help them sell their homes and relocate before property prices plummeted. By promoting a panic sale, Bob's license could be revoked.

Franchise Investment Law

A licensee may not violate any of the provisions of the Franchise Investment Law or any regulations of the Corporations Commissioner Franchise Investment Law. *Section 10177(m)*

Corporations Code

A licensee may not violate any of the provisions of the Corporations Code or of the regulations of the Commissioner of Business Oversight relating to securities as specified by the Corporations Code. *Section 10177(n)*

Failure to Disclose Conflict of Interest

A licensee must disclose to the buyer of real property, in a transaction in which the licensee is an agent for the buyer, the nature and extent of a licensee's direct or indirect ownership interest in that real property. *Section 10177(o)*

> Example: Gary had a cousin, Gayle, who asked him to help her buy a home. Gary had another client with whom he was romantically involved, Lori, who was trying to sell her home.

Gayle did not know that Gary and Lori were seeing each other, and Gary did not inform Gayle of their relationship. A conflict of interest is present because Gary has familial ties with Gayle and romantic interests in Lori. Failure to disclose close relationships, in writing, in a real estate transaction could bring disciplinary action against Gary.

Obtaining a License by Fraud

Within 90 days of issuing a license, the Commissioner may without a hearing, suspend the license of any person who procured the issuance of the license by fraud, misrepresentation, deceit, or by the making of any material misstatement of fact in his or her application for such license. *(Section 10177.1)*

Mobilehome Sales Violations

When dealing with mobilehomes, licensees could have their licenses suspended or revoked if fraudulently completed an application for the registration of a mobilehome. They must deliver a properly endorsed certificate of ownership from the seller to the buyer. They cannot knowingly purchase or sell a stolen mobilehome, or give the Department of Housing and Community Development a bad check. *(Section 10177.2)*

Receiving Compensation for Referring Customers

Receipt or payment of a referral fee from parties related to a real estate transaction are prohibited and may lead to the suspension or revocation of a real estate license. **Referral fees** are considered any claim, demand, or receipt of a commission, fee, or other consideration for referral of customers to an escrow agent, structural pest control firm, home protection company, title insurer, controlled escrow company, or underwritten title company. *Section 10177.4*

> Example: Tom is a real estate agent. His friend Pam owns an escrow company. They have an arrangement, whereby for every transaction Tom refers to Pam, she gives him 5% of the escrow costs back as a way of saying thank you for the patronage. This is considered to be a kickback and is illegal.

Fraud in a Civil Action

Being found liable in an action for civil fraud in connection with a real estate transaction can lead to adverse consequences for the licensee. If a final judgment is obtained in a civil action against any real estate licensee upon grounds of fraud, misrepresentation, or deceit with reference to any transaction for which a license is required, the Commissioner may, after hearing, suspend or revoke the license of such real estate licensee. *Section 10177.5.*

Example: Tim was sued by his former client, Gary, for monetary damages in connection with the sale of a property. The prior property owner did not have clear title, and Tim altered the title with correction fluid to induce Gary to complete the sale. Ultimately, Gary discovered the problems with the title, and brought suit against Tim for the fraud, in order to recover the monies Gary had to spend to acquire clear title to the property. Gary won his suit against Tim, and now Tim will face disciplinary action for having committed fraud.

———— ABC Real Estate Company ————

REAL ESTATE HALL OF SHAME VIOLATIONS

FALSE PROMISE — Section 10176(b)

MISREPRESENTATION — Section 10176(a)

COMMINGLING — Section 10176(e)

Other Provisions

There are several other items specified in the Business and Professions Code that could adversely affect either someone's application for a real estate license or his or her current standing as a licensee. This list is not exhaustive, but it highlights some important key items to keep in mind:

False Advertising

Every broker, associate licensee, officer, or employee of any company, who knowingly authorizes or directs the publication, distribution, or circulation of any written statement that is false or fraudulent regarding subdivided lands or government patents, is guilty of a public offense. Punishment includes a $1,000 fine, imprisonment up to one year, or both. In addition, a real estate licensee may have his or her license revoked by the Commissioner. The district attorney of each county prosecutes all violations in the counties in which the violations occur. *Section 10140*

Example: Judy takes out an advertisement in the local phone directory. Her ad says she handles residential and commercial transactions, that she is a REALTOR®, and that she has been in real estate since 1968. Truthfully, in 1968, Judy was in nursery school. Unless Judy can prove that the printer made a typo, she may face discipline and a fine.

Disclosure of Licensed Status in Advertising

Blind advertising is the failure to disclose licensee status in advertising and solicitation materials.

Advertisements placed in newspapers, periodicals, mailers, or the like by real estate agents for any activity that requires a real estate license must also include a designation disclosing that the agent is performing acts that require a real estate license. [§10140.6(a)]. When advertising, licensees may use the terms broker, agent, REALTOR®, loan correspondent or the abbreviations "bro.", "agt.", or other similar terms or abbreviations to indicate the persons license status. Reg. 2770.1

> Example: Sarah takes out an ad in the local newspaper. She says that she is in real estate sales, but fails to identify herself as an agent or broker. She could face disciplinary action.

A real estate licensee must disclose his or her license identification number on all solicitation materials and on real property purchase agreements when acting as an agent in those transactions. [§10140.6(b)]. **Solicitation materials** include business cards, stationery, websites owned or controlled by the license, advertising fliers, and other promotional materials designed to solicit a professional relationship between the licensee and a consumer. Solicitation material does not include promotional materials (e.g., refrigerator magnets), advertisements in print or electronic media (e.g., radio, cinema and television ads, and the opening section of streaming video and audio), and "For Sale" signs. However, if the solicitation materials also include the name the salesperson's employing broker, the license number of the employing broker does not need to be included on the solicitation materials. Reg. 2773(a).

Selling Price Disclosure

A broker must notify the buyer and the seller of the selling price within one month after completion of the sale. It is usually done by the escrow company. *Section 10141*

Recording Trust Deed

A broker (or escrow company) must record a trust deed created on the sale of a property within one week of closing. *Section 10141.5*

Delivery of Agreement

A broker must give a copy of any contract to the party signing it at the time that it is signed. *Section 10142*

Real Estate Commissions are Negotiable

All printed agreements that determine the amount of commission to be paid a real estate licensee for the sale of residential (1-4) property or manufactured homes must have a statement in 10-point (or larger) boldface type stating that commissions are negotiable.

> **Notice: The amount or rate of real estate commissions is not fixed by law. They are set by each broker individually and may be negotiable between the seller and broker.**

In addition, the amount of compensation or commission rate cannot be printed in the agreement. *Section 10147.5*

Document Retention

A broker must retain several types of documents for 3 years from the date of the closing or, if the transaction is not closed, from the date of the listing. These documents include listings, deposit receipts, cancelled checks, trust records, disclosure documents, correspondence, email, and other related documents. However, brokers do not have to retain electronic messages of an **ephemeral nature** such as text messages, instant messages, or tweets. [Civil Code §1624(d)]. For example, a Mortgage Loan Disclosure Statement needs to be kept for 3 years. In addition, if a broker acts as a property manager, in addition to the documents listed above, he or she should keep records of rental agreements, rent collection receipts, and property management agreements with clients. The Bureau of Real Estate can suspend or revoke the license of any real estate licensee who knowingly destroys, alters, conceals, mutilates, or falsifies any of the documents that are required to be retained.

A broker should maintain personnel files for as long as a salesperson or employee works for the brokerage and archive the files for at least 3 years after the person leaves. Since these records are confidential, brokers should secure the files and provide limited accessibility to the information. *(Section 10148)*

Violations are Misdemeanors

Any person including officers, directors, agents, or employees of corporations who willfully violates or knowingly participates in the violation of this division shall be guilty of a misdemeanor punishable by a fine not exceeding $10,000, or by imprisonment in the county jail not exceeding six months, or by a fine and imprisonment. *(Section 10185)*

SUMMARY

California has long been a leader in real estate trends with the passing of the nation's first real estate licensing law in 1917. To create and maintain higher professional standards combined with public trust, the real estate industry has supported legislation that protects consumer interests. The bulk of the laws concerning licensing of real estate professionals are included in Division 4 – Real Estate, Parts I through IV in the Business and Professions Code (B&P Code).

Parts I and II are the most important part for real estate licensees. Part 1 is titled "Licensing of Persons" and is called the Real Estate Law, Part 2 is titled "Regulation of Transactions" and is called the Subdivided Lands Law. The Real Estate Law, sometimes referred to as the License Law, is designed mainly for the protection of the public in real estate transactions involving a licensee.

The Real Estate Commissioner is the head of the Bureau of Real Estate (CalBRE).

The two main types of real estate licenses are the broker's license and the salesperson's license. A real estate broker is someone who holds a broker license issued by the Bureau of Real Estate. A real estate salesperson is someone who holds a salesperson license issued by the Bureau of Real Estate. Before an applicant for a real estate salesperson or broker license may obtain a license, he or she must fulfill certain real estate education requirements, pass a real estate examination, and apply for the license.

The License Law is only effective if enforced. Persons who violate the licensing law may be subject to a variety of penalties. Licenses may be suspended, revoked, or otherwise restricted. In addition, violators may be subject to civil injunctions, criminal penalties, or fines as the result of being found guilty of unethical conduct.

UNIT 8 REVIEW

⬜ Matching Exercise

Instructions: Write the letter of the matching term on the blank line before its definition.
Answers are in Appendix A.

Terms

A. Administrative Law Judge

B. agent

C. blockbusting

D. branch office

E. Business & Professions Code

F. commingling

G. DBA

H. eLicensing

I. false advertising

J. moral turpitude

K. Order to Desist and Refrain

L. payment of child support

M. real estate broker

N. Real Estate Commissioner

O. Real Estate Law

P. Recovery Account

Q. referral fees

R. restricted license

S. secret profits

T. solicitation materials

Definitions

1. _____ Portion of codified California law covering real estate professionals

2. _____ Law that affects the licensing and conduct of real estate brokers and
   salespeople

3. _____ Head of the Bureau of Real Estate

4. _____ If not paid by an obligor, his or her license will be suspended

5. _____ Account to pay otherwise uncollectible court judgments against licensees who
   have committed fraud or misrepresentation in a real estate transaction

6. _____ Person with a real estate license who can employ someone who holds a
   salesperson or a broker license

7. _____ Role of a broker to his or her client

8. _____ Any business location other than the main office

9. _____ Acronym for a fictitious business name

10. _____ Type of probationary license issued when a license has been suspended, revoked, or denied after a hearing

11. _____ Interactive online system used for license renewal and change transactions

12. _____ Court-ordered demand that prohibits a business or individual from carrying on a particular activity

13. _____ Person who makes recommendations to the Commissioner concerning discipline, after a formal hearing

14. _____ Mixing of the principal's funds with the broker's own

15. _____ Money obtained by buying property from a client and reselling it quickly to someone else, rather than allowing the client to reap the benefits of the greater sale

16. _____ Conduct considered contrary to community standards of justice, honesty, or good morals

17. _____ Promoting sales with inaccurate information

18. _____ Term for inducing panic sales

19. _____ Money paid illegally in exchange for generation of business

20. _____ Business cards, stationery, advertising fliers, and other materials designed to solicit a professional relationship between the licensee and a consumer

Multiple Choice Questions

Instructions: Circle your response and go to Appendix A to read the complete explanation for each question.

1. The main purpose of the Real Estate Law is to:
   a. uphold the good standing of ethical real estate agents from actions of unscrupulous agents.
   b. offer financing alternatives for low-income borrowers who want to purchase real estate.
   c. protect consumers from losses caused by unethical agents.
   d. do both (a) and (c).

2. Which of the following acts requires a real estate license?
    a. Solicitation of real estate buyers
    b. Negotiating sales transactions
    c. Negotiating leases
    d. All of the above

3. Charles is a construction worker who owns a home that he wishes to sell. By law, he must hire _____ to help him.
    a. a broker
    b. a broker-associate
    c. no one
    d. a salesperson

4. Which is not a type of license issued by the California Bureau of Real Estate?
    a. Property Management License
    b. Real Estate Broker License
    c. Real Estate Salesperson License
    d. Restricted License

5. A licensee who violates the Real Estate Law can be subject to:
    a. monetary fines.
    b. license suspension or revocation.
    c. civil injunctions.
    d. all of the above.

6. Complaints filed against a licensee with CalBRE are investigated by the:
    a. Administrative Law Judge.
    b. Commissioner.
    c. Enforcement and Audit Section.
    d. Department of Housing and Urban Development.

7. Rose is a real estate salesperson who did not disclose a dual agency relationship. If a party later complains, an Administrative Law Judge will:
    a. order her to pay a fine.
    b. preside over the hearing.
    c. revoke her license.
    d. suspend her license.

8. Robert is handling several different transactions at once. He has six different homes being sold by six different people, and six separate buyers buying them. During the course of these transactions, he receives money from all the buyers and puts all the funds into a trust account. Robert has:

    a. acted unethically because he handled too many transactions simultaneously.
    b. commingled funds.
    c. engaged in blockbusting.
    d. done none of the above.

9. Andy is a real estate broker. Charles listed a rundown apartment building through Andy, asking one million dollars. Andy knew that Donna, a real estate investor, would readily pay twice that amount for the land alone due to its choice location. Andy had his fiancée purchase the property for him, and then immediately resold the property to Donna. All three parties got what they sought: Charles got the one million dollars he wanted, Donna got the property she wanted, Andy got the commission plus the difference between the two sales. Did Andy act ethically?

    a. No, he advertised falsely.
    b. No, he engaged in secret profits.
    c. No, he failed to disclose listing-option profits.
    d. Yes, everyone received what he or she expected.

10. Bob is a broker who employs Sally, a salesperson. Sally has made several careless and significant errors on the last four transactions she has handled. The various clients in all four transactions separately filed complaints against Sally with CalBRE. What may be the outcome?

    a. Bob will not be disciplined for improper supervision of his sales associate because Sally is the one who was negligent.
    b. Both Bob and Sally may be disciplined.
    c. Neither Bob nor Sally will be disciplined.
    d. Sally will not be disciplined for negligence, because it is Bob's responsibility to supervise her actions.

Agency Law

Unit **9**

INTRODUCTION

When a person hires another to act on his or her behalf, an agency relationship is created. **Agency** is a legal relationship in which a principal authorizes an agent to act as the principal's representative when dealing with third parties. The simplest agency relationship involves three parties—the principal, the agent, and a third person or entity. Agency is an essential part of real estate transactions because of the complexities of buying and selling real property and the potentially devastating results of mishandling these transactions. Lay people usually do not feel knowledgeable and confident enough to handle these transactions without assistance. Therefore, real estate brokers—usually as agents of the sellers—step in.

Agency is an area with its own unique set of laws. Special and specific duties are owed by the agent to the principal and vice versa. Because legal ramifications attach to the principal for the decisions and actions the agent makes, there are substantial danger areas of which to be wary. This unit examines the law of agency and its legal effect on real estate licensees.

Learning Objectives

After completing this unit, you should be able to:

9A   identify the types of agency law.

9B   choose the types of agency relationships in real estate.

9C   select the ways to create an agency relationship.

9D   identify how to terminate an agency relationship.

LAW OF AGENCY

Agency relationships are part of the body of law called the law of agency. The **law of agency** is based on the Latin maxim *Qui facit per alium, facit per se,* which means, "He who acts through another is deemed in law to do it himself." Agency, in its legal definition, usually relates to commercial or contractual dealings, such as real estate transactions. Agency involving real property should be in writing, such as listings, trusts, and powers of attorney.

If a principal authorizes an agent to act on his or her behalf when dealing with third parties, this creates a fiduciary relationship. A **fiduciary relationship** implies a position of trust and confidence. This applies to agency relationships in various types of industries, not just real estate.

Throughout the United States, with the exception of Louisiana, English common law forms the basis of each state's legal system. In addition, each state has passed statutes to codify, clarify, change, limit, or expand common law principles. California is no exception. Two types of laws are used for guidance regarding agency relationships.

Two Types of Agency Law

1. **Common law agency** gets its authority from the customs that originated from pre-colonial England, the laws that were common, and from the subsequent judgments and case law that have enforced and re-affirmed the customs.

2. **Statutory law agency** draws from the statutes and rules created by various legislative and governing bodies. These rules directly affect and regulate agency relationships. In California, the law of agency is found in Civil Code sections 2295 et seq.

Roles in Agency Relationships

The people involved in an agency relationship are the agent, principal (client), and third party (customer). The **agent** is a person who has the authority to act on the behalf of another, representing the business interests of that person. The **principal** is the client who gives authority to an agent to represent his or her interests in dealing with third parties. A **third party** is a customer who may be affected by the terms of an agreement but who is not a part of the agreement.

The principal hires the agent to perform a service and gives the agent authority to act for or on behalf of the principal. The agent is in a position of trust with the principal and owes the principal certain fiduciary duties. This creates a fiduciary relationship between the agent and the principal.

Agent's Scope of Authority

The authority given an agent is determined by the principal. Depending upon the agency classification, the scope of authority delegated to the agent by the principal may vary greatly. Usually, the agent's authority is categorized as general agency or special agency.

General Agency

General agency is a relationship in which a principal delegates ongoing tasks or duties to an agent under his or her employ. A **general agent** is authorized by a principal to perform all tasks associated with the continued operation of a particular project. A general agent may have significant responsibilities and liabilities and, as a result, the principal is liable and accountable for all of the agent's actions.

Authority Given to a General Agent
- Limited scope to specific business or job
- Act on a continuing basis
- Multiple transactions
- Bind contracts

General agency is applicable in all sorts of industries. For example, the officers of a corporation act as the corporate agents who can enter into contracts, which legally bind the corporation. A sports agent, for example, is responsible for negotiating an athlete's contracts and securing endorsements. The agent provides continued services that generate income and exposure for the athlete. A literary agent works on the behalf of an author to sell the author's works to publishers. A writer's guild agent helps writers sell their screenplays to television and movie producers. In the real estate business, a property manager is a good example of a general agent. He or she is responsible for preserving the value of the real estate investment while generating income for the owner.

Special Agency

Special agency is a relationship in which a principal delegates limited tasks or specific duties to an agent under his or her employ. A special agent is sometimes referred to as a **limited agent** because this is the most restricted agency relationship. A **special agent** is a person employed to perform a particular task or transaction for a specified amount of time.

Authority Given to a Special Agent
- Limited scope
- Single transaction
- One-time basis
- No authority to bind contracts

An example of a special agent is an attorney hired for a specific purpose, such as drawing up a will for a client. The duties are limited in both duration and nature of the task.

Similarly, a real estate broker under a signed listing agreement is the special agent of the owner of the property. A special agency also exists between the broker and buyer under a signed buyer representation agreement. These agreements give the broker permission to act on the client's behalf. With a listing agreement, the broker is given the authority to list, market, and sell the client's property. With a buyer representation agreement, the broker is given the authority to represent the client on the purchase of a property. In both examples, the agents are not able to bind the principal to a contract. Rather, they are hired to represent the client for a certain amount of time for a specified task.

Actual or Implied Agency

If the agency relationship is described in a written agreement, it is called **actual authority**. A principal is not responsible for the acts of the agent if those acts are beyond the agent's actual authority. If the relationship is created through words or actions, without actual authority, an **implied agency** relationship is created. An implied agency is created through words, actions, inference, and deduction from other factors rather than a written agreement.

Agency by estoppel, also known as **ostensible agency**, is created when a principal causes a third party to believe another person is the principal's agent. Ostensible means apparent; therefore, if someone from the public believes an agency is in place between two parties even though the relationship does not exist, an agency by estoppel or ostensible agency could exist. If the principal does not give the agent written or implied authority to do the act, a third party cannot hold the principal responsible.

AGENCY RELATIONSHIPS IN REAL ESTATE

Real estate brokers are involved in broker/client and broker/associate agency relationships. For example, the broker would be the agent of the seller who is the principal in the agency relationship. That same broker is the principal to his or her associate licensees who are his or her agents.

Broker/Client Agency Relationships

As stated earlier, every agency relationship has a principal (client), an agent, and a third party (customer). In a real estate transaction, the principal (buyer or seller), agent (real estate broker), and third party (customer) are bound together in a legal relationship, with all the duties and rights that go with that connection. Most frequently, the principal is a seller who employs an agent to find a buyer for his or her property. Sometimes the principal is a buyer who employs an agent to locate a property.

The agent is always a licensed real estate broker. That is why a listing broker is also called a listing agent; a selling broker is also called a selling agent; and a buyer's broker is also called a buyer's agent. When a broker represents only the buyer or the seller in the transaction, it is called **single agency**. A **dual agency** exists if one broker represents both principals in the transaction.

Listing Agent

A **listing agent** is a broker who obtains a listing from a seller to act as an agent for compensation. A **listing** is a contract between an owner of real property and an agent who is authorized to obtain a buyer.

Subagent

A **subagent** is a broker delegated by the listing agent (if authorized by the seller) who represents the seller in finding a buyer for the listed property.

Buyer's Agent

A **buyer's agent** is a broker employed by the buyer to locate a certain kind of real property.

Selling Agent

A **selling agent** is the broker who finds a buyer and obtains an offer for the real property. Usually a cooperating broker, the selling agent (broker) may act as a subagent of the seller, as an agent of the buyer, or as a dual agent.

Cooperating Broker

A **cooperating broker** is a selling agent who assists another broker by finding a buyer. A cooperating broker participates in the multiple listing service (MLS) and finds a buyer for a property listed in MLS. A **multiple listing service** (MLS) is a cooperative listing service conducted by a group of brokers, usually members of a real estate association. A cooperating broker may represent either the seller or the buyer.

Review – Agency Relationships

- In a real estate transaction, the agent is always a broker.
- In a listing agreement:
    - the agent of the seller (principal) is the listing agent or listing broker.
    - a subagent represents the seller.
    - a broker who works with the buyer (third party) can be the selling agent or cooperating broker.
- Broker representing and working for both buyer and seller is a dual agent.
- In a buyer representation agreement:
    - the agent of the buyer is the buyer's agent or buyer's broker.

Dual Agent

A **dual agent** is a broker acting as agent for both the seller and the buyer in the same transaction. A broker can legally be the agent of both the seller and the buyer in a transaction, but the broker must have the informed, written consent of both the seller and the buyer. The dual agent is a broker who may be working independently or through an

associate licensee. A real estate broker who has a listing agreement with a seller may establish an agency with a buyer as well. In this case, the broker is acting as a dual agent whether the broker is the actual agent of both the seller and the buyer or is the agent of the seller and the ostensible or implied agent of the buyer. Dual agency commonly occurs when two associate licensees employed by the same broker represent two or more parties to a transaction. The real estate broker is then a dual agent.

A real estate broker who represents both buyer and seller must act with extreme care because the broker owes fiduciary duties to both principals. The broker would have conflict with the negotiation of price and terms between seller and buyer and the negotiation of loan amount and terms between lender and borrower. A real estate broker functioning as a dual agent may not disclose to the seller that the buyer is willing to pay more than the buyer's written offer to purchase. A dual agent cannot disclose to the buyer that the seller will take less than the listing agreement, without the express written consent of the party authorizing the disclosure.

Disclosure of Dual Agency - B&P Section 10176(d)

A licensee must inform all principals if the licensee is acting as an agent for more than one party in a transaction. Failure to disclose a dual agency, by providing written notice or obtaining a written consent concerning dual agency, has been a costly mistake for many licensees. The consequences can include substantial monetary loss and action against the agent's real estate license.

Broker/Associate Agency Relationship

A general agency relationship exists between sales associates and their employing real estate brokers. A **sales associate** (also called an **associate licensee**) is a licensed real estate salesperson or broker whose license is held by an employing licensed broker. The sales associate works for an employing broker and the employing broker is responsible for the acts of the sales associate.

The salesperson is a general agent of his or her employing broker and a subagent to the principal. The employing broker authorizes his or her agents to list and sell real estate multiple times, on a continuing basis, and bind the broker to these contracts. Because the salesperson is the agent of the broker, the broker owns all listings. Consequently, the broker has the right to reject the listing agreement if certain terms of the agreement, such as the listing price or broker's fee, are not acceptable to the broker.

> Example: Pam, a sales associate in the employ of broker Dan, listed a property owned by Joe Green. Under the law, the agency has been created between Joe Green and broker Dan. Pam is bound by the agency because she represents Dan.

Employment Status

Employment status refers to the relationship between an associate licensee and his or her broker—as an employee or self-employed. For purposes of California real estate law, an associate licensee is considered an employee of the broker. Additionally, the broker must have a written independent contractor agreement with each of his or her associate-licensees. This agreement allows the associate-licensees to be *self-employed*.

However, an associate licensee is NOT considered an employee for federal income tax purposes—nor does the IRS consider real estate licensees independent contractors. In fact, since 1982, real estate licensees have been classified by the IRS as **statutory nonemployees**. If an employing broker and real estate salesperson meet the following tests, the broker is **not treated as**

an employer and the salesperson is **not treated as an employee** for federal income tax purposes.

Tests Used to Determine Statutory Nonemployee Status

- The salesperson or broker-salesperson must be duly licensed;
- The salesperson or broker-salesperson must be compensated on the basis of the number of sales closed and commissions earned—not on the basis of the number of hours worked; and
- There must be a written contract between the broker and the salesperson providing that the salesperson will not be treated as an employee for federal tax purposes. 26 USC §3508

Statutory nonemployees are treated as *self-employed* for all federal tax purposes, including income and employment taxes. Therefore, they must pay the full amount of Social Security and Medicare taxes, and not just a matching amount. Statutory nonemployees receive 1099s (instead of a W-2 form) and must file a Schedule C to report their income and expenses. Additionally, they must make quarterly estimated tax payments.

Despite these factors, brokers are still liable for torts committed by an agent. Business and Professions Code §10177(h) requires that a broker exercise "reasonable supervision over the activities of his or her salespersons" and do so with respect to contracts filled out by salespersons working under the broker's license. A broker also can be liable if the salesperson is required to have a license for a task that the salesperson performs and it turns out that the person is unlicensed.

Employment Agreement

Regardless of whether an employee is a salesperson or a broker-associate, he or she must have a written employment agreement with the broker for whom he or she works. The **employment agreement** is an agreement that specifies the important aspects of the employment relationship, including the supervision of licensed activities, licensee's duties, and the compensation arrangement. The compensation arrangement or split of commissions is a key provision in the employment agreement. Typically, for every sale a salesperson makes, he or she receives a percentage of the commission paid to the broker.

Example: Tara is a salesperson who works for Sally, a broker. Tara sells a home for $2.4 million for Gary. Tara's agreement with Gary is that Tara earns a six percent commission on the sale. Therefore, the commission equals $144,000. Tara's employment agreement with Sally states that Tara splits 50-50 any commission earned while in Sally's employ. Therefore, Tara's portion of the commission is $72,000 and Sally's half is $72,000.

The agreement must contain signatures and dates by both parties. The broker needs to keep a copy for a minimum of three years after the employment ends. Specific language is required in the employment agreement if the employee is an independent contractor.

CREATING AN AGENCY RELATIONSHIP

When a person hires another to act on his or her behalf, an agency relationship is created. The agency relationship commences at the time that the licensee undertakes to provide real estate brokerage services to a principal. The principal's liabilities and the agent's duties begin when the relationship is established. Agency relationships are created by agreement, ratification, or estoppel.

Agreement

An agency relationship may be created by agreement with or without a written contract. However, real estate agreements must be in writing to be enforceable in a court of law. The typical ways to create a written agreement are by a power of attorney, listing agreements, and buyer representation agreements.

Power of Attorney

A **power of attorney** is a written document that gives a person legal authority to act on behalf of another person. A power of attorney creates a particular kind of agency. The principal executes a document that gives a specific person "power of attorney" to act on his or her behalf in certain circumstances.

Typically, there are two types: special and general. A **special power of attorney** authorizes the agent to do certain specific acts. The agent is then known as an **attorney-in-fact** under a limited power of attorney. A **general power of attorney** allows the agent to transact all the business of the principal (within the agreed upon area), but this is not common in real estate transactions. Another kind of power of attorney, known as a **durable power of attorney** for health care, can allow someone to make medical decisions if the principal becomes incapable of doing so for himself or herself.

Listing Agreement

In real estate, a listing agreement is the most common way to create an agency relationship. A **listing agreement** is a written contract by which a principal, or seller, employs a broker to sell real estate. When the seller signs a listing agreement promising payment for service by the listing broker and the broker promises to "use due diligence" in finding a buyer, it is a **bilateral contract**—in that a promise is given in exchange for a promise.

Buyer Representation Agreement

Buyers may employ a real estate broker to represent them using a **buyer representation agreement**. In this instance, the buyer is the principal and the seller of a property is the customer (third party).

Ratification

Ratification means acceptance of an act already performed. Ratification of an agency relationship is created by approving acts after performance. Agency by ratification is created when a person gains some benefit from a previously unauthorized act of an agent, and the person, upon learning of the act, does not deny that the agent had the authority to perform the act. Otherwise, ratification authority is given if the beneficial act is self-evident or expressly approved.

Requirements for Agency by Ratification

- The agent performs an unauthorized act for a person
- The person learns of the act
- The person does not deny the agent's authority to act
- The person benefits from the act

Example: Tom is a busy business executive and barely has time to mow his lawn. He casually mentions this to a neighbor who notices the growing grass. The next day, the neighbor begins to mow Tom's lawn. Tom sees this as an act of courtesy and allows the neighbor to continue this for several months. At the end of that time, Tom's neighbor bills him for several hundred dollars. Tom may have to pay the bill because he saw the unauthorized act and did not deny the authority of his neighbor to perform the act. Therefore, Tom authorized the neighbor's actions by ratification.

Ratification can be voided under certain circumstances. For instance, if the principal is not fully aware of all the terms and conditions of the transaction and such items are of a material nature affecting the transaction, the principal may be able to void the agency.

Estoppel

An agency relationship can be created by estoppel. **Estoppel** is a legal bar that prevents a person from asserting facts or rights that are not consistent with what was implied by the person's previous behavior. Agency is created when the principal causes a third party to believe another person is the principal's agent. What the principal has implied by his or her behavior is barred, or stopped, from being denied. Authority is given when a principal allows a third party to believe that another person is the agent, even if the third party is unaware of the appointment. That is why this is also called an **implied, ostensible,** or **apparent agency.**

Example: If a seller allows a buyer to believe that a broker represents the seller and the buyer believes that to be so, the existence of an agency cannot be denied by the seller, who will be bound by the actions of the broker. This is known as the Doctrine of Estoppel.

While an ostensible agency occurs when the principal gives the impression to a third party that someone is his or her agent, it does not have to be intentional. Ostensible agency can be created by "want of ordinary care," according to the California Civil Code.

Example: Homeowner Donna is at home gardening when her friend, real estate broker Sam, drives up with Tim. Sam tells Donna he has a prospective buyer for the property and introduces Tim as such. Donna never listed her property for sale and did not retain Sam to act as her agent for purposes of selling her property. Meanwhile, Donna tells Sam to show him around the place and he takes Tim inside. An ostensible agency has been created.

Had Donna, in Tim's presence, stated to Sam that she has not listed the property for sale or that she has not asked Sam to procure a buyer for the property, there would have been clear communication that an agency did not exist. Donna, however, acted in "want of ordinary care" by failing to mention any of these facts and allowed Tim to believe that the property was for sale and that she had enlisted Sam to show the property.

Duties in a Fiduciary Relationship

The broker and client are bound together in a fiduciary relationship with all the duties and obligations that go with that connection. An agent may not unduly gain any financial advantage over the principal. In fact, even if an agent decides to purchase property the principal has listed for sale, the agent must still act as a fiduciary even though he or she is thereafter acting not only as an agent.

Example: A seller lists a property with an agent and tells the agent the price he wants. The agent later finds a potential purchaser who would be willing to purchase at a significantly higher price. The agent fails to disclose that information to the seller. Instead, the agent himself purchases the property from the seller at the seller's price and then resells it to the other party, reaping a nice profit. Even though the seller obtained the price that he originally requested, the agent has breached his fiduciary duty to the seller.

Real estate brokers have specific duties and responsibilities to their clients and an obligation to act fairly and honestly with customers. The duties are not limited to brokers—clients have certain duties, responsibilities, and obligations to their brokers.

Duties Agents Owe Clients

Agents owe several special duties to their principals. These duties and obligations are: Obedience, Loyalty, Disclosure, Confidentiality, Accounting, and Reasonable Care.

Obedience

Obedience is the willingness to follow the orders of others. As a fiduciary, a licensee must perform all lawful actions requested by his or her client. However, if the principal asks to do anything illegal, the licensee must explain the law and inform the client that all agents must obey the law in all transactions. If a client still wants or asks a licensee to do anything illegal, the licensee should terminate the agency relationship and walk away from the transaction immediately.

A client may reasonably expect a licensee to arrange certain services to be performed on a property, such as an appraisal or inspection. Regardless of the service ordered, the licensee should give the client an opportunity to choose the service provider. This avoids any accusations of unfair dealings. If clients do not have a service provider of their own, the licensee may select one for them, with their permission. After a service provider has been selected, it would then be appropriate for the licensee to arrange the requested service.

Loyalty

Loyalty refers to the duty of a licensee to his or her client's best interests first. Disloyalty can allow a principal to rescind a transaction and any commission earned could be returned. In addition, the client could be sued for damages and the licensee could lose his or her license. If a client asks a licensee to treat others dishonestly or unfairly, he or she should refuse. In this case, the licensee is not being disloyal to the client.

Disclosure

Disclosure refers to any statement of fact that is required by law. Every party to a transaction has the right to expect disclosure of material facts about the property. However, the client in an agency relationship can expect to know much more from his or her agent. The licensee involved in the transaction must know

everything that the client knows, whether it is favorable or not.

A client should receive full disclosure of all information relating to the other parties in the transaction and the transaction itself. This information may include what the broker thinks the home is worth, negotiation techniques that may be used to help the client achieve his or her goals, and the motivation of the other party including his or her financial condition.

Typical Disclosures to Clients

- Relationships between the agent and other parties to the transaction
- Agent's opinion of the property's value
- Type of the earnest money deposit received
- Financial condition of the buyer
- Existence of other offers
- Commission split agreements between a listing broker and another broker
- Meaning of the statements in the contract

A customer is entitled to know any material facts about the property, such as the condition of the property, ownership or title information, restrictions, liens, encroachments, and the presence of any environmental issues.

Because an agent acts as a representative of the principal, it is necessary for the agent to communicate thoroughly with the principal. The duty of full disclosure ensures that the principal is given the opportunity to give thoughtful consideration to all decisions. Failure to disclose fully all pertinent matters to the principal unfairly puts him or her in a position of making a poor decision with undesirable consequences.

Example: Kate is interested in buying a large parcel of undeveloped realty. Fred is the agent for Gary, who owns the property. Kate tells Fred she will pay Gary's asking price, but Gary has to run water and sewer lines throughout so that she can later subdivide the land into  a residential community of homes. Fred communicates to Gary that he has a buyer, but anxious to obtain his commission, he neglects to tell Gary the important conditions of the sale. Relying on his agent, Gary accepts the offer, unaware that he will be responsible for many tens of thousands of dollars of improvements to the land, effectively destroying any profit he would have realized on the sale. Fred breached his duty of full disclosure to Gary and both suffer the consequences of this breach in disclosing the conditions of sale.

Confidentiality

Confidentiality refers to discretion in holding privileged information. Any confidential information an agent has about his or her client must be kept confidential unless the client provides written permission for it to be disclosed. The only information that should be disclosed to the other party is what is required by law.

In other words, a client's motivation for buying or selling and his or her acceptable price or bargaining position should not be disclosed to the other party. That is because a client's motivation, for example, is not a material fact. It is a personal detail and when disclosed in confidence, it must remain in confidence. When confidential information seems to conflict with disclosure duties, a licensee's duty of confidentiality should always take precedence in these situations.

The duty of confidentiality is not limited to the transaction. It extends even after the transaction has been completed.

Accounting

Accounting refers to the systematic recording of monies in a transaction and giving accurate reports to the owner(s) of the money. Many times in a transaction, funds are held in trust for a client or a customer. These funds must be placed in a separate account set up for this purpose. Any agent who puts a client or customer's money into his or her own bank account is guilty of commingling. **Commingling** is the illegal practice of mixing a client or customer's funds with a broker's personal or general business account. If a broker actually uses the client or customer's money in a manner that it was not intended, it is **conversion**.

The broker, or salesperson associated with the broker, must deposit the earnest money funds promptly in an escrow account. It is customary for buyers and sellers to agree upon a neutral agent, usually an escrow or title company, to hold any funds. However, as long as all funds held in the account are accurately recorded, a real estate broker is legally permitted to have an escrow account.

Once the earnest money deposit has been placed in an escrow account, the neutral party will hold the funds until the transaction closes. If for some reason the transaction does not close, the money is to be refunded to the appropriate party, providing all the parties have agreed to this in writing. The neutral agent cannot release the funds without written permission from both buyer and seller.

Reasonable Care

Reasonable care, also known as due care or diligence, refers to the amount of care that an average, rational person would take under the same or similar circumstances. Professionals and specialists are held to a higher standard of care than the public when dealing with situations related to their field of specialization. Clients hire real estate professionals to provide skilled and knowledgeable service and advice about buying and selling real estate.

> Example: Gayle contacts Ted to sell her home. She tells him the price she would like and he creates a listing. However, he did not check what prices comparable homes in the area are fetching and allowed her to list the home for significantly less than it is worth, to her financial detriment. Ted did not exercise due care in advising his client of the value of her home compared to similar properties in the vicinity.

The courts use a **standard of care** to decide whether an agent has used reasonable skill and care in a disputed transaction. The judge or jury (trier of fact) must determine if, under similar circumstances, a reasonably prudent broker would use the same amount of care to protect the best interests of the client. If the answer is yes, then the agent has not acted negligently.

Clients expect real estate agents to do more than simply locate a suitable property or find a ready, willing, and able buyer. Real estate agents need an understanding of title, physical characteristics of the land, and the improvements of the property under contract. Clients further expect agents to keep abreast of financing trends and market conditions. Additionally, to fulfill the obligation of serving their clients and customers, real estate professionals must keep informed on national, state, and local issues in the real estate industry.

Fiduciary Duties of a Real Estate Agent

DUTIES	SELLERS AGENT	EXCLUSIVE BUYERS AGENT
Obedience	Must obey all lawful instruction of the Seller; is not obligated to obey instructions from the Buyer	Must obey all lawful instruction of the Buyer; is not obligated to obey instructions from the Seller
Loyalty	Must do everything possible to gain an advantage for the Seller	Must do everything possible to gain an advantage for the Buyer
Disclosure	Must reveal any known material defects in the property Must NOT reveal information about traffic problems, poor school system, declining property values, etc. since these items might make the property less desirable to Buyers	Must tell Buyer everything known about the Seller including the motivation for selling and any reasons the Seller may have for wanting a quick sale Must tell Buyer everything known about the property, including traffic problems, poor school system, high crime rates, etc.
Confidentiality	Must tell the Seller everything known about the Buyer, including all financial details obtained Must conceal anything about the Seller that would help the Buyer gain an advantage, such as impending foreclosure, need to move in a hurry, need to sell to settle a divorce, etc.	Must keep all information about the Buyer confidential, including the Buyer's ability or willingness to pay more for the property than offered, as well as the Buyers' motivation for buying
Accounting	Must account to the Seller for any money or documents entrusted to them	Must account to the Buyer for any money or documents entrusted to them
Reasonable Care (Dilligence)	Must prepare themselves through education and study to represent the Seller competently in all matters	Must prepare themselves through education and study to represent the Buyer competently in all matters

Duties Agents Owe Third Parties

In addition to those duties to the seller, the listing broker owes a duty of fair and honest dealing to the buyer, including the duty of full disclosure. The duty to disclose requires that the listing broker conduct a reasonably competent and diligent inspection of the property and note anything that would affect its value or desirability.

It is important to understand that while dealing fairly, an agent does not represent a third party equally. The duties owed to a third party should not be at the expense of the duties owed to the client. For example, it would be a breach of confidence to disclose what a seller is willing to accept or what a buyer is willing to pay. Those are negotiation positions rather than material facts.

Material Facts

A listing broker may not withhold any material facts that are known to the seller or broker, from a prospective buyer. A **material fact** is any fact that would seem likely to affect the judgment of the principal in giving consent to the agent to enter into the particular transaction on the specified terms. As a result of the Easton decision (*Easton v. Strassburger*, 1984), real estate agents can be held liable, not only for defects they know about, but for defects about which they should have known as a result of careful investigation. These facts include any known physical defects in the property, conditions of title, or conditions affecting the area surrounding the property. For example, if a licensee knows that a property is located in a floodplain and the seller is not aware of this fact, the licensee must disclose this information.

On the other hand, a buyer's agent has the duty to disclose any facts that could affect a seller's decision to enter into or proceed with a transaction. These facts are generally relevant to the buyer's financial ability. For example, if a purchase is contingent on the buyer selling his or her existing home, this is considered a material fact. The seller has the right to know that the buyer's ability to purchase is contingent upon selling another home.

If an agent has substantive knowledge of a defect, unfavorable condition, or material fact, but fails to disclose it, he or she could be liable to both parties (buyer and seller). This liability extends to facts that an agent should have known, based on what is expected of a real estate professional. The duty to disclose and investigate extends to his or her actual and expected knowledge of matters affecting the transaction.

Review —

A material fact is any fact that would seem likely to affect the judgment of the principal in giving consent to the agent to enter into the particular transaction on the specified terms.

Misrepresentation

A great majority of the complaints received are about misrepresentation on the part of the broker or salesperson. **Misrepresentation** is making a false statement or concealing a material fact. The failure of a broker or salesperson to disclose to his or her principal material facts of which the principal should be made aware is included as a cause for discipline under Section 10176(a) of the Business and Professions Code.

The line between truth and fiction can be blurred either innocently or with malice intended. It is easy for an agent to misrepresent a fact to a client or third party if the agent is not careful. The types of misrepresentations are innocent misrepresentation, negligent misrepresentation, and fraudulent misrepresentation.

Innocent Misrepresentations

Innocent misrepresentations are statements not known to be untrue at the time they are made and usually they carry no criminal liability for an agent. However, a buyer or seller could cancel a contract as a result.

Negligent Misrepresentations

Negligent misrepresentations are untrue statements made without facts to back them up in circumstances where care should have been taken.

Example: Sarah is a real estate agent showing a home to Teri. Teri inquires as to improvements to the front and back yards, which are lush, expertly manicured, and maintained. Sarah says that there is a sprinkler system in both yards. In truth, only the front yard has visible sprinkler heads, but Sarah never checked to see if there were any in the back yard. Sarah has committed negligent misrepresentation, because although she genuinely believed her statement to be true, she had no reasonable grounds for her belief. She never bothered to verify that the back yard was indeed equipped with a sprinkler system.

Fraudulent Misrepresentations

Fraudulent misrepresentations are untrue statements made by an agent who knows that he or she is not telling the truth. The agent may be liable for committing fraud.

Fraud is an act meant to deceive in order to get someone to part with something of value. Fraud is an intentional misrepresentation of statements made by an agent who knows that he or she is not telling the truth. Fraud extends to the intentional nondisclosure of material facts. An agent may be liable for damages, if the client or customer suffers a loss as a result of committing fraud.

> Example: Don is a real estate broker who is eager to make his first sale. Gayle is a prospective buyer, touring a home in a Marina del Rey development with Don. She asks him what features and amenities come with the home. Flustered and eager to close the deal, he blurts out that the purchase of the home comes complete with a dock slip on the Marina suitable for a small yacht. Don knows this is not true and is an intentional misrepresentation of the facts, but Don is too embarrassed to admit his lie. He allows Gayle to believe that a dock slip is included in the purchase price of the home and she buys the home based on his representations. Don has committed fraud, for which he would be civilly liable and most likely would face disciplinary action under the Business and Professions Code.

Puffing

Puffing is an exaggerated statement of opinion about property that is not factual. Puffing is different from misrepresentation in that it describes an opinion made by an agent who honestly believes that the inflated statement about the condition of a property is just another innocent way to make a sale.

Tort

Tort is a violation of a legal right, or a civil wrong, such as negligence, libel, or nuisance. It is a breach of duty created legally rather than by contract. If an agent fails to carry out his or her contractual obligation, the agent could be liable for breach of contract. It is not a tort if the breach of duty does not include negligent wrongdoing. If a principal directs an agent to commit a tort, the agent will be liable for carrying out that directive. Even though an agent owes a duty to follow the instructions of his or her principal, there is a caveat that the duty is limited to lawful directions.

> Example: Jo owns an apartment building and wishes to sell it. One of her tenants, Dawn, breeds and raises guinea pigs in one of the units. Unfortunately, although Jo has asked Dawn to stop her activities and to clean up her very messy situation, Dawn has not done so. As a result, a horrendous stench emanates from the unit around the clock. A potential buyer, Alex, is interested in touring the property. Before Alex visits, Jo directs her agent, Paul, to get a cleaning crew over to Dawn's unit, clean it out, and dispose of all her animals to make the property more attractive to Alex. Paul carries out Jo's directions, much to Dawn's shock and dismay.
>
> In so doing, Paul has broken several laws. While Dawn's activities might themselves also have violated different laws, Paul and Jo failed to follow lawful procedures to make her clean up the property and instead took the law into their own hands. As Jo's agent, Paul is liable to Dawn for monetary damages on several different grounds, including monetary loss of property, conversion, trespass, and infliction of emotional harm.

By law, an agent is not liable for torts committed by a principal, only his or her own torts. If a seller were negligent in disclosing a material fact and non-disclosure of that fact results in damages, the agent would not be held liable for what he or she did not or could not have known.

Review – Types of Misrepresentation

Misrepresentation is making a false statement or concealing a material fact.

Puffing is a statement of opinion that is not factual about a piece of property.

Fraud is an act meant to deceive in order to get someone to part with something of value.

Tort is a violation of a legal right, or a civil wrong, such as negligence, libel, or nuisance.

Duties Clients Owe Agents

Agents are not the only ones in the transaction with duties and responsibilities. Principals also have certain obligations to fulfill by recognizing the respondeat superior doctrine, indemnification, and providing compensation to the broker.

Respondeat Superior

There are legal ramifications for the principal in all transactions. The principal is responsible or liable for the actions of his agent, because he is the agent's employer. The legal doctrine of **respondeat superior** means, "let the superior answer." The doctrine makes principals liable for agents acting within the scope of their authority. Not only does this concept apply to things the agent does, but it also applies to things the agent neglects to do.

> Example: Kris is a principal who hired Tracy to be his agent. While negotiating a deal on Kris' behalf, Tracy hired an inspector to look at the premises in question. Tracy neglected to pay the inspector. Kris refused to pay the inspector and the inspector brought a lawsuit against Kris. The court orders Kris to pay for the inspection because under the doctrine of respondeat superior, Kris is liable for the expenses his agent incurs on his behalf while acting within the scope of his authority.

The principal is not liable for everything an agent does and there are exceptions to the respondeat superior concept. The agent's actions or omissions must be in the course and scope of the agency. This would mean that the agent must conduct business for the principal. However, if the agent goes beyond the scope of the agency, liability may not rest on the principal's shoulders.

Indemnification

When entering into a listing agreement, a seller is agreeing to indemnify the broker. **Indemnification** means to protect against damage, loss, or injury, or to make compensation for damage, loss, or injury.

A seller must hold the broker harmless from any damage, costs, attorney's fees, and expenses that:

- are caused by seller, negligently or otherwise.
- arise from seller's failure to disclose any material or relevant information about the property.
- are caused by seller giving incorrect information to any person.

Compensation for Performance

An agent has earned a commission if he or she procures a ready, willing, and able buyer. Though a seller can opt out of a sale, he or she must still pay a commission if the agent has performed per contract. If the broker brings about a "meeting of the minds" of the buyer and seller on price and other terms for the transaction, the agent has earned the commission. Thus, if buyer and seller enter into a valid contract, the agent is entitled to a commission even though the sale is never completed.

The broker has earned the commission if he or she presents an accepted offer to the seller during the term of the listing. After a listing has expired, the broker may still earn a commission if the listing has a protection period clause.

The amount of commission is decided by the seller and the broker and is included in the listing agreement. Usually it is a percentage of the sales price, but does not necessarily have to be mentioned in this manner. Commissions and fees are always subject to negotiation between the parties. If a group of brokers or brokerage firms attempts to set the commission rates in their area, it is considered price fixing, which is illegal. Commissions are not set by the Board of REALTORS®, between competitors, or by CalBRE.

Review – Commissions

- The amount of commission is not set by law and is always negotiable.
- It is a violation of the Sherman Anti-Trust Law for brokers to discuss or set commission rates in a community.

Procuring Cause

Disputes regarding procuring cause of a sale are the source of most litigation over payment of commissions. **Procuring cause** refers to an agent who produces a buyer ready, willing, and able to purchase the property for the price and terms specified by the seller, regardless of whether the sale is completed. A procuring cause is that which produces the desired results. The agent must be the procuring cause of the sale to earn a commission.

The commission does not depend on the amount of work completed by a competing broker. It is dependent upon who has performed the agency and who has procured a ready, willing, and able buyer.

Occasionally, determining procuring cause of a sale becomes a matter of significant dispute between real estate agents. When more than one agent has shown a prospective buyer a property, with or without the knowledge of the other agent's involvement, each may feel they have earned the commission when the buyer authorizes one of them to write up an offer, which is accepted by the seller.

The law states that the agent who is the procuring cause of the sale has earned the commission. The procuring cause is the person who starts an uninterrupted chain of events that leads to a sale. The others were unable to bring the buyer to the point of sale and, therefore, did not earn a commission.

Protection Period Clause

Listing agreements have a **protection period clause** that protects the listing broker's commission if the owner sells the property to any person whose attention has been called to the property during the listing. At the time the listing agreement is signed, the seller and agent agree to the length of the protection period (starting the day after the listing ends and continuing for an agreed-upon number of days). This prevents the seller from waiting for the listing to end and then accepting an offer and refusing to pay the broker (the procuring cause) a commission.

> ### Review – When an Agent's Commission is Earned
> - Agent produces a ready, willing, and able buyer to purchase on the terms and at the price asked by the seller
> - Agent secures from a prospective buyer a binding contract with terms and conditions acceptable to the seller

Suit for Commission

In order for an agent to enforce payment of his or her commission, he or she must satisfy special requirements.

- The agent must have an employment agreement, which includes a promise to pay a commission and is signed by the party to be charged (usually, the seller). More information on the employment is available later in this unit.
- The agent must hold a valid real estate broker's license.
- The agent must be the procuring cause of the sale.
- The agent must provide a ready, willing, and qualified buyer who agrees to the sale terms required by the seller. The buyer may not be under duress.

The licensee must have informed the buyer that he or she should either have the abstract examined by an attorney or should be given a title policy.

TERMINATING AN AGENCY RELATIONSHIP

An agency relationship can be terminated by the actions of the parties to the agency or by operation of law. Since the relationship between a principal (client) and agent (broker) is a personal one, at any time during the agency, the principal or agent may terminate the agency.

If agency is cancelled for any reason, it is very important to keep the entire client file. Whether a problem exists or not, always put in writing the reason for the termination of the agent-client relationship. If the client sought new representation, document the circumstances that led to the client's actions. Document any conversations or actions of all the parties related to the cancellation and the outcome. If problems occur after the cancellation, continue to document everything in writing. Keep this documentation in the client file for as long as there are problems existing in relation to the termination of the agency relationship.

If the broker cancels the agency without good cause, the broker could be liable for any expenses the client has incurred. If a seller cancels an agency created by a listing agreement without good cause, the seller may be liable for breach of contract and may be liable to pay a broker's fee to the listing broker. A seller cannot terminate a listing agreement if it is coupled with an interest. An **agency coupled with an interest** is one in which the agent gets an interest in the subject of the agency, which is the property.

> Example: The listing broker advanced funds to pay for a defaulted loan on the property to keep it out of foreclosure. The seller cannot revoke the listing after the broker has cured the loan.

Full Performance. Once the property is sold and closed, the agency relationship with the owner (or the buyer) terminates. Even after termination of agency, an agent or broker must still keep confidential any personal client information received during the transaction.

Expiration of its term. The agency terminates when the listing or buyer representation agreement ends. Every employment agreement must have a definite termination date according to CalBRE. When that time is reached, the obligations of all parties to the agreement end.

Mutual Agreement. If two parties agree to make a contract, both can agree to terminate it.

Example: An owner is being transferred out of state and lists the home for sale. If the transfer is cancelled, the owners no longer need to move. It would be poor business practice for a broker to require clients to follow through with the sale of their home in this situation, because selling is no longer in the clients' best interest.

Conceivably, a buyer representation agreement could be cancelled, based on similar circumstances.

Revocation. The client may unilaterally revoke the listing or buyer representation agreement and "fire" the broker. If the broker is negligent, does not perform, or does not properly represent the client, the client would have the right to terminate the agency relationship with the current broker.

Renunciation. The broker may unilaterally renounce the listing or buyer representation agreement and "fire" the client. Clients have obligations and duties of performance, under the terms of a listing agreement or a buyer representation agreement. If they are not fulfilling these duties, the broker has the right to terminate the agency agreement.

Operation of Law. Incapacity or death of either the client or the broker terminates an agency relationship because agency is a contract for personal services. If the property is destroyed, condemned, or no longer controlled by the owner, the agency relationship terminates. A listing agreement is a personal services contract in that a licensed real estate broker agrees to provide services for a seller. If the broker were to lose his or her license, the broker would not legally be able to perform under the terms of the listing agreement.

SUMMARY

Agency is a legal relationship in which a principal authorizes an agent to act as his or her representative when dealing with third parties. This creates a fiduciary relationship between the agent and the principal. A fiduciary relationship relies on trust and confidence.

The parties involved in an agency relationship are the agent, principal, and third party. The agent is a person who has the authority to act on the behalf of another, representing the business interests of that person. The principal in a real estate transaction is the client and is the person or persons being represented. In contrast, the customer is the person who a broker or salesperson works with, but does not represent. A third party is a person who may be affected by the terms of an agreement but who is not a part of the agreement.

The principal determines the authority given to the agent. The types of authority are actual and ostensible. Actual authority is obtained when the authority to act is intentionally given by the principal to the agent. Ostensible authority, also known as agency by estoppel, is created when a principal causes a third party to believe another person is the principal's agent. Usually, the agent's authority is categorized as general agency or special agency. General agency is a relationship in which a principal delegates ongoing tasks or duties to an agent under his or her employ. Special agency is a relationship in which a principal delegates limited tasks or specific duties to an agent under his or her employ.

Real estate brokers are involved in broker/client and broker/associate agency relationships. In a broker/client relationship, the principal (buyer or seller), agent (real estate broker), and third party (customer) are bound together in a legal relationship with all the duties and rights that go with that connection. In a broker/associate relationship, a general agency exists between sales associates and their employing real estate brokers.

When a person hires another to act on his or her behalf, an agency relationship is created. The principal's liabilities and the agent's duties begin when the relationship is established. Agency relationships are created by agreement, ratification, or estoppel. An agency relationship can be terminated by the actions of the parties to the agency or by operation of law. Since the relationship between a principal (client) and agent (broker) is a personal one, at any time during the agency, the principal or agent may terminate the agency.

UNIT 9 REVIEW

Matching Exercise

Instructions: Write the letter of the matching term on the blank line before its definition. Answers are in Appendix A.

Terms

A. agency

B. agent

C. confidentiality

D. cooperating broker

E. dual agent

F. estoppel

G. fiduciary relationship

H. general agency

I. indemnification

J. material fact

K. misrepresentation

L. obedience

M. power of attorney

N. principal

O. ratification

P. respondeat superior

Q. right to control

R. sales associate

S. special agency

T. third party

Definitions

1. _____ Legal relationship in which a principal authorizes an agent to act as the principal's representative when dealing with third parties

2. _____ Implies a position of trust and confidence

3. _____ Person who has the authority to act on the behalf of another, representing the business interests of that person

4. _____ Client who gives authority to an agent to represent his or her interests in dealing with third parties

5. _____ Customer who may be affected by the terms of an agreement but who is not a part of the agreement

6. _____ Relationship in which a principal delegates ongoing tasks or duties to an agent under his or her employ

7. _____ Relationship in which a principal delegates limited tasks or specific duties to an agent under his or her employ

8. _____ Selling agent who assists another broker by finding a buyer

9. _____ Broker acting as agent for both the seller and the buyer in the same transaction

10. _____ Licensed real estate salesperson or broker whose license is held by an employing licensed broker

11. _____ How much direction the broker exercises over the person the broker has hired

12. _____ Written document that gives a person legal authority to act on behalf of another person

13. _____ Acceptance of an act already performed

14. _____ Legal bar that prevents a person from asserting facts or rights that are not consistent with what was implied by the person's previous behavior

15. _____ Willingness to follow the orders of others

16. _____ Discretion in holding privileged information

17. _____ Any fact that would seem likely to affect the judgment of the principal in giving consent to the agent to enter into the particular transaction on the specified terms

18. _____ Making a false statement or concealing a material fact

19. _____ "Let the superior answer."

20. _____ Protect against damage, loss, or injury, or to make compensation for damage, loss, or injury

Multiple Choice Questions

Instructions: Circle your response and go to Appendix A to read the complete explanation for each question.

1. Statutory law agency is governed by:
   a. statutes and rules created by legislative organizations.
   b. common law.
   c. authority from customs originating in pre-colonial England.
   d. industry-specific standards of practice.

2. Which of the following is one of the parties involved in an agency relationship?

    a. The agent

    b. A third party or customer

    c. The principal or client

    d. All of the above

3. An agency relationship created by actual authority requires:

    a. actions.

    b. words.

    c. inferences.

    d. a written agreement.

4. Which of the following is a type of agency relationship in real estate?

    a. Client/spouse

    b. Broker/associate

    c. Third party/client

    d. Broker/spouse

5. In a broker/associate relationship, a licensed _____ is employed by a licensed broker.

    a. salesperson

    b. broker

    c. appraiser

    d. both (a) and (b)

6. How is an agency relationship created?

    a. By agreement

    b. Through ratification

    c. Estoppel

    d. All of the above

7. Which of the following written agreements can create an agency relationship?

    a. Listing agreement

    b. Power of attorney

    c. Buyer representation agreement

    d. All of the above

8. Which of the following is not one of the fiduciary duties that an agent owes to his or her principal?

   a. Accounting
   b. Confidentiality
   c. Misrepresentation
   d. Reasonable Care

9. An agent who is unaware that he or she is presenting false statements is guilty of:

   a. fraud.
   b. negligent misrepresentation.
   c. innocent misrepresentation.
   d. puffing.

10. Which of the following would terminate an agency relationship?

   a. Revocation
   b. Full performance
   c. Operation of law
   d. All of the above

Fair Housing Laws

Unit 10

INTRODUCTION

Every person who wants to purchase or rent real property hopes that he or she will be treated ethically and fairly during that transaction. Hopefully, the person's prospective purchase or rental will be based on objective factors such as income and credit, rather than subjective factors such as ethnicity or gender. To protect prospective buyers or renters from illegal discrimination in obtaining housing, both state and federal law require those who work in the real estate business, including related industries such as finance, to make decisions based only on a buyer's objective fitness to enter into a real estate agreement.

Real estate licensees are required to practice within the guidelines of many federal and state fair housing laws. They should never consider violating a person's rights to buy, sell, rent, or lease real property.

Learning Objectives

After completing this unit, you should be able to:

10A   recognize federal fair housing laws.

10B   identify the protected classes under federal fair housing laws.

10C   indicate the applicability of the Americans with Disabilities Act.

10D   recall California fair housing laws.

10E   identify the protected classes under California fair housing laws.

FEDERAL FAIR HOUSING LAWS

Anti-discrimination legislation from the 1800s was relatively ineffective in combating private discrimination in housing. It was not until nearly 100 years later that the Civil Rights Act of 1968 was enacted to protect the rights of individuals to secure housing without the threat of discrimination.

The 1800s

Following the end of the Civil War in 1865, two amendments were added to the Constitution that have had increasingly important implications for fair housing and civil rights. One could say that the civil rights movement in America began with the passage of the Thirteenth and Fourteenth Amendments to the United States Constitution. These were reinforced by legislation, starting with the Civil Rights Act of 1866.

The Thirteenth Amendment

Prior to the Civil War, in the case of *Dred Scott v. Sandford* 60 U.S. 393 (1857), the U.S. Supreme Court ruled that slaves were property and did not lose that status just because a slave had lived for a time in a free (non-slave) state. In 1866, once the Civil War was over and the Union had triumphed, Congress passed and a sufficient number of states ratified the **Thirteenth Amendment** to the Constitution, which in effect overruled the *Dred Scott* case by amending the Constitution.

The Thirteenth Amendment prohibits slavery or other "involuntary servitude" except as punishment for a crime anywhere in the United States. Because most former slaves had been private property, the impact of this amendment was primarily on private citizens—i.e., it in effect abolished what had formerly been a lawful form of property.

For this reason, the significance of the Thirteenth Amendment is that, unlike the Fourteenth Amendment (the other important post-Civil War Constitutional amendment), the Thirteenth Amendment has no "state action" requirement—that is, it is not limited just to restricting what the U.S. Congress or the state governments may do. The Civil Rights Act of 1866 (discussed below) was adopted before the Fourteenth Amendment became part of the

Constitution. It is, therefore, one of the few federal statutes that can prohibit private acts of discrimination without having to rely on the Commerce Clause.

Civil Rights Act of 1866

The earliest law protecting individuals in the lease or purchase of real property was the **Civil Rights Act of 1866**. The act prohibited discrimination based on race and is in the 42 U.S. Code §1982, granting all citizens equal rights in the purchase or lease of ALL real property.

Because the 1866 law was adopted to deal with a specific situation—providing for equal treatment for former slaves in the aftermath of the Civil War—the act addressed discrimination based on race. The act does not cover other types of discrimination such as color, sex, religion, national origin, disability, or familial status.

The 1866 law is both broader and narrower than its more modern counterpart, the Fair Housing Act of 1968, discussed later in the Unit. Unlike that law, which does not apply to the sale of commercial or even the sale of residential property if the owner owns fewer than three other such properties, the 1866 Act applies to race discrimination in the sale or lease of ALL real property. Thus, if someone refused to sell commercial property to a buyer because of his or her race, the 1866 law would allow the buyer to bring a lawsuit even though the 1968 law would not.

The Fourteenth Amendment

There had been some hope that the Thirteenth Amendment might settle the matter of making former slaves equal members of American society. But there were lingering concerns about whether merely abolishing slavery had done enough to accomplish this goal, and many of the former Confederate states had responded by passing laws known as "Black Codes" that tried to limit the rights of former slaves to do such things as travel freely. This led Congress to propose another amendment to the Constitution, which became the **Fourteenth Amendment** when it was ratified in 1868. The Fourteenth Amendment has had more far-reaching effects than any other amendment to that document.

Due Process and Equal Protection Clauses

Among the provisions of the Fourteenth Amendment are the **Due Process Clause** and the **Equal Protection Clause**. The exact language of the Amendment states: ". . . nor shall any State deprive any person of life, liberty, or property, without due process of law; nor deny to any person within its jurisdiction the equal protection of the laws."

Because this language specifically provides that citizens are protected against something done by the "State," in a number of cases the U.S. Supreme Court has interpreted both the Due Process Clause and the Equal Protection Clause as having a **state action requirement**. This means that Congress can pass laws prohibiting the state governments or local public entities from passing laws that discriminate, or prohibiting state or local employees from committing acts of discrimination. The federal courts can also find that actions of the states or local governments violate Due Process or Equal Protection. Unlike the Thirteenth Amendment, however, Congress or the federal courts cannot use either of those clauses to do anything about *private* discriminatory conduct.

One rare exception took place when the Supreme Court struck down private **restrictive covenants**—that is, clauses in deeds that prohibited the sale of real property to members of certain races or religious groups.

Shelley v. Kraemer

In *Shelley* v. *Kraemer*, 334 U.S. 1 (1948), the Shelleys, a black family, bought a house in St. Louis, Missouri. The property had a restrictive covenant that had been recorded several decades earlier barring "people of the Negro or Mongolian Race" from owning the property. The neighbors sued to prevent the Shelleys from moving onto the property, and the lower courts held that the covenant was enforceable. The Supreme Court acknowledged that the covenant was a private agreement that ordinarily would "run with the land" and be enforceable against subsequent owners. The court concluded, however, that because the neighbors had to use the power of the state courts to enforce the covenants, the involvement of the courts in enforcing such covenants was still a violation of the Equal Protection Clause.

The 1900s

With the exception of *Shelley* and a few other cases, most Supreme Court decisions have held that the Fourteenth Amendment does not allow Congress to pass legislation prohibiting private acts of discrimination by relying on or any provisions of the Fourteenth Amendment. When Congress wanted to pass civil rights legislation in the 1960s, therefore, it relied not on the Fourteenth Amendment, but on the Commerce Clause.

The **Commerce Clause** is found in Article I of the original text of the Constitution where the powers of Congress are enumerated. It gives Congress the authority to "regulate commerce with foreign nations, and among the several states, and with the Indian tribes."

Commerce by its very nature involves private conduct. The Supreme Court accepted Congress' statement of its intent in adopting these laws—that private discriminatory conduct places a burden on interstate commerce, and therefore private discrimination should be outlawed. Persons who are discriminated against are prevented from buying or selling things because of their race, national origin, and so forth are prevented from participating in the commercial life of the nation, including when the commodity involved in the discriminatory conduct is real property.

Therefore, most of the federal civil rights legislation adopted during the twentieth century relies on the Commerce Clause—not on provisions of the Fourteenth Amendment like the Due Process Clause or the Equal Protection Clause.

Jones v. Mayer

Jones v. Alfred H. Mayer Co. 392 U.S. 409 (1968), is a United States Supreme Court case which held that Congress could regulate the sale of private property in order to prevent racial discrimination. The court stated that under the Thirteenth Amendment (ending slavery), Congress may outlaw not only slavery, but the manifestations of slavery as well. It left it to Congress to define those manifestations. Therefore, ***Jones v. Mayer*** prohibits discrimination based on race by upholding the 1866 Civil Rights Act and the 13th Amendment to the U.S. Constitution.

Civil Rights Act of 1968

Almost one hundred years after passage of the Civil Rights Act of 1866, a new law—the **Civil Rights Act of 1968** was passed. Title VIII of the Civil Rights Act of 1968 is found beginning at 42 U.S.C. §3601. It provides for some things that the 1866 law lacked, while also providing exemptions for some actions that are nevertheless covered by the 1866 law. There are differences between the 1866 and the 1968 laws, but together they formed "a complete arsenal of federal authority" in the area of housing discrimination.

The Civil Rights Act of 1968 became a law only one week after the assassination of Martin Luther King, Jr. This act constituted landmark legislation in the United States. It provided anti-discriminatory protection in education, housing, and employment for five protected classes of people based on their race, color, religion, sex, or national origin. A **protected class** is a group that is protected from discrimination under federal or state law.

Title VI of the Civil Rights Act of 1968 prohibits discrimination in programs and activities receiving federal financial assistance. Programs and activities under the act mean all of the operations of government, institutions of higher education, and local educational agencies. It also includes businesses receiving federal assistance that principally engage in providing education, health care, housing, social services, or parks and recreations.

Part of Title VII of the Civil Rights Act of 1968 extended the Commission on Civil Rights and prevented discrimination in federally assisted programs. Overall, the Civil Rights Act of 1968 had positive sweeping affects across the country and instituted new protections of individual civil rights under the law.

Federal Fair Housing Act

Despite the breadth of the Civil Rights Act of 1968, Congress has amended the law over the years. Title VIII of the Civil Rights Act of 1968 and the Fair Housing Amendments Act of 1988, taken together, constitute the **Fair Housing Act**. The Fair Housing Act makes it illegal for anyone to refuse to sell or rent a property to a person because of race or any other protected group.

Protected Classes

The Fair Housing Act protects specific groups of people. The Fair Housing Amendments Act of 1988 added disability and familial status to bring the total to seven protected classes.

Seven Protected Classes under the Federal Fair Housing Act

1. Race
2. Color
3. Familial status
4. Sex
5. National origin
6. Disability
7. Religion

Persons with disabilities are those with physical conditions that impair them, including those with AIDS and mental disorders. Under this law, a person with a disability may make minor modifications to allow safe access and use of a property, as long as the property is returned to its original design when the tenant vacates the property. **Familial status** refers to the relationship of people in a family, and protection under the Fair Housing Act includes children under the age of 18 living with parents or legal custodians, pregnant women, and people securing custody of children under the age of 18.

Included or Exempt Property

The Fair Housing Act prevents discrimination in specific types of housing.

Types of Housing Covered by the Fair Housing Act

- All residential property owned or operated by the Federal Government

- Single-family homes owned by private persons, including corporations or partnerships, even if a broker is not used to sell or rent the home

- Multi-family dwellings with four or more units, including rooming houses

- Multi-family dwellings with four or less units, if the owner does not live in one of the units

Types of Property Exempt from the Fair Housing Act

- Commercial and industrial properties

- Unimproved land, unless the land is specifically offered for construction for residential purposes

- Single-family home sold by the owner provided the owner resides at the unit for sale and does not own more than three single-family homes at one time and does not use a real estate broker for the sale. This exception applies once within 24 months.

- Rental of one-to-four dwelling units (e.g., fourplex or the rental of rooms in a home) that the owner occupies who is not utilizing the services of a real estate broker

Exempt Organizations and Groups

- Religious organizations that are selling or leasing the organization's own property may limit the sale or lease to members of the same religion, if this is the only basis for preference.

- Private clubs that do not rent to the public at large may limit the rental of the organization's property to its members.

- Certain senior citizen housing is exempt from what would otherwise amount to familial status discrimination. This housing must be occupied exclusively by those 62 and older or be specifically designed for elderly persons under a federal, state, or local government program. In addition, the  housing must include at least one person who is 55 or older in at least 80% of the occupied units and adhere to a policy that demonstrates intent to house persons who are 55 or older.

Prohibited Practices

In addition to refusing to sell or rent a property to a person of a protected class, it is also illegal to tell a person that the dwelling is unavailable for inspection, if in fact it is available. The act prohibits coercing, threatening, intimidating, or interfering with a person's enjoyment or exercise of housing rights, based on discriminatory practices, or retaliating against a person or organization that aids or encourages the exercise or enjoyment of fair housing rights.

One of the most noteworthy features of the Fair Housing Act is that it specifically prohibits, by definition if not by name, a number of practices that had informally amounted to discrimination. These practices include: (1) refusing to make a mortgage loan; (2) refusing to provide information regarding loans; (3) imposing different terms or conditions on a loan, such as different interest rates, points, or fees; (4) discriminating in appraising property; (5) refusing to purchase a loan; (6) setting different terms or conditions for purchasing a loan; and (7) redlining.

Redlining

Redlining is the practice of designating, usually although not exclusively on a map, certain neighborhoods as areas where loans will not be made, or at least will not be made to members of certain minority groups. The term "redlining" comes from a practice that originated in the 1930s when lenders would sometimes rate various parts of a city according to whether it was desirable to make loans within each area. The least desirable areas were either colored in red or had a red line around them, hence the term.

Redlining is not so much a problem in the sale of real estate as it is in the practices of lenders. There is a related kind of redlining that involves the reluctance of insurance carriers to make loans within certain neighborhoods, once again making it difficult for homeowners or business owners to acquire property and casualty insurance. Without such insurance, home and business owners face increased risks that a fire or similar calamity will cost them the equity in their property; and, because property loans are almost always required as a condition of obtaining financing for a home loan, the lack of property insurance makes a purchase-money loan, as a practical matter, unavailable.

Harrison v. Otto G. Heinzeroth Mortgage Co.

In *Harrison v. Otto G. Heinzeroth Mortg. Co.*, 414 F.Supp. 66 (D.Ohio, 1976), the plaintiffs were white persons who attempted to purchase a home in an integrated or predominantly black neighborhood. They alleged that they were refused a mortgage loan with terms and conditions equal to those of loans on homes in predominantly white neighborhoods solely because of the racial composition of their intended neighborhood. In other words, the plaintiffs alleged not that they were denied a loan because they were being discriminated against because of their race, but rather because the company did not want to make loans based on the company's perception of the

Harrison v. Otto G. Heinzeroth Mortgage Co. (continued)

"character" of the neighborhood where they wanted to live. The defendant company tried to dismiss the case, arguing that the Fair Housing Act only applied if the plaintiff alleged discrimination based on the plaintiff's race. The district court disagreed. The court found that nothing in the Fair Housing Act limited its applicability to discrimination on the basis of the complainant's race. Rather, it was enough that the plaintiff could demonstrate a denial of housing opportunities solely on the basis of racial considerations—here, the racial composition of the neighborhood, or what would today be called redlining. The case was allowed to proceed forward to trial.

Blockbusting

Blockbusting is a tactic used by some real estate brokers to induce panic selling by making property owners believe that the "character" of a neighborhood was likely to change because one or two properties had been acquired by members of a minority group, usually African-American. The tactics included supposedly mistaken phone calls for "the black family that just moved in." Sometimes, a business card was left on properties adjacent to a house that had recently been sold to a member of a minority group. Another tactic was to contact a non-minority family stating that a nearby home had recently been sold to a non-white family, and then attempting to induce a sale by the non-minority owners, sometimes at less than fair market value.

Zuch v. Hussey

In *Zuch v. Hussey*, 394 F.Supp. 1028 (D.Mich, 1975), the various real estate firms conducted campaigns to solicit business involving door-to-door canvassing, fliers, and telephone calls. The fliers contained such statements as "We think you may want a friend for a neighbor" and "Know Your Neighbors." A mailing addressed to "Resident" supposedly contained "neighborhood news." It informed the recipients that the real estate agency had purchased a home in the recipient's neighborhood, that the firm had paid cash, and that the recipients of the mailing might receive the same service.

> ### *Zuch v. Hussey* (continued)
>
> Because residents would have been aware that the racial character of the neighborhood had been changing and that black families had been moving into the area, the implication was that white families worried about the changes could "cash out" quickly if they were willing to accept the firm's offer. The federal district court concluded that this conduct amounted to blockbusting.

Steering

Steering is the practice of directing members of certain racial or ethnic groups to certain neighborhoods and directing members of other groups to different neighborhoods. Steering is based on assumptions that persons of a given ethnic background will only want to live in neighborhoods with persons of the same ethnic backgrounds. Conversely, people of one ethnic background prefer not to live in neighborhoods where the predominant group has a different background.

In a chicken-and-egg kind of way, of course, steering may itself create the very situation that its practitioners claim to be the justification for their action. Because a given agent or broker may assume for example, that people of a Hispanic background prefer to live only around people who are also Hispanic, the agent's or broker's actions in steering people to certain neighborhoods reinforces those very patterns *because of* their actions, and not the other way around.

> ### United States v. Real Estate One, Inc.
>
> One of the most notorious steering cases of all time was *United States v. Real Estate One, Inc.*, 433 F.Supp. 1140 (E.D. Mich, 1977). A brokerage in the Detroit area assigned new sales agents to its field offices based solely on whether they were white or black. Certain offices were essentially all white or all black depending on the neighborhoods where these agents would be showing housing. Furthermore, houses in certain neighborhoods that were mostly black were only advertised in certain publications that had a mostly black readership. A separate phone number was used for the advertisements in these newspapers, so that when the call came in, the person answering the phone would know that it was coming on the "black" line and could assume that the call was coming from someone who was black. If the call did come in on that line, it was assigned to a black sales agent.

> **United States v. Real Estate One, Inc. (continued)**
>
> The court ordered that Real Estate One conduct an educational program and to make no assignments to agents on the basis of race or the composition of the neighborhood where a house was to be sold. The court also ordered that the company change its practices of advertising to ensure that advertising was not based solely on the racial composition of the target readership of the newspaper or of the neighborhoods where particular houses were located.

Advertising Guidelines

The Fair Housing Act also made it illegal for advertisements of housing offered for sale or rental to show preference or discrimination based on race, color, religion, or national origin.

Certain kinds of advertising and the use of certain words or phrases can be a violation of civil rights laws, even if the person who placed the advertisement had no intent to discriminate. It is illegal to advertise in such a way that indicates a preference, restriction, or intention to discriminate. This applies to all types of advertising media whether it is in print or on the Internet.

The use of certain terminology in an advertisement is often a red flag. For example, describing a certain neighborhood as exclusive, private, or restricted implies that certain applicants for sale or rental of such property might not be welcome. Likewise, using terms that are too specific are also potentially troublesome. Describing a house as "great for a single person" (implying potential discrimination against married couples) or "great for an active person" (implying potential discrimination against a person with a disability), or even describing a neighborhood as "integrated" (implying that a neighborhood is changing from one racial group to another) can be a violation of the Fair Housing Act.

Even referring to the incidental presence of nearby religious, racial, ethnic, or similar landmarks, buildings, or monuments can be deemed a violation because of the implication that specific buyers might be drawn to purchase because of those attractions. Examples would include "walk to nearby church," "down the street from Italian-American cultural center," or "close to the Mormon Temple."

Example: Ad using *inappropriate* words or phrases: Example: Ad using appropriate words or phrases:

■ **Lovely 2Br, 2Ba with garage**
Gym, pool. Near hiking trails. Ideal for young, physically fit. Garage. Starts $1,500. Call Now! (555) 231-5564

■ **Lovely 2Br, 2Ba with garage**
Gym, pool. Near parks, hiking trails. Garage. Starts $1,500. Call Now! (555) 123-5564

In addition, if someone uses print or television advertising that depicts potential buyers or sellers by using models, care must be taken that, over time, a cross-section of models are used that imply only adults are being targeted or only members of a specific group.

Models, if used, should vary according to age, sex, ethnicity, and social settings, so that there is an implication that persons belonging to all groups, sexes, and ages are welcome.

Even consistently using members only of a minority group would potentially cause a problem here—e.g., using only persons of Hispanic background would be just as much of a problem as using only Caucasian models, because of the potential implications that steering one group is taking place.

Recall *United States v. Real Estate One* in which potential Fair Housing Act violations were found from advertising in a strategically limited geographic area, or using particular editions of newspapers to reach a particular segment of the community, or advertising only in small newspapers targeted to specific religious, racial, or ethnic groups. (Alternatively, of course, a broker or agent could simply dispense with the use of models and avoid that problem entirely.)

On the other hand, certain terms that indicate intent not to discriminate are acceptable. For example, the Fair Housing Act permits statements that property is accessible to handicapped persons or is intended for persons over the age of 55.

Equal Housing Opportunity Poster

The Fair Housing Act requires businesses, such as real estate brokers and real estate lenders, to display the **Equal Housing Opportunity Poster** that depicts the equal housing logo. The poster is based on a form detailed in the regulations of the Department of Housing and Urban Development (HUD). A copy of the poster is available from HUD or from one of various commercial vendors.

U.S. Department of Housing and Urban Development

**EQUAL HOUSING
OPPORTUNITY**

We Do Business in Accordance With the Federal Fair Housing Law

(The Fair Housing Amendments Act of 1988)

It is Illegal to Discriminate Against Any Person Because of Race, Color, Religion, Sex, Handicap, Familial Status, or National Origin

---

- In the sale or rental of housing or residential lots

- In advertising the sale or rental of housing

- In the financing of housing

- In the provision of real estate brokerage services

- In the appraisal of housing

- Blockbusting is also illegal

Anyone who feels he or she has been discriminated against may file a complaint of housing discrimination:
    1-800-669-9777 (Toll Free)
    1-800-927-9275 (TDD)

**U.S. Department of Housing and
Urban Development
Assistant Secretary for Fair Housing and
Equal Opportunity
Washington, D.C. 20410**

Previous editions are obsolete

form HUD-928.1A(8-93)

Care should be taken to display the most recent version; failure to display the poster at all or to display the most recent version can be used as prima facie evidence of discrimination by someone alleging that a brokerage has violated the Fair Housing Act. Failure to display the Equal Housing Opportunity Poster can also be used in an anti-discrimination lawsuit to find that the defendant has waived the statute of limitations; that is, a lawsuit that might be dismissed if it is too old could nevertheless move forward if the poster was not placed as required.

The equal housing logo should also be used in any print or display advertising (e.g., on handbills or flyers) with the exception of classified advertising, which is normally covered by a given newspaper's own nondiscrimination banner before or after the housing listings in the newspaper.

Avoiding Risk

Although a broker or agent may avoid violating the law or committing discriminatory conduct, he or she may confront prospective clients or buyers who are not so conscientious. A client may instruct a broker or agent not to sell to persons of certain races or religions, or a buyer may ask questions that would lead the broker to violate the law merely by answering them. For example, a buyer may ask a broker about the racial composition of a given neighborhood, or be told that the buyer does not want to live near people belonging to a certain group.

Caution is important in such situations—if the person making such statements is a client or prospective client, the safest course may be to decline the representation or to withdraw from representing this person. The potential distractions, expense, and harm to reputation from a lawsuit is never worth the profit from a single sale. Alternatively, the broker can explain the requirements of the law and inform the client that if the professional relationship is to continue, the broker cannot engage in such conduct or even discuss the client's preferences. Similar caution also applies to the representation of buyers. If asked about the racial composition of a neighborhood or for similar information prohibited by law, the broker or agent should respond that the law prevents the licensee from answering the question.

Brokers and agents should also recognize that, because subjective intent to discriminate is difficult to prove, housing advocacy organizations and government agencies occasionally employ testers who may be persons of different racial or ethnic backgrounds inquiring with a brokerage about buying or renting property.

Example: Bernice, an agent, manages rental units for specific clients. Bernice harbors certain discriminatory beliefs even though she is aware of the fair housing laws. An applicant, who does not carry the same religious beliefs as Bernice, goes to her office one day and asks to

> fill out an application for an advertised rental unit. Bernice, aware of the applicant's religious background, tells him that the advertised unit expired. An hour later, an applicant from the same religious sect as Bernice shows up inquiring about the same unit. Bernice gives him the rental application and offers to show the unit.
>
> Some time thereafter, both Bernice and the owner of the apartment building receive a fair housing complaint. It turns out that the two applicants were testers working together and were able to compare their experiences in her real estate office. Her statement to the first applicant of the expired rental advertisement coupled with her willingness to show it to the second applicant is compelling evidence that Bernice intended to discriminate. She should have treated all applicants alike at all times, regardless of religion, race, ancestry, or other protected characteristics.
>
> The best way to avoid failing such a test, of course, is to treat all applicants alike at all times, regardless of their race, religion, ancestry, or other protected characteristics.

Complaint Procedures

The Fair Housing Act provides for a variety of remedies, both by the government and private individuals. A person who wants to bring a civil rights complaint based on housing discrimination must begin by filing an administrative complaint with the appropriate government agency.

Complaints regarding practices that violate fair housing laws are filed with the U.S. Dept. of Housing and Urban Development (HUD), or a person may file his or her own lawsuit in federal or state court.

The Fair Housing Act authorizes the Department of Justice to bring a lawsuit, if it believes a person or entity, or group of persons, is engaged in a pattern or practice of unlawful conduct, or a denial of rights granted to a group of persons under the Act raises an issue of public importance. A complaint must be filed with HUD within one year of an incident related to housing discrimination. There is a two-year limit for filing a federal civil court action.

If proof exists that discrimination occurred, the Fair Housing Act entitles the victim to receive compensation for damages. If the victim wins a federal civil court lawsuit, the law may also allow the victim to receive substantial compensation in the form of punitive damages for humiliation, pain, anger, embarrassment, or emotional distress.

Conciliation

An initial process known as **conciliation** is sometimes used to resolve disputes. This is an attempt to resolve the matter informally at the administrative level, with the accuser and the party accused of discrimination agreeing to one or more of a variety of remedies. These can include payment of money damages, attorney's fees, or some other form of equitable relief. Participation in this process is voluntary and used only if both parties elect to participate.

Civil Penalties

If the conciliation process is unsuccessful or the parties choose not to use it, the person who files the accusation may request that the Department of Justice (DOJ) investigate the allegations. The DOJ is empowered to impose fines of up to $10,000 for a first violation, up to $25,000 for a second offense within 5 years, and up to $50,000 for more than two violations within 7 years. Because these are penalties imposed by the DOJ itself, they are payable to the United States rather than the person alleging the harm. If the DOJ finds a "pattern and practice" of discrimination, it can also seek civil penalties of $50,000 for a first violation and $100,000 for each subsequent violation.

Private Lawsuit

Given the limited resources of the DOJ as compared to the thousands of civil rights complaints filed annually, most persons who believe they have been the victims of discrimination do not ask for a DOJ-sponsored investigation. Rather, they typically seek a **right to sue letter**, which bypasses the administrative process entirely and allows the person to pursue a remedy before an administrative law judge, in the state superior court, or the United States District Court. An individual can pursue federal civil rights violations in the state courts and violations of state law in federal courts if the violation includes at least one federal law.

In federal or state court, the person alleging discrimination has the burden of proving that the discrimination took place. If the judge or jury finds that the complaint has merit, they can award **actual damages** to the aggrieved person. They can also award **punitive damages** against the person accused of discrimination to punish that person and to make an example of him or her, although this requires a finding that the discrimination was deliberate. The court can also award attorney's fees.

Avoiding Risk

Attorney's fees are calculated based on what a court finds to be the reasonable rate in the community where the case was filed (which can be as much as $250 to $400 per hour in some urban areas). Therefore, the attorney's fees in civil rights cases can be many times the amount of actual damages awarded to the successful plaintiff, even if the plaintiff's recovery itself is relatively modest. The potential exposure to liability for attorney's fees often leads defendants who do not subjectively believe that they have committed discriminatory conduct to resolve the case early rather than risk a substantial award of attorney's fees.

Example: In City of Riverside v. Rivera (1986) 477 U.S. 561, 91 L.Ed.2d 466, 106 S.Ct. 2686 (1986) a large number of police officers broke up a party using what the trial court later found to be "unnecessary physical force." Later, eight individuals sued the city and were awarded a total of just over $33,000. The court then awarded their two attorneys $245,000 (approximately 8 times the total award to the plaintiffs and about 60 times what each of the individual plaintiffs, on average, recovered). The Supreme Court upheld this decision, concluding that in civil rights cases, attorney's fee awards do not have to be proportional to the amount recovered by the plaintiff—even though a private client presumably would have balked at paying an attorney almost $250,000 in order to recover $30,000.

Civil Rights Restoration Act (1988)

The **Civil Rights Restoration Act**, passed in 1988, broadened the reach of the law relating to discriminatory practices to include all organizations receiving federal dollars. In order to ensure equal rights and protection under the law, anti-discrimination legislation has undergone a number of revisions over time.

Americans with Disabilities Act (1990)

Congress passed the **Americans with Disabilities Act of 1990** (ADA) to provide a clear, enforceable, and comprehensive national mandate for the elimination of discrimination against individuals with disabilities. A **disability** is "any physical or mental impairment that substantially limits one or more of an individual's major life activities."

With respect to fair housing, however, the Fair Housing Act Amendments of 1988 had already added handicapped individuals as one of the protected classes. Consequently, a person who alleges discrimination on the basis of handicap with respect to the sale or rental of real property would probably rely on the Fair Housing Act and would not have needed the ADA.

It was designed so that the federal government would play a central role in enforcing these standards on behalf of individuals with disabilities. The Americans with Disabilities Act gives civil rights protections to individuals with disabilities similar to those provided to individuals based on race, color, sex, national origin, age, and religion. The definition of a disability under the ADA is quite broad.

Nevertheless, there are a number of other kinds of discrimination involving disabled persons that would be covered by the ADA but would not necessarily have been covered by the Fair Housing Act. The ADA protects individuals with disabilities by providing a guarantee of equal opportunity in public accommodations, commercial facilities, employment, transportation, state and local government services, and telecommunications. A **public accommodation** is a private entity that owns, operates, leases, or leases to, a place designed to provide products or services to the public. Although it appears to refer to property and facilities owned by a public entity (such as a city), a public accommodation actually includes any private entity that owns, operates, or leases a place open to the public if the operation of that place affects commerce. Most businesses that are open to the public meet this definition, and thus, a real estate broker's office would be a public accommodation under this definition.

Private clubs and religious organizations are exempt from the ADA's Title III requirements for public accommodations. The ADA does not cover the majority of residential private apartments and homes. However, if a place of public accommodation, such as a doctor's office or day care center, is located in a private residence, those portions of the residence used for that purpose are subject to the ADA's requirements.

Requirements of the Americans with Disabilities Act

The Americans with Disabilities Act requires that anyone who operates a public accommodation take a variety of steps, as long as they are **readily achievable**. The ADA and the regulations promulgated by the Department of Justice define "readily achievable" to mean that something is "easily accomplishable and able to be carried out without much difficulty or expense."

The ADA prohibits discrimination on the basis of disability in the full and equal enjoyment of goods, services, facilities, privileges, advantages, or accommodations of any place of public accommodation by any private entity that owns, leases or leases to, or operates a place of public accommodation. A public accommodation must make **reasonable modifications**—in other words, change its policies, practices, or procedures if they are necessary to afford persons with disabilities the enjoyment of goods, services, or accommodations provided by that business. The only exception is if the owner of the public accommodation (business) can demonstrate that making the modifications would fundamentally alter the nature of the goods, services, facilities or accommodations it provides if it makes the modifications.

Fortyune v. American Multi-Cinema, Inc.

In *Fortyune* v. *American Multi-Cinema, Inc.*, 364 F.3d 1075 (9th Cir. 2004), a quadriplegic movie patron and his wife attempted to view the defendant's sold-out screening of a film. They were unable to do so when a man and his son refused to vacate the wheelchair companion seats they occupied. The theater's manager informed the Fortyunes that, under company policy concerning the use of wheelchair companion seats at sold-out screenings, he could not require the man and his son to change seats.

The Fortyunes sued, arguing that the theater chain's policy violated the ADA. The trial court issued a court order directing the theater chain to modify its policies regarding companion seating, and the Ninth Circuit affirmed. The court order directed that wheelchair-bound patrons should receive priority in the use of companion seats.

Because there were only four such seats in the theater, patrons in wheelchairs had limited opportunities for alternative seating in a full theater. The court order directed the company to ensure that the companion seat was made available to the wheelchair-bound patron and his or her companion if they arrived at least 10 minutes prior to show time.

When a broker is involved in the leasing or sale of commercial real property, knowledge of ADA standards is important. If an existing commercial building does not satisfy ADA requirements, needed alterations to accommodate the client's use of the building may be a consideration of the purchase or lease. The broker or salesperson should counsel the buyer to seek bids from contractors to determine ADA costs associated with any needed remodel or alteration.

Possible violations of ADA may be filed with the United States Department of Justice (DOJ).
The DOJ has authorization to bring a lawsuit when there is a pattern or practice of discrimination. The website is www.usdoj.gov.

STATE CIVIL RIGHTS LAWS

The federal government faces some limits in the discriminatory conduct it can regulate because its powers are constrained by specific grants of power in the Constitution. Thus, while the 13th Amendment of the Constitution allows Congress to pass laws outlawing private acts of racial discrimination, the **state action requirement** of the 14th Amendment limits the power of Congress to reach other kinds of private discriminatory conduct.

The state governments, however, have no such limitations. Like each of the other states, California has the **police power**, which is the power of the state to enact laws, within constitutional limits, to promote the order, safety, health, morals, and general welfare of the society. Over the years, California has used the police power to pass numerous statutes prohibiting both public and private discrimination in the purchase and sale of real property, as well as in offering property for rental housing.

The State of California has enacted laws directly related to the practice of real estate. State laws are often fashioned after federal law such as the Fair Housing Act. California includes other protected classes to complement the protections of the federal law.

Protected Class	Federal Fair Housing Protections	California Fair Housing Protections
Race	X	X
Color	X	X
National Origin	X	X
Religion	X	X
Sex	X	X
Disability	X	X
Familial Status	X	X
Age		X
Ancestry		X
Genetic Information		X
Marital Status		X
Medical Condition		X
Sexual Orientation		X
Source of Income		X

Fair Employment and Housing Act

California's **Fair Employment and Housing Act (FEHA)** is intended to prevent discrimination in the sale, rental, or financing of practically all types of housing. It is found at Government Code §12900 et seq. and prohibits discrimination on a wide variety of bases, including some added only in recent years.

FEHA is derived from an earlier law that dealt specifically with housing discrimination known as the **Rumford Act**. California voters attempted to overturn this law in 1964 with an amendment to the California Constitution that would have allowed anyone to decline the sale, lease, or rental of property to anyone whom the seller or lessor chose. Three years later, in the landmark case of *Reitman v. Mulkey*, the U.S. Supreme Court invalidated this provision, finding that the amendment was not a neutral repeal of an anti-discrimination law, but consciously intended to abet or encourage private racism. The Rumford Act was later expanded into FEHA, covering both housing and employment discrimination.

Major Provisions

FEHA, insofar as it applies to housing discrimination, is broader than the federal law because it applies to certain kinds of discrimination that are not covered by federal law.

Primary Provisions of the Fair Employment and Housing Act

- Provides protection from harassment or discrimination in housing based on race, color, religion, sex, national origin, disability, familial status, age, ancestry, marital status, sexual orientation, medical condition, or source of income

- Exemption: Housing that meets the legal definition of senior housing or housing for older persons (62 years or older)

- Prohibits discrimination and harassment in all aspects of housing including sales, rentals, evictions, terms and conditions, mortgage loans, insurance, land use, and zoning

- Requires housing providers to make reasonable accommodations in rules and practices to permit persons with disabilities to use and enjoy a dwelling. In addition, FEHA allows persons with disabilities to make reasonable modifications of the premises.

- Prohibits retaliation against any person who filed a complaint with the department, participated in a department investigation, or opposed any activity prohibited by the act

In addition to the discriminatory characteristics outlined in the federal law, the California law also protects its citizens against discrimination based on sexual orientation, source of income, and medical condition. Thus, a person whose discrimination is based on one of these characteristics, but not under the federal law, would sue in the state forum rather than the federal forum.

Smith v. Fair Employment & Housing Commission

In *Smith v. Fair Employment & Housing Commission*, Evelyn Smith owned four rental units (two duplexes) in Chico, California. Ms. Smith belonged to a Christian church and believed that sex outside of marriage is sinful. This included a belief that it was a sin for her to rent to unmarried people living together.

An unmarried couple found one of her units attractive and made a deposit to rent it. However, when Ms. Smith learned that they were not married, she told them of her religious objections to their unmarried cohabitation and sent their deposit back. They filed a complaint with the Fair Employment and Housing Commission.

> *Smith v. Fair Employment & Housing Commission* (continued)
>
> The Commission ruled in their favor, but a lower court found that the law could not be enforced against Ms. Smith because of her honestly held religious beliefs.
>
> However, the California Supreme Court reversed the decision. It held that discrimination based on marital status violated FEHA. FEHA prohibits a landlord from asking prospective tenants whether they are married and from refusing to rent to them because they are not. The court accepted that Ms. Smith's religious beliefs were genuine, but concluded that the law did not allow her to discriminate. It stated that if she did not want to comply with anti-discrimination laws that conflicted with her religious beliefs, she could sell the rental units and invest her capital elsewhere.

Unruh Civil Rights Act

The **Unruh Civil Rights Act** was named after its primary author, former California Speaker of the Assembly Jess Unruh. It is a comprehensive anti-discrimination law covering a variety of businesses, including the business of real estate. The Act is found at California Civil Code §§51 et seq. Section 51 now incorporates any violation of the Americans with Disabilities Act as a violation of the Unruh Act as well.

The Unruh Act requires that all business establishments provide equal accommodations to the seven protected classes in the Federal Fair Housing Act as well as age, ancestry, sexual orientation, and medical condition. Protections are not limited to these classes and can extend to other personal characteristics that are similar in nature.

The Unruh Act not only requires that all business establishments provide equal accommodations to persons regardless of race, color, sex, ancestry, etc., but it has several provisions dealing specifically with housing.

Important Provisions in the Unruh Act

§ 51   This is the primary provision of the law stating that business establishments cannot discriminate based on various categories set forth therein

§ 51.2   Business establishments cannot discriminate in the sale or rental of housing based upon age, with the exception of senior housing. It includes an exception for seniors-only housing (62 or older), and acknowledges that its provisions are intended to clarify the California Supreme Court's decision in *Marina Point, Ltd. v. Wolfson* (1982) 30 Cal.3d 72 and *O'Connor v. Village Green Owners Association* (1983) 33 Cal.3d 790. (In *Marina Point*, the Supreme Court found that an apartment owner's policy of excluding families with children was invalid under the Act, even though discrimination against families with children is not mentioned specifically in the Act. In *O'Connor*, the court likewise invalidated a homeowners' association's declaration of conditions, covenants, and restrictions (CC&Rs) as also being in violation of the Act.)

§ 51.8   Prohibits a franchisor from discrimination in the granting of franchises. In effect, it prohibits the equivalent of redlining in the granting of franchises just as the law prohibits redlining in other areas of the real estate business.

§ 52   Allows a person injured by a violation of the Unruh Act to seek damages up to three times the actual damages or a maximum of $4,000 per violation, as well as attorney's fees. It also provides for an award of civil penalties of up to $25,000 for cases brought by various public attorneys' offices and allows injunctive relief to prevent future occurrences.

§ 53   Outlaws restrictive racial covenants and other covenants that attempt to bar the transfer of real property based on anything that would constitute discrimination under §51.

Auburn Woods v. Fair Employment & Housing Commission

In *Auburn Woods v. Fair Employment & Housing Commission* (2004) 121 Cal.App.4th 1578, a condominium association had a rule prohibiting residents from keeping a dog as a pet (even though it allowed birds and cats). A couple, Mr. and Mrs. Elebiaris, nevertheless kept a dog, which they claimed helped them because they suffered from depression, and supported this claim with notes from their treating physicians.

The Elebiarises initially got rid of their dog when threatened with a fine by the association. The association refused to allow them to take the dog back. They said that because it was not a service animal (such as a seeing-eye dog), there was no legal basis for the Elebiarises to keep it. The couple then filed a complaint with the State, alleging that the refusal to allow them to keep the dog, even though it improved their mental health, violated the law.

> *Auburn Woods v. Fair Employment & Housing Commission (continued)*
>
> The State FEHC found in the couple's favor, and the association sued. The trial court ruled in favor of the association, but the court of appeal reinstated the FEHC's decision, finding that the state administrative body had sufficient medical evidence to support its conclusion that the failure to accommodate Mr. and Mrs. Elebiaris was a violation of state law. It upheld the State's award of $12,500, plus attorney's fees, to the couple.

California Civil Code (Section 54-55.1)

This section of the Civil Code prohibits discrimination in the rental, leasing, or sale of housing accommodations to the visually impaired, deaf, or otherwise physically disabled. It also precludes restrictions on seeing-eye dogs and signal dogs from "No Pet" clauses in lease agreements.

Commissioner's Regulations

The California Real Estate Commissioner has made it very clear that a person's real estate license will be restricted, suspended, or revoked for any violation of the fair housing laws. The Commissioner regulates all aspects of the real estate transaction from prospecting for listings through the closing of the transaction. In fact, every conceivable activity is regulated.

Activities Prohibited by Regulation 2780

- Refusing to list and show properties to selected people
- Processing some applications more slowly than others
- Stating to some people that property is not available when it is
- Using special codes on applications
- Actively discouraging other licensees from working with minorities
- Charging more for the cleaning or security deposit to some applicants
- Assisting other licensees to discriminate

Regulation 2781 Prohibits Blockbusting

Licensees are prohibited from creating fear, alarm, or transmitting written or oral warnings regarding the present or prospective entry of one or more persons of another race, color, sex, religion, ancestry, marital status, or national origin into an area or neighborhood.

SUMMARY

While home ownership has become a reality for many Americans over the last 140 years, the process has not always been fair to everyone. Over the years, laws have been created to make the housing market equitable to level the playing field for all Americans. Many of these laws have been aimed at discriminatory practices in the sale, financing, and rental of homes. Both the federal and state governments have taken action to prohibit discriminatory housing practices.

Real estate licensees must be aware of and practice under the guidelines of fair housing laws on a regular basis. The earliest fair housing law was the Civil Rights Act of 1866, which prohibited discrimination based on race. Almost one hundred years later, the Civil Rights Act of 1968 provided anti-discriminatory protection in education, housing, and employment for five protected classes of people based on race, color, religion, sex, or national origin. The Fair Housing Amendments Act of 1988 added disability and familial status to bring the total to seven protected classes.

The Fair Housing Act prohibited certain practices such as redlining, blockbusting, and steering. In addition, it banned advertising that contained civil rights violations and required real estate businesses to display the Equal Housing Opportunity Poster. Complaints for violation of fair housing laws are filed with the U.S. Dept. of Housing and Urban Development (HUD), or a person may file his or her own lawsuit in federal or state court.

Fair housing laws were further supplemented with the Americans with Disabilities Act of 1990, which provided a clear, enforceable, and comprehensive national mandate for the elimination of discrimination against individuals with disabilities.

The State of California has enacted laws directly related to the practice of real estate. State laws are often fashioned after federal law such as the Fair Housing Act. Anti-discrimination laws in California include the Fair Employment and Housing Act (FEHA), the Unruh Civil Rights Act, the California Civil Code, and Commissioner's Regulations.

UNIT 10 REVIEW

Matching Exercise

Instructions: Write the letter of the matching term on the blank line before its definition. Answers are in Appendix A.

Terms

A. Americans with Disabilities Act

B. Civil Rights Act of 1866

C. Civil Rights Act of 1968

D. Commerce Clause

E. Equal Housing Opportunity Poster

F. Fair Employment and Housing Act

G. Fair Housing Act

H. familial status

I. Fourteenth Amendment

J. *Jones v. Mayer*

K. police power

L. protected class

M. public accommodation

N. reasonable accommodation

O. redlining

P. Regulation 2780

Q. restrictive covenant

R. steering

S. Thirteenth Amendment

T. Unruh Civil Rights Act

Definitions

1. _____ First federal law outlawing discrimination on the basis of race

2. _____ Part of the Constitution that outlawed slavery and allows Congress to pass laws prohibiting private acts of race discrimination

3. _____ Clauses in deeds that prohibited the sale of real property to members of certain races or religious groups

4. _____ Part of the Constitution that includes the Due Process Clause and the Equal Protection Clause

5. _____ Provision of the Constitution giving Congress the authority to regulate commerce among the several states

6. _____ Court case that upheld the 1866 Civil Rights Act

7. _____ Act that expanded protected classes to include not only race, but also color, religion, sex, and national origin

8. _____   Group that is guarded from discrimination under federal or state law

9. _____   Title VIII of the Civil Rights Act of 1968 and the Fair Housing Amendments Act of 1988, taken together

10. _____   Relationship of people in a family

11. _____   Practice of not making loans for property in certain neighborhoods, or to members of certain minority groups

12. _____   Practice of directing members of certain racial or ethnic groups to certain neighborhoods

13. _____   Document that displays the equal housing logo

14. _____   Federal law requiring that persons with handicaps be given equal access to goods and services

15. _____   Any private entity that owns, operates, or leases a place open to the public if the operation of that place affects commerce

16. _____   Change in a business' policies, practices, or procedures if necessary to afford persons with disabilities the enjoyment of goods, services, or accommodations

17. _____   California law that prohibits discrimination by employers and in real estate sales and rentals

18. _____   California Legislature's authority to pass any law that it believes is necessary to protect its citizens' health, safety, welfare, or morals

19. _____   California law providing that all persons in California are free and equal and entitled to the full and equal accommodations by all business establishments

20. _____   Commissioner's Regulation prohibiting licensees to violate fair housing laws

Multiple Choice Questions

Instructions: Circle your response and go to Appendix A to read the complete explanation for each question.

1. Arthur, who is African-American, wants to buy a house in a particular neighborhood in a California city. During the title search, a restrictive covenant in a deed recorded in the 1920s states that no person other than a member of the Caucasian race can buy property in the neighborhood where the house he wants to buy is located. What, if anything, can Arthur do about it?
    a. Arthur can safely ignore it and proceed with the purchase because under both federal and state law, the clause would be unenforceable.
    b. Arthur must bring a lawsuit to quiet the title to the deed, and hope that a judge will agree that the racial clause cannot be enforced.
    c. Arthur will be unable to buy the property because of the clause in the deed.
    d. Arthur will have to pay the seller additional compensation to have the clause in the deed waived, if the seller elects to do so.

2. Which court case upheld the 1866 Civil Rights Act and the 13th Amendment to the U.S. Constitution?
    a. *Easton v. Strassburger*
    b. *Jones v. Mayer*
    c. *Ragin v. New York Times*
    d. *Shelley v. Kraemer*

3. As a federal law, the 1866 Civil Rights Act was largely ignored until another law provided anti-discriminatory protection in education, housing, and employment. This law covers the financing, leasing, or selling of residential property. What is this federal law?
    a. Title VI of the Civil Rights Act of 1966
    b. 13th Act to the U.S. Constitution
    c. Title VIII of the Civil Rights Act of 1968
    d. Fair Housing Amendments Act of 1988

4. Bill, who is Hispanic, wants to buy a parcel of commercial land to open a restaurant in the city where he lives. He speaks to the seller on the telephone and the seller seems interested. When he and the seller meet on the premises, though, the seller reacts with surprise when he meets Bill, and makes a comment that he "didn't realize" Bill was Hispanic, then changes the subject. The next day, he calls Bill to tell him that he has decided he does not want to sell him the property. Can Bill bring a complaint under the federal Fair Housing Act?

   a. No, because the seller will probably deny that he made the comment, and it is Bill's word against his.

   b. Yes, because the seller made a comment about Bill's ethnic background and then told him he was not going to sell the next day.

   c. Yes, because the Fair Housing Act prohibits discrimination on the basis of national origin.

   d. No, because the Fair Housing Act does not apply to sales of commercial property.

5. Assume that in the previous question, Bill were African-American and the seller refused to sell to him because of his race. Is there any federal law under which Bill would be able to bring a lawsuit alleging that he was the victim of unlawful discrimination?

   a. Yes, under the Federal Trade Commission Act.

   b. Yes, under the Civil Rights Act of 1866.

   c. Yes, under the Civil Rights Act of 1968.

   d. No, because the property in question was commercial.

6. The First Avenue Church owns a small apartment building a few blocks from its church building. It has a policy that limits the lease of apartments in the building to members of the same First Avenue Church and affiliated churches. Assuming that someone is a member of the church, however, it places no other restrictions on to whom it will rent. What is the status of the Church's policy under the federal Fair Housing Act?

   a. The Church's policy violates the Fair Housing Act because it discriminates on the basis of religion.

   b. The Church's policy does not violate the Fair Housing Act because the Church does not discriminate on any other basis.

   c. The Church's policy would not violate the Fair Housing Act even if the Church discriminated on the basis of race, sex, color, and so forth.

   d. The Church's policy must sell its property and invest the proceeds elsewhere.

7. Paul listed a property located in an area where the ethnic makeup is changing from one racial group to another. Paul wants to emphasize this change by adding the word, "integrated", into the property listing for an advertisement. Is this a violation of the Fair Housing Act?

    a. No, as long as Paul is telling the truth.

    b. No, since Paul uses the proper word to describe the changing area.

    c. Yes, because this is an example of commingling.

    d. Yes, because the term can imply potential discrimination.

8. The Fair Employment and Housing Act would prohibit a property owner from refusing to rent to an otherwise eligible tenant based on:

    a. that the person's income comes from public assistance.

    b. low income.

    c. a poor credit history.

    d. past tenancies that resulted in evictions through court process.

9. A property owner has sincerely held religious beliefs. She does not want to rent to an unmarried couple who want to live together in her apartment building. What must she do in order to avoid violating California's fair housing laws?

    a. Obtain a certificate from her minister attesting to the sincerity of her faith that she can present to the fair housing authorities.

    b. Only allow persons who are members of her local church to rent in her building.

    c. Prominently advertise this restriction in all advertisements for this rental property.

    d. Allow unmarried couples to cohabit in her building or sell the property and invest her money elsewhere.

10. Which rule would not violate the Fair Employment and Housing Act, the Unruh Act, or the Fair Housing Act? A rule prohibiting occupancy in a particular housing development by persons under the age of:

    a. 10.

    b. 18.

    c. 45.

    d. 62.

Consumer Protection Laws

Unit 11

INTRODUCTION

There is a variety of federal and state laws, such as antitrust laws, prospecting laws, and lending laws that are intended to protect consumers in commercial transactions. Because the real estate industry is a commercial enterprise, it is subject to the provisions of the consumer protection laws.

A broker's professionalism and his or her handling ethical and legal situations are critical in maintaining a sound real estate business. Fortunately, by following the various consumer protection laws, licensees can limit their risk to groundless, protracted lawsuits. It is important to know and follow the various consumer protection laws that are relevant to the real estate industry. This unit reviews the most significant consumer protection legislation that applies to the business of real estate.

Learning Objectives

After completing this unit, you should be able to:

11A specify actions prohibited by federal and state antitrust laws.

11B recognize laws that regulate prospecting.

11C recall protections under the Equal Credit Opportunity Act.

11D identify the main provisions of the Truth in Lending Act.

11E name the main features of RESPA.

ANTITRUST AND UNFAIR COMPETITION LAWS

Like most real estate services, the real estate brokerage industry contains a certain level of competitiveness. Certain firms will offer a variety of services at certain prices in an effort to outlast their competition. Some go to extremes when competing for business, which calls for regulatory measures by the federal and state governments.

Federal and state antitrust laws prohibit unwarranted restraints on free and open competition. Antitrust violations are not just ways of doing business–they are serious crimes for which the penalties are severe. Licensees who violate the antitrust laws are committing a felony for which they could go to prison. Additionally, licensees found guilty of violating the antitrust laws are liable to their victims for three times the amount of the injury.

Real estate is a competitive industry, which can foster illegal acts by licensees who are vying for business and seeking a competitive advantage. As a result, federal and state laws exist to uphold fair competition among licensees.

Actions Prohibited by Federal & State Antitrust Laws

Federal and state antitrust laws are created to protect and preserve business competition. The laws prohibit businesses from forming a monopoly and restrict the way businesses interact with their competitors and customers. These laws cover many specific actions including horizontal and vertical arrangements.

Monopolies

A **monopoly** exists when a person or group has exclusive control over a product or service within a given region. It is illegal for businesses to conspire with others to drive its competitors out of business in order to create a monopoly.

Sometimes a natural monopoly occurs. A **natural monopoly** results from circumstances over which the business has no control, e.g. the product or service is so specialized that only one provider is needed to meet the demand. Natural monopolies are not illegal. A **legal monopoly** occurs when the government gives the exclusive control over a specified commercial activity to a single party, e.g. providing utility service.

Horizontal and Vertical Arrangements

Business agreements between competitors are called **horizontal arrangements**. According to antitrust law, some horizontal arrangements conflict with antitrust laws. All business agreements for the intentional purpose of restraining trade or gaining a monopoly in the market are illegal. These agreements could include price fixing, boycotting, dividing the market, and tying.

Price Fixing

Price fixing is the collaboration or agreement of one or more persons to set a fixed price for goods or services, thereby removing the ability of a free market to influence prices. A real estate company is not allowed to collaborate with another real estate company to set a standard commission to be charged. The agreement does not need to be in writing–even an informal understanding concerning commission rates between competing brokers is illegal. This is considered **horizontal price fixing**, which is the agreement between competitors to set their prices at the same amount or within the same range.

Group Boycotting

Group boycotting, also called a collective refusal to deal, is the deliberate exclusion of a particular business or group from the benefits of competition and inclusion. An example of boycotting in real estate would be two brokers who decide to collaborate and refuse to show any of the properties listed by another broker, in an effort to force the broker out of business. Unlike a boycott by consumers of a particular business, a group boycott is unlawful because it has the effect of restraining freedom of trade.

Occasionally, a joint venture is in violation of antitrust laws. For example, there may be an antitrust violation if several competitive brokerage firms form a joint venture and exclude others—particularly if there are more businesses included in the joint venture than those that are excluded.

Market Division

Market division (allocation of customers) occurs when two or more competing businesses agree to divide the market among themselves. This is an illegal arrangement because it limits the ability of the public to negotiate for the best price and services.

Usually, the market division is geographic. The businesses agree not to enter into the geographic area assigned to their competitors to sell their products or services. In real estate, this could occur if two brokers agree that one will only take business from one section of town and the other will only take business from another section of town. The market can be divided by product. In real estate, this could occur if one broker agrees 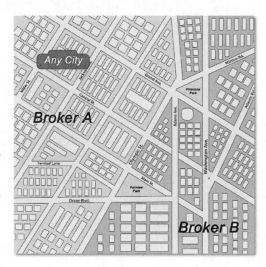 to specialize only in townhouses and condominiums and the other broker only handles the single-family residences.

Tying

Tying is the illegal action of requiring buyers to purchase one product or service (tied product or service) in order to obtain another product or service (tying product or service). This practice is more common in consumer products. For example, a consumer may purchase a breadbox that is guaranteed to keep bread fresh for two weeks at a reduced rate provided a specific loaf of bread is purchased. An example of tying in real estate would be for a mortgage broker to require a buyer to use an affiliated insurance company in order for the buyer to obtain a loan with favorable interest rate and terms.

Federal Antitrust Laws

The U.S. Congress passed the **Sherman Antitrust Act** of 1890. The Sherman Antitrust Act is the basic federal antitrust statute. The act prohibits collaboration between companies and individuals, when the collaboration has the affect of restraining trade. For many years, the federal authorities did not enforce the act due to various Supreme Court rulings. President Theodore

Roosevelt invoked the Sherman Antitrust Act in his trust-busting campaigns, and in 1904, the Supreme Court upheld the government's suit dissolving the Northern Securities Company.

In 1914, the **Clayton Antitrust Act** was enacted to supplement the Sherman Antitrust Act. This law specifically prohibits leases, sales, contracts for sale, or other conditions, agreements, or understandings that have the effect of substantially lessening competition or creating a monopoly in a line of commerce. Price fixing, price discrimination, tying, and exclusive dealing are covered by this law. In 1936, Congress passed the **Robinson-Patman Act** to amend the Clayton Act and strengthen prohibitions on price discrimination.

The federal antitrust acts are regulated and enforced by the Department of Justice (DOJ) and the Federal Trade Commission (FTC).

Federal Trade Commission Act

The **Federal Trade Commission Act** (FTC Act), found at 15 U.S.C. § 41 et seq., indirectly provides various protections to consumers. The primary goal of this statute is to protect the public from anti-competitive acts. Unlike many of the other statutes discussed in this unit, the FTC Act is intended to give power to the Commission itself to protect consumers, not to allow consumers to bring lawsuits on their own behalf. Thus, only the FTC itself can bring suit, in state or federal court, to obtain compensation from the defendant on behalf of all consumers or injunctive relief, for the unfair business practice under consideration, the deceptive advertisement, or the violation of the privacy rule.

Unfair Business Practices. The FTC Act prohibits unfair business practices. The law provides a three-part test to determine if something constitutes an unfair business practice.

> **Three Tests of Unfair Business Practices**
> 1. The practice causes a substantial consumer injury.
> 2. The harm of the injury outweighs a countervailing benefit.
> 3. The consumer could not reasonably avoid the injury.

In addition, an unfair business practice may be established if the FTC finds that the practice violates public policy, even if it does not meet the three tests.

Advertising. The Act regulates advertisements that contain significant misrepresentations likely to mislead a **reasonable consumer.** Such advertisements are considered deceptive and hence, actionable.

Privacy Rule. The FTC enacted the **FTC Privacy Rule,** which safeguards the privacy of an individual's personal information by mandating companies to provide a disclosure to consumers prior to passing personal information to unaffiliated third parties. Part of a property manager's duties is to screen prospective tenants and check their rental history for qualification purposes. A property management firm may ask another firm to provide this and other personal information in order to determine whether the prospect will make a worthy tenant. The property manager disseminating the information must obtain a written statement from the other property manager that the personal information requested will not fall in the hands of unaffiliated third parties. These parties can include credit card companies and other financial institutions in the business of extending credit. If the property manager reveals the personal information to these unaffiliated third parties, written permission from the tenant is necessary.

State Laws

California's antitrust and unfair competition laws include the Cartwright Act, Unfair Practices Act, and the Unfair Competition Act. The California Attorney General prosecutes antitrust and unfair trade law violations in California.

Cartwright Act

California's **Cartwright Act,** found in the Business and Professions Code, Sections 16720-16728, is the state's general antitrust law. The Cartwright Act prohibits monopolies, price fixing, and group boycotting. In addition, the Cartwright Act prohibits illegal tying. The prohibition against tying in the Cartwright Act applies to services as well as products.

Unfair Competition Law

In 1933, the California Legislature enacted the **Unfair Competition Law** (UCL), found in the Business and Professions Code Sections 17200 through 17209. California courts have used various names to identify the UCL including the Unfair Business Practices Act, the Unfair Practices Act, and the Unfair Competition Act. However, the California Supreme Court has determined to use the Unfair Competition Law and most recent cases follow that decision.

The UCL is California's most frequently used consumer protection statute. It is similar to the Federal Trade Commission Act discussed above, though it has some important differences. Section 17200 of the UCL prohibits business practices that are "unlawful," "unfair," and "fraudulent" while also prohibiting "unfair, deceptive, untrue, or misleading advertising." Its sister statute, §17500, prohibits false and misleading advertising. California's UCL allows government and private parties to initiate and prosecute actions. California's UCL is unique because it permits plaintiffs to borrow other codes, statutes, regulations, and ordinances to create liability.

Perhaps the most important difference between the UCL and the FTC Act is that, unlike the FTC Act, the UCL has a provision allowing "private attorney general" enforcement against a business that has committed a business practice in violation of one of its provisions. During the 1990s, this led to a rash of lawsuits—or threats of lawsuits—by law firms that relied on the "citizen suit" provisions, as well as the UCL's lax standard for "standing" to bring a suit.

As it was written at that time, a person initiating a lawsuit under the UCL was not required to show that he or she had suffered injury or lost money or property due to the allegedly unfair business practice. Some attorneys, relying on state databases of businesses that were already under investigation for some unlawful practice, would send letters to each business in the database and threaten to bring a citizen lawsuit against the business unless it "settled" for a payment of attorney's fees in the range of several thousand dollars.

As a result of these perceived abuses of the UCL, a statewide initiative measure adopted in 2004 limited the reach of the UCL. As amended, a suit can be brought under the UCL only by public attorneys, such as a district attorney or the Attorney General, or by a citizen who alleges that he or she lost money or property, or was injured, as a result of the unfair business practice. Such a lawsuit initiated on behalf of someone other than a named plaintiff in the lawsuit must be brought as a class action. Civil penalties, which also were available under the "citizen suit" provisions of the former law, now can only be brought by public attorney's offices. The Attorney General vigorously enforces the antitrust laws and acts upon any information indicating antitrust violations that affect the California public. Such actions can include formal or informal investigation and when necessary, a court action.

PROSPECTING LAWS

As with any business, success in real estate depends upon effective prospecting for new clients. **Prospecting** is the process of identifying potential customers. The majority of sales associates prospect by cold calling or sending text through mailings, faxes, or emails.

Anytime real estate solicitation involves the use of the telephone, cell phone, fax, or email, licensees must comply with applicable federal and state Do Not Call, Do Not Fax, and anti-spam laws. These laws were passed to give consumers an opportunity to limit the amount of telemarketing calls and spam emails received. Anytime real estate solicitation involves the use of the telephone, cell phone, fax, or email, the sales associate must comply with any Do Not Call, Do Not Fax, and CAN-SPAM laws.

Do Not Call Laws

In 1991, Congress passed the **Telephone Consumer Protection Act** (TCPA). In 2003, the FCC established, together with the Federal Trade Commission (FTC), a national Do Not Call Registry. This **registry** is nationwide in scope, applies to all telemarketers (with the exception of certain non-profit organizations), and covers both interstate and intrastate telemarketing calls. Commercial telemarketers are not allowed to call you if your number is on the registry, subject to certain exceptions. Today there are some 150 million numbers on that list.

All real estate licensees are subject to the legislation. If a telephone number is on the national Do Not Call Registry (DNC) list, you may not make an unsolicited telephone call to that number. The fines for violations range from $500 up to $11,000.

Do Not Call Rules

Do Not Call rules apply to calls containing a commercial solicitation (most cold calls). The rules do not apply to calls made if an established business relationship already exists. With an **established business relationship**, the caller had a transaction with the receiver within the last 18 months; or the customer has made an inquiry with the caller's firm in the last 3 months. Because you can call individuals who have given you permission, use any opportunity to secure that permission—for example, when conducting open houses, presenting agency disclosures and securing listing agreements.

Generally, to make a cold call, the real estate licensee must scrub the number against the national Do Not Call list and the real estate company's internal Do Not Call list. If the number does not appear on either list, the licensee may call.

Do Not Call Rules

- Real estate licensees may make calls between 8:00 a.m. and 9:00 p.m.

- Licensees must identify themselves before making the solicitation, must identify that the call is a solicitation, and disclose all material information related to the solicited service.

- Licensees may not use caller ID blocking.

- Telemarketers must scrub their contact lists against the national Do Not Call registry every month.

Company Do Not Call Procedures

If a company's marketing plan includes telemarketing, the company will have to establish a profile with the DNC Registry and obtain the official Do Not Call list. There is an annual fee based on the number of area codes requested although the first five area codes are free. It is against FCC rules to sell the list or share the cost with other companies.

Any company making telephone solicitations must have a procedure in place to maintain a list of persons requesting not to receive telemarketing calls. Potential contacts in a database will have to be scrubbed against the official list every 30 days to accommodate the request of any contacts that wish to be removed from the list. These requests must be maintained for five years.

A consumer's Do Not Call request terminates the established business relationship for purposes of telemarketing calls even if the consumer continues to do business with the seller.

Company Do Not Call Procedures

- A written policy for maintaining a Do Not Call list must be available upon demand.

- Personnel involved in any aspect of telemarketing must be trained on the existence and use of the Do Not Call list.

- Requests by called parties not to be called must be recorded at the time of the request and available upon demand for disclosure. Requests must be honored for five years from the time the request is made.

- Anyone making a call for telemarketing purposes must identify the name of the caller, the name of the person/ entity on whose behalf the call is being made, and the toll-free telephone number or address at which the person/entity may be contacted.

It is also important to note that some states continue to maintain their own Do Not Call lists, which are not integrated into the federal list. In those states, if you make telephone solicitations, you will have to consult both the state and federal lists. However, here is the infamous catch-22. The FCC action preempts state law that is less restrictive. Although many states require an exemption for real estate licensees, that law is considered less restrictive than the federal law and is preempted by the federal law and real estate professionals are prohibited from making intrastate calls to persons on the federal list.

Do Not Fax Laws

In addition, the Telephone Consumer Protection Act of 1991 (TCPA) created the rules and regulations regarding unsolicited faxes. The TCPA prohibits the sending of faxes containing unsolicited advertisements. **Unsolicited advertisements** are defined as any material advertising the commercial availability or quality of any property, goods, or services that is transmitted to any person without that person's prior express invitation or permission. The penalties for violating the TCPA are $500 per fax with treble damages for willful violations.

Summary of the TCPA Do Not Fax Rules

- Sender must have an established business relationship with the recipient or written consent from the recipient prior to sending unsolicited advertising faxes.

- Sender must have voluntarily received recipient's fax number.

- Sender must provide the recipient with the right to opt-out of receiving future unsolicited advertising faxes. Opt-out procedures should be clear and conspicuous on the fax.

- Sender must honor opt-outs received from recipients within 30 days of receipt.

Bulk faxing has been largely eclipsed by email but the rules are still in place and enforceable.

Anti-SPAM Laws

The **CAN-SPAM Act** of 2003 (Controlling the Assault of Non-Solicited Pornography and Marketing Act) establishes requirements for those who send commercial email. It also gives consumers the right to ask emailers to stop sending them emails. A **commercial email message** is "any electronic mail message with the  primary purpose of which is the commercial advertisement or promotion of a commercial product or service." Emails sent as part of an ongoing commercial transaction, called **transactional email messages**, are excluded from the Act.

Types of Transactional Email Messages

- Facilitating or confirming an existing commercial transaction

- Giving notice about product updates or upgrades

- Providing notice about certain changes in a subscription, membership, account, or loan

- Providing warranty information, product recall information, or safety or security information with respect to a commercial product or service used or purchased by the recipient

- Providing information directly related to an employment relationship in which the recipient is currently involved

An unsolicited email message sent by a real estate agent to people on a mailing list offering that agent's services is a commercial email message. However, an email sent to a client concerning an existing listing or sales transaction is a transactional email message and is exempt from the rules.

Items Required in a Commercial Email Message
- A legitimate return email and a physical postal address
- A clear and conspicuous notice of the recipient's opportunity to opt-out or decline to receive any future messages
- Opt out mechanism active for at least 30 days after the transmission of the message
- Clear and conspicuous notice that the message is an advertisement or solicitation

The Act does not apply to purely informational messages, such as a newsletter without advertisements. It also does not apply to an email to a client or customer in an ongoing transaction.

FAIR LENDING LAWS

Financing is a huge business. Annually, lenders extend billions of dollars in credit to people to finance consumer products and to purchase or refinance real estate. Therefore, it is very important to understand laws pertaining to consumer credit and finance in order to be in compliance and avoid lawsuits.

Since federal, state, and local governments have passed laws that require fair and equal treatment of all consumers, more people are able to buy their own homes now than at any time in history. These federal laws are organized into three categories: credit protection, fair lending, and settlement procedures.

Credit Protection

Real estate finance is based on credit so it makes sense that consumers must have certain protections and guarantees. Good credit is a valuable intangible asset. Since 1968, many laws have been written to reduce the problems and confusion and to protect consumer credit.

Equal Credit Opportunity Act

The **Equal Credit Opportunity Act** (ECOA), found at 15 U.S.C. 1691 et seq., ensures that all consumers are given an equal chance to obtain credit. The law protects borrowers when they deal with any creditor who regularly extends credit, including banks, small loan and finance companies, retail and department stores, credit card companies, and credit unions. The law covers anyone involved in granting credit, such as mortgage brokers who arrange financing. The law also protects businesses applying for credit.

Because credit is so important in this society in making the decision whether to grant credit, a creditor is prohibited from taking a number of actions based on certain characteristics. In 1974, the Act made it unlawful for creditors to discriminate in any aspect of a credit transaction based on sex or marital status.

In 1976, amendments to the Act made it unlawful to discriminate based on race, color, religion, national origin, age, and receipt of public assistance. For example, a creditor may not ask if someone is widowed or divorced. When permitted to ask marital status, a creditor may only use the terms "married," "unmarried," or "separated" (as relevant to whether an applicant is applying for credit jointly or in his or her own name).

Creditors may not use any appraisal of the value of the property that considers the race of the people in the neighborhood. A borrower is entitled to receive a copy of an appraisal report that he or she paid for in connection with an application for credit if he or she submits a written request for the report.

In addition, a consumer may exercise his or her rights under the Consumer Credit Protection Act without fear of discrimination.

Regulation B

The Board of Governors of the Federal Reserve System issued **Regulation B** to implement the provisions of the Equal Credit Opportunity Act (ECOA). The primary purpose of the ECOA is to prevent banks and other creditors from discriminating when granting credit by requiring them to make extensions of credit equally available to all creditworthy applicants with fairness, impartiality, and without discrimination on any prohibited basis. The regulation applies to consumer and other types of credit transactions.

Handling Borrowers' Applications

Creditors must treat all potential borrowers equally and fairly when handling loan applications. Therefore, it is inappropriate and illegal to question potential borrowers about their age, gender, marital status, national origin, religion, race, sexual orientation, or because they receive public assistance income.

Creditors may ask borrowers to disclose this information voluntarily (except religion) if the borrower is applying for a real estate loan. This information helps federal agencies enforce anti-discrimination laws. The creditor may ask a borrower about his or her residence or immigration status.

Usually, creditors may not ask a borrower's gender on an application form (one exception is on a loan to buy or build a home). A female borrower does not have to use Miss, Mrs., or Ms. with her name on a credit application.

When permitted to ask marital status, a creditor may use only the terms married, unmarried, or separated. Unmarried includes single, divorced, or widowed. A creditor may ask that the borrower to provide this information if the borrower lives in a community property state. These states are Arizona, California, Idaho, Louisiana, Nevada, New Mexico, Texas, Washington, and Wisconsin. A creditor in any state may ask for this information if the borrower is applying for a joint account or one secured by property.

Creditors must not ask about the borrower's plans for having or raising children.

Even though a creditor may not ask if the borrower receives alimony, child support, or separate maintenance payments, the creditor may ask if the borrower pays any of them.

Extending Credit

Creditors must act fairly and cannot refuse loans to qualified, creditworthy borrowers. Creditors cannot lend borrowers money on terms that differ from those granted others with similar income, expenses, credit history, and collateral.

The race of people in the neighborhood in which the borrower wants to buy or refinance a house cannot be used in consideration for a loan.

The borrower's age is immaterial unless he or she is too young to sign contracts (generally under 18 years). If the borrower is 62 or older, a creditor can use the borrower's age to determine if income might drop because of retirement.

Evaluating Borrowers' Income

Creditors must evaluate the source of income objectively. Creditors may not refuse to consider or discount income from alimony, child support, part-time employment, pensions, social security, or public assistance. Income from child support and alimony payments does not have to be disclosed unless the borrower wants the creditor to include it as income. A creditor may ask the borrower to provide proof of consistent payment.

The amount of income cannot be discounted because of the borrower's sex or marital status. For example, a creditor cannot count a man's salary at 100% and a woman's at 75%. A creditor may not assume a woman of childbearing age will stop working to raise children.

Credit Application Denial

A creditor must tell the applicant if the application was accepted or rejected within 30 days of having received a complete application. After analyzing the risk factors of the borrower and the property, a creditor may deny the loan. This is legal as long as all potential borrowers are assessed according to the same underwriting guidelines.

If the application is rejected, the applicant must be given the reasons for the rejection. Acceptable reasons include inadequate income, length of employment, or a low credit score. Indefinite or vague reasons are illegal so the lender should be specific.

Creditors must give borrowers a notice of the rejection. It must state the specific reason(s) for the rejection or tell the borrower he or she has the right to learn the reason within 60 days of receipt of the letter.

Fair Credit Reporting Act

The **Fair Credit Reporting Act** (FCRA) is one of the most important laws that protect consumer identity and credit information. It is designed to promote the accuracy, fairness, and privacy of the information collected and maintained by credit reporting agencies.

The FCRA establishes procedures for correcting mistakes on a person's credit record and requires that a consumer's record only be provided for legitimate business needs. It also requires that the record be kept confidential. A credit record for judgments, liens, suits, and other adverse information may be retained for 7 years. The exception is bankruptcies, for which the record may be retained for 10 years. If a consumer has been denied credit, a cost-free credit report may be requested within 60 days of denial.

A consumer may sue any credit reporting agency or creditor for breaking the rules regarding who may see his or her credit records or for failing to correct errors in a credit file. If the violation is proved to have been intentional, a consumer may be entitled to actual damages plus punitive damages allowed by the court, as well as court costs and attorney's fees. Any person who obtains a credit report without proper authorization, or a credit reporting agency employee who gives a credit report to an unauthorized person, may be fined up to $5,000 or imprisoned for 1 year, or both.

Consumers must be told if personal credit information is used against them. If a consumer is denied credit, employment, or insurance because of information in the credit report, the denying party must alert the consumer and provide the name, address, and phone number of the credit reporting agency used to support the denial.

A consumer has access to his or her file. Upon request, a credit reporting agency must give a consumer the information in the file and a list of everyone who has requested it within a certain time period. There is no charge for the credit report if the consumer has been denied credit, employment, or insurance because of  items in the file (if a request is made within 60 days). Additionally, a consumer is entitled to one free credit report from each of the three credit bureaus every 12 months.

A consumer can dispute inaccurate information and a credit reporting agency must investigate those items reported as inaccurate by the consumer. The consumer should receive a full copy of the investigation report. If the dispute is not settled to his or her satisfaction, the consumer may add a statement to the report. Inaccurate information must be corrected or deleted. Credit reporting agencies are required to remove or correct inaccurate or unverified information. They are not required to remove accurate data unless it is outdated.

Access to a consumer's file is limited. Only people and institutions with needs recognized by the FCRA may legally access a credit file. This normally includes creditors, government agencies, insurers, employers, landlords, and some businesses.

A consumer can remove his or her name from credit reporting agency lists used for unsolicited credit and insurance offers. Unsolicited offers must include a toll-free phone number the consumer can call to be removed from credit reporting agency lists.

Fair and Accurate Credit Transactions Act

The **Fair and Accurate Credit Transactions Act** (FACTA) in 2003 amends the FCRA to give borrowers the right to see what is in their credit file and to have any errors corrected.

If a lender refuses credit to a borrower because of unfavorable information in his or her credit report, a borrower has a right to get the name and address of the agency that keeps the report. A borrower may request information from the credit bureau by mail or in person. The law also says that the credit bureau must help a borrower interpret the data in the report because the raw data may be difficult for the average person to analyze. If a borrower is questioning a credit refusal made within the past 60 days, the bureau cannot charge a fee for explaining the report. The Fair and Accurate Credit Transactions Act of 2003 allows consumers to request and obtain a free credit report once every 12 months from each of the three nationwide consumer-credit reporting companies—Equifax®, Experian®, and TransUnion™. The three major credit-reporting agencies maintain a website (www.annualcreditreport.com) that provides free access to annual credit reports.

If a borrower notifies the bureau about an error, generally the bureau must investigate and resolve the dispute within 30 days after receiving the notice. The bureau contacts the creditor who supplied the data and removes any information that is incomplete or inaccurate from the credit file. If a borrower disagrees with the findings, he or she can file a short statement (100 words) in the record that gives the borrower's side of the story. All future reports to creditors must include this statement or a summary of its contents.

Right to Financial Privacy Act

The **Right to Financial Privacy Act** states that customers of financial institutions have a right to expect that their financial activities have a reasonable amount of privacy from federal government scrutiny. The Act specifies that, before any information is released to the federal government, certain procedures, exemptions, limitations, and requirements concerning the release of customer financial records must be met.

Lending Laws

Lending laws are necessary to the protection of individual rights as the process of making and funding real estate loans occurs across the country. Together, these laws set a standard of how individuals should be treated in their financial dealings. Since the 1960s, laws that protect consumers in real estate financial transactions have multiplied rapidly. The concepts of fair and equal financing have been written into lending laws that prohibit unfair discrimination, protect consumers' credit rights, and clarify settlement procedures.

Federal Truth in Lending Act

The federal **Truth in Lending Act** (TILA) is found at 15 U.S.C. § 1601 et seq.—Title 1 of the **Consumer Credit Protection Act** of 1968. The Truth in Lending Act is implemented by **Regulation Z**, which is an administrative regulation enforced by the Consumer Financial Protection Bureau (CFPB).

The Truth in Lending Act is aimed at promoting the informed use of consumer credit by requiring disclosures about its terms and costs. This landmark legislation forces a creditor to state the cost of borrowing in a common language so that consumers can figure out what the charges are, compare the costs of loans, and shop for the best credit deal. A **creditor** is a lender (person or company) who regularly makes real estate loans that are secured by a dwelling.

TILA only pertains to certain loans—those subject to a finance charge or that are payable in more than four installments, excluding the down payment. Because most real property purchases are financed through federally-regulated lenders or by federally insured or guaranteed loans, it applies to virtually every loan that is issued for the purchase of a parcel of real property.

One of the consequences of a lender failing to provide the proper disclosures as required by the TILA is that if the borrower can successfully challenge the loan as violating this statute, the borrower can void the security agreement that the lender otherwise would have in the real property. This makes the lender an **unsecured creditor** rather than a **secured creditor**.

This creates two problems for the lender. First, without a valid security interest in the real property, the lender cannot foreclose its security interest in the property as an alternative to bringing a lawsuit against the creditor if the creditor defaults on the loan. Second, if the creditor files bankruptcy, the lender would no longer have the right to take back the property with the permission of the bankruptcy court and sell it to recover the losses on the loan. Rather, the lender would be just another general unsecured creditor who must receive a percentage of the total value of the creditor's assets when the debtor's property is liquidated.

Main Provisions of TILA

- The Act requires creditors to give certain disclosures to the consumer before making a loan contract.

- The Act establishes disclosure standards for advertisements that refer to certain credit terms. It requires disclosure of the finance charge, the annual percentage rate, and certain other costs and terms of credit. This allows a consumer to compare the prices of credit from different sources.

- The Act gives consumers the right to cancel certain credit transactions that involve a lien on a consumer's principal dwelling. If credit is extended for business, commercial, or agricultural purposes, Regulation Z does not apply. For more detailed information go to www.ecfr.gov.

Disclosures

In 2015, The Consumer Financial Protection Bureau (CFPB) adopted the TILA-RESPA Rule (TRID) creating new mortgage disclosures (integrated mortgage disclosure forms) that are provided to BORROWERS for closed-end mortgage loan transactions. The TRID rule applies to most closed-end residential mortgages, construction-only loans, and loans secured by vacant land or by 25 or more acres. However, some home loans are exempt and still use the GFE and HUD-1 disclosures discussed later. [12 CFR §1026.19]. The disclosure forms are written in readily understandable, plain language and are designed to help borrowers understand complicated real estate loan and closing transactions.

The integrated mortgage disclosure forms are the Loan Estimate and the Closing Disclosure. The **Loan Estimate** is designed to highlight the most important information that borrowers need on the first page (e.g., interest rate, monthly payment, and the closing costs). The **Closing Disclosure** contains the actual terms and costs of the transaction.

Lenders must ensure that BORROWERS receive the Closing Disclosure at least **3 business days before consummation** (the day the loan closes). The settlement agent is responsible for preparing and providing the seller's Closing Disclosure to the seller, reflecting the actual fees and terms related to the seller's transaction. The seller's Closing Disclosure must be provided to the seller **at or before consummation.**

Finance Charge and Annual Percentage Rate

TILA requires lenders to disclose the important terms and costs of their loans, including the annual percentage rate, finance charge, the payment terms, and information about any variable rate feature. The **finance charge** is the dollar amount the credit will cost. As a condition to obtain credit, the finance charge is composed of any direct or indirect charges. Those include interest, loan fees, finder fees, credit report fees, insurance fees, and mortgage insurance fees (PMI or MMI).

In real estate loans, the finance charge does not include appraisal fees or credit report fees. The **annual percentage rate (APR)** is the relative cost of credit expressed as a yearly rate. Expressed as a percentage, it is the relationship of the total finance charge to the total amount financed.

Regulation Z requires that the following **material disclosures** must be displayed to allow consumers ease of comparison. [§1026.18].

- **Amount financed** – *The amount of credit provided to you or on your behalf*
- **Finance charge** – *The dollar amount the credit will cost you*
- **Annual Percentage Rate** – *The cost of your credit expressed as a yearly rate*
- **Total of payments** – *The amount you will have paid when you have made all the scheduled payments*
- **Payment schedule** – The number, amount, and timing of payments
- **Name of the lender** – Creditor making the disclosure

In addition to the previously mentioned disclosure, the regulation also requires disclosures regarding due-on-sale clauses, prepayment penalties, late payment charges, description of the property, insurance requirements, and loan assumptions.

The penalties for failure to comply with the Truth in Lending Act can be substantial. A creditor who violates the disclosure requirements may be sued for twice the amount of the finance charge. In the case of a consumer lease, the amount is 25% of the total of the monthly payments under the lease, with a minimum of $100 and a maximum of $1,000. Costs and attorney's fees may also be awarded to the consumer. The consumer must begin a lawsuit within a year of the violation.

Adjustable-Rate Loan Disclosure

A lender offering adjustable-rate residential mortgage loans must provide prospective borrowers with a copy of the most recent CFPB publication, which provides information about adjustable-rate loans. The *Consumer Handbook on Adjustable-Rate Mortgages* helps consumers understand the purpose and uses of adjustable-rate mortgage loans. The lender must give the publication to the borrower upon his or her request or when the lender first provides information concerning adjustable-rate mortgages. Lenders, who adopted or are subject to federal rules, may provide the disclosures at the same time and under the same circumstances as when the lender makes the federally required disclosures pursuant to the Truth in Lending Act.

Closed-End and Open-End Loan Disclosure

Open-end credit includes types of credit arrangements, such as revolving credit cards and home equity lines of credit. Home equity plans require that disclosures and a brochure also be given to the consumer along with the application.

Closed-end credit includes any credit arrangement that does not fall within the definition of an open-end credit transaction, such as a real estate loan. Closed-end credit has a stated maturity date. Usually, disclosure is required before any closed-end credit transaction is completed.

The type and timing of disclosures required under Regulation Z for closed-end and open-end loans are provided on the FDIC's website at www.fdic.gov.

Advertising

The Truth in Lending Act establishes disclosure standards for advertisements that refer to certain credit terms. If the annual percentage rate (APR) is disclosed in the advertisement, no other disclosures are required.

For example, if the APR is not stated, then the specifics of all credit terms must be disclosed. An advertisement that discloses the number of payments must also disclose the amount or percentage of the down payment, amount of any payment, finance charge, interest rate, property description, and so forth. In fact, if the advertisement

states the interest rate, it must also disclose the APR. For example, ads that require complete disclosure include *No money down* or *100% financing*.

Advertising Guidelines

The questions and answers below illustrate some aspects of advertising regulations under Regulation Z. Advertising includes newspapers, electronic media, signs, handouts, brochures, and other similar mediums.

1. *Can the advertisement include only the interest rate?*

    No.

2. *Can the annual percentage rate be advertised without disclosure of other terms?*

    Yes, but if the rate varies, that must be disclosed.

3. *Is using APR in place of the term annual percentage rate allowed in advertising?*

    No, use the annual percentage rate.

4. *Is advertising $10,000.00 down without disclosing other terms allowed?*

    No, the annual percentage rate and other terms must be disclosed.

5. *Is advertising no closing costs without disclosing other terms permitted?*
    Yes.

6. *Is advertising that mentions a small down payment without disclosing other terms allowed?*

    Yes.

7. *Can advertising disclose liberal rates without disclosing other terms?*

   Yes.

8. *Can terms be advertised without disclosing other terms?*

   Yes.

9. *Can the deferred payment price or the total of loan payments be disclosed in any residential real estate advertisement?*

   No.

10. *If only the sales price or loan amount and the annual percentage rate are advertised, must the advertisement include other terms?*

    No, but if the rate is advertised, the advertisement must expressly state whether it is an annual percentage rate or a variable rate.

11. *Can a $350.00 monthly payment be advertised?*

    Yes, but the additional disclosure requirements must be met.

12. *Can an advertisement state, "Assume a 9% loan" or "11.9% Financing Available"?*

    Yes, but ALL additional disclosure requirements must be met.

13. *Can MLS sheets be used as credit advertising?*

    No.

Right of Rescission

The **right to rescind** (cancel) a real estate loan applies to most consumer credit loans (hard money loans) or refinance loans. Loans used for the purchase or construction of the borrower's personal residence (purchase money loans) have no right of rescission. The lender must provide a written rescission disclosure to every borrower who is entitled to rescind.

Rescission Disclosure

- Lender's security interest in the consumer's principal dwelling
- Consumer's right to rescind the transaction
- Consumer's rescission process including a form for that purpose, designating the address of the lender's place of business

When the right of rescission applies, the borrower has a right to rescind the agreement until midnight of the 3rd business day after the promissory note is signed.

Federal Home Ownership and Equity Protection Act

The **Home Ownership and Equity Protection Act** of 1994 (HOEPA) deals with high-rate, high-fee home loans that are refinance or home equity installment loans. The law addresses certain deceptive and unfair practices in home equity lending. It amends the Truth in Lending Act (TILA) and establishes requirements for certain loans with high rates and/or high fees. Since the rules for these loans are contained in Section 32 of Regulation Z, they are called **Section 32 Mortgages**.

HOEPA rules include most types of mortgage loans secured by a consumer's principal dwelling, including purchase money mortgage loans, refinances, closed-end home-equity loans, and open-end credit plans (i.e., home-equity lines of credit, or HELOCs). Reverse mortgages and construction loans would still be excluded.

A **high-cost mortgage** is a consumer credit transaction secured by a consumer's 1-4 unit principal dwelling, including purchase and non-purchase money closed-end credit transactions and HELOCs that meets certain thresholds.

Section 32 Mortgage Threshold Triggers
- The annual percentage rate (APR) exceeds the average prime offer rate (APOR) for a comparable transaction by more than:
    - 6.5% for first liens;
    - 8.5% for first liens less than $50,000 secured by a dwelling that is personal property (e.g., manufactured home); or
    - 8.5% for junior liens;
- The total points and fees exceed:
    - 5% of the total loan amount if the loan amount is $20,350 or more; or
    - The lesser of 8% of the total loan amount or $1,017 for a loan amount less than $20,350 (the figures are adjusted annually); or
- A prepayment penalty may be charged more than 36 months after consummation or account opening, or may exceed, in total, more than 2% of the amount prepaid.

Required Disclosures for High-Cost Loans

If a loan meets the above requirements, a borrower must receive several disclosures at least 3 business days before the loan is finalized. These disclosures must be given in addition to the other TILA disclosures that the borrower must receive no later than the closing of the loan. If the disclosure becomes inaccurate, a creditor must provide new disclosures and begin a new 3-day waiting period.

As part of the additional disclosures, the lender must give borrowers a written notice stating that the loan need not be completed even though they have signed the loan application and received the required disclosures. Borrowers have 3 business days after receiving the special Section 32 disclosures to decide if they will sign the loan agreement.

The notice must warn borrowers that the lender will place a lien on their home and, if the borrowers fail to make payments, they can lose the residence and any money put into it. In addition, the lender must disclose the APR, the regular payment amount (including any balloon payment when the law permits balloon payments), and the loan amount. If the borrowed amount includes credit insurance premiums, that fact must be stated. For variable rate loans, the lender must disclose that the rate and monthly payment may increase and state the amount of the maximum monthly payment.

> **Banned Features on High-Cost Mortgages**
> - Balloon payments unless permitted by law
> - Negative amortization
> - Financing points and fees
> - Most prepayment penalties

In addition, creditors cannot make loans based on the collateral value of the secured property regardless of the borrower's ability to repay the loan. They cannot refinance a HOEPA loan into another HOEPA loan in the first 12 months of origination unless the new loan is in the borrower's best interest. Creditors cannot document a closed-end, high-cost loan as an open-end loan. For example, a high-cost loan may not be structured as a home equity line of credit if there is no reasonable expectation that repeat transactions will occur.

Lenders may be sued if they violate these requirements. Additionally, a violation of the high-rate, high-fee requirements of TILA may enable the borrower to rescind the loan for up to 3 years.

Federal Home Equity Loan Consumer Protection Act

The **Home Equity Loan Consumer Protection Act** of 1988 requires lenders to disclose terms, rates, and conditions (APRs, miscellaneous charges, payment terms, and information about variable rate features) for home equity lines of credit with the applications and before the first transaction under the home equity plan. If the disclosed terms change, the consumer can refuse to open the plan and is entitled to a refund of fees paid in connection with the application. The Act also limits the circumstances under which creditors may terminate or change the terms of a home equity plan after it is opened.

California Housing Financial Discrimination Act

The **Housing Financial Discrimination Act** of 1977, better known as the Holden Act and sometimes referred to as the Fair Lending Law, is similar to the federal Fair Employment and Housing Act or the California Unruh Civil Rights Act. The Holden Act can be found at Health and Safety Code § 35800 et seq.

The **Holden Act** bans the consideration of race, color, religion, sex, marital status, national origin or ancestry, as well as trends, characteristics or conditions in the neighborhood or geographic area where a house is located, with regard to the making of a real estate loan. In particular, the act forbids **redlining**— the practice of disapproving real estate loans in economically or physically blighted areas—unless it is based on sound business practice.

In addition, a lender can refuse to neither make a loan nor require stricter terms for a loan (e.g., a higher interest rate) based on such characteristics. However, a lender can refuse to make a loan or require stricter terms based on any generally accepted lending practice, such as the fair market value of a property or the borrower's credit history.

Furthermore, the act only applies to the purchase, construction, rehabilitation, or refinancing of one-to-four unit family residences occupied by the owner and/or the home improvement of any one-to-four unit family residence. Violations may be reported to the state Secretary for Business and Transportation, who must act on the complaint within 30 days.

Real Estate Settlement Procedures Act

Settlement, or closing, is the process by which ownership of real property or title to the property is passed from seller to buyer. The federal **Real Estate Settlement Procedures Act (RESPA)** is found at 12 U.S.C. § 2601 et seq. and is implemented by Regulation X, an administrative regulation enforced by the Consumer Financial Protection Bureau (CFPB). Both RESPA and Regulation X are remedial consumer protection statutes that are liberally construed by the courts. RESPA protects consumers by mandating a series of disclosures that prevent unethical practices by mortgage lenders and that provide consumers with the information to choose the real estate settlement services most suited to their needs. The disclosures must take place at various times throughout the settlement process. For example, failure of a lender to give proper notice as required by its provisions can subject the lender to liability for actual damages and even to criminal penalties, potentially leading to a fine of up to $10,000 and/or one year in jail.

RESPA applies to all federally related home loans used to purchase or refinance real property or improved real property of one-to-four units, provided the property includes the principal residence of the borrower. These include most purchase loans, assumptions, refinances, property improvement loans, and equity lines of credit. The Consumer Financial Protection Bureau (CFPB) is responsible for enforcing RESPA.

The U.S. Department of Housing and Urban Development's (HUD) Federal Housing Administration (FHA) administers several regulatory programs to ensure equity and efficiency in the sale of housing. The Real Estate Settlement Procedures Act (RESPA) applies to almost all home loans and lenders, not just FHA-insured loans.

RESPA's Purposes

- To help consumers get fair settlement services by requiring that key service costs be disclosed in advance
- To protect consumers by eliminating kickbacks and referral fees that will unnecessarily increase the costs of settlement services
- To further protect consumers by prohibiting certain practices that increase the cost of settlement services

RESPA requires lenders or servicers to provide a disclosure statement, give proper notice when the loan servicing is going to be transferred, grant a grace period during the transfer of the loan servicing, and respond promptly to written inquiries.

Timing of Disclosures

RESPA requires that borrowers receive disclosures at various times. Some disclosures spell out the costs associated with the settlement, outline lender servicing and escrow account practices, and describe business relationships between settlement service providers.

Disclosures at the Time of Loan Application

When a potential homebuyer applies for a home loan, the lender must give the buyer a special information booklet, the Loan Estimate, and a Mortgage Servicing Disclosure Statement.

The disclosures must be provided at the time a written application is submitted, or no later than 3 business days after the application is received. However, if the application is denied before the end of the 3-business day period (or the application is withdrawn), the loan originator is not required to provide the disclosures.

The special information booklet, *Your Home Loan Toolkit*, contains consumer information on various real estate settlement services.

The **Loan Estimate** summarizes key loan terms and gives an estimate of loan and closing costs. The lender is generally required to provide the Loan Estimate within 3 business days of the receipt of the borrower's loan application. Lenders must allow applicants to have a **7-business day waiting period** after mailing or delivering the Loan Estimate prior to closing the loan.

The **Mortgage Servicing Disclosure Statement** states whether the lender intends to sell the real estate loan servicing immediately, if the loan servicing can be sold at any time during the life of the loan, and the percentage of loans the lender has sold previously. The lender must also provide information about servicing procedures, transfer practices, and complaint resolution. The borrower may file a complaint with with the CFPB at www.consumerfinance. gov/complaint/process.

The RESPA statute does not provide an explicit penalty for the failure to provide the disclosures. However, bank regulators may choose to impose penalties on lenders who fail to comply with federal law.

Disclosures before Settlement (Closing) Occurs

An **Affiliated Business Arrangement Disclosure** is required whenever a settlement service refers a buyer to a firm with which the service has any kind of business connection, such as common ownership. Usually, the service cannot require the buyer to use a connected firm.

Lenders must ensure that BORROWERS receive the Closing Disclosure at least **3 business days before consummation** (the day the loan closes). The seller's Closing Disclosure must be provided to the seller **at or before consummation**.

Disclosures during Settlement

The Closing Disclosure must show the actual charges at settlement. In addition, an **Initial Escrow Statement** is required at closing or within 45 days of closing. This statement itemizes estimated taxes, insurance premiums, and other charges to be paid from the escrow account during the first year of the loan.

Disclosures after Settlement

The servicer must deliver an **Annual Escrow Loan Statement** to the borrower. This statement summarizes all escrow account deposits and payments during the past year. It also notifies the borrower of any shortages or surpluses in the account and tells the borrower how these can be paid or refunded. A **Servicing Transfer Statement** is required if the servicer transfers the servicing rights for a loan to another servicer.

Prohibited Practices under RESPA

Certain practices are prohibited under the Real Estate Settlement Procedures Act.

> **Kickbacks, Fee Splitting, and Unearned Fees:** The Act prohibits anyone from giving or accepting a fee, kickback, or anything of value in exchange for referrals of settlement service business involving federally related mortgage loans. A **kickback** is an illegal payment made in return for a referral that results in a transaction. This applies to almost every loan made for residential property. RESPA also prohibits fee splitting and receiving fees for services not actually performed. Violation of these RESPA provisions can be punished with criminal and civil penalties.

Seller-Required Title Insurance: A seller is prohibited from requiring a homebuyer to use a particular title insurance company. A buyer can bring a lawsuit against a seller who violates this provision.

Unlimited Deposits into Escrow Accounts: A limit is set on the amount that a lender may require a borrower to put into an escrow account to pay taxes, hazard insurance, and other property charges. RESPA does not require lenders to impose an escrow account on borrowers, but some government loan programs or lenders do require an escrow account. During the loan term, RESPA prohibits a lender from charging excessive amounts for the escrow account. The lender must notify the borrower annually of any escrow account shortage and return any excesses of $50 or more.

Borrowers who believe a settlement service provider has violated RESPA, in an area in which the CFPB has enforcement authority, may file a complaint. The complaint should outline the violation and identify the violators by name, address, and phone number. The name and phone number of the person filing a complaint should be provided for follow-up questions from the CFPB. The CFPB honors confidentiality requests from those filing complaints.

SUMMARY

Other state laws that prohibit various forms of discrimination in transactions related to real estate transactions include the Holden Act (sometimes called the Fair Lending Law) and the Unfair Competition Law, which regulates advertising and incorporates a number of other state and federal statutes in determining whether a business has engaged in unfair, deceptive, untrue, or misleading advertising. Unlike the Federal Trade Commission Act, the Unfair Competition Law allows citizens to bring their own suits for violations of the law, but only if the person bringing the suit was injured. Besides the Federal Trade Commission Act, the federal government also provides consumer protection through the Real Estate Settlement Procedures Act (RESPA) and the Truth in Lending Law (TILA). The former regulates costs and disclosure requirements at closings on certain kinds of real estate loans; the latter requires that consumer loan agreements in which a security interest is acquired by the lender contain certain disclosures; as a practical matter, it applies to virtually all loans for real estate.

These laws set a standard for how individuals are to be treated in their financial dealings, including real estate.

Credit

Since 1968, the number of credit protection laws has multiplied rapidly. Some of these laws are the Truth in Lending Act, the Equal Credit Opportunity Act, the Fair Credit Reporting Act, and the Fair and Accurate Credit Transaction Act. The concepts of fair and equal credit have been written into laws that prohibit unfair discrimination in credit transactions, require that consumers be told the reason credit is denied, give borrowers access to their credit records, and set up ways for consumers to settle billing disputes. For more information on TILA, visit www.fdic.gov. For more information on the ECOA, FCRA, and FACTA, go to www.ftc.gov.

Settlement Issues

Settlement (closing) is the process by which ownership of real property or title to the property is passed from seller to buyer. The federal Real Estate Settlement Procedures Act (RESPA) applies to all federally related home loans used to purchase or refinance real property or improved real property of one-to-four units. Certain practices are prohibited under RESPA, such as kickbacks, fee splitting, unearned fees, seller-required title insurance, and unlimited deposits into escrow accounts. Borrowers may file a complaint with the lender if they believe the lender has violated RESPA. For more details regarding RESPA, go to www.hud.gov.

The National Flood Insurance Act requires federally regulated lenders to compel borrowers to purchase flood insurance in certain designated areas and to disclose to borrowers if the property is located in a flood hazard area. Additional information about this Act may be found at www.fema.gov.

UNIT 11 REVIEW

Matching Exercise

Instructions: Write the letter of the matching term on the blank line before its definition. Answers are in Appendix A.

Terms

A. annual percentage rate

B. Clayton Antitrust Act

C. commercial email message

D. creditor

E. Equal Credit Opportunity Act

F. established business relationship

G. Fair Credit Reporting Act

H. Federal Trade Commission Act

I. finance charge

J. group boycotting

K. Holden Act

L. horizontal arrangements

M. market division

N. monopoly

O. price fixing

P. redlining

Q. Regulation B

R. Regulation Z

S. right to rescind

T. settlement

U. Sherman Antitrust Act

V. transactional email messages

W. Truth in Lending Act

X. tying

Y. Unfair Competition Law

Definitions

1. _____ Person or group with exclusive control over a product or service within a given region

2. _____ Business agreements between competitors

3. _____ Agreement of one or more persons to set prices for goods or services

4. _____ Deliberate exclusion of a particular business or group from the benefits of competition

5. _____ Two or more competing businesses agree to allocate the market among themselves

6. _____ Illegal action requiring buyers to purchase one product or service in order to obtain another product or service

7. _____ Basic federal antitrust statute

8. _____ Antitrust act enacted to supplement the Sherman Antitrust Act

9. _____ Federal law enacted to protect the public from anti-competitive acts

10. _____ California's most frequently used consumer protection statute found in the B&P Code, Section 16720

11. _____ Caller had a transaction with the receiver within the last 18 months; or the customer has made an inquiry with the caller's firm in the last 3 months

12. _____ Any electronic mail message with the primary purpose of which is the commercial advertisement or promotion of a commercial product or service

13. _____ Emails sent as part of an ongoing commercial transaction

14. _____ Act ensuring that consumers have an equal chance to obtain credit

15. _____ Regulation that implements the provisions of the Equal Credit Opportunity Act

16. _____ Act promoting the accuracy of information collected by credit reporting agencies

17. _____ Federal law requiring consumer loan agreements in which a security interest is acquired by the lender to contain certain disclosures

18. _____ Regulation that implements the Truth in Lending Act

19. _____ Lender who regularly makes real estate loans secured by a dwelling and whose loans are subject to a finance charge

20. _____ Amount charged to the consumer for the credit

21. _____ Relative cost of credit expressed as a yearly rate

22. _____ Right to cancel a real estate loan

23. _____ California law referred to as the "fair lending law"

24. _____ Illegal use of a property location to deny financing or insurance

25. _____ Process by which ownership of real property or title to the property is passed from seller to buyer

Multiple Choice Questions

Instructions: Circle your response and go to Appendix A to read the complete explanation for each question.

1. Four brokers decided to collaborate and refuse to show any of the properties listed by a new broker in the area in an effort to force the new broker out of business. This is an example of:

    a. allocating customers.
    b. group boycotting.
    c. monopolizing the market.
    d. price fixing.

2. Eric believes that an advertisement for the sale of a house in his neighborhood is deceptive. He is not interested in buying the property himself, but is concerned that a prospective buyer will be misled by the seller's advertisement. Can he bring a lawsuit under the Unfair Competition Law for penalties and a court order because of the deceptive advertisement?

    a. No, because Eric is not trying to buy the house in question, he cannot show that he has been harmed or lost money because of the advertisement.
    b. Yes, assuming that he is correct that the advertisement is deceptive.
    c. Eric can bring a lawsuit under the Unfair Competition Law for a court order but not for damages.
    d. Yes, because he lives in the same neighborhood as the house that is for sale and has an interest in protecting his prospective neighbors from harm.

3. In general, the Do Not Call rules do not apply to calls made:

    a. containing a commercial solicitation.
    b. if an established business relationship already exists.
    c. for business purposes.
    d. during normal business hours.

4. What type of email is excluded from the CAN-SPAM Act of 2003?

    a. Business email message
    b. Commercial email message
    c. Transactional email message
    d. Written email message

5. Which act has the primary purpose of preventing banks and other creditors from discriminating when granting credit by requiring them to make extensions of credit equally available to all creditworthy applicants with fairness, impartiality, and without discrimination on any prohibited basis?

    a. ECOA
    b. FHLMC
    c. RESPA
    d. TILA

6. A few years ago, Bill became a victim of identity theft. Recently, Bill received a corrected credit clearance from Indent Credit Reporting Services. Indent accurately cleared Bill's credit records of the harmful credit originating from the identity theft. The theft originated due to their incorrect maintenance of information collection procedures. Which federal law protected Bill's consumer rights?

    a. Consumer Creditor Law
    b. Equal Consumer Law
    c. Fair Credit Reporting Act
    d. Truth in Lending Act

7. Consumers can request and obtain a free credit report once every 12 months from each of the three nationwide consumer-credit reporting companies. This was made possible by the:

    a. Fair Credit Reporting Act.
    b. Fair and Accurate Credit Transactions Act.
    c. Fair Housing Act.
    d. Fair Housing Amendments Act.

8. What is the commonality of finance charge, APR, payment schedule, and amount financed?

    a. Holden Act
    b. Home Ownership and Equity Reduction Act
    c. Real Estate Settlement Procedures Act
    d. Truth in Lending Act

9. You are a business that provides loans to consumers seeking to finance the purchase of residential property. Which state statute most directly regulates your business?

    a. The Fair Credit Reporting Act
    b. The Housing Financial Discrimination Act
    c. The Real Estate Settlement Procedures Act
    d. The Truth in Lending Act

10. Broker Tom offers extensive sales training classes in his office. During a recent office session, he discussed a Federal act, which protects consumers from unfair closing practices. Tom, placed emphasis on kickback fees, fee splitting, referral fees and non-disclosure of closing costs. In addition, he mentioned that the HUD's Office of Consumer Regulatory Affairs is responsible for enforcing the program. What Federal program is Tom discussing?

    a. National Credit Protection Law

    b. Real Estate Settlement Procedures Act

    c. Regulatory Credit Settlement Act

    d. Right to Credit Settlement Act

Contract Law

Unit 12

INTRODUCTION

The law of contracts governs which agreements the law will enforce and those that it will not. Those abstract legal principles are important to the business of real estate because every real estate transaction involves a promise by at least one party to sell real property and a promise by someone else to buy it. Brokers and salespeople are in the business of completing contracts day in and day out. The related liability is obvious. Therefore, it is important to understand how a contract is created, what makes a contract valid or invalid, and how a contract can be terminated or voided. The concepts of contract law will be covered in this unit.

Learning Objectives

After completing this unit, you should be able to:

12A   recall classifications of contracts.

12B   identify the elements of a valid contract.

12C   recognize factors, which would allow a party to disaffirm a contract.

12D   recall principles in the interpretation of contracts.

12E   choose methods of discharging contracts.

12F   recognize remedies for breach of contract.

OVERVIEW OF CONTRACT LAW

Unlike many of the other legal principles discussed in this book, contract law is a comparatively new area of the law. There was a process during the Middle Ages when someone, usually a member of the nobility, could write down a promise and then "seal" the document with a wax impression created with a signet ring or other distinctive object that had a symbol, such as a coat of arms. This process eventually reached the lower strata of society and binding oneself "under seal" became the only kind of promise that was enforceable during that time.

During the seventeenth and eighteenth centuries, as a middle class developed in England (and later in the United States), and as commerce began to flourish, merchants began to require a way to enforce agreements without resorting to the cumbersome medieval notion of the "binding seal." Instead, new understandings of the way that merchants dealt with one another came to be recognized by the courts and a new area of law developed to meet the needs of those involved in mercantile dealings.

At the most basic level, the term contract today refers to an agreement that is enforceable by law. California Civil Code §1549 defines a **contract** as "an agreement to do or not to do a certain thing." Our modern capitalist society, of course, could not exist today without contracts. As will be discussed, most such contracts are two-way agreements that are enforceable by an exchange of promises by each side. Both parties to the agreement assume that the other party will live up to that party's end of the bargain and each side makes plans in reliance on those assumptions.

Classification of Contracts

Contracts may be express or implied, bilateral or unilateral, and executory or executed.

Express or Implied Contracts

In an **express contract**, the parties declare the terms of the agreement and put their intentions in words, either orally or in writing. An example of an express contract is a lease or rental agreement in which the landlord agrees to allow the tenant to live on the property and the tenant agrees to pay rent in return.

When a contract is implied, the agreement is demonstrated by conduct rather than by words. For example, when a person goes into a restaurant and orders food, it creates an **implied contract**. By requesting a service, it is implied that the person will pay for the service.

Bilateral or Unilateral Contracts

Contracts are classified as bilateral (two-sided) or unilateral (one-sided).

Bilateral Contracts

A bilateral contract is what most people think of when referring to an agreement as a "contract." A **bilateral contract** is an agreement in which each party promises to perform an act in exchange for the other party's promise to perform his or her part of the agreement. The mutual promises made by the parties are the actual consideration that supports a bilateral contract—not the underlying things of value or other action or performance to which the promises relate.

> Example: Paul has a house on the market. Alice, a prospective buyer, offers to buy the property at a price close to the asking price in the listing. Paul reviews her offer and decides to accept. He delivers a written acceptance to Alice. Paul and Alice now have a bilateral contract: Alice's promise to pay a certain price for the property and Paul's promise to deliver title to the property in exchange for the property provide the consideration on each side of the transaction to support the contract.

Of course, almost any contract—and especially a real estate contract—will have multiple promises by each party. Once there is an exchange of offer and acceptance, the agreement between Paul and Alice will typically be combined into a single document that sets forth in some detail the terms of their mutual understandings.

Unilateral Contracts

A **unilateral contract** is a contract in which a party promises to perform without the expectation that the other party will perform. The second party is not obligated to act, but if he or she does, the first party must keep his or her promise.

A reward, such as the finder's fee is one of the most common kinds of offers for a unilateral contract. Someone who offers a reward does not want the offeree to "agree" to the terms of the offer; he or she seeks the performance of an act that meets the terms of the offer.

> Example: A neighbor who is missing a pet may post signs offering a reward for the return of the pet. If the pet is returned, the neighbor is required to pay the promised reward.

Thus, the consideration for a unilateral contract is the PERFORMANCE of whatever act constitutes acceptance of the offer, whether providing information leading to the capture of a criminal, the return of a lost pet—or the introduction of the eventual buyer of a parcel of property to the seller.

> Example: Janet has a house on the market. She lets it be known that she is willing to pay a "finder's fee" of $1,000 to anyone who introduces her to the person who eventually buys her property. Janet's friend Sharon hears of her offer and knows that another acquaintance, Terry, is interested in relocating to the area where Janet's house is located.

> Sharon tells Terry that he might want to consider Janet's house if he decides to move to the area. Terry visits Janet's property and decides that it will be suitable for his needs. He makes an offer on Janet's house. When the property closes escrow, Sharon has "accepted" Janet's offer of a finder's fee because she introduced Janet to Terry, who eventually bought her house. Sharon is entitled to the $1,000 that Janet offered now that Terry's transaction with Janet is complete.

A typical unilateral contract sometimes encountered in the real estate business is an open listing. An open listing would denote that a parcel of real property is for sale for which no broker is formally representing the seller.

Executory or Executed Contract

A contract that remains to be performed by one or both parties is referred to as an **executory contract**. An example of an executory contract is a contract that has not yet closed or a contract that has not been signed by both parties.

A contract is executed when all parties have performed according to the agreement. Performance may be as simple as signing the document, but a typical real estate contract requires much more than signatures. An **executed contract** is a sales agreement that has been signed by all parties involved in the transaction.

ELEMENTS OF A VALID CONTRACT

As in other areas of the law, contracts are composed of elements. By way of explanation, a series of events must occur in order to say that two people or entities are parties to a contract.

The California Civil Code §1550 states that "it is essential to the existence of a contract that there should be: (1) parties capable of contracting, (2) their consent, (3) a lawful object, and (4) a sufficient cause or consideration."

Although Section 1550 lists four required elements, some authors describe five elements that must exist in order for a valid contract to exist. The five elements are competent parties, an offer, an acceptance, a lawful object, and consideration. In essence, the Section 1550 element of "consent" is separated into two parts—offer and acceptance.

Competent Parties

Parties entering into a contract must be legally capable of contracting or competent. Civil Code §1556 states the principle in this way: "All persons are capable of contracting, except minors, persons of unsound mind, and persons deprived of civil rights."

Minors

Civil Code §1557, subdivision (a) refers to Family Code §6500 regarding who is a minor. Family Code §6500 in turn defines a **minor** straightforwardly as "an individual who is under 18 years of age." However, an individual who is under the 18 years of age can enter into a legally binding contract if he or she is emancipated. Family Code §7050 defines an **emancipated minor** as a person under 18 who is or has been married, is on active duty with the armed forces, or has been declared emancipated by

the court. An emancipated minor can "Buy, sell, lease, encumber, exchange, or transfer an interest in real or personal property, including, but not limited to, shares of stock in a domestic or foreign corporation or a membership in a nonprofit corporation." [Family Code §7050 (e)(2)]

If a person is foolish enough to enter into a contract with a minor and fails to check that person's age before making the agreement, that party may be in for a rude awakening if he or she tries to enforce the contract against the minor.

Because the contract was not valid when it was created, the minor can **disaffirm**—that is, set aside—the agreement at any time. Although the other party cannot enforce the agreement according to its terms, that party at least can demand the return of any property that was the basis for the contract (in whatever condition it is found).

Persons of Unsound Mind

As noted above, Civil Code §1557 also refers to "persons of unsound mind." Normally, this refers to someone who is the subject of a conservatorship proceeding. There are two kinds of conservatorship: one is established under the Welfare and Institutions Code because the person has a mental illness; the other, more common kind is established under the Probate Code because a person has become too aged or ill to manage his or her affairs. The person who is the subject of the conservatorship is called a **conservatee** and the person appointed by the court (often, though not always, a public official) is called the **conservator**.

In both kinds of conservatorship, the conservator's duty is to manage the conservatee's property for as long as the conservatee needs a conservatorship. During that time, the conservatee has various legal disabilities imposed by the court, including the right to enter into contracts. Anyone wanting to buy property owned by the conservatee, therefore, will have to deal directly with the conservator and sometimes to have the transaction approved by the court, in order for the agreement to be lawful. As with a minor, even if the conservatee nevertheless appears well-enough to a third party to enter into a contract, that contract can be disaffirmed later by the conservator.

In some instances, if a person makes a contract while intoxicated or under the influence of legal or illegal drugs, the contract is voidable. However, when the individual regains sobriety, he or she may choose to ratify (or approve) the contract.

Persons Deprived of Civil Rights

Penal Code §§2600 and 2601 deal with the loss of certain civil rights by persons who are sentenced to imprisonment in the state prison. Section 2601, subdivision (a) provides that such prisoners normally have the right "to inherit, own, sell, or convey real or personal property." On the other hand, another part of that same subdivision states that the state Department of Corrections "may restrict or prohibit sales or conveyances that are made for business purposes."

Should such a prisoner own real property and desire to sell it, there is a possibility that these provisions could come into play. Both the agent for such a seller and the buyer should seek legal advice and contact the Department of Corrections to ensure that there is no legal impediment to the sale because of these statutes.

Mutual Consent between the Parties

In a valid contract, all parties must mutually agree. **Mutual consent** (or mutual assent) is sometimes called a **meeting of the minds**. It is an offer by one party and acceptance by the other party. At the point, an offer is accepted and the acceptance is communicated to the offeror, there is a meeting of the minds and a bilateral contract is created.

Offer

An offer is the starting point for many contracts. Of course, there are contracts (e.g., the purchase of groceries or other goods in a retail store) that do not involve anyone saying the words of "offer" or "accept." Most large purchases and almost all real property transactions, do involve such formalities. An **offer** is a proposal from one party (offeror) that is conveyed to another party (offeree) that, if accepted, would create a binding contract between the two parties. The **offeror** is the person making the offer to enter into a contract and the **offeree** is the person to whom the offer is being made.

In order for a proposal to be deemed an offer, it must indicate a present intent by the person making the offer to be bound by a contract if the offer is accepted. It must be communicated to the offeree and must be definite and certain in its terms so that a reasonable person in the offeree's position would realize that an offer for a contract has been made.

Lucy v. Zehmer

In *Lucy* v. *Zehmer*, 196 Va. 493, 84 S.E.2d 516 (1954), a case from Virginia, Mr. Lucy and his brother had attempted to convince Mr. and Mrs. Zehmer to sell their farm, which consisted of approximately 470 acres, for some time. Shortly before Christmas in 1952, Lucy again approached Mr. Zehmer at the restaurant and filling station that Zehmer operated with his wife and offered him $50,000 for the property.

Zehmer said that he doubted Lucy could raise that much money, but after 30 or 40 minutes of discussion, they wrote out a contract that both Zehmers and Mr. Lucy signed. The contract had a provision allowing Lucy to verify that the property's title was good, but otherwise appeared on its face to be a complete contract. Zehmer later claimed that he thought the whole matter was a joke and that he and his wife had no intention of selling the farm.

When Lucy tendered the $50,000 and the Zehmers refused to accept it, he instituted a lawsuit to enforce the contract. Besides claiming that he did not think Lucy was serious in wanting to buy the property, Mr. Zehmer claimed that he "was high as a Georgia pine" during the discussions and that the transaction "was just a bunch of two doggoned drunks bluffing to see who could talk the biggest and say the most."

The court, however, found that Mr. Zehmer's claims were inconsistent with his attempt to testify in great detail as to what was said and done. He also was contradicted by other evidence, including that the two men discussed the matter for more than half an hour and that the agreement was written up twice to address issues, such as whether Mrs. Zehmer should be included in the agreement. The court found that Zehmer was not so intoxicated as to be unable to comprehend the nature and consequences of the instrument he executed and ultimately ruled in Lucy's favor.

Whether one party has made an offer to another is a factual question based on all the surrounding circumstances of the transaction. Merely listing a parcel of land for sale is not an offer. Although a listing will often contain some of the terms that will eventually go into a contract, such as the sales price, a listing is not itself an offer. Rather, a sales listing, like a newspaper advertisement, is a solicitation to interested buyers to step forward to make offers to buy the listed property. The prospective seller in effect indicates a willingness to sell, combined with a suggested selling price.

Termination of an Offer

Once an offer has been communicated to the offeree, it does not stay open forever. An offer can be terminated by the offeror at any time prior to acceptance by the offeree. The offeror usually has an expectation that the offer he or she makes will be accepted or rejected by the offeree in a timely manner.

Methods to Terminate an Offer
- Lapse of time
- Death or incapacity of either party
- Destruction of the subject matter
- Revocation by the offeror
- Rejection by the offeree
- Qualified acceptance or counteroffer by the offeree

Lapse of Time An offer terminates if the offeree fails to accept it within a period of time stated in the offer. If the offeree does nothing (i.e., completely ignores the offer) then it eventually will be deemed to have been rejected by the lapse of time. Some offers have a built-in "fuse"—that is, the offer will state that it is open only for a period of time and, if the offeror hears nothing from the offeree, then the offeror will deem it to be rejected automatically. On the other hand, even if the offer itself does not state that it will be deemed rejected if the offeree does nothing, it will also be deemed rejected after the lapse of a "reasonable" period of time.

Death or Incapacity of Either Party. A binding contract must have living parties. If either the offeror or offeree dies or becomes incompetent before the offer is accepted, the offer is terminated.

Destruction of the Subject Matter. If the parties are negotiating about something that is destroyed before the offeree responds to the offer, then there is no longer a legal object. An offer is terminated if the subject of their negotiations is destroyed before the offeree responds and it can no longer be accepted.

> Example: Ted makes an offer to buy Krista's home. While Krista is considering whether to accept it, the house burns to the ground. The fire automatically terminates Ted's offer. The destruction of the legal object (house) prevents Krista from trying to "snap up" Ted's offer that she was considering if she finds out about the fire before he does.

Revocation by the Offeror. The offer is terminated if the offeror revokes the offer before the offeree provides a response. In California, a revocation is effective as soon as it is sent to the offeree.

> Example: Mary has a house on the market. On August 1, Bill makes an offer to purchase it and gives Mary 5 days to respond to his offer. While Mary is considering Bill's offer, Bill finds another house that he deems to be more desirable for less money. On August 2, Bill mails Mary a note revoking his offer, which she receives on August 5. Because Mary does not yet know of Bill's revocation, she accepts his offer on August 4.

> In this example, there is no contract because Bill's offer was revoked effective August 3, when it was mailed—not August 5, when Mary received it.

Rejection by the Offeree. An offer is terminated if the offeree rejects it. In most cases, the offer is rejected by some action on the part of the offeree.

> Example: Sam's house is listed for $350,000. Tom knows that the market has been weak and that the house has been on the market for several months. He makes a "low-ball" offer to buy the house for $275,000. Sam responds a day later with a letter stating, "I'm sorry, but $275,000 is too little money. Your offer is rejected." At that point, Sam's dealings with Tom are at an end unless one of them makes a new offer.

Note that Sam's rejection of Tom's offer terminates the offer for all purposes—including later "remorse" on Sam's part. If more time goes by and Tom's offer is the only one that he has received, Sam cannot change his mind and "pick up" the $275,000 offer after rejecting it. His only recourse would be to make Tom his own, new offer, which Tom can then accept or reject—or ignore.

> Example: In the previous situation, Tom makes the "low-ball" offer to buy Sam's house for $275,000. Assume that Sam, instead of simply rejecting the offer, responds with a counteroffer stating, "$275,000 is too little, but I'd be willing to

sell on the same terms as your offer for $325,000." At that point, Tom's $275,000 offer is still rejected, but Tom is now in the position of the offeree and can either accept, reject, or make a counter-counteroffer to Sam's $325,000 offer.

Acceptance

As noted above, an offer is a proposal that, if conveyed to another party and accepted, would create a binding contract between the two parties. Once a valid offer has been made, the offeree normally has three choices: (1) to accept the offer, (2) to reject the offer (either directly or by making a counteroffer), or (3) to take no action. If the offeree takes no action, the offer will eventually be deemed rejected by lapse of time (based on either a time limit stated in the offer itself or after a reasonable period of time).

As the three choices above should make clear, unlike the offeror—whose only choice is whether to make an offer at all and to select its terms—the offeree always has a range of options. These choices put the offeree, at least initially, in somewhat of a superior position *vis-à-vis* the offeror and why sometimes the offeree is referred to as the "master of the offer."

An **acceptance** is an unqualified agreement to the terms of an offer. Once an offer has been accepted, that phase of contract negotiation is over and the offer and acceptance merge into the newly formed contract. In order for an acceptance of an offer to become a binding contract, it must meet four basic requirements.

Requirements for Unconditional Acceptance
- Offer accepted only by the offeree
- Terms of the acceptance cannot vary from the offer
- Acceptance must be communicated to the offeror
- Acceptance must be made in the manner specified

Acceptance by the Offeree. The offer must be accepted only by the offeree. An offeree cannot assign his or her position in the offer to someone else.

Unconditional Acceptance of the Terms of the Offer. In order for a contract to be formed, the offeree must accept the offer without making any changes to it. Sometimes this is called the mirror image rule. The **mirror image rule** states that an offer must be accepted exactly and without modification. The acceptance must be a mirror image of the offer given. Any changes would result in a termination of the first offer and a new offer would be formed.

If the offeree does make a change, then the purported "acceptance" has really become a counteroffer. A **counteroffer** is just what it sounds like—the offeree responds to the offer not with a rejection but with a different offer. [C.C. §1583]

> Example: Ron sent Larry an offer to buy Larry's house for $240,000. The offer includes a provision that "escrow is to close on or before October 31." Larry responds, "I accept your offer, but escrow must close by October 15." Despite what either of them may think, Ron and Larry do not yet have a contract, because the change to the one term—the date of the proposed close of escrow—has effectively rejected Ron's original offer. Larry has now made a counteroffer, which Ron can either accept or reject.

Communication of Acceptance of the Offer. Once an offeree decides to accept an offer, he or she should communicate the acceptance to the offeror. Unless the acceptance is communicated to the offeror directly (over the telephone or in person), it is considered effective when the acceptance is sent. Under what has come to be known as the **mailbox rule**, the acceptance or rejection of an offer is deemed complete the moment that it is deposited in the mail. The actual receipt of the communication is not required, even if the letter communicating the acceptance or rejection is lost.  It is still effective (assuming that the offeree can establish that the acceptance was deposited in the mail and when that deposit took place). One way to think of this is to imagine the offeree "reaching through" the mailbox to hand the acceptance or rejection directly to the offeror the moment it is mailed, regardless of when it is actually received. The date of the postmarked acceptance would establish the exact date of acceptance.

> Example: Rob hand-delivers an offer to buy Sarah's property to Sarah on June 15. On June 19, Sarah mails her acceptance of Rob's offer to him at his business address. On June 20, Rob—having heard nothing and having found another property in which he is interested—mails a revocation of his offer to Sarah. He receives Sarah's acceptance on June 21.
>
> Rob's June 20 revocation was ineffective, because Sarah already accepted his offer on June 19 when she mailed her acceptance. Even though Rob did not receive her acceptance until a day after he mailed his revocation, her acceptance was effective on June 19 as soon as she deposited her acceptance in the mail.

The mailbox rule does not apply to instantaneous communications, such as fax or telephone. The normal rule that such messages must be received by the offeror still applies. There has not been a definitive court ruling on whether the mailbox rule applies to e-mail. On the one hand, unlike the telephone, e-mail is sometimes delayed by network congestion or does not arrive at all and is subject to being put in an "inbox" like conventional mail. On the other hand, for most practical purposes, it is as "instantaneous" as telephonic communications and appears within the recipient's inbox almost as soon as it is sent. The best approach is probably to rely on the telephone or fax if instantaneous communication is desirable or to use the postal service (or personal delivery) of an acceptance, rejection, or revocation if one wants to ensure the most effective and immediate results.

Communication in the Manner Specified. Acceptance of an offer must be communicated to the offeror in the manner specified, before a contract becomes binding between the parties. If an offer specifies the means of communication, no other method is acceptable. If the offer does not specify the means of communicating the acceptance, then any reasonable method will qualify, such as mail, e-mail, fax, telegram, or personal delivery.

Lawful Object

Even if the parties are capable and mutually agreeable, the object of the contract must be lawful. A contract requiring the performance of an illegal act is not a valid contract. An example in real estate would be someone attempting to sell a piece of property that he or she does not own and has no reasonable expectation to own prior to the closing date.

The contract must also be legal in its formation and operation. For example, a note bearing an interest rate in excess of that allowed by law would be void. Contracts opposing general public policy, called **contracts of adhesion**, may also be unenforceable.

Consideration

Assuming that all of the parties are competent to enter into a contract and that the object of the contract is lawful, there is still one more condition—consideration. Consideration is an element that makes the contract legally enforceable.

Consideration refers to the mutual exchange of something that is a legal benefit to one party for something that is likewise a legal benefit to the other party. Consideration can also be a legal detriment to one of the parties—that is, the person may agree to give up something that he or she has a legal right to do in exchange for something offered by the other party. Civil Code §1605 defines **consideration** as "Any benefit conferred, or agreed to be conferred, upon the promisor, by any other person, to which the promisor is not lawfully entitled, or any prejudice suffered, or agreed to be suffered, by such person."

Consideration may be a promise for a promise, money for a promise, money for property, or goods for services. Legally, every contract must have acceptable consideration. Terms that denote **acceptable consideration** include valuable, adequate, good, or sufficient consideration. Forbearance, or forgiving a debt or obligation, or giving up an interest or a right, qualifies as valuable consideration. Gifts, such as real property based solely on love and affection, are good consideration. These gifts meet the legal requirement that consideration be present in a contract.

In a bilateral contract, a promise of one party is consideration for the promise of another. For example, in the sale of real property, the buyer promises to pay a certain amount and the seller promises to transfer title.

On the other hand, certain promises, although they may appear to be satisfactory to support a contract, in fact are only **illusory promises** because the promisor is agreeing to do something that is not, in fact, valid consideration.

> Example: Edna has worked for a corporation for 30 years. The corporation offers no pension plan. Shortly before Edna is planning to retire, the president of the company calls her into his office. He tells her that, in gratitude for her years of service, the corporation has decided to pay her a lifetime stipend of $2,500 per month. Edna thanks him and, somewhat in a daze, begins to make her retirement plans in earnest.

The problem is that the only consideration for the president's "promise" of lifetime compensation is work that Edna has already performed for the corporation in the past. This is sometimes referred to as "past consideration," i.e., it is work that Edna already has done in the past (for which she has already been paid) and cannot provide new consideration.

If Edna had been promised a pension plan at the time she began to work for the company, then receipt of it would have been part of her compensation over the years. But because all of her services have been completed before she was offered the "promise" of the monthly payments, the president's offer to make the payments here is illusory. If a future company president or board of directors decided to stop making the payments, Edna, having given the company no new consideration, would be unable to make them continue paying.

VOID AND VOIDABLE CONTRACTS

Two terms that sometimes confuse newcomers to the area of contract law are void and voidable. In one sense, they do not really describe two different kinds of contracts, because a "void contract" is really a contradiction in terms. On the other hand, the concept of voidable contracts provides one party, but not both, with the right to set aside a contract.

Void Contracts

As just noted, the term **void contract** is an oxymoron. It refers to a "contract" that is not really a contract at all. If two parties have entered into what they believe to be a contract but it is either lacking an element or violates the law, then what they believe to be a contract is not, in fact, a contract. If such an agreement truly is "void," then there is no contract and the court will not enforce it. Such a contract is sometimes referred to as a "void contract" in order to distinguish it from a **valid contract**, which is a contract that has all required elements and is therefore binding and enforceable.

Voidable Contracts

A **voidable contract** is a contract that has some barrier to the formation or validity of the contract that does not appear on the face of the agreement itself. However, a contract that is voidable is not unlawful under all circumstances. Like a contract entered into with a minor, a voidable contract can be disaffirmed by one party, but is valid until the party with the right to disaffirm does so.

Until that party exercises its right to disaffirm the contract, it is presumptively valid and can be performed by either party.

When creating a contract, mutual consent must be genuine, which means that an offer and acceptance must be genuine and freely made by all parties. Genuine assent does not exist if there is fraud, misrepresentation, mistake, duress, menace, or undue influence involved in reaching an agreement.

Duress

Duress is the making of threats or coercion to get someone to enter into an agreement. If one party is induced to enter into an agreement by such tactics (as made famous in the motion picture *The Godfather* when someone is given an "offer he can't refuse"), then the party subjected to those threats can later set aside the contract.

This is a straightforward application of Civil Code §1550, subdivision (2), which as noted requires both parties to give "their consent" to enter into a contract. If the consent is obtained by force or threats of force, then there is not a valid acceptance of the offer. Therefore, no contract was legally formed.

Civil Code §§1569 and 1570 respectively define duress and menace that will vitiate (impair) the consent required by §1550. Duress includes such things as unlawful confinement of the party, the party's spouse, or other close relatives; it can also include withholding property that belongs to the person. **Menace** as defined in §1570 as a threat to do one of the acts that constitutes duress, threats of violence, or a threat to harm the reputation of the person.

Whether the behavior of one party meets these definitions is a factual question and therefore a judge or jury will ultimately have to decide if the person was subjected to menace or threats that induced the person to enter into the contract. Perhaps, a person subjected to duress might conclude after the fact, that the contract is, in fact, beneficial and decide to go through with it anyway. Because these questions turn on subjective assessments by one party, such contracts are voidable, not void.

Undue Influence

Like duress and menace, undue influence is defined in the Civil Code. Section 1575 provides that **undue influence** consists of such things as a person who holds a real or apparent influence over another person, taking advantage of another person's "weakness of mind," or taking oppressive or unfair advantage of another person's necessities or distress.

Undue influence most commonly involves a person who, although of sound mind and capable of entering into a contract, has become dependent on a relative or other caregiver and is pressured by that person to enter into agreements that benefit the caregiver. Because a caregiver may take advantage of the position of power that being in such a position may provide, a court will carefully examine the consent given by the person who later claims undue influence. It can also apply in situations when, because of something like a natural disaster, a person charges another an outrageous sum for something that normally would not be so expensive (sometimes referred to as "gouging").

Civil Code §39 provides that if a court finds a person is substantially unable to manage his or her own financial resources or to resist fraud or undue influence, this creates a presumption that the person was of unsound mind. Therefore the person would be unable to enter into a contract, just as if that person was subject to a conservatorship. This places the burden on the person trying to uphold the contract of proving that, in fact, the person who entered into the agreement did so voluntarily.

Intoxication

A person making an offer or accepting an offer to enter into a contract must do so knowingly and intelligently. If a party to a contract is so intoxicated that he or she cannot understand all the terms of the agreement or does not realize that a contract has even been entered into, then the agreement again does not have the consent of both parties and the party who was intoxicated can try to disaffirm the agreement on that basis.

As with duress, the court will examine the degree of the party's alleged intoxication, as well as such factors as whether the contract is objectively unjust, in order to determine if the person was actually so intoxicated that he or she could not enter into the agreement consensually.

> Example: Recall that in *Lucy* v. *Zehmer*, 196 Va. 493, 84 S.E.2d 516 (1954), Mr. Zehmer tried to claim he "was high as a Georgia pine" during his discussion with Mr. Lucy and that the transaction "was just a bunch of two doggoned drunks bluffing to see who could talk the biggest and say the most." The court disbelieved his claims, including his claim of intoxication, because he nevertheless attempted to testify in great detail as to what was said and done; the court also noted (somewhat ironically) that Mrs. Zehmer actually suggested that Mr. Zehmer should drive Lucy home that night.
>
> The court summarized its findings: "The record is convincing that Zehmer was not intoxicated to the extent of being unable to comprehend the nature and consequences of the instrument he executed, and hence that instrument is not to be invalidated on that ground." As a result, the court ruled in Lucy's favor and upheld the validity of the contract.

Fraud

Fraud is an act done with intent to deceive, in order to get someone to part with something of value. Although it sounds like it might make a bargain unlawful at the outset, fraud is in the same category as undue influence, duress, intoxication et al. in making a contract voidable and not automatically illegal. Fraud is either "actual" or "constructive." (Civil Code §1571.)

Actual Fraud As Defined By Civil Code §1572

"1. The suggestion, as a fact, of that which is not true, by one who does not believe it to be true;

2. The positive assertion, in a manner not warranted by the information of the person making it, of that which is not true, though he believes it to be true;

3. The suppression of that which is true, by one having knowledge or belief of the fact;

4. A promise made without any intention of performing it; or,

5. Any other act fitted to deceive."

For example, the intentional failure to disclose a material fact or latent defect in order to entice a prospective buyer into making an offer is a fraudulent act.

According to Civil Code §1573, fraud is **constructive fraud** when someone breaches a duty, without any actually fraudulent intent, gaining an advantage over another person that misleads him to his prejudice, or if the person commits any other act that the law provides is "fraudulent" even if it does not amount to actual fraud.

Mutual Mistake

Another basis upon which a contract can be voidable is a mutual mistake, of either fact or law. Mutual mistake often arises when someone believes in the existence of something that is material to a given contract, which does not actually exist.

A mistake of law is a misunderstanding by both parties of the law that applies to something, with all of them making substantially the same mistake; it can also be a misapprehension of the law by one party that the other party is aware of, but does not rectify. Thus, if both parties made assumptions about the facts or the law that applied to the transaction and those beliefs later turned out to be incorrect, then the law will "put the parties back where they started out."

The **doctrine of mistake** arises from the principle that, in order for the parties to give their "consent" to a contract, the promises that make up the contract cannot be based on both parties' erroneous assumptions. This is referred to as a **mutual mistake** because if only *one* party made such an error (e.g., miscalculated the cost of a subcontract in bidding on a construction project), then that party will be left to deal with the consequences of his or her own carelessness.

INTERPRETATION OF CONTRACTS AND PROTECTIONS

Once the parties have entered into a written agreement, this action does not end the possibility of disputes. Although a written contract may prevent misunderstandings once both parties have signed it, disputes may still arise about how certain terms or phrases in the agreement are to be interpreted. There are a number of principles for the interpretation of contracts, many of which have been enacted into the Civil Code.

Statute of Frauds

One such principle provides that certain contracts must be put into writing in order to be enforceable. Most contracts, of course, do not have to be in writing. Many contracts—the purchase of goods at a store, for example, or a month-to-month rental agreement—are often performed with little or nothing in writing to memorialize their existence.

On the other hand, certain contracts are required by law to be in writing. The law that requires such a writing is known as the **statute of frauds**. The term comes from the English statute that first imposed this requirement in the seventeenth century. Prior to that time, when most people were illiterate and deeds were rarely used to transfer land, land conveyances—like a wedding today—were done in a public ceremony with a number of live witnesses who could later give testimony of the transfer of the land. Because the statute was intended to prevent false testimony about such transfers, it was given the name that is still used today.

There are a number of agreements subject to the statute of frauds that are beyond the scope of this work. The principal agreements of interest in the real estate business are found in Civil Code §1624.

Contracts That Must Be in Writing
- An agreement for the sale of real property
- An agreement that cannot be performed within a year from its making. This includes a lease for longer than one year
- An agreement to employ an agent, broker, or other person to purchase, sell, or to lease real estate for longer than one year, for compensation or a commission
- An agreement by a purchaser of real property to pay an indebtedness secured by a mortgage or deed of trust upon the property purchased, unless the purchaser's assumption of the indebtedness is provided for in the conveyance of the property

Merger Clause

A primary duty for a real estate agent is to make sure all contract language conveys the parties' wishes and agreements. A written contract is the most reasonable way to ensure mutual assent. Once a contract has been reduced to writing and has been signed, the law normally will presume that all oral discussions that led up to the agreement have been "merged" or "integrated" into the four corners of the written contract.

The **four corners doctrine** is the principle stating that the whole document rather than its individual parts convey the purpose or meaning of a contractual document. The courts will make every effort to enforce a contract by determining the intent of the parties from within the four corners of the contract itself, with all provisions considered together in the original context.

Many standard written contracts, in fact, explicitly contain a merger clause. A **merger clause** (sometimes referred to as an **entire agreement clause** or an **integration clause**) is a term in the contract declaring this is the complete and final agreement between the parties. The paragraph usually states that both parties acknowledge that the written agreement constitutes the entire agreement between the parties relating to the subject matter of the contract, superseding all previous discussions and agreements between them. It also will often state that, by signing the agreement, both parties agree that they have not relied on anything stated orally before the execution of the contract that is not set forth in the written contract itself. In essence, if it is not stated in the written contract, any promise or other statement does not exist and the parol-evidence rule typically will prevent either party from trying to claim that there were such "other promises" or a "side agreement" that is not set forth in the final written contract.

Parol-Evidence Rule

Another rule relating to the interpretation of contracts is known as the parol-evidence rule. Parol evidence refers to the oral discussions that precede the parties' reduction of those discussions into a written agreement. The **parol-evidence rule** is not really a rule of courtroom evidence. Rather, it is a substantive rule of contract law relating to when such discussions can and when they cannot, be considered by a court when it interprets a contract. Occasionally a contract is ambiguous or vague. Under these circumstances, a judge might allow prior agreements to be entered into evidence in order to clarify the contract that is under dispute.

> Example: A written contract states that the seller is to move out at funding and closing. The buyer and seller verbally agree that the seller may have a few extra days to move out. Just after closing, the buyer demanded the seller surrender possession or be sued. The seller will probably have to move, because the agreement amending the original contract was oral. The written agreement normally prevails, absent an ambiguity in the written contract.

Despite the apparent sweep of this rule, as well as the standard language of most pre-printed contracts, there are a number of exceptions that can allow parol evidence to be introduced by one party.

Exceptions to the Parol-Evidence Rule

- To determine the subject matter of the agreement if it is not clear from the contract itself.

- To introduce evidence that would make the contract voidable, such as duress, undue influence, mutual mistake, or fraud.

- To establish that a contract term that appears to be unambiguous was, in fact, different from how it is expressed in the final agreement. This can be used by one party to try to obtain **reformation** of the contract—that is, to have the contract interpreted (or even re-written) by a court according to the parties' intentions and not according to the strict written language expressed.

- To prove that consideration that the written agreement states has been paid, in fact has not been paid.

- To allow for the interpretation of a contract term that is ambiguous.

Seck v. Foulks

In *Seck* v. *Foulks* (1972) 25 Cal. App. 3d 556, Seck, a real estate broker was a personal friend of Foulks. In 1965, Foulks and his parents were interested in selling a ranch in Sacramento County. Foulks declined to give Seck a conventional listing agreement claiming he feared the wrath of neighbors if surrounding property values (and taxes) were driven up if it became known the Foulks' ranch was for sale, a possibility in the days before Proposition 13.

Seck took out one of his business cards and wrote down the terms of their agreement, getting Foulks to date and initial the card.

> ### *Seck v. Foulks* (continued)
>
> Seck eventually located a company that made an offer that Foulks initially accepted. When that transaction fell through, Foulks eventually sold the property to a buyer not referred by Seck.
>
> Seck sued for his commission anyway, relying on the notations on the back of the business card. The case was dismissed because the buyer who eventually bought the property was not the one referred by Seck. The court of appeal, however, concluded Seck might be entitled to a commission and discussed why the contract between Seck and Foulks was valid even though it had been written on the back of a business card.
>
> The appeals court also found it was permissible for Seck to testify at length about the meaning of the notations on the back of the card, most of which were cryptic. For example, he testified that the entries "310 M/L; 2000 per acre; ½ down; bal 5 years; 5% int.," meant that Foulks was selling a 310-acre ranch, "more or less," at an offering price of $2,000 per acre; the buyer would have to deposit half the sales price as a down payment, paying the balance over five years at 5% interest. The card also stated, "6% comm," which meant that Seck was to get a six percent commission if he found a buyer by "10/1/65" —which he testified was the date by which a buyer had to be found.

Determining Conflicts in a Contract

When drafting a contract, there may be conflicts or contradictions that exist within the details. In this case, there are certain rules to follow in order to resolve these conflicts.

Order of Resolving Contradictory Statements in Contracts

1. Handwritten content
2. Typewritten content
3. Attached addenda
4. Preprinted material

Anything that is handwritten in a written contract that contradicts any other term of that contract will overrule and take precedence. Anything typewritten will overrule any addendum and any addendum will overrule the preprinted contract. Each one up the scale shows more effort by the parties and that effort demonstrates the meaning and intent of the parties.

> Example: In the main body of a contract, a preprinted form clearly states that the buyer will pay for the appraisal. In the special provisions section, the buyer wrote that the seller would be responsible for paying for the appraisal, which the seller acknowledged. In this situation, the handwritten condition overrules the preprinted material.

Conditions Precedent and Subsequent

Many of the terms of a contract can be placed into one of two groups: either a contract term is a condition precedent or it is a condition subsequent. Many people who work in the real estate business refer to all such conditions—whether conditions precedent or conditions subsequent—as **contingencies**, because the successful completion of a sale often hinges on whether one of these "contingent" requirements comes about. It is important to recognize that there is a distinction and that it governs whether one party is obligated to perform or is excused from further performance.

A **condition precedent** is a term within a contract that must arise before the other party's duty to perform arises.

> Example: Philip has a life insurance contract with a major national insurance company. The contract provides $500,000 of term life coverage. As long as he pays his monthly payments (premiums) according to the terms of the contract, the insurance policy will remain in force.
>
> The contract provides that the insurance company does not have a duty to pay the beneficiary, Philip's wife, unless Philip dies while the life insurance contract is in force. The requirement that the insurance company pay her the $500,000 is a condition precedent to the insurance company's obligation to perform; but if the condition arises while the policy is in force (i.e., if Philip dies), then the insurance company will have an obligation to make the payment.

A **condition subsequent**, on the other hand, is a condition that, if it arises, cuts off further obligation by one party to perform. In effect, this is an "escape hatch" that the party in whose favor the condition runs can use to get out of the contract if the enumerated condition arises.

Example: Nathan has a contract to sell his house to Phyllis. The contract has a provision that, within 45 days of the execution of the contract, Phyllis can undertake various due diligence steps to verify that the property is in marketable shape. For example, she is entitled to have a termite inspection performed; to have access to the property for an inspection by a building contractor to inspect the foundation and other physical aspects of the property; and to have a preliminary title report prepared by the title insurance company. The contract provides that if any of these inspections or other steps shows that there are problems, Phyllis is entitled to cancel the agreement.

As it happens, the preliminary title report shows that there is a problem with the title to the property. During the 1920s, one of the people who drafted the title description for the property left out a portion of the property that eventually was dedicated to the city for an alleyway. This was not a problem when Nathan bought the property, but during the previous year, the city abandoned the alleyway, leaving a "hiatus" between Nathan's property and the neighboring property on the other side of the alley.

Phyllis does not want to spend the funds to have an attorney file a quiet title action to clear up title to the strip of land. She gives Nathan notice that, according the paragraph of the agreement that requires her to find the title to be satisfactory, she is electing to cancel their contract. Nathan will either have the title problem cleared before selling the property or find a buyer for whom this is not as important.

Time is of the Essence Clause

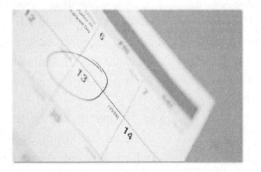

Many contracts also have a provision stating that "time is of the essence." What this somewhat ambiguous-sounding phrase means is that if a term of the contract calls for performance by one party or the other by a certain date, then the failure of that party to comply with that requirement by that date is a material breach of the contract.

If one party is confronted by the other party's failure to meet such an obligation and wants to be excused from further performance, then that can be a basis to cancel the entire contract. (To use the terminology from the preceding section, the "time is of the essence" clause would be a condition subsequent because it will excuse the party not in breach from further performance.) Conversely, the party who could take advantage of the other party's failure to meet a time deadline could choose instead to treat the breach as immaterial and allow the contract to go forward as if there had not been such a failing.

On the other hand, if time is NOT of the essence, then time deadlines within the contract are to be treated merely as goals, not as binding obligations.

> Example: Bill, a buyer, has entered into a real estate contract that provides he will complete the termite inspection by November 1. Bill's contract, however, does not provide that "time is of the essence." If the contract does not state that time is of the essence, the seller would not be able to invalidate the contract even if on November 2 the inspection had not yet been performed.

Liquidated Damages Clause

Finally, because contract damages are sometimes difficult to ascertain, many contracts include a provision for liquidated damages. **Liquidated damages** are a sum set forth in a contract that the parties agree in advance will be their maximum exposure if one party or the other breaches the contract. Courts assume that such clauses give the parties certainty regarding their potential legal liability if either side breaches the agreement and consequently usually uphold them.

Liquidated damages can be a specific total amount. For example, the contract could provide that in the event either party breaches the agreement, that party will owe the other liquidated damages up to a maximum of $5,000 provable damages (regardless of how much one side or the other might be able to prove). Liquidated damages provisions also can provide for payment of a daily amount up to a certain ceiling. Therefore, the contract could provide for liquidated damages of $100 for each day one party is in breach, for a maximum of 30 days.

If the parties intend to use a liquidated damages clause, it is important that they use the phrase "liquidated damages" and not refer to the payment as a forfeiture or a penalty; even though the law favors liquidated damages, it abhors forfeitures. Courts generally support liquidated damage clauses even though this can cause a hardship to the party whose provable damages are much higher.

H. S. Perlin Co. v. Morse Signal Devices

In *H. S. Perlin Co. v. Morse Signal Devices* (1991) 209 Cal.App.3d 1289, Perlin, a stamp and coin shop, entered into a contract with Morse, an alarm company, for which Perlin paid Morse a $300 start-up fee and $50 per month. Morse was supposed to contact the police if a signal from the store indicating a break-in had occurred. The contract had a clause stating that if Morse failed to comply with its obligations under the agreement, it owed Perlin $250 as liquidated damages.

Six years after Perlin and Morse entered into the agreement, burglars broke into the store. The burglars cut the phone line to the alarm and a signal informed Morse that a break-in was occurring at Perlin's store. Despite this, Morse's employees failed to notify the police about the burglary. Perlin, who carried no insurance, lost nearly $1 million in stolen merchandise.

The trial court awarded Perlin the $250 provided for in the liquidated damages provision. The court of appeal upheld the award, noting that one of Perlin's owners had testified that insurance would have cost $25,000 per year to insure just one-half the inventory that had been stolen and that Morse could not have intended to accept such a large liability for the relatively small monthly fee paid by Perlin to Morse.

Quasi-Contract

A **quasi-contract** is a contract that exists by order of a court, not by agreement of the parties. It is created by law for equity and fairness in order to prevent the unjust enrichment of a party in a dispute over payment for a good or service. Quasi contracts are also called implied-in-law contracts. Actually, a quasi-contract is not a contract, but rather a remedy allowing the plaintiff to recover a benefit that was conferred on the defendant.

In some cases, the parties may believe that they have a contract, even though no contract really existed. Alternatively, a person may induce someone to perform a service through an offer for a unilateral contract, but revoke the offer after the offeree has performed substantial services in reliance on that offer. In situations where one person would otherwise be unjustly enriched by services performed by another person, even though no contract actually existed between them, the person who performed the services can still be compensated through the doctrine of quasi-contract. In effect, quasi-contract allows a court to provide a substitute for the contract that would otherwise have protected the innocent party.

> Example: Fred has a large, grassy athletic field that is in need of mowing. On Wednesday, he tells Bob, "I'll pay you $1,000 if you can mow my entire athletic field by Saturday at 5:00 p.m."
>
> Bob spends three days mowing the field. He has about a tenth of an acre left at 4:30 p.m. on Saturday when Bob comes running up to him and says, "I've changed my mind and I revoke my offer. I'm going to hire a professional landscape company instead."
>
> At the point that Fred revoked his offer, no contract existed between him and Bob. Bob was attempting to accept Fred's offer for a unilateral contract by performing an act—by mowing the entire field. However, Bob reasonably relied on Fred's offer to begin the work and even though there was no contract, a court would probably conclude that because Fred would otherwise be unjustly enriched by Bob's efforts, Bob should still be compensated for the work he completed.

The measure of damages under quasi-contract, however, is not based on the contract that turns out not to have existed; rather, it is the reasonable value of the services performed, even if the contract price (had there been a contract) would have been much greater.

For example, assume that Bob goes to court and proves that he spent an average of 8 hours per day for the three days mowing the athletic field. If the court determines that a reasonable hourly rate for similar services would be $25.00 per hour, Bob would be entitled to $600.00 for the work he performed ($25.00 x 24 hours worked), not a percentage of the $1,000 contract price he thought he was going to get.

Doctrine of Promissory Estoppel

The doctrine of **promissory estoppel** provides that if a party changes his or her position substantially either by acting or forbearing from acting in reliance upon a gratuitous promise, then that party can enforce the promise although the essential elements of a contract are not present.

When one party misleads another by making a promise that, it later turns out, was not binding at all, a court will often enforce the promise anyway. If the person has relied on the promise to that person's detriment, the court will treat the promise as if it was supported by consideration. The result would not be the same if the person to whom the promise was made did not rely on it.

DISCHARGE OF CONTRACTS

Discharge of contract refers to the cancellation or termination of a contract. Typically, contracts are terminated by performance, mutual rescission, cancellation, release, revocation, assignment, novation, accord and satisfaction, and breach.

Performance

Commonly a contract is discharged or terminated through **performance**. Seller's performance would be to sell the property. Buyer's performance would be to purchase the property. If everyone performs and the contract closes, then everyone wins.

A **tender of performance** is an offer by one of the parties to carry out his or her part of the contract. A buyer's tender would be his or her willingness and ability to pay the purchase money. A seller's tender would be his or her offer to deliver marketable title to the property. Usually, a tender is made at the time to close escrow. The person to whom the tender is made must state any objections at that time or they are waived.

> Example: A tender of performance by the buyer, for example, by depositing the purchase money into escrow, places the seller in default, if the seller refuses to accept it and deliver a deed. The buyer could rescind the transaction or sue for breach of contract or for specific performance.

Mutual Rescission

If all parties agree to make a contract then all parties can agree to terminate a contract. A **mutual rescission** occurs when all parties to a contract agree to cancel the agreement and put themselves back where they started. This is sometimes referred to as returning the parties to the *status quo ante*—a Latin term meaning the situation that existed before the contract was created. Executory contracts can be mutually rescinded by a written or oral agreement. [C.C. §1689]

Cancellation

Contracts can be terminated by a cancellation agreement. With cancellation, the parties to the contract are abolishing all remaining unperformed (executory) terms of the contract. However, the parties are still responsible for any claims for breach of contract that have already occurred (executed). [C.C. §1699] Therefore, a cancellation agreement should include a release clause to extinguish any obligations.

Release

The person in the contract to whom an obligation is owed may release the other party from the obligation to perform the contract. [C.C. §1541] The release can be a partial release whereby certain terms of a contract are released but not the contract entirely.

In real estate listing agreements, there are two types of releases—conditional and unconditional. A **conditional release** would release the seller from the property being marketed until its expiration time. However, if the seller sold the property to anyone during the remaining listing time, the broker is still entitled to the commission. An **unconditional release** is a complete release and no further obligations are owed by either party.

Revocation

One party can revoke a contract. **Revocation** is typically done when one party has been defrauded or some type of misrepresentation has occurred. Without fault, unilateral revocation could cause the revoking party financial liability.

Assignment

An **assignment** will transfer all the contractual rights and duties of one of the parties (assignor) to another party (assignee). The assignee in every respect takes over the assignor's rights and obligations in the contract, but the assignor is not released from his or her obligations. Unless released from liability, the assignor remains secondarily liable on the contract.

Novation

If the assignor wants to be released entirely from any obligation or secondary liability for the contract, it may be done by novation. **Novation** is the substitution, by agreement, of a new obligation for an existing one, with the intent to terminate the original contract. For example, novation occurs when a buyer assumes a seller's loan and the lender releases the seller from the loan contract by substituting the buyer's name on the loan.

Accord and Satisfaction

Accord and satisfaction is an agreement to settle a contract dispute by accepting less than what is owed in exchange for extinguishing the debt. The accord is the agreement and the satisfaction its execution or performance. Typically, this is used by creditors who are attempting to collect as much money as possible from a debtor who cannot pay the full amount owed.

Breach

Even when a contract between two parties meets all the requirements of the law, that does not end the possibility of disputes. Besides disagreements about the interpretation of the agreement, there will be situations in which one party or the other will be unable to live up to the terms of the contract. Someone who fails to comply with a contractual obligation is said to be in breach of the agreement. A **breach of contract** is a failure to perform on part or all of the terms and conditions of a contract without a legal excuse.

A BREACH OF CONTRACT DOES NOT AUTOMATICALLY LEAD TO THE TERMINATION OF THE AGREEMENT OR THE INITIATION OF LITIGATION. When one party or the other concludes that the other party has breached a term of a contract (e.g., by not making a required payment or not performing under the contract within the time required), the party who is not in breach is put to an election. That party can treat the breach as a material breach or as an immaterial breach. With a **material breach**, the party in breach is put on notice of this fact and the person harmed by non-performance may seek an appropriate remedy. On the other hand, the non-breaching party can treat the breach as an **immaterial breach** and continue to treat the contractual relationship as being unaffected by the other party's failure to live up to the terms of the contract.

> Example: Dan has a contract to purchase Kate's residential real property. The contract provides that Dan is to deposit $10,000 into escrow by Monday, July 15. On July 16, Dan has still not deposited these funds into escrow.
>
> At this point, Kate could decide that pursuing the contract with Dan is not worth it. She could send him written notice that she considers his breach of the requirement to deposit the funds into escrow to be a material breach of the contract and that she will deem their agreement no longer in force. She could then re-list the property and try to find a new buyer.
>
> Suppose, instead, that Kate believes that there is no reason to terminate her relationship with Dan based on this one failure to meet a contractual obligation.

She and her broker will then have to go to the trouble of finding another prospective buyer, possibly taking many more months to reach this point in the process. Instead, she contacts Dan by telephone and points out that he has failed to meet the date. Dan apologizes and tells her that he had put the incorrect date on his calendar. By Friday, he has deposited the $10,000 into escrow. By treating Dan's inaction as an immaterial breach, Kate has allowed the process to move forward as if he had met the July 15 date.

An agent can be liable to third parties for breach of contract, too. The third party may seek damages from the agent, the principal, or both. Breach of a contract, however, is subject to different legal rules from the commission of a tort. The third party will not receive compensation greater than that contemplated under the contract.

Example: Pat is a principal and Sam is his agent. Together, they entered into a legal contract with Tom, a third party, concerning a property valued at $450,000. Later, Tom sues both Pat and Sam for breach of the contract and seeks the full $450,000 that he spent. After a trial, the court finds that Pat and Sam are both liable and orders them each to pay a portion of the $450,000, not $450,000 each. Tom will get restitution but will not reap any greater benefit than the full value of the contract (or else Tom would be unduly enriched).

Types of Remedies

Merely determining that a breach of contract has occurred is also not the end of the process. One possibility is that the party who is not in breach can treat this as excusing further performance by that party under the contract. However, the party who has suffered the breach may have damages as a result.

Example: In the sale of real property, a person who is trying to sell his or her property might receive an attractive offer from a buyer who appears to have the ability to purchase the property. The seller might turn down other offers in reliance on the first offer from a buyer that meets his or her terms. Later, if that buyer refuses to go through with the contract, the seller will be left with an unsold property. The seller cannot accept the offers that were turned down because of the initial buyer's offer. Being able to enforce the promises that someone has made in a contract, therefore, is one of the most important parts of contract law.

The remedies for a breach of contract, as for remedies for most injuries for which one seeks redress in court, are normally divided into two categories—legal remedies and equitable remedies.

Legal Remedies

Legal remedies, also referred to as **remedies at law**, are usually money damages of some kind. Money damages may be classified as compensatory damages, nominal damages, and punitive damages.

Compensatory Damages

The most basic kind of money damages available to a plaintiff for a breach of contract are **compensatory damages**. This is the amount of money that will put the plaintiff in the same position that the plaintiff would have been in if the other party had not breached the contract. This is sometimes referred to as making the plaintiff whole.

> Example: Brenda has a contract with Allen to buy Allen's residence for $300,000. After they have signed the agreement, Brenda discovers that because the market is in decline, she can buy another property for less money that she decides will suit her needs. She sends Allen a letter informing him that she has decided not to go through with her purchase. She does not cite anything in their contract that would allow her to cancel it unilaterally.
>
> After receiving Brenda's note, Allen's broker must put the property back on the market. Allen incurs an additional $1,000 in advertising and related expenses to do so. After several months, the only offer he receives is for $270,000. He reluctantly accepts it and eventually concludes the sale of the property at that price. He then sues Brenda for $31,000—$1,000 for the additional expenses he would not have incurred and $30,000 for lost profit he would have realized if Brenda had gone through with the original contract.

Punitive Damages

If someone does something to injure another person intentionally, that conduct will sometimes also support an award of punitive damages. **Punitive damages** are awarded not to compensate the plaintiff, but to punish the defendant. They are sometimes referred to as **exemplary damages**. In a breach of contract action in California, punitive damages are not available in a breach of contract lawsuit (except for the breach of an insurance contract). Because most contracts arise in a commercial context, it is generally assumed that a party can always elect to breach a contract and pay contract damages without having to risk more than the amount that the plaintiff lost as result of the breach.

Nominal Damages

Nominal damages are contract damages awarded by a judge or jury as a way to recognize that some legally protected right of the plaintiff has been violated, even if there are no provable damages to which a dollar figure can be assigned. While it is usually a token amount to acknowledge that damage has been done, it can support other kinds of damages.

> Example: In the situation described in the previous example, assume that after Brenda backed out of her contract with Allen, he managed to sell the property for the same $300,000 that she originally agreed to pay. Allen cannot receive any provable damages from Brenda because he received the same amount from a subsequent buyer. However, he had to take the time and go to the trouble of re-listing the property and incurred the additional $1,000 in expenses. Allen could sue Brenda just for the $1,000 in extra expenses in small claims court, where he could get a small additional recovery to acknowledge that she breached the contract when she had no right to do so.
>
> Or, if their contract had an attorney's fee clause—a provision that the losing side pays the other side its attorney's fees if the winning side goes to court because of a breach of contract—Allen could sue her using the assistance of an attorney and recover his attorney's fees as well. He or his attorney could also use the mere threat of possible attorney's fees (which would almost certainly be much more than the $1,000 in extra expenses) as a way to get Brenda to pay those expenses before he has to file suit; otherwise, she risks much more than the $1,000 if Allen is represented by an attorney and wins.

Equitable Remedies

In some situations, money damages alone will not be enough to restore the plaintiff to the position that he or she would have been in before the contract was breached. In those cases, because the legal remedy is inadequate, the plaintiff can invoke the court's **equitable powers** to seek an **equitable remedy**, typically a court order of some kind. Common equitable remedies include unilateral rescission, specific performance, and reformation.

Unilateral Rescission

When one party believes that performance under the contract has been excused because a condition subsequent has come to pass, but the other side refuses to acknowledge this, then the party who believes that the contract has become inoperative can unilaterally file a lawsuit for rescission. **Unilateral rescission** is an equitable remedy because the plaintiff asks the court to set aside the contract as if it had never been entered into. Unilateral rescission is available to a person who enters a contract without genuine assent because of fraud, mistake, duress, undue influence, or faulty consideration. [C.C. §1689]

Specific Performance

One rare equitable remedy for a breach of contract is a **lawsuit for specific performance**. Generally, this remedy occurs when money cannot restore an injured party's position. If the plaintiff can demonstrate that forcing the defendant to go through with the contract, instead of paying money to the plaintiff, is the only way to make the plaintiff whole, then a court may invoke this remedy. Specific performance is one form of an injunction—a court order. The court order that the party seeks in a lawsuit for specific performance is also called a "mandatory injunction"—that is, the court is ordering (mandating) that the party who refuses to comply with his part of the contract in fact do so.

> Example: Amy has a contract with Fred to buy Fred's residence for $250,000. The market has been going through an upswing and after Fred accepts Amy's $250,000 offer, he receives a belated offer for $300,000. Deciding to take advantage of the steep increase, he notifies Amy that he intends to back out of their agreement. He accepts the offer for $300,000 and goes into escrow with the second offeree.

> Amy could try to look elsewhere, but she, too, is aware that prices are rising and cannot easily find a comparable house for the price she thought she had settled on with Fred. More importantly is that land is unique; it is not just a cliché that, in real estate, the three most important things are "location, location, and location." Amy cannot really obtain a "comparable" property even if she could find a similar house for the same or less money.

> Every house has a unique street address, will have different construction and configuration, different surrounding views, and may be in a different neighborhood or a different school district. In short, no amount of money from Fred will give Amy the benefit she had bargained for under their original contract. Amy therefore sues Fred for specific performance and obtains a  court order canceling the second contract he signed with the later offeror and compelling him to go through with the contract he had signed with Amy.

Lawsuit for Reformation

In some situations, the parties may have agreed to one thing during their negotiations, but either through error or an intentional action on the part of whoever set down the final discussions in writing, the written language of the contract differs from the parties' agreement. As noted above regarding the merger clause often found in real estate contracts, even when the language of a contract is clear, a party who claims that the written contract does not accurately set forth the parties' agreement can challenge those written terms.

If the other party disagrees that the written terms of the contract are inaccurate, then the party challenging the written language can bring a lawsuit for **reformation** of the contract—that is, to have the contract interpreted (or re-written) by a court so that it expresses the parties' intentions and not the strict written language expressed.

Statute of Limitations

When someone decides to go to court, there is normally a time limit during which a lawsuit must be filed. This is known as the **statute of limitations**, because it places a limit on the length of time a plaintiff has to file a lawsuit. Once the statute of limitations has expired, any lawsuit that could have been brought to enforce one's contractual rights is terminated just as completely as if they had not existed in the first place. Conversely, once the lawsuit has been filed, this stops or "tolls" the statute of limitations and the lawsuit proceeds from that point.

The purpose behind the statute of limitation is to encourage someone who believes his or her rights have been violated to enforce those rights promptly, while witnesses' memories are relatively fresh and documentary evidence is available. As time passes, written documents are purged or become mislaid and witnesses will forget details, move away, or die. Statutes of limitation also allow people not to have to worry about potentially expensive and distracting lawsuits over old disputes.

The statute of limitations in California is long for contract matters and therefore for real estate matters, because they usually involve written contracts.

Time Limits for Filing Some Real Estate Civil Actions

1 Year	Action for libel or slander, injury or death caused by wrongful act, or loss to depositor against a bank for the payment of a forged check. [C.C.P. §340]
2 Years	Action for breach of an oral contract or an action based upon the rescission of a contract not in writing. [C.C.P. §339]

3 Years	Action on a liability created by statute; action for trespass on or injury to real property, such as encroachment; action for relief on the grounds of fraud or mistake; attachment. [C.C.P. §338]
4 Years	Action on any written contract, which includes most real estate contracts. [C.C.P. §337]
4 Years	Action for breach of a written lease. [C.C.P. §337.2]
5 Years	Action for violation of a restriction. The period prescribed in this subdivision runs from the time the person seeking to enforce the restriction discovered or, through the exercise of reasonable diligence, should have discovered the violation. [C.C.P. §336]
10 Years	Action on a judgment or decree of any court in the United States. [C.C.P. §337.5]

The reason for the lengthy statute of limitations for written contracts is perhaps an assumption that, because such disputes involve written documents, witness testimony will not be as important to the court as the language of the documents themselves. Also, records today are often converted to computer files, which can both be stored and retrieved more easily than paper files once were. As discussed below, these limitations apply to lawsuits for money damages or for interpretation of a contract when there is a dispute as to the interpretation of a term in the contract.

Avoiding Risk

Although the general statutes of limitation are lengthy, certain kinds of lawsuits have much shorter time limits. For example, to sue a public entity, one first has to file what is called a "claim" on a special form that one obtains from the public entity that one intends to sue. Depending on the type of lawsuit, the time limit to file the claim is only six months (which is actually twice as long as it once was—for many years, the time limit was only 100 days!) There is also a requirement that, before the plaintiff can go to court after filing the claim, the plaintiff must wait for the public entity to reject it or to take no action on it for a certain period of time.

For those reasons, anyone who is seriously contemplating filing a lawsuit should at least consult an attorney. The attorney can review the statutes of limitation to determine whether a lawsuit must be filed immediately or if it is more cost-effective to try to resolve the dispute informally at first by corresponding with the other side before a lawsuit drives up the costs for both parties.

Laches

Laches is the delay or negligence in asserting one's legal rights. Most lawsuits involve one party seeking money damages from the other. However, when equitable remedies are sought, this not only invokes the court's special powers of equity, it also involves a special rule regarding how long someone has to go to court. Because the rules of equity are flexible and are intended to achieve "substantial justice" between the parties, equitable remedies are not governed by a strict statute of limitations in the way that a damages lawsuit would be.

Instead, a defendant who believes that the plaintiff has waited "too long" can invoke the equitable defense of **laches**. This rather odd term is expressed somewhat more eloquently in Civil Code §3527 (one of the "maxims of jurisprudence") that "The law helps the vigilant, before those who sleep on their rights." Normally, a party who tries to defend an equitable lawsuit on the grounds of laches will have to show some prejudice—that is, that he or she relied on the plaintiff's failure to seek an equitable remedy promptly, so that the defendant changed his or her position to his or her detriment.

> Example: George has a contract with Sam to buy Sam's residence for $275,000. After they signed the agreement, Sam receives an offer for $350,000 from David, who did not realize that the property had already been sold. Rather than honoring his agreement with George, Sam decides that the extra $75,000 is too good to pass up and notifies George that he intends to back out of their agreement. He accepts David's offer for $350,000 and opens escrow with David.
>
> George could seek specific performance while Sam is in escrow with David, but initially decides not to do so. Escrow closes, the deed is recorded, and David moves in. A year goes by and George and Sam have a chance meeting one day. They become involved in an argument over an unrelated matter. The argument revives the hurt feelings of the previous year and George decides to sue seeking specific performance of the sale that Sam had earlier not honored.
>
> By this time, David has established himself in Sam's former house and Sam had assumed that George had forgotten about the earlier matter. Although George is well within the four-year statute of limitations, a court eventually dismisses George's lawsuit for specific performance on the ground of laches. By not trying to seek specific performance promptly the previous year, George has allowed Sam's and David's expectations to become settled that their transaction was final.

SUMMARY

California law defines a contract as "an agreement to do or not to do a certain thing." A contract must have certain elements—competent parties, mutual consent, a lawful object, and consideration. The Civil Code combines the offer and acceptance into the mutual consent of the parties to enter into the agreement. The person who makes the offer is the offeror, while the person to whom the offer is made is the offeree. Contracts that lack any of the required elements are void.

An offer is terminated in a number of ways. These include the lapse of time, the death of either the offeror or offeree, the destruction of the subject matter of the contract, and rejection by the offeree. Rejection by the offeree includes the making of a counteroffer, which turns the former offeror into the offeree, and vice versa. Before it is accepted, an offer can be revoked by the offeree.

Contracts are either unilateral or bilateral. If they are unilateral, the offeree will have to perform some act in order to accept the offer, at which point the contract has been formed. If the contract is bilateral, the parties exchange mutual promises to bind one another to perform the various obligations under the contract.

The parties are competent if both are over 18, and are of sound mind, and have not been deprived of civil rights. A person who is under a conservatorship is by law of unsound mind, and someone in prison following a felony conviction has usually been deprived of civil rights. A lawful object means that the subject matter of the contract is not illegal to own or to bargain for, such as illegal drugs or, in many states, gambling debts.

The statute of frauds requires real estate contracts to be in writing. It also requires anything related to a real estate contract, such as the listing agreement between the seller and broker, to be in writing in order to be enforceable.

Breach of a contract occurs when one party fails to comply with a contractual obligation. The party that is not in breach can treat a breach as material or immaterial. Depending on the circumstances, a material breach of contract may entitle the other party to money damages or may excuse further performance by the party who is not in breach.

UNIT 12 REVIEW

Matching Exercise

Instructions: Write the letter of the matching term on the blank line before its definition. Answers are in Appendix A.

Terms

A. acceptance

B. bilateral contract

C. breach

D. competence

E. condition precedent

F. condition subsequent

G. consideration

H. contract

I. counteroffer

J. laches

K. lapse of time

L. liquidated damages

M. mailbox rule

N. minor

O. mutual rescission

P. offer

Q. parol evidence

R. statute of limitations

S. unilateral contract

T. valid contract

Definitions

1. _____ Agreement to do or not to do a certain thing

2. _____ Contract in which the offeror bargains for the performance of an act as the acceptance of the offer

3. _____ Contract in which the promises mutually exchanged by each party constitute the consideration for the contract

4. _____ Element of all valid contracts that requires the parties to be over 18, of sound mind, and not deprived of civil rights

5. _____ Person under the age of 18

6. _____ Proposal indicating a present intent by the person making the proposal to be bound by a contract

7. _____ Way an offer is deemed to be terminated because the offeree failed to respond within a reasonable period after the offer

8. _____ Manifestation on the part of the offeree to agree to the terms of an offer unconditionally

9. _____ Response to an offer that changes some term of the offer

10. _____ Exception to the rule that an offer must be communicated to an offeree, making an acceptance binding upon deposit in the U.S. Mail

11. _____ Any benefit conferred upon the promisor in a contract that will support the formation of a contract

12. _____ Contract with all required elements and is therefore binding and enforceable

13. _____ Oral statements made during the negotiation of a contract that are "merged" into a written agreement upon its execution

14. _____ Event, which if it occurs, excuses one party from further obligations to perform under a contract

15. _____ Something that must happen before one party to a contract is obligated to perform

16. _____ Term in a contract by which the parties agree that if one party breaches the agreement, their liability is limited to a specific amount

17. _____ All parties to a contract agree to cancel the agreement and put themselves back where they started

18. _____ Failure by one party to comply with his or her obligations under a contract

19. _____ Time limit for someone to file a lawsuit or be forever barred from enforcing a legal right in court

20. _____ Flexible time limit within which someone must seek an equitable remedy from a court

Multiple Choice Questions

Instructions: Circle your response and go to Appendix A to read the complete explanation for each question.

1. Ted, Pat, and Molly are selling a property they own as tenants in common. They received a full price offer. Both Ted and Pat have signed the purchase offer, but Molly has not yet signed. How would this contract be classified?
    a. Executed
    b. Executory
    c. Implied
    d. Unilateral

2. Of the following, who legally would be considered competent to contract?
    a. Person who is under 18 years of age.
    b. Divorced person who is under 18 years of age.
    c. Person who is the subject of the conservatorship.
    d. Person who is sentenced to imprisonment in the state prison.

3. Once an offer has been communicated to the offeree, it does not stay open forever. Which is not a way to terminate an offer?
    a. Destruction of the subject matter
    b. Capacity of either party
    c. Rejection by the offeree
    d. Revocation by the offeror

4. On April 20, Fred submits a written offer to buy Andrew's house. The offer states that it will remain open until May 1. On April 28, the house is destroyed by fire. On April 29, Andrew, unaware of the fire, mailed a letter accepting the offer. Which of the following is true?
    a. The acceptance created a binding contract, because the offer was irrevocable until May 1.
    b. No contract was formed, because the offer was terminated by the fire.
    c. A contract was formed because of the "mailbox rule."
    d. The acceptance created a binding contract, because a written offer is not terminated by the destruction of the subject matter of the offer.

5. On October 1, Kelly sends Bill a letter stating, "I offer to sell you my property for $250,000. This offer is irrevocable for 14 days." On October 6, she receives a written offer from Sarah for this same property for $300,000. Kelly immediately delivers a letter to Bill stating, "I revoke my offer to sell as of October 1," and accepts Sarah's offer. On October 10, despite having received the October 6 revocation, Bill sends a written acceptance of the October 1 offer, citing the language in the original letter. If this matter ends up in court, what is likely to occur?

    a. Kelly will have to pay Bill damages, but will not have to sell the house to him.

    b. Kelly will have to sell the house to Bill because her October 1 offer stated that it was irrevocable.

    c. Bill will not be able to compel Kelly to sell the house, nor can he receive damages, because there was no consideration for the statement that her offer was "irrevocable" for 14 days.

    d. Sarah will owe Bill damages for interference with contract.

6. Fred induced his aunt, Nancy, who was completely dependent upon Fred for her daily needs, to enter into a contract to sell her house to Fred on highly favorable terms. Which of the following is a court likely to conclude about this transaction?

    a. Fred and Nancy have an unconditionally enforceable bilateral contract.

    b. The contract is voidable by Nancy, because Fred used duress to make her sign.

    c. The contract is void because it has an unlawful purpose.

    d. The contract is voidable by Nancy, because Fred used undue influence to make Nancy sign.

7. Tom and Pam have been negotiating a real property deal for some time. Each has rejected offers that the other has made through their respective brokers. Tom runs into Pam at a restaurant one day and says, "I think we can work out the terms of this deal ourselves." After an hour, they have reached an agreement. Tom scribbles the terms on a cocktail napkin, which he signs and has Pam sign. What is the status of their agreement?

    a. Tom and Pam have no contract because it was written on a cocktail napkin.

    b. Tom and Pam have no contract because they acted without the assistance of their respective brokers.

    c. Tom and Pam have a binding contract assuming that all terms are set forth on the napkin.

    d. Tom and Pam would have a binding contract whether or not it was in writing.

8. Ron, a broker, has an exclusive agency listing with Sam, the owner of a parcel of real estate. Their listing agreement provides that Ron must find a ready, willing, and able buyer who will pay a minimum of $390,000 for Sam's house. If he does so, Ron will receive a 6% commission. Ron finds such a buyer and informs Sam of the offer, recommending that he accept it. After thinking it over, Sam decides that he cannot bring himself to sell and instructs Ron to reject the offer. Which of the following legal actions would most likely result from this?

   a. Ron could sue for Sam for specific performance to compel him to go through with the sale.
   b. The buyer that Ron found could sue Sam for specific performance to compel him to go through with the sale.
   c. The buyer could sue Sam for monetary damages.
   d. Ron could sue Sam for his 6% commission.

9. Broker Donna released Bob from a listing agreement with no further obligations to broker Donna. What type of release is this?

   a. Consideration
   b. Conditional
   c. Unilateral
   d. Unconditional

10. Shortly after purchasing a home, Sam realized he paid more for the property than for what other comparable homes in the neighborhood were selling. He discovered later that the broker-owner of the property and the appraiser were related. He decided to sue the broker for a breach of fiduciary duty. However, Sam became involved in his business and before he knew it, over four years had passed. He was still angry with the broker, so he called his attorney to start a lawsuit against the broker. After the lawyer learned the facts of the case, the attorney told Sam that he could not file a lawsuit because the time had expired according to the:

   a. statute of frauds.
   b. doctrine of promissory estoppel.
   c. statute of limitations.
   d. parol-evidence rule.

Real Estate Contracts

Unit 13

INTRODUCTION

An agent must know how to fill out a contract and be able to explain the contract in understandable terms to his or her client. The listing agreement and purchase contract are two key contracts that agents complete when representing a seller or buyer.

The most common types of contracts a licensee encounters are listing agreements, buyer representation agreements, purchase agreements, and options. The real estate licensee should be familiar with the content of these contracts and be able to explain them to clients.

Learning Objectives

After completing this unit, you should be able to:

13A   recognize specifics of real estate contracts.

13B   classify types of listing agreements.

13C   designate the main functions of a deposit receipt.

13D   recall the rights of the optionor and optionee in an option.

OVERVIEW OF REAL ESTATE CONTRACTS

Real estate contracts must have all the elements of a valid contract. Additionally, the statute of frauds requires that all real estate contracts must be in writing to be enforceable. The law states that the contracts that violate the statute of fraud are unenforceable—not void. This means that all parties may agree to move forward with the contract, if they choose to do so.

A broker must give a copy of any contract to the party signing it at the time that it is signed. [B&P §10142]. The agreement is still enforceable if the broker fails to comply with this requirement, but the broker can be disciplined for not doing so. In addition, brokers must keep copies of contracts and documents associated with real estate transactions for three years from the date of the closing or, if the transaction is not closed, from the date of the listing. Documents that must be retained include listings, purchase offers, counter offers, options, cancelled checks, trust records, disclosure documents, and other related documents. [B&P §10148].

Since real estate transactions depend on a variety of contracts, it is important to know which contracts to use and their proper completion. Real estate brokers and their agents often deal with relatively unsophisticated buyers and sellers during a real estate transaction. Therefore, brokers and their agents will help negotiate the terms of the agreement that will ultimately become the contract between the buyer and seller.

Perhaps even more important is that in transferring the terms of the parties' oral negotiations into written form, licensees should use care not to try to write specialized contract terms for the contract. This activity can constitute the **unauthorized practice of law** (a misdemeanor under Business and Professions Code §6125). The drafting of complicated language specific to a particular contract is what attorneys—not real estate agents or brokers—are licensed to do. In addition, when completing contracts avoid ambiguity. The *contra proferentem* (Latin for "against the proffering party") rule states that any term in a contract that is ambiguous should be interpreted against the party that drafted the document. For example, if a buyer's agent drafts a purchase offer and some term is not clear, then the seller will benefit.

Standardized Contract Forms

It is for these reasons that many standard form real estate contracts use checkbox and fill-in-the-blank formats. Standardized contracts used in California real estate transactions are available from the California Association of

REALTORS® (e.g. zipForm®), Professional Publishing in Novato, California, and from other providers, such as U.S. Legal Forms, Inc. In addition, some brokerage firms use contracts prepared specifically for their company by an attorney.

When using standardized forms, all that a real estate broker or salesperson has to do is to check a box to indicate a subject (e.g., financing, if the buyer needs financing) and then fill in the boxes related to the terms of that subject. By using a variety of standard contract forms, licensees can cover nearly every conceivable topic necessary to summarize the parties' agreement, while avoiding actions that might constitute practicing law. In this role, a real estate licensee in effect becomes merely the scrivener or recorder of the parties' agreements, without having to create specific language for any of the covenants in the contract.

Electronic Real Estate Contracts

The **California Uniform Electronic Transactions Act** (UETA) codified California Civil Code; Division 3; Part 2, Contracts; Title 2.5, Electronic Transactions *Cal. Civ. Code §§1633.1–1633.17* became effective January 1, 2000. This act provides that documents establishing contracts and agreements in a real estate transaction may be electronically written and signed. UETA legitimizes electronic contracting and "removes the barriers without affecting the underlying legal rules and requirements." UETA does not formally mandate electronic contracts, but leaves it to the option of the parties involved whether or not to contract electronically or by traditional means. It expressly provides that it "applies only to transactions between parties each of which has agreed to conduct transactions by electronic means." The Act also makes it clear that "[a] party that agrees to conduct a transaction by electronic means may refuse to conduct other transactions by electronic means."

Section 2 of the UETA defines contract, electronic record, and electronic signature as they relate to the act. A **contract** means the total legal obligation resulting from the parties' agreement as affected by this chapter and other applicable law. An **electronic record** means a record created, generated, sent, communicated, received, or stored by electronic means. An **electronic signature** means an electronic sound, symbol, or process attached to or logically associated with a record and executed or adopted by a person with the intent to sign the record.

Section 7. Legal Recognition of Electronic Records, Electronic Signatures, and Electronic Contracts.

(a)　A record or signature may not be denied legal effect or enforceability solely because it is in electronic form.

(b)　A contract may not be denied legal effect or enforceability solely because an electronic record was used in its formation.

(c)　If a law requires a record to be in writing, an electronic record satisfies the law.

(d)　If a law requires a signature, an electronic signature satisfies the law.

LISTING AGREEMENTS

A **listing agreement** is a written contract by which a principal, or seller, employs a broker to sell real estate. As a contract, a listing agreement must meet each element of a contract, including mutual consent and consideration. (Presumably, in most situations, both the seller and broker will be age 18 or older, both will be mentally competent to enter into the agreement and the object of the agreement—the sale of the client's real property—will be lawful.) A bilateral contract is created when the seller signs a listing agreement promising payment for service by the listing broker and the broker promises to use due diligence in finding a buyer.

Under agency law, the listing broker is a special agent who deals in the name of the principal to negotiate the sale of property. The broker does not have control over the property itself, while acting within the course of a special agency, but only has the right to represent that principal. The seller does not promise to sell the house, nor can the seller be forced to sell, even after signing a listing agreement. The seller simply promises to pay a commission to the broker if he or she brings a ready, willing, and able buyer.

> Example: Ellen, a licensed real estate broker, spoke to everyone in her area at least once a month. Since she was well known, owner Sam called her when he wanted to sell his home. Ellen met with him and completed a listing agreement. An agency by express, written agreement was created.

Any listing agreement between the broker and the seller is subject to the statute of frauds. That is, because it is related to the purchase and sale of real estate, the listing agreement must be in writing or it is not enforceable by the broker. The requirement that the listing agreement be in writing is found in Civil Code §1624, subdivision (5).

Broker's Right to Compensation

A listing agreement is similar to an employment contract between the seller and the broker. It gives the broker the right to be paid only after doing the job or producing results. In general, a broker earns his or her commission by producing a mirror offer or by presenting an offer that the seller accepts. However, some contracts expressly state that no commissions are paid unless the property actually sells. This is the **no deal, no commission clause**. As the term implies, under this arrangement the seller is not obligated to pay a commission unless a sale of the property is actually consummated.

Broker Earns the Commission

1. Broker produces a buyer who is ready, willing, and able to purchase the property at the terms and price set by the seller, regardless of whether the sale is completed. A **ready, willing, and able** buyer is one who is prepared to enter into a purchase contract, eager to buy, and meets the financing requirements of purchase.
2. Seller accepts an offer from a buyer secured by the broker. In essence, the broker is the procuring cause.

Procuring Cause

A procuring cause is that which produces the desired results. *Black's Law Dictionary* defines **procuring cause** (proximate cause) as the "cause that directly produces an event and without which the event would not have occurred." In real estate, a broker must be the procuring cause—the person who brought about the ultimate sale of the property—in order to be entitled to a commission from such a listing.

A real estate broker is not entitled to a commission from a seller (or from the principal if the principal is not a seller) merely by entering into a listing agreement and trying to find a buyer. Unless the client has agreed to pay the broker on an hourly basis for the broker's services, the broker must meet the terms of the listing and show that the broker has complied with those terms through an uninterrupted sequence of events in order to be entitled to a fee.

In some cases, such as an exclusive-right-to-sell listing, the broker's job will be easier than in others. On the other hand, if the broker does not find a ready, willing, and able buyer—and in most cases, bring the transaction to a sale—then the broker is not entitled to a commission. A broker's ability to show that he or she has met the terms of the listing is ordinarily most difficult when an open listing is involved, because there is no agreement between the broker and principal. Rather, the broker must demonstrate that he or she was the procuring cause.

Safety Clause

Most listing agreements have a safety clause, sometimes called a protection or extender clause. The **safety clause** protects the listing broker's commission, if the owner personally sells the property to someone who was shown the property or made an offer during the term of the listing. At the time the listing is signed, the seller and broker need to agree on a length of time for the protection period. The protection clause applies only if the broker has given the seller a list containing the names of the protected buyers within three calendar days of expiration of the listing. This prevents a seller from waiting for a listing to end before accepting an offer and then refusing to pay the original broker (the procuring cause) a commission.

The assumption underlying a safety clause is that the broker's efforts in marketing the property during the term that the listing was in force was part of the causation behind the buyer's eventual decision to buy the property, and the broker should be rewarded for those efforts even though the listing technically had expired.

Specific Requirements for Listings

The law imposes some specific requirements on the formalities of a listing agreement. Real estate brokers and sales associates who do not comply with the following obligations could be fined or have their licenses suspended or revoked.

Definite Termination Date. If the listing is exclusive (either exclusive right to sell or exclusive agency), the exclusive listing must specify a definite termination date. [B&P §10176(f)]. Without a specified termination date, the seller may disaffirm the executory listing.

Listing-Option. A licensee who has both a listing and an option to buy on a property must inform the principal of the amount of profit the licensee will make and obtain the written consent of the principal approving the amount of such profit, before the licensee may exercise the option. [B&P §10176(h)]

Negotiability of Real Estate Commission. If a listing agreement is for one-to-four residential units (a single-family dwelling, or up to the size of a four-plex), the agreement must contain a statement in 10-point boldface type:

> **"Notice: The amount or rate of real estate commissions is not fixed by law. They are set by each Broker individually and may be negotiable between Seller and Broker."**

[B&P §10147.5]. The rate or the amount of a commission may not be pre-printed in a listing contract for such property.

Types of Listing Agreements

In California, there are four commonly used listing agreements: exclusive right to sell listing, exclusive agency listing, open listing, and net listing.

Exclusive Authorization and Right-to-Sell

An **exclusive authorization and right-to-sell listing** is an exclusive contract where the seller must pay the listing broker a commission if the property is sold within the time limit by the listing broker, any other person, or even by the owner. This is the most favorable kind of listing for a broker because the broker gets a commission regardless of who obtains a buyer—even if the seller locates the buyer! Because this arrangement is so favorable to the broker—it truly gives the broker a "right to sell" because the broker is entitled to a commission as long as the property actually changes hands during the term of the listing—one might wonder why a seller would agree to such terms.

The answer depends upon two things: the reputation a particular broker has and the conditions of the market. When real estate is moving quickly, some brokers have enough business to pick the properties they want to try to sell and can insist upon such a listing as a condition of handling a seller's property. In addition, if a given broker has a favorable reputation for being able to sell property quickly, that will also give that broker bargaining leverage when negotiating the listing agreement with a client. Obviously, when the market slows down, if a given broker does not have such a reputation, being able to obtain such a listing arrangement with a client may not be possible in every case. Every exclusive authorization and right-to-sell listing must specify a definite termination date.

Exclusive Agency Listing

If a broker and a seller enter into an **exclusive agency listing**, the broker is the only one entitled to a commission upon the procurement of a buyer meeting the requirements of that listing agreement, unless the owner finds a buyer on his or her own. Because that broker is the only one who can obtain a commission for the transaction, the broker must use his or her best efforts to procure a buyer. This listing agreement must have a definite termination date or allow the seller to terminate the listing at will. If the seller cancels the listing, then this agreement commonly entitles the broker to a commission based on the original listing price (assuming that the broker has been acting with due diligence).

Open Listing

An **open listing**, unlike other kinds of listings, is not exclusive to one broker. The owner provides notice that a parcel of property is for sale and will pay a stated commission to any broker who procures a ready, willing, and able buyer. An open listing is really an **offer for a unilateral contract**.

The first broker to obtain a buyer who meets the terms of the listing, and whose offer is accepted by the seller, earns the commission. That agent is known as the procuring cause of the sale. Unlike an exclusive listing agreement, an open listing does not require a specific termination date. The owner may sell the property without an agent, owing no commission.

Net Listing

A **net listing** is an employment contract in which the commission is not definite. Instead of the broker being entitled to a percentage of the sales price, the seller and the broker agree to a minimum amount that the seller wants for the property and the broker is entitled to anything that the broker can negotiate above that price. The broker must disclose the selling price to both buyer and seller within 30 days after closing the transaction.

> Example: Sam wants to sell his property and retains Bruce as his broker. Sam wants $250,000 for the property. He and Bruce agree to a net listing that and will guarantee Sam the $250,000 and allow Bruce to keep anything above this that he can negotiate as the sale price for his fee. If Bruce ultimately closes a sale for $350,000, then he would be entitled to $100,000 as his sales commission.

Avoiding Risk

Unlike other arrangements between the broker and seller, a net listing carries with it the potential to create conflict of interest between the broker and seller. A potential buyer, especially in a weak market, might try to "lowball" the property, with an offer that either matches (or perhaps comes in just above) the minimum price the seller wants. Although the broker might be tempted to reject such an offer immediately, as a fiduciary, the broker must inform the seller of all offers that meet the minimum terms of the client's agreement, even if that means that the broker will get little or no fee.

> Example: Sally wants to sell her property and retains Ted as her broker. Sally wants $250,000 for the property. She and Ted agree to a net listing that will guarantee Sally $250,000 and allow Ted to keep anything above this that he can negotiate as the sale price for his fee. Ted lists the property for $300,000. However, Charles makes an offer for $255,000. If Sally accepts this offer, she will owe Ted $5,000 for his fee because the offer is above the minimum that Sally said she wanted. The difference ($5,000) is all that Ted will earn. Had Ted found Sally a buyer under a traditional 6% commission, his fee would have been more than $15,000.

A net listing comes close to converting the broker into an optionee rather than a true representative of the seller. Because of the potential conflict of interest, brokers who choose to work under a net listing should be aware of the risks involved.

Rattray v. Scudder

In *Rattray v. Scudder* (1946) 28 Cal.2d 214, Rattray was a real estate agent in Bakersfield. He told his client, for whom he was attempting to sell some commercial property, that he was having difficulty achieving the seller's requested price of $13,000, and suggested that the seller accept $10,000. The seller was reluctant, but finally agreed to accept $10,250, but later learned that Rattray actually had negotiated a sale with a buyer for $13,500, and that immediately upon getting the seller's permission to accept $10,250, Rattray sold the property for that sum and his brokerage kept more than $2,000.

> ### *Rattray v. Scudder* (continued)
>
> The Supreme Court, by a 4-3 vote, overturned a lower court decision and reinstated the Real Estate Commissioner's revocation of Rattray's license. The majority found that Rattray had violated his fiduciary duties to his client by double-dealing: in effect, he bought the property for $10,250 and then immediately re-sold it for a profit. The minority would have found that Rattray was really an optionee and had simply exercised the option to buy the property himself before re-selling it.

Handling Buyer's Deposits

A listing broker cannot accept a deposit from a buyer unless specifically authorized to do so in the listing agreement. When a listing broker does so without authorization from the seller, he or she is acting as an agent of the buyer and not the seller. Any misappropriation of these funds by the listing broker would result in loss to the buyer and not the seller. However, most listing agreements give express authority to the broker to receive the buyer's deposit on behalf of the seller. This authority given to the broker also applies to any subagents, unless the subagent is working as the agent of the buyer. If a seller accepts an offer, the buyer's deposit becomes the responsibility of the seller. A listing broker may not return a buyer's deposit after the seller accepts the offer, without the consent of the seller.

The acceptance of a check, rather than cash or a promissory note, as an earnest money deposit must be disclosed to the seller at the time the offer is presented. In addition, if the buyer instructs the listing broker to hold the check uncashed until the offer is accepted, the fact must be disclosed to the seller when the offer is presented.

Any broker who puts a client's money in his or her own personal bank account is guilty of commingling. [B&P §10176(e)]. **Commingling** is the illegal practice of depositing client's funds in a broker's personal or general business account. Checks must be deposited within three business days after receiving them, either into a trust account or a neutral escrow account. If a broker uses the client's money, it is known as conversion.

BUYER REPRESENTATION AGREEMENTS

A **buyer representation agreement** is an employment contract between a buyer and a broker. The buyer representation agreement is to the buyer as the listing agreement is to the seller. As single agency becomes more prevalent, more brokers represent the buyer to locate a property rather than represent the seller. A **buyer's agent** is a broker employed by the buyer to locate a certain kind of real property.

As with all exclusive agreements, a definite termination date is specified. Also, the manner of the broker's compensation is described, stating that all real estate commissions are negotiable.

PURCHASE AGREEMENTS

A **purchase agreement** or sales contract is the original agreement between the buyer and seller. When signed by both buyer and seller, it is a legally binding written contract that indicates the terms and conditions of the purchase and sale of the piece of real estate. Because of this, it reflects the mutual and agreed-upon desires of the parties when it becomes the actual escrow instructions.

In California, most real estate agents use the Residential Purchase Agreement and Joint Escrow Instructions, commonly known as a **deposit receipt** or **purchase offer** because it is an offer to purchase real property. In most cases, a standard California Residential Purchase Agreement and Joint Escrow Instructions (RPA-CA) contract is used by real estate agents when a buyer makes an offer anywhere in California. It was created by the California Association of REALTORS® (C.A.R.). The Bureau of Real Estate does not officially recommend this form nor is any type of specific form required by law. Real estate agents do have an alternative, however, among the standard C.A.R. forms, depending on the custom in their area of the state. Real estate practices differ significantly in different parts of California and some of those differences are not reflected in the commonly used deposit receipt. An alternate form, Area Edition Residential Purchase Agreement (AERPA11) is available to real estate agents who desire features not included in the other form.

Elements of Purchase Agreements

The purchase agreement covers more than just the purchase price and closing date. It covers contingencies, various inspections, mandatory disclosures, buyer's rights to investigate the property, how the buyer will take title, damages and dispute resolution, escrow instructions, compensation to the brokers, and acceptance of the offer.

Multi-Purposes of the Deposit Receipt

Offer. It is an offer to purchase a specific parcel of real property described by street address, legal description, and/or assessor's parcel number. Most buyers stipulate a timeframe within which the seller must accept the offer. However, anytime before the seller accepts the offer, the buyer may revoke the offer. If the seller takes no action of the offer, the offer terminates due to lapse of time.

Receipt for Deposit. It is the buyer's receipt for the earnest money deposit. Until the seller unconditionally accepts the offer and signs the deposit receipt, the deposit belongs to the buyer. [*Sarten v. Pomatto* (1963) 192 C.A.2d 28].

Acceptance of Offer. Once the deposit receipt is accepted unconditionally and signed by the seller, it becomes a legally binding bilateral contract. A conditional acceptance creates a counteroffer, thus terminating the original offer. Death or incapacity does not automatically cancel a contract. If the seller dies or becomes incapacitated after acceptance of the offer, the seller's heir(s) must complete the sale.

Joint Escrow Instructions. The written contract acts as joint escrow instructions to the escrow holder.

Agency. The contract reconfirms the agency relationships.

Broker Compensation from Seller. The seller agrees to pay the broker compensation, which is specified in a separate, written agreement. Additionally, if escrow does not close, the broker is paid according to the terms of the separate, written agreement.

Dispute Resolution. The contract provides for dispute resolution. The buyer and seller must agree to mediation by a neutral mediator in the attempt to resolve disputes. If a party does not attempt mediation prior to filing an arbitration or court action, he or she will not be awarded attorney's fees even if he or she is the prevailing party. In contrast to mediation, both buyer and seller must agree to be bound by mutual arbitration in order for the arbitration clause to be effective.

Handling Contingencies

The majority of purchase agreements are conditional—that is, they have contingencies. Although the most common contingency in a purchase agreement may be financing, others include appraised value, marketability of title, sale of the buyer's property, and various disclosures and inspections.

> Example: Barney makes an offer to buy Sylvia's real estate that she has for sale for $500,000. When Barney made this offer, he had not arranged financing from his local bank. He puts a condition into the contract that he has 30 days to arrange financing. Because Barney's offer is higher than any other offer she has received, Sylvia agrees to the condition. If he fails to arrange the financing, however, Sylvia will not be obligated to sell him the property.
>
> Three weeks after the contract is signed, Barney's bank approves the loan for $500,000. Barney informs the broker handling the transaction for Sylvia that he has obtained financing and that he will arrange for the loan to be funded at the close of escrow. Obtaining the loan for $500,000 is a **condition precedent** to Sylvia being obligated to sell Barney the property. Now that he has satisfied the condition, Sylvia is obligated to comply with the other terms of the contract and, barring any other problems, will have to go through with the sale to Barney.

Contingency Time Periods. Buyers and sellers are given specific amounts of time to meet the various conditions of the contract. In the C.A.R. RPA-CA form, sellers have seven days, or a specified number of days, to deliver all reports and disclosures for which he or she is responsible. Buyers are given 17 days or a specified number of days to complete all investigations and review of reports. This may include reviewing lead-based paint and hazard disclosures, scheduling a home inspection, and investigating insurability). The buyer must request that the seller make repairs, which the seller may or may not agree to make. Additionally, within the 17 days, the buyer must either remove the contingency or cancel the agreement.

Seller's Right to Cancel. If the buyer does not meet certain obligations provided for in the contract, such as making a deposit, providing a preapproval letter or signing a receipt for uninsured deposit; the seller may cancel the agreement and return the buyer's deposit.

Effect of Buyer's Contingency Removal. If the buyer's contingency or cancellation rights are removed, in essence the buyer agrees to continue without contingencies, proceed with the transaction, and assume responsibility for repairs or corrections pertaining to that contingency or cancellation right.

Cancellation. The buyer and seller agree that if the agreement is cancelled, the buyer's deposit, less costs and fees, will be returned. The buyer and seller will sign a notice of cancellation and it will be given to the holder to release the deposit. This is not automatic.

OPTIONS

An **option** is a contract to keep open, for a set period of time, an offer to purchase or lease real property. An option is a written, unilateral contract between the owner of real property and a prospective buyer, stating the right to purchase, a fixed price, and timeframe. The person who owns the property (seller, lessor) is the **optionor**. The person who wants to purchase or lease (lessee) the property is called the **optionee**.

An option comes about when one party has made an offer that the other party believes is attractive but is unsure whether to accept it or to reject it immediately. Rather than choosing either one immediately, the offeree may instead suggest paying the offeror separate consideration for the right to accept or reject the offer at some time in the future.

Example: Oscar has a parcel of property that has been on the market for some time. He has not received many offers for it. Then he receives an offer from Lewis that is $30,000 below the listing price. Oscar thinks about rejecting the offer immediately, but because this is the first offer he has received in several weeks, he hesitates.

Finally, he contacts Lewis and says, "I'd like some time to think about your offer for my place. How much would it cost to keep it open for a couple of weeks?" Lewis is not in a hurry to find a place to buy, and he is hoping that Oscar will accept his offer. He responds, "Two hundred bucks."

Oscar visits Lewis and gives him a check for $200. He also has Lewis sign a receipt indicating that the money is for an option that will keep his offer open for two weeks; it also states that, if Oscar decides to accept the offer, Lewis will get a credit against the purchase price for the $200, but if Oscar turns him down, Lewis will keep the money. Oscar now has two weeks to mull over Lewis' offer without making a hasty decision either way.

Elements of a Valid Option

An option must be in writing and must have actual monetary consideration paid to the owner (optionor). The consideration may be in the form of cash, a check, or something else of value. If the optionee decides not to buy the property during the term of the option, the consideration remains with the optionor. In a lease option, payment of rent and the provisions of the lease are acceptable as the consideration.

Rights of the Optionor and Optionee

An option contract actually restricts the rights of the seller (optionor) because he or she cannot sell or lease the property during the option period. While the option is in existence, the optionor cannot accept any other offers for the property. For example, if a more attractive offer comes in, the optionor cannot revoke the option in order to accept the second offer.

The buyer (optionee) is the only one who has a choice, once the contract is signed and the consideration given. The option does not bind the optionee to any performance—he or she does not have to exercise the option. It merely provides the right to demand performance from the optionor, who must sell if the optionee decides to buy the property during the course of the option.

The option does not give the optionee a legal interest in the title and the optionee does not have any right to use the land. The optionee may assign or sell the option without the permission of the optionor during the term of the option. The optionee may find another buyer for the property to exercise the option.

SUMMARY

A listing agreement is a written contract by which a principal, or seller, employs a broker to sell real estate. There are various kinds of listing agreements; some, like an open listing, are highly favorable to the seller and require the broker to prove that he or she was the one who was the procuring cause of the sale. Other listings, such as the exclusive agency or exclusive right to sell, will normally entitle the broker to a fee as long as the property changes hands during the term of the listing agreement.

An option occasionally arises at the beginning of a real estate negotiation. An option is really a separate contract that governs whether an offer by one party will remain open—and therefore irrevocable—while the other party considers it. An option can be a flexible tool for the party entitled to exercise the option, especially the buyer, while exploring other opportunities. The party who grants the option will at least be entitled to the fee for the option if the party who pays for it ultimately declines to exercise it.

Real estate purchase contracts have various conditions that impose obligations on each party to the agreement. A condition precedent is one that, if the condition occurs, it requires the other party to perform as provided in the agreement. A condition subsequent, on the other hand, cuts off further obligation to perform by the party in whose favor the condition runs. Both conditions precedent and conditions subsequent are referred to by the terms contingencies among those who practice in the real estate industry.

UNIT 13 REVIEW

◻ Matching Exercise

Instructions: Write the letter of the matching term on the blank line before its definition. Answers are in Appendix A.

Terms

A. buyer representation agreement

B. contra proferentem

C. electronic record

D. electronic signature

E. exclusive agency listing

F. listing agreement

G. net listing

H. no deal, no commission clause

I. open listing

J. option

K. optionee

L. procuring cause

M. purchase agreement

N. safety clause

O. unauthorized practice of law

Definitions

1. _____ Misdemeanor under Business and Professions Code §6125

2. _____ Ambiguous terms in a contract should be interpreted against the party drafting the document

3. _____ Record created, generated, sent, communicated, received, or stored by electronic means

4. _____ Electronic sound, symbol, or process attached to or logically associated with a record and executed or adopted by a person with the intent to sign the record

5. _____ Written contract by which a principal, or seller, employs a broker to sell real estate

6. _____ Clause expressly stating that no commissions are paid unless the property actually sells

7. _____ Person responsible for the ultimate sale of real property so as to be entitled to a commission

8. _____ Clause protecting listing broker's commission, if the owner personally sells the property to someone who was shown the property or made an offer during the term of the listing

9. _____ Listing in which the broker is entitled to a fee only if the seller does not find a buyer on his or her own

10. _____ Listing, not exclusive to one broker

11. _____ Listing between a broker and a seller setting the broker's fee above a certain minimum amount

12. _____ Employment contract between a buyer and a broker

13. _____ Original purchase contract between the buyer and seller

14. _____ Contract to keep an offer open for a set period of time

15. _____ Person who wants to purchase or lease property under an option

Multiple Choice Questions

Instructions: Circle your response and go to Appendix A to read the complete explanation for each question.

1. If an agent failed to give a property owner a copy of an exclusive listing at the time it was signed, this would:
    a. allow the owner to refuse to pay a commission to the broker.
    b. make the listing void.
    c. make the listing voidable.
    d. subject the agent to disciplinary action.

2. Broker Mary enters into a listing to handle a sale for Sally for property that Sally has just inherited. One week after entering the listing, Sally contacts Mary and tells her, with some embarrassment, that she has changed her mind and is not ready to part with her late parents' former home. Does Mary have to maintain a record of this listing?
    a. No, because the listing was so short.
    b. Yes, but only because the listing lasted at least a week.
    c. Only if Sally insists upon it in case she again decides to sell.
    d. Yes, because it was a listing, even though it was so short.

3. Seller Sam signed a 90-day exclusive authorization and right to sell listing agreement with broker, Pam. Thirty days later, Pam presented an offer from a buyer, which Sam accepted. Escrow was opened, but the buyer and seller could not agree on some termite work so the sale did not go through. The listing had a specific clause that prohibited Pam from earning a commission, even though she found a ready, willing, and able buyer. What is the clause?

    a. Assignment clause
    b. Contra proferentem
    c. No deal, no commission clause
    d. Safety clause

4. A safety clause is a:

    a. common provision in a real estate contract allowing either party to withdraw within three days of the contract's formation.
    b. requirement that the seller ensure that there are no hazards on property that is the subject of a real estate contract.
    c. requirement that the property owner ensure that there are no hazards on a property that is the subject of a residential tenancy.
    d. provision allowing a real estate broker to receive a fee under certain conditions even if the listing has expired.

5. Which statement is incorrect regarding listing agreements?

    a. Commissions are negotiable between seller and broker.
    b. Exclusive listings must specify a definite termination date.
    c. The rate of real estate commissions is set by law.
    d. The rate or the amount of a commission may not be pre-printed in a listing contract for such property.

6. Jack, a real estate broker, enters into an exclusive agency listing with Mike, who is selling his house. A few weeks later, Mike is at a party and mentions to another partygoer that he is selling his property, and suggests that they go by the property after the party. Mike's friend is taken with the property during this visit and contacts Jack the next day asking him to draw up a contract. Is Jack entitled to a fee?

    a. Yes, because he had an exclusive agency listing with Mike.
    b. No, because Mike found the eventual buyer of the property.
    c. Yes, because Jack still had to prepare the sales agreement.
    d. No, because Jack had already performed other services for Mike.

7. If a seller accepts the deposit receipt unconditionally, the deposit receipt:

    a. becomes a legally binding bilateral contract.

    b. acts as joint escrow instructions to the escrow holder.

    c. reconfirms the agency relationships.

    d. does all of the above.

8. Buyer Pat presented an offer to Seller Sam for the purchase of Sam's 10-year-old home in a quiet neighborhood. Pat gave Sam three days from the date of the offer to respond. Sam had another offer to consider, but finally accepted Pat's offer four days later and asked his broker to communicate his acceptance to Pat. Under these circumstances:

    a. a legally binding bilateral contract has been created.

    b. Sam created a counteroffer.

    c. Pat has no obligation under his original offer.

    d. Pat is obligated to make a new offer to seller Sam.

9. A prospective buyer made an offer and gave the seller's broker a $1,000 check as a deposit for the sale of a residence. Before the seller accepted the offer, the buyer contacted the broker and withdrew the offer. What should the broker do with the $1,000 check?

    a. Deposit it in escrow

    b. Return it immediately

    c. Hold it until the seller is notified

    d. Keep it to be reimbursed for out-of-pocket expenses

10. On October 1, Donna sends Bill a letter stating, "I offer to sell my property to you for $250,000. This offer shall remain irrevocable for 14 days." On October 6, she receives a written offer from Sarah for this same property for $300,000. Donna immediately sends Bill a fax stating, "I revoke my offer to sell as of October 1," and accepts Sarah's offer. On October 10, despite having received the October 6 revocation, Bill sends a written acceptance of the October 1 offer, citing the language in the original letter. If this matter ends up in court, what is likely to occur?

    a. Donna will have to sell the house to Bill because her original offer created an option that he could exercise for ten days.

    b. Donna will have to pay damages to Bill, but will not have to sell him the house.

    c. Bill did not have an enforceable option because there was no consideration for the statement in Donna's original letter that her offer was "irrevocable."

    d. Sarah will have to pay Bill damages for interfering with his contract with Donna.

Disclosures in Real Estate Transactions

Unit **14**

INTRODUCTION

One of the biggest pitfall areas for real estate professionals concerns the subject of disclosures. Inadequate or insufficient disclosure of information can and often is a major source of litigation. Ultimately, failure to provide disclosure can cost a real estate professional dearly. Failure to disclose can be financially devastating to the real estate professional if a judgment is entered against him or her. Moreover, failure to disclose can lead to immeasurable damage to professional reputation and most significantly, a loss of license in some instances.

Consequently, a real estate professional cannot be too cautious when dealing with sensitive information and important factual data. It is imperative that, as a real estate professional, you make absolutely certain you have given full and fair disclosure to the client on every conceivable matter that might arise. Failure to do so endangers you and your client substantially.

The list of disclosures in this unit is not and cannot be exhaustive because of the specific and individual nature of various parcels of property. Not every conceivable item can be covered here; however, the most common and significant items are included in the sections that follow. It is up to real estate professionals to give thoughtful consideration to each parcel and to give thorough and diligent service to their clients. In other words, be proactive, know the listing, know the client, and do not hesitate to be overly cautious by having clients sign disclosures for issues that may or may not ever arise. As the old adage says, "Better safe than sorry."

Learning Objectives

After completing this unit, you should be able to:

14A   identify why it is important to make appropriate disclosures in real estate transactions.

14B   recognize disclosures required of real estate agents.

14C   recall disclosures that are required in the process of transferring real estate.

WHY DISCLOSE?

California is a litigious state. People sue for the slightest insult or infraction. The news reports are peppered with stories of people who sue for coffee being too hot or for being offended by a silk-screened t-shirt. People sue for the sake of suing.

When large sums of money and/or homes are involved, the likelihood of being involved in litigation increases significantly. Litigation is expensive for all parties concerned and takes an immeasurable toll on people. Nonetheless, the court dockets are overloaded with increasing numbers of lawsuits. When people get "buyer's remorse" following the expenditure of hundreds of thousands of dollars or more, sometimes the only way they can assuage the "buyer's remorse" is by bringing litigation, trying to recoup some of the expenditure at the expense of a defendant. Somehow, reclaiming some of the outlaid money helps alleviate the feelings of regret.

Unfortunately, for the other parties involved, their feelings do not usually factor into the equation. Consequently, anything and everything parties can do to protect themselves to avoid litigation is a prudent choice. The only way to avoid the risk of litigation completely is not to engage in any transactions whatsoever. But, that behavior defeats the very purpose of becoming a real estate professional and trying to make a lucrative living.

Easton v. Strassburger

As mentioned earlier, real estate licensees are often held to a higher standard of disclosure than the seller is. This not only requires agents to disclose known facts, but to investigate suspected problems as well. This was not always the case, however. A seminal legal decision in 1984 imposed upon real estate professionals the duty to make a reasonable inspection of property. No longer was an eyeball inspection of the premises sufficient; rather, the professional *qua* professional, had to make a more specific inspection and disclose the findings to the buyer.

The case of *Easton v. Strassburger*, 152 Cal. App. 3d 90, is about a home built on a landfill that had not been properly compacted, but was listed for sale. The Strassburgers owned a one-acre parcel of land that contained a residence, a pool, and a guesthouse. During the time the Strassburgers owned it, there were two landslides on the property, one of which caused considerable damage. The Strassburgers repaired the damage and listed the property for sale the following year, but did not tell the real estate agent about the problem.

The listing agents inspected the property. According to the court, there was evidence that the agents "were aware of certain red flags which should have indicated to them that there were soil problems." A **red flag** is something that alerts a reasonably observant person of a potential problem. However, the agents did not test the soil stability of the property. Neither did they inform prospective buyers that there were potential soil stability problems.

Easton purchased the property from the Strassburgers for $170,000. Not long after escrow closed, a landslide occurred, followed by several subsequent, smaller slides. The damage was extensive. After the damage occurred, the value of the property was reduced to approximately $20,000 and the estimated cost of repairing and preventing further slide damage was more than $200,000.

Ultimately, the real estate agents were held to be liable for not performing an inspection in the face of the physical signs indicating poorly compacted fill. The court indicated that although the

> ### *Easton v. Strassburger* (continued)
>
> evidence did not establish that the agents had actual knowledge of the property's history of slides and soil problems; they were still negligent. All that the jury needed to hold them liable was to conclude that a reasonably competent and diligent inspection of the property would have uncovered the history of soil problems.
>
> In short, ignorance was not bliss. It is incumbent upon all professionals to rise to the highest level of competence and act in the most honorable and truthful manner. Failing to do a thorough job and claiming that there was insufficient reason to suspect a problem is inadequate.

The only option for those professionals who wish to press forward and succeed in their chosen vocation is to do their utmost to protect themselves. One way that this is performed is to document the disclosure of **material facts**—namely, those items that would affect the value or desirability of the property. While there is no bright line rule for what constitutes a material fact, generally, a fact is considered "material" if its existence or nonexistence would have affected whether the parties would have entered into or completed the transaction. Real estate licensees have a duty to disclose to the buyer all material defects that the buyer would not discover with diligent observation and attention. This can be and often is subjective. Examples of obvious material facts would be the presence of an easement across the land or presence in a hazard zone, such as an earthquake fault.

Because of the subjectivity in determining what might be a material fact, courts have developed guidelines to help alleviate the subjectivity based on individual sensitivities. The guidelines are more detailed and examine the gravity of the harm caused by nondisclosure—whether it is fair to impose on the buyer a duty to discover material facts instead of imposing on the seller a duty to disclose it and the impact on the stability of contracts if the court permits the buyer to rescind. These guidelines help reduce the likelihood of the irrational rescission of agreements.

Sometimes it seems the documentation is overdone to a ridiculous detail, which may be true. Every document and disclosure form, however, has been created as the result of some dispute that cost someone a lot of money in a prior litigation. Hence, every disclosure document represents the proverbial "ounce of prevention" to obviate the painful "pound of cure."

Moreover, the real estate professional is just that—a professional—and as such is held to a higher standard than the layperson because real estate professionals are presumed to have greater knowledge about the field than the public. Consequently, the standard of care imposed on the licensee is higher than that for the layperson. In fact, courts have held that the standard is even higher than that imposed on the actual seller, as we will see later in this unit. The real estate licensee's superior knowledge means that the licensee therefore must adhere to a higher standard of care.

We often hear the phrase, "Some things are better left unsaid." Such is not the case in the world of real estate transactions. Tempting as it may be not to shine a light on items that might hinder or even kill a potential sale, the repercussions of not doing so are potentially far worse. Examples throughout this unit help illustrate why it is crucial to "cross your T's" and "dot your I's" in every real estate transaction. It is essential to be diligent about ensuring that every possible risk—no matter how slight—be adequately disclosed and documented.

DISCLOSURES REQUIRED OF REAL ESTATE AGENTS

Real estate agents have the responsibility to disclose agency relationships, the negotiability of sales commissions, and sales price information to their clients. They are required to conduct a visual inspection of the listed property and disclose any material defects. They are not, in most instances, required to disclose a death on the property.

Agency Relationship Disclosure

Brokers work with clients in agency relationships, which exist between the broker (agent), the principal (client), and the third party (customer). As of January 1, 1988, the **Agency Relationship Disclosure Act** became effective in an attempt to clarify the agency relationships between sellers, brokers, and buyers. It applies to every residential property transaction of one-to-four units. [C.C. §2079.13 et. seq.] The law requires that real estate licensees supply a written document, called **Disclosure Regarding Real Estate Agency Relationships**, explaining the nature of agency. This agency disclosure must be made **prior** to taking a listing or writing an offer. Failure to make full disclosure can result in a breach of the relationship and subject the agent to litigation, should the principal's decision prove to be flawed based on the agent's insufficient communication.

Disclosure Process

The steps in the disclosure process are disclose, elect, and confirm.

Disclose the Relationship

The agency disclosure describes the obligations of an agent as seller's agent, buyer's agent, or dual agent. At this point, all parties are made aware that they do have a choice of who is to represent them as their own agent.

Who Presents a Written Disclosure?

- Listing agent (or his or her sales associate) must deliver the form to the seller before entering into a listing agreement.

- Selling agent (who may also be the listing agent) must provide the form to the buyer before the buyer makes an offer to purchase.

- Selling agent (if different from the listing agent) must provide the form to the seller before the offer to purchase is accepted.

Elect the Agency

The second part of the agency disclosure form requires all parties involved to confirm that they understand the agent's role. In other words, the first part of the disclosure reveals that the agent may represent only the buyer, only the seller, or both. All parties acknowledge their understanding at this point.

Confirm the Agency

All parties to the transaction (buyer, seller, and agents) are required to acknowledge that they understand who is representing whom and sign the agency confirmation form. One more time, the relationship will be confirmed in the sales contract, which is signed by all parties.

A licensee must use the Disclosure Regarding Real Estate Agency Relationships form and be able to explain it to clients and customers. The law is very clear about a licensee's responsibility for full disclosure. Misunderstanding or ignorance of the law is not a defense. A real estate license may be revoked or suspended for violation of the agency disclosure law.

Commission Disclosure

The Business & Professions Code §§10147.5, 10176(g) requires a written disclosure concerning commissions to all clients of a real estate licensee for transactions involving not more than 4 residential units (or mobile homes). The law is very specific about the size and type font that must be used and that the language must be prominent enough so as not to be hidden amongst other language. The text must be at least 10-point boldface type and must state:

> **NOTICE: The amount or rate of real estate commissions is NOT fixed by law. They are set by each broker individually and may be negotiable between the seller and broker.**

This notice must be physically placed before the provision in the agreement for compensation of the broker and the amount or rate of compensation cannot be preprinted.

Visual Inspection and Disclosure of Material Facts

The *Easton v. Strassburger* case findings stated real estate agents could be liable for defects in property that they know about as well as defects that they should know about as a result of a visual investigation. As a result of the 1985 amendments to Civil Code sections 2079 et seq., all listing brokers of a residential property and any cooperating brokers must conduct a reasonably competent and diligent visual inspection of the property. Additionally, they must disclose to a prospective buyer all material facts that may affect value, desirability, and intended use of the property.

They are not required to seek out latent defects in areas of the property that are not reasonably accessible. They are not required to inspect areas offsite of the property or public records or permits concerning the title or use of the property. If the property is a condominium, the real estate agent is responsible for inspecting the unit, not the common area.

Selling Price Disclosure

A broker must notify the buyer and the seller, in writing, of the selling price of real property within one month after completion of the sale. If a neutral escrow closes the transaction, a closing statement from the escrow holder will constitute compliance on the part of the broker. [B&P §10141].

Disclosure of Death and/or AIDS

Real estate agents must be very careful when making disclosures of death and/or AIDS on the property. Civil Code § 1710.2 states that the owner or the owner's agent (or any cooperating broker) do NOT have to disclose the occurrence of a death provided it occurred more than 3 years prior to the buyer's/lessor's offer to purchase or lease the property. Owners and the agents do NOT have to disclose that a person has or has died from Acquired Immune Deficiency Syndrome (AIDS). [C.C. §1710.2(1)(B)].

However, if a death occurs on a property within 3 years and the circumstances of that death are material (gruesome, offensive, or affected the reputation of the property), it must be disclosed. For example, under the case of *Reed* v. *King*, (1983) 145 Cal.App.3d 261, a death that occurred on a property was a material fact. In the *Reed* case, the court allowed the purchaser to rescind a contract on a home when she discovered that a woman and her four children were murdered there.

DISCLOSURES REQUIRED IN A REAL ESTATE TRANSFER

The area of real estate practice that probably has the most significant amount of disclosure requirements involves transfers. The buying and selling of real property typically involves hundreds of thousands—sometimes millions— of dollars and invokes multiple and complex considerations. The average layperson is ill equipped to research all the potential problems any given property may possess and therefore the law has increasingly required sellers to be forthright with information about possible problems on the property.

Caveat emptor—the old Latin phrase that means, "Let the buyer beware"— may apply to sales of used appliances at a flea market, but when a sale involves real property and large amounts of cash, *caveat emptor* does not apply in most circumstances (at least in California).

The variety of terms of a transaction that might warrant disclosure statements seems to grow all the time. Years ago, a seller might have had to disclose a septic tank that needed replacing. Now, a plethora of issues require disclosure and as previously stated, it is always better to err on the side of extreme caution (and hence, to disclose) than to withhold disclosure and risk litigation down the line.

Required Disclosures When Transferring Real Property

- Real Estate Transfer Disclosure Statement (TDS)
- Local Option Real Estate Transfer Disclosure Statement (LORETDS)
- Natural Hazard Disclosure Statement (NHD)
- Environmental Hazard Disclosures
- Property Tax Disclosures
- Miscellaneous Disclosures

Real Estate Transfer Disclosure Statement

Under California Civil Code section 1102 et seq., a seller of a residential property (one-to-four units) must deliver a written disclosure statement (Real Estate Transfer Disclosure Statement) about the condition of the property to the prospective buyer. The **Real Estate Transfer Disclosure Statement (TDS)** is a document that the seller must provide to any buyer of residential property (one-to-four units). It is a detailed statement telling what the seller knows about the condition of the property. The statement must list all known defects as well as any potential problems that might affect the property value.

The seller reveals any information that would be important to the buyer regarding the condition of the property in the TDS and states that to the seller's knowledge—everything important has been disclosed. Many facts about a residential property could materially affect its value and desirability.

Material Facts Affecting Desirability and Value of a Property

- Age, condition, and any defects or malfunctions of the structural components and/or plumbing, electrical, heating, or other mechanical systems
- Easements, common driveways, or fences
- Garage door openers that do not have the safety reverse feature
- Room additions, structural alterations, repairs, replacements, or other changes, especially those made without required building permits
- Flooding, drainage, or soil problems on, near, or in any way affecting the property
- Zoning violations, such as nonconforming uses or insufficient setbacks
- Homeowners' association obligations and deed restrictions or common area problems
- Citations against the property, or lawsuits against the owner or affecting the property

Material Facts Affecting Desirability and Value of a Property (continued)

- Location of the property within a known earthquake zone
- Major damage to the property from fire, earthquake, or landslide

Applicability of TDS

This requirement extends to most residential sales and some subdivided interests. The TDS applies to any transfer by sale, exchange, installment land sale contract, lease with an option to purchase, any other option to purchase, or ground lease coupled with improvements. Some transfers of realty are exempt.

Transfers Exempt from the Disclosure Requirement

- Transfers pursuant to a court order
- Transfers by a foreclosure sale
- Transfers court-ordered by a fiduciary in the administration of a probate estate or a testamentary trust
- Transfers to a spouse or another related person resulting from a judgment of dissolution of marriage or of legal separation or from a property settlement agreement incidental to such a judgment
- Transfers from one co-owner to another
- Transfers by the state controller for unclaimed property
- Transfers as a result from the failure to pay taxes
- Transfers from or to any governmental entity
- Transfers of the first sale of a residential property within a subdivision and a copy of a public report is delivered to the purchaser or if such a report is not required

Timing of Delivery

The seller, listing broker, and cooperating broker have the obligation to prepare and deliver the disclosure. If more than one real estate agent is involved in the transaction (unless otherwise instructed by the seller), the agent obtaining the offer is required to deliver the disclosure to the prospective buyer.

Usually, a broker obtains this statement at the time of the listing and provides a copy to a buyer before an offer to purchase the property is presented. If the real estate agent gives a copy of the disclosure statement to the buyer after the offer to purchase the property is presented, the buyer can terminate the sale. The buyer must act timely, however. If the disclosure was made by personal delivery, the buyer can terminate within three days. If the disclosure was sent by mail, the buyer has five days to terminate.

Realmuto v. Gagnard

> *In Realmuto v. Gagnard*, 110 Cal.App.4th 193 (2003), prospective buyers of a parcel of real property and its seller entered into a standard form residential purchase agreement. The written agreement contained provisions about the TDS and that the TDS had to be delivered to the buyer before the offer is signed or else the buyer had the right to cancel and rescind. During the course of the sale, the buyers did not request and the seller did not provide, the TDS. When the buyers did not complete the sale, the seller sued the buyers for specific performance. At trial, the court ruled in favor of the buyers, saying that the seller had an obligation to supply the TDS and the buyers could not waive their right to receive it by failing to request it. The trial court's decision to that effect was upheld on appeal.

If the prospective buyer receives a report or an opinion prepared by a licensed engineer, land surveyor, geologist, structural pest control operator, contractor, or other expert (with a specific professional license or expertise), the liability of the seller and the real estate agents may be limited when making required disclosures. The overall intention is to provide meaningful disclosures about the condition of the property being transferred. A violation of the law does not invalidate a transfer; however, the seller may be liable for any actual damages suffered by the buyer.

Avoiding Risk

Real Estate Transfer Disclosure Statement Violations B&P §10176.5(a). The commissioner may suspend or revoke a real estate license if the licensee has willfully or repeatedly violated any of the provisions of the Transfer Disclosure Statement.

Do not rely on the standard Real Estate Transfer Disclosure Statement to be a catchall for any possible problems. The disclosure statement is an important tool, but it is not exhaustive and does not cover all possible disclosure needs. Use it as a starting point and then continue to add other disclosure statements as necessary. As you will see in examples later in this unit, the failure to use supplemental disclosure forms can be tragic.

CalBRE has published a booklet, approximately 70 pages long, about the TDS which can be found on the Internet at CalBRE's website.

The TDS Itself

The TDS must be completed as soon as possible but certainly before transfer of title. Both the seller and the real estate licensee are required to make disclosures. The most critical items about the TDS are summarized below and a sample TDS is included for your convenience:

Information Disclosed by the Seller on the TDS Form

- Inclusion of other inspection reports
- Seller occupies the property
- Specific fixtures, appliances, improvements and features of the property, and whether they are in working order
- Any defects or malfunctions of the property, such as hazardous materials or conditions on the property
- Any features shared in common with adjoining owners
- Any encroachments or easements
- Additions, alterations, or modifications made without permits or to disclose additions, alterations, or modifications that do not comply with building codes
- Any fill on the property, soil problems, flooding, or any major damage to the property from floods, earthquakes, etc.
- Zoning violations
- Noise problems or nuisances
- Deed restrictions or the presence of a homeowner's association
- Common area facilities
- Any legal issues or actions affecting the property

In addition, there may be local requirements for disclosure and a Local Option form is included as well, which describes the property. Furthermore, natural hazards disclosures (floods zones, high fire risk, wildlands, earthquake fault zones, seismic hazard zones) are also prudent. The booklet also discusses Mello-Roos, property taxes, and other conditions that are significant, including methamphetamine contamination, lead-based paints, smoke detectors, water heaters, security against earthquakes, sex offenders, etc.

CALIFORNIA ASSOCIATION OF REALTORS®

REAL ESTATE TRANSFER DISCLOSURE STATEMENT
(CALIFORNIA CIVIL CODE §1102, ET SEQ.)
(C.A.R. Form TDS, Revised 4/14)

THIS DISCLOSURE STATEMENT CONCERNS THE REAL PROPERTY SITUATED IN THE CITY OF _____ , COUNTY OF _____ , STATE OF CALIFORNIA, DESCRIBED AS _____ .
THIS STATEMENT IS A DISCLOSURE OF THE CONDITION OF THE ABOVE DESCRIBED PROPERTY IN COMPLIANCE WITH SECTION 1102 OF THE CIVIL CODE AS OF (date) _____ . IT IS NOT A WARRANTY OF ANY KIND BY THE SELLER(S) OR ANY AGENT(S) REPRESENTING ANY PRINCIPAL(S) IN THIS TRANSACTION, AND IS NOT A SUBSTITUTE FOR ANY INSPECTIONS OR WARRANTIES THE PRINCIPAL(S) MAY WISH TO OBTAIN.

I. COORDINATION WITH OTHER DISCLOSURE FORMS

This Real Estate Transfer Disclosure Statement is made pursuant to Section 1102 of the Civil Code. Other statutes require disclosures, depending upon the details of the particular real estate transaction (for example: special study zone and purchase-money liens on residential property).

Substituted Disclosures: The following disclosures and other disclosures required by law, including the Natural Hazard Disclosure Report/Statement that may include airport annoyances, earthquake, fire, flood, or special assessment information, have or will be made in connection with this real estate transfer, and are intended to satisfy the disclosure obligations on this form, where the subject matter is the same:

☐ Inspection reports completed pursuant to the contract of sale or receipt for deposit.
☐ Additional inspection reports or disclosures: _____

II. SELLER'S INFORMATION

The Seller discloses the following information with the knowledge that even though this is not a warranty, prospective Buyers may rely on this information in deciding whether and on what terms to purchase the subject property. Seller hereby authorizes any agent(s) representing any principal(s) in this transaction to provide a copy of this statement to any person or entity in connection with any actual or anticipated sale of the property.

THE FOLLOWING ARE REPRESENTATIONS MADE BY THE SELLER(S) AND ARE NOT THE REPRESENTATIONS OF THE AGENT(S), IF ANY. THIS INFORMATION IS A DISCLOSURE AND IS NOT INTENDED TO BE PART OF ANY CONTRACT BETWEEN THE BUYER AND SELLER.

Seller ☐ is ☐ is not occupying the property.

A. The subject property has the items checked below: *

☐ Range
☐ Oven
☐ Microwave
☐ Dishwasher
☐ Trash Compactor
☐ Garbage Disposal
☐ Washer/Dryer Hookups
☐ Rain Gutters
☐ Burglar Alarms
☐ Carbon Monoxide Device(s)
☐ Smoke Detector(s)
☐ Fire Alarm
☐ TV Antenna
☐ Satellite Dish
☐ Intercom
☐ Central Heating
☐ Central Air Conditioning
☐ Evaporator Cooler(s)

☐ Wall/Window Air Conditioning
☐ Sprinklers
☐ Public Sewer System
☐ Septic Tank
☐ Sump Pump
☐ Water Softener
☐ Patio/Decking
☐ Built-in Barbecue
☐ Gazebo
☐ Security Gate(s)
☐ Garage:
  ☐ Attached ☐ Not Attached
  ☐ Carport
  ☐ Automatic Garage Door Opener(s)
    ☐ Number Remote Controls _____
☐ Sauna
☐ Hot Tub/Spa:
  ☐ Locking Safety Cover

☐ Pool:
  ☐ Child Resistant Barrier
☐ Pool/Spa Heater:
  ☐ Gas ☐ Solar ☐ Electric
☐ Water Heater:
  ☐ Gas ☐ Solar ☐ Electric
☐ Water Supply:
  ☐ City ☐ Well
  ☐ Private Utility or
    Other _____
☐ Gas Supply:
  ☐ Utility ☐ Bottled (Tank)
☐ Window Screens
☐ Window Security Bars
  ☐ Quick Release Mechanism on Bedroom Windows
☐ Water-Conserving Plumbing Fixtures

Exhaust Fan(s) in _____ 220 Volt Wiring in _____ Fireplace(s) in _____
☐ Gas Starter _____ ☐ Roof(s): Type: _____ Age: _____ (approx.)
☐ Other: _____

Are there, to the best of your (Seller's) knowledge, any of the above that are not in operating condition? ☐ Yes ☐ No. If yes, then describe. (Attach additional sheets if necessary): _____

(*see note on page 2)
Buyer's Initials (_____)(_____)   Seller's Initials (_____)(_____)

TDS REVISED 4/14 (PAGE 1 OF 3)   Reviewed by _____ Date _____

REAL ESTATE TRANSFER DISCLOSURE STATEMENT (TDS PAGE 1 OF 3)

Agent: _____ Phone: _____ Fax: _____ Prepared using zipForm® software
Broker:

Property Address: _____ Date: _____

B. Are you (Seller) aware of any significant defects/malfunctions in any of the following? ☐ Yes ☐ No. If yes, check appropriate space(s) below.

☐ Interior Walls ☐ Ceilings ☐ Floors ☐ Exterior Walls ☐ Insulation ☐ Roof(s) ☐ Windows ☐ Doors ☐ Foundation ☐ Slab(s) ☐ Driveways ☐ Sidewalks ☐ Walls/Fences ☐ Electrical Systems ☐ Plumbing/Sewers/Septics ☐ Other Structural Components
(Describe: _____
_____)

If any of the above is checked, explain. (Attach additional sheets if necessary.): _____
_____

*Installation of a listed appliance, device, or amenity is not a precondition of sale or transfer of the dwelling. The carbon monoxide device, garage door opener, or child-resistant pool barrier may not be in compliance with the safety standards relating to, respectively, carbon monoxide device standards of Chapter 8 (commencing with Section 13260) of Part 2 of Division 12 of, automatic reversing device standards of Chapter 12.5 (commencing with Section 19890) of Part 3 of Division 13 of, or the pool safety standards of Article 2.5 (commencing with Section 115920) of Chapter 5 of Part 10 of Division 104 of, the Health and Safety Code. Window security bars may not have quick-release mechanisms in compliance with the 1995 edition of the California Building Standards Code. Section 1101.4 of the Civil Code requires all single-family residences built on or before January 1, 1994, to be equipped with water-conserving plumbing fixtures after January 1, 2017. Additionally, on and after January 1, 2014, a single-family residence built on or before January 1, 1994, that is altered or improved is required to be equipped with water-conserving plumbing fixtures as a condition of final approval. Fixtures in this dwelling may not comply with section 1101.4 of the Civil Code.

C. Are you (Seller) aware of any the following:

1. Substances, materials, or products which may be an environmental hazard such as, but not limited to, asbestos, formaldehyde, radon gas, lead-based paint, mold, fuel or chemical storage tanks, and contaminated soil or water on the subject property . . . . ☐ Yes ☐ No
2. Features of the property shared in common with adjoining landowners, such as walls, fences, and driveways, whose use or responsibility for maintenance may have an effect on the subject property . . . . ☐ Yes ☐ No
3. Any encroachments, easements or similar matters that may affect your interest in the subject property . . . . ☐ Yes ☐ No
4. Room additions, structural modifications, or other alterations or repairs made without necessary permits. . . . . . . ☐ Yes ☐ No
5. Room additions, structural modifications, or other alterations or repairs not in compliance with building codes. . . . ☐ Yes ☐ No
6. Fill (compacted or otherwise) on the property or any portion thereof . . . . ☐ Yes ☐ No
7. Any settling from any cause, or slippage, sliding, or other soil problems . . . . ☐ Yes ☐ No
8. Flooding, drainage or grading problems . . . . ☐ Yes ☐ No
9. Major damage to the property or any of the structures from fire, earthquake, floods, or landslides . . . . ☐ Yes ☐ No
10. Any zoning violations, nonconforming uses, violations of "setback" requirements . . . . ☐ Yes ☐ No
11. Neighborhood noise problems or other nuisances . . . . ☐ Yes ☐ No
12. CC&R's or other deed restrictions or obligations . . . . ☐ Yes ☐ No
13. Homeowners' Association which has any authority over the subject property . . . . ☐ Yes ☐ No
14. Any "common area" (facilities such as pools, tennis courts, walkways, or other areas co-owned in undivided interest with others) . . . . ☐ Yes ☐ No
15. Any notices of abatement or citations against the property . . . . ☐ Yes ☐ No
16. Any lawsuits by or against the Seller threatening to or affecting this real property, claims for damages by the Seller pursuant to Section 910 or 914 threatening to or affecting this real property, claims for breach of warranty pursuant to Section 900 threatening to or affecting this real property, or claims for breach of an enhanced protection agreement pursuant to Section 903 threatening to or affecting this real property, including any lawsuits or claims for damages pursuant to Section 910 or 914 alleging a defect or deficiency in this real property or "common areas" (facilities such as pools, tennis courts, walkways, or other areas co-owned in undivided interest with others) . . . . ☐ Yes ☐ No

If the answer to any of these is yes, explain. (Attach additional sheets if necessary.): _____
_____
_____

D. 1. The Seller certifies that the property, as of the close of escrow, will be in compliance with Section 13113.8 of the Health and Safety Code by having operable smoke detector(s) which are approved, listed, and installed in accordance with the State Fire Marshal's regulations and applicable local standards.
    2. The Seller certifies that the property, as of the close of escrow, will be in compliance with Section 19211 of the Health and Safety Code by having the water heater tank(s) braced, anchored, or strapped in place in accordance with applicable law.

Buyer's Initials (_____) (_____)

| Reviewed by _____ Date _____ |

☖ EQUAL HOUSING OPPORTUNITY

TDS REVISED 4/14 (PAGE 2 OF 3)
REAL ESTATE TRANSFER DISCLOSURE STATEMENT (TDS PAGE 2 OF 3)

Property Address: _____ Date: _____

Seller certifies that the information herein is true and correct to the best of the Seller's knowledge as of the date signed by the Seller.

Seller _____ Date _____

Seller _____ Date _____

III. AGENT'S INSPECTION DISCLOSURE
(To be completed only if the Seller is represented by an agent in this transaction.)

THE UNDERSIGNED, BASED ON THE ABOVE INQUIRY OF THE SELLER(S) AS TO THE CONDITION OF THE PROPERTY AND BASED ON A REASONABLY COMPETENT AND DILIGENT VISUAL INSPECTION OF THE ACCESSIBLE AREAS OF THE PROPERTY IN CONJUNCTION WITH THAT INQUIRY, STATES THE FOLLOWING:

☐ See attached Agent Visual Inspection Disclosure (AVID Form)
☐ Agent notes no items for disclosure.
☐ Agent notes the following items: _____
_____
_____
_____

Agent (Broker Representing Seller) _____ By _____ Date _____
                                          (Please Print)   (Associate Licensee or Broker Signature)

IV. AGENT'S INSPECTION DISCLOSURE
(To be completed only if the agent who has obtained the offer is other than the agent above.)

THE UNDERSIGNED, BASED ON A REASONABLY COMPETENT AND DILIGENT VISUAL INSPECTION OF THE ACCESSIBLE AREAS OF THE PROPERTY, STATES THE FOLLOWING:

☐ See attached Agent Visual Inspection Disclosure (AVID Form)
☐ Agent notes no items for disclosure.
☐ Agent notes the following items: _____
_____
_____
_____

Agent (Broker Obtaining the Offer) _____ By _____ Date _____
                                          (Please Print)   (Associate Licensee or Broker Signature)

V. BUYER(S) AND SELLER(S) MAY WISH TO OBTAIN PROFESSIONAL ADVICE AND/OR INSPECTIONS OF THE PROPERTY AND TO PROVIDE FOR APPROPRIATE PROVISIONS IN A CONTRACT BETWEEN BUYER AND SELLER(S) WITH RESPECT TO ANY ADVICE/INSPECTIONS/DEFECTS.

I/WE ACKNOWLEDGE RECEIPT OF A COPY OF THIS STATEMENT.

Seller _____ Date _____   Buyer _____ Date _____

Seller _____ Date _____   Buyer _____ Date _____

Agent (Broker Representing Seller) _____ By _____ Date _____
                                          (Please Print)   (Associate Licensee or Broker Signature)

Agent (Broker Obtaining the Offer) _____ By _____ Date _____
                                          (Please Print)   (Associate Licensee or Broker Signature)

SECTION 1102.3 OF THE CIVIL CODE PROVIDES A BUYER WITH THE RIGHT TO RESCIND A PURCHASE CONTRACT FOR AT LEAST THREE DAYS AFTER THE DELIVERY OF THIS DISCLOSURE IF DELIVERY OCCURS AFTER THE SIGNING OF AN OFFER TO PURCHASE. IF YOU WISH TO RESCIND THE CONTRACT, YOU MUST ACT WITHIN THE PRESCRIBED PERIOD.

A REAL ESTATE BROKER IS QUALIFIED TO ADVISE ON REAL ESTATE. IF YOU DESIRE LEGAL ADVICE, CONSULT YOUR ATTORNEY.

Published and Distributed by:
REAL ESTATE BUSINESS SERVICES, INC.
a subsidiary of the California Association of REALTORS®
525 South Virgil Avenue, Los Angeles, California 90020

Reviewed by _____ Date _____

EQUAL HOUSING
OPPORTUNITY

TDS REVISED 4/14 (PAGE 3 OF 3)

REAL ESTATE TRANSFER DISCLOSURE STATEMENT (TDS PAGE 3 OF 3)

Local Option Real Estate Transfer Disclosure Statement

A city or county may require that the seller provide specific information about the neighborhood or community. If there is some local condition, which may materially affect a buyer's use and enjoyment of residential property, an optional disclosure form may be required, called the **Local Option Real Estate Transfer Disclosure Statement** (LORETDS). Residential properties in cities and counties throughout California are typically subject to specific local ordinances on occupancy, zoning and use, building code compliance, fire, health and safety code regulations, and land subdivision descriptions. The various requirements for compliance as well as who and what is affected should be disclosed to the prospective buyer of the property by the seller or the seller's agent and any agent acting in cooperation with such agent. For example, based on the Farm Practices Protection Act of 1996, many jurisdictions in the Central Valley have enacted Right to Farm ordinances to protect existing agricultural uses adjacent to new residential uses. [B&P §11010; C.C. §§1102.6a, 1103.4, 1353].

Natural Hazard Disclosure Statement

A joke says that while America enjoys four seasons—Spring, Summer, Winter and Fall, California has four of its own: Fire, Flood, Earthquake, and Drought. Geologic surveys find more and more fault lines, some of them active that could lead to earthquakes. Year after year, we see wildfires that devastate homes and even entire communities. Burn areas that have not had a chance to generate new growth are susceptible to extensive flooding when heavy rains follow. Landslides often accompany and complicate the issue. Increasingly, we see areas of the state that are prone to devastating natural disasters. Certainly, these could and would affect the salability and desirability of a home.

California standardized natural hazard disclosure requirements in real property transactions with the passage of the Natural Hazard Disclosure Law in 1998. In addition to the usual Transfer Disclosure Statement, the sellers must give the prospective buyer a separate **Natural Hazard Disclosure Statement** (NHD) if the residential property lies within any of six statutorily specified areas.

Areas Subject to NHD Disclosures

1. **Special flood hazard zone** (Zone A or Zone V) area designated by the Federal Emergency Management Agency (FEMA).
2. **Area of potential flooding** in the event of a dam failure, designated by the California Office of Emergency Services.
3. **Very high fire hazard severity zone** designated by the California Department of Forestry and Fire Protection (CDF).
4. **Designated wildland fire area** that may contain substantial forest fire risks and hazards, designated by the State Board of Forestry.
5. **Earthquake fault zone** designated by the State Geologist.
6. **Seismic hazard zone** designated by the State Geologist.

The law prescribes the contents of the Natural Hazard Disclosure Statement including a checklist. The statement warns prospective buyers: "These hazards may limit your ability to develop the real property; to obtain insurance; or to receive assistance after a disaster." It also advises buyers and sellers that they "may wish to obtain professional advice regarding those hazards." The disclosure must be made as soon as practicable before the transfer of title, unless the purchase contract provides for an earlier deadline. It is in the seller's and listing agent's best interest to disclose early because the buyer can annul the purchase contract during a certain period after getting the information. The rescission period is 3 days if the disclosures are hand-delivered or 5 days if the disclosures are mailed.

If the NHD report is prepared by a third-party expert on behalf of a seller or real estate agent, additional disclosures regarding "Airport in Vicinity", "Farm and Ranch Proximity", and "Notice of Mining Operations" must be included in the report. [Civil Code §1103.4].

Special Flood Hazard Area (Any type Zone "A" or "V")

Flood hazard boundary maps identify the general flood hazards within a community. They are also used in flood plain management and for flood insurance purposes. These maps, developed by the **Federal Emergency Management Agency (FEMA)** in conjunction with communities participating in the
National Flood Insurance Program (NFIP), show areas within a **100-year**

flood boundary, termed **special flood zone areas**. Also identified are areas between 100 and 500-year levels termed areas of moderate flood hazards and the remaining areas above the 500-year level termed areas of minimal risk.

A seller of property located in a special flood hazard area or the seller's agent and/or any agent cooperating in the deal, must disclose to the buyer that federal law requires flood insurance as a condition of obtaining financing on most structures located in a special flood hazard area. Since the cost and extent of flood insurance coverage may vary, the buyer should contact an insurance carrier or the intended lender for additional information.

The Local Option Real Estate Transfer Disclosure Statement (LORETDS) also lists disclosures, providing the local jurisdiction has mandated the use of this form.

National Flood Insurance is available to any property owner whose local community participates in the national program by adopting and enforcing flood plain management. The **National Flood Insurance Act** states that federally regulated lenders are required to compel borrowers to purchase flood insurance in certain designated areas. Lenders also must disclose to borrowers if the property is located in a flood hazard area.

Areas of Potential Flooding

Designated on an **inundation map** are areas that may flood as the result of a dam failure. If the property is on a list of properties posted at the County Public Works/Engineering Offices, Assessors Office, Water Agencies, or Planning Agency, the seller or listing broker must disclose this information to a prospective buyer. If the owner has received federal flood disaster assistance, the seller must tell the buyer to buy flood insurance. This is disclosed on the NHD.

Very High Fire Hazard Zone

The seller must disclose if the property is in this zone. Properties in this zone are subject to property maintenance requirements, such as clearing brush and maintaining firebreaks. Generally, the CDF requires a 30-foot clearance area around dwellings per the Public Resources Code. This disclosure is made on the NHD.

State Fire Responsibility Area

The Department of Forestry and Fire Protection has produced maps identifying rural lands classified as **state responsibility areas**. In such an area, the state, as opposed to a local or federal agency, has the primary financial responsibility for the prevention and extinguishing of fires. Maps of State Responsibility Areas and any changes, including new maps produced every five years, are to be provided to planning agencies in the affected counties.

If the property is located in a State Responsibility Area or is included on a map given by the department to the county assessor or planning agencies, the seller must disclose the possibility of substantial fire risk in such **wild land areas** and that the land is subject to certain preventative requirements.

With the department's agreement and by ordinance, a county may assume responsibility for all fires, including those occurring in State Responsibility Areas. If there is such an ordinance, the seller of property located in the area must disclose to the buyer that the state is not obligated to provide fire protection services for any building or structure unless such protection is required by a cooperative agreement with a county, city, or district.

Earthquake Fault Zones

Geologists describe the surface of the earth as always changing. Some of these geological changes are relatively unimportant and do not require a disclosure. Other changes are apparent by casual inspection, i.e. they are of a nature that a potential buyer should be able to judge the impact of the existing geological condition on the intended property's use.

In some cases, disclosure of a geological condition must be made. This is true of potential hazards from earthquakes, flooding, landslides, erosion, and expansive soils. One condition requiring such disclosure is **fault creep**, which is movement along an earthquake fault caused by stress and/or earthquake shaking.

Geology, in the context of the required disclosures, refers to the type of soil and how that soil will respond to earthquakes. Soft sediments tend to amplify shaking, whereas bedrock soils tend to lessen the shaking. Generally, the closer in location to the fault, the more intense the shaking will be. However, soil types and conditions may be more important than distance from the epicenter.

The state geologist is in the process of identifying areas of the state susceptible to fault creep, which is shown on maps prepared by the State Division of Mines and Geology. These maps also identify known historic landslides. The seller or the seller's agent and any agent acting in cooperation with such agent may usually rely on the identification of the designated earthquake fault zones by the state geologist for disclosure purposes.

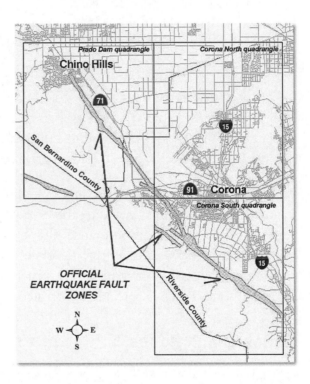

In some instances, additional investigation may be required. Construction on real property of any structure for human occupancy may be subject to the findings and recommendations of a geologic report prepared by a geologist or soils engineer registered in or licensed by the state of California.

A seller of real property situated in a delineated earthquake fault zone (called special studies zones prior to 1994), or the agent of the seller and any agent acting in cooperation with such agent, must disclose to the buyer that the property is, or may be situated in such a zone as designated under the Alquist-Priolo Earthquake Fault Zoning Act.

This disclosure must be made on either the Natural Hazard Disclosure Statement (NHDS) or the Local Option Real Estate Transfer Disclosure Statement (LORETDS).

Seismic Hazards Zone

The California Seismic Safety Commission developed a **Homeowner's Guide to Earthquake Safety** for distribution to real estate licensees and the public. The guide includes information on geologic and seismic hazards for all areas, explanations of related structural and nonstructural hazards, and recommendations for mitigating the hazards of an earthquake. The guide states that safety or damage prevention cannot be guaranteed with respect to a major earthquake and that only precautions, such as retrofitting can be undertaken to reduce the risk of various types of damage.

If the buyer of real property receives a copy of the *Homeowner's Guide to Earthquake Safety*, neither the seller nor the agent is required to provide additional information regarding geologic and seismic hazards. Sellers and real estate agents must disclose that the property is in a designated earthquake fault zone and that there are known hazards affecting the real property being transferred.

Requirement: *Homeowner's Guide to Earthquake Safety* Booklet

- Transfer of any real property with a residential dwelling built prior to January 1, 1960 and consisting of one-to-four units any of which are of conventional light-frame construction.
- Transfer of any masonry building with wood-frame floors or roofs built before January 1, 1975.

Certain exemptions apply to the obligation to deliver the booklet when transferring either a dwelling of one-to-four units or a reinforced masonry building. These exemptions are essentially the same as those that apply to delivery of the Real Estate Transfer Disclosure Statement described earlier in this section.

The buyer and/or agent may be responsible for making further inquiries of appropriate governmental agencies. The obligation of the buyer and/or agent to make further inquiry does not eliminate the duty of the seller's agent to make a diligent inquiry to identify the location of the real property in relationship to a designated earthquake fault zone—and to determine whether the property is subject to any local ordinance regarding geological and soil conditions. Full and complete disclosure is required of all material facts regarding a designated earthquake fault zone, local ordinances, or known structural deficiencies affecting the property.

The Seismic Safety Commission also has published the booklet *Commercial Property Owner's Guide to Earthquake Safety*. Each buyer receives a copy of CalBRE/OEHHA or the Seismic Safety Commission booklet from the seller or seller's agent.

Environmental Hazard Disclosures

Numerous federal, state, and local laws have been enacted to address the problems created by environmental hazards. Responsible parties for the improper disposal of hazardous waste and owners of contaminated property may be held liable for contamination cleanup.

Several disclosure laws relating to the transfer of land affected by hazardous waste contamination have been enacted. The California Real Estate Transfer Disclosure Statement requires sellers to disclose whether they are aware of the presence of **hazardous substances**, materials, or products including—but not limited to—asbestos, formaldehyde, radon gas, lead-based paint, fuel, or chemical storage tanks, contaminated soil, water, or mold.

Any owner of nonresidential property who knows or suspects that there has been a release of a hazardous substance or that it may occur on or beneath the property must notify a buyer, lessee, or renter of that condition prior to the sale, lease, or rental of that property. Failure to give written notice may subject the owner to actual damages and/or civil penalties.

Under Proposition 65, certain businesses may not expose knowingly or intentionally any individual to a cancer-causing chemical or reproductive toxin without first giving clear, reasonable warning to such individuals. Proposition 65 has also imposed extensive asbestos disclosure requirements on owners of commercial buildings constructed prior to January 1, 1979.

Environmental Hazards Booklet

The Bureau of Real Estate and Office of Environmental Health Hazard Assessment have developed a booklet on environmental hazards to help educate and inform consumers about environmental hazards that may affect real property. The booklet identifies common environmental hazards, describes the risks involved with each, discusses mitigation techniques, and provides lists of publications and sources from which consumers can obtain information that is more detailed. The seller or seller's agent should give each buyer a copy of this booklet.

Hazards Discussed in the Environmental Hazard Booklet

Asbestos: A mineral fiber used in construction materials, which has been found to cause lung and stomach cancer.

Radon: A colorless gas known to cause cancer. Radon can be detected with a spectrometer.

Lead: A mineral that causes major health problems.

Formaldehyde: A chemical organic compound found in building materials, which may be a carcinogen.

Hazardous waste: Materials—chemicals, explosives, radioactive, biological—whose disposal is regulated by the Environmental Protection Agency (EPA).

Household hazardous waste: Consumer products, such as paints, cleaners, stains, varnishes, car batteries, motor oil, and pesticides that contain hazardous components.

Once the booklet is provided to a prospective buyer of real property, neither the seller nor a real estate agent involved in the sale has a duty to provide further information on such hazards. Although not required to, the buyer should read the booklet. However, if the seller or agent has actual knowledge of environmental hazards on or affecting the subject property, that information must be disclosed.

Lead-Based Paint

Paint containing lead poses a serious health risk, especially for children. Children have eaten the paint chips and suffered major health problems. As a result, disclosure of lead-based paint is required. The Residential Lead-Based Paint Hazard

Reduction Act of 1992 (Title X) became effective on September 6, 1996 for owners of property with four or fewer units. A lead-hazard information brochure and a disclosure form must be provided to a buyer or lessee by a seller or landlord. Additionally, the presence of any known lead-based paint must be disclosed. The seller is not required to remove the lead-based paint, but is required to disclose it.

This disclosure pertains to residential housing built before 1978, called **target housing**, because the Act banned lead based paint for residential use in that year. Target housing does not include housing for the elderly or persons with disabilities, a 0-bedroom dwelling, such as a studio apartment, or vacation housing.

The seller, landlord, and real estate agent involved in the sale or rental of pre-1978 housing each have certain obligations under the new law.

Obligations Imposed on Seller/Landlord

- Give buyers/tenants *Protect Your Family from Lead in Your Home* pamphlet.

- Disclose all known lead-based paint and lead-based paint hazards in the dwelling and provide buyer/tenants with any available reports.

- Include standard warning language as an attachment to the contract or lease.

- Complete and sign statements verifying completion of requirements.

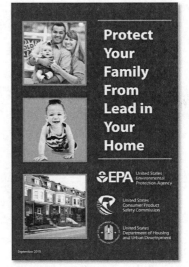

- Retain the signed acknowledgment for three years.

- Give buyers a 10-day opportunity to test for lead (for sale transactions only).

Real estate agents must comply with the law if the seller or landlord fails to do so. However, the agent is not responsible if an owner conceals information or fails to disclose information.

Real Estate Agent Responsibilities

- Seller/landlords are aware of their obligations.
- Seller/landlords disclose the proper information to buyers and tenants.
- Leases and sales contracts include proper disclosure language and signatures.
- Sellers give buyers the opportunity to conduct an inspection for 10 days or another mutually agreed-upon time.

Toxic Mold

There is always a little mold everywhere—in the air and on many surfaces. **Mold** is a fungus that reproduces by means of spores. Molds themselves are not toxic or poisonous. However, certain molds are toxigenic because they can produce toxins (called mycotoxins).

Currently, standards for judging what is an acceptable quantity of mold have not been established to determine toxicity.

The **Toxic Mold Protection Act**, enacted in 2001, gave the California Department of Public Health (CPDH) the task of developing permissible exposure limits (PELs) for indoor molds. After considerable research into this issue, CDPH scientists concluded that although recent studies have strengthened the evidence between  living or working in a damp environment and increased risk for respiratory symptoms, the role of mold growth in these complex environments is still unclear. Damp buildings also encourage the growth of bacteria, dust mites, and cockroaches, as well as degradation of wet building materials that can also release irritant chemicals indoors. Some or all of these chemicals or biological organisms may contribute to occupant illness. After considerable research into this question, CDPH staff has determined that sound, science-based permissible exposure limits for indoor molds cannot be established at this time. A complete report by the CPDH is available online at www.cdph.ca.gov. Therefore, no special disclosure requirements are in effect for **toxic mold**.

However, the Transfer Disclosure Statement has been modified to add the word mold in paragraph II.C.1 and any transferor must disclose actual knowledge of mold on the property.

Drug-Lab Illegal Controlled Substance

The seller must inform the buyer in writing of toxic contamination by **illegal controlled substance** on the property, receipt of notice from the Department of Toxic Substance Control or another agency.

If the owner has actual knowledge of the presence of an illegal controlled substance release and knowingly and willfully fails to provide written notice to the buyer, the owner is liable for a civil penalty not to exceed five thousand dollars ($5,000) for each separate violation, in addition to any other damages provided by law. [CA. Health & Safety §25400.10 et. seq.].

Former Military Ordnance Locations

Federal and state agencies have identified certain areas once used for military training, which still may contain live ammunition and potentially explosive munitions as part of the ordnance (military supplies).

A seller of residential property located within one mile of such a hazard must give the buyer written notice as soon as possible before transfer of title. This obligation depends upon the seller having actual knowledge of the hazard. [C.C. §1102.15]

Industrial Uses

The seller must disclose actual knowledge that the property is affected by or zoned for industrial use of the property. Examples of industrial use disclosure are manufacturing, commercial, or airport use. A seller who has actual knowledge must disclose this information. [C.C. §1102.17]

Taxes

When property transfers, it may be subject to supplemental taxes or be in a Mello-Roos District. Prospective buyers need to know this information before finalizing the negotiations to purchase a home.

Mello-Roos Disclosure

Currently on purchase property, Proposition 13 limits property taxes to a maximum of 1% of the assessed value of the property. Mello-Roos Community Facility District taxes predominantly apply to new homes built after 1982. This tax typically supports the construction of infrastructure to allow the development of formerly undeveloped land. The city, through the sale of municipal bonds, can include the cost and maintenance of infrastructure items in the property tax bill as a special assessment, exempt from the limitations of Proposition 13.

The Mello-Roos Community Facilities Act of 1982 authorizes the formation of community facilities districts, the issuance of bonds, and the levying of special taxes, which will finance designated public facilities and services. A **Mello-Roos District** is an area where a special assessment is imposed on those real property owners within a Community Facilities District. Public services, such as roads, sewers, parks, schools, and fire stations in new developments may be financed under this law.

A Mello-Roos lien is placed on each parcel in a new development by the developer to pay off municipal bonds issued to fund off-site improvements for the development. The developer must make the payments on the bond until the homes are sold and then the new owners are responsible. Mello-Roos liens are a way a developer can make improvements and have each homeowner pay for them, without charging the improvements to property taxes.

Effective July 1, 1993, the seller of a property consisting of one-to-four dwelling units subject to the lien of a Mello-Roos community facilities district must make a good faith effort to obtain from the district a disclosure notice concerning the special tax and give the notice to a prospective buyer.

Exempt from this requirement are the various transfers listed earlier for the Transfer Disclosure Statement. According to the California Tax Data website, Mello-Roos information should be on the property tax bill. Mello-Roos funds are used to finance subdivision costs. The transferor (seller) of residential property (one-to-four units) is responsible to disclose if a property is subject to a Mello-Roos assessment.

ANY CITY, CALIFORNIA

Mello Roos Disclosure Statement
Notice of Special Tax

Community Facilities District 20___-1
ABC Public Facilities Financing Agency
County of _____, State of California

To: The Prospective Purchaser of the Real Property Known as:

Address: Assessors Parcel Number:

_____

THIS IS A NOTIFICATION TO YOU PRIOR TO YOUR PURCHASING THIS
PROPERTY.

1. This property is subject to a special tax, which is in addition to the regular property
taxes and other charges and benefit assessments on the parcel. This special tax may not
be imposed on all parcels within the city or county where the property is located. If you
fail to pay this tax when due each year, the property may be foreclosed upon and sold.
The tax is used to provide public facilities or services that are likely to particularly
benefit the property. **You should take this tax and the benefits from the facilities and
services for which it pays into account in deciding to whether to buy this property.**

2. The maximum annual tax to which this property is subject is $_____ during the
20___ tax year and thereafter. The special tax will be levied each year until all of the
authorized facilities are built and all special tax bonds are repaid.

3. The authorized facilities which are being paid for by the special taxes, and by the
money received from the sale of bonds which are being repaid by the special taxes, are
set forth on Exhibit A attached hereto. These facilities may not yet have all been
constructed or acquired and it is possible that some may never be constructed or acquired.

4. The obligation to pay the special tax, attached to this property, was a condition
required in order to permit this property to be developed. The payment of tax is intended
to insure that there will be adequate capacity in the school district for the children that
may come from this property. However, the payment of the special tax does not
guarantee attendance at any particular school, nor does it guarantee attendance at a newly
constructed school. School attendance boundaries are set by the School Board and are
based on many criteria, only one of which is whether a property pays the special tax.

You may obtain a copy of the resolution of formation which authorized creation of the
community facilities district, and which specifies more precisely how the special tax is
apportioned and how the proceeds of the tax will be used, from the Comptroller of ABC
Public Facilities Financing Agency by telephoning (555) 123-4567. There may be a
charge for this document not to exceed the reasonable cost of providing this document.

I (we) acknowledge that I (we) have read this notice and received a copy of this
notice prior to entering into a contract to purchase or deposit receipt with respect
to the above-references property. I (we) understand that I (we) may terminate the
contract to purchase or deposit receipt within three days after receiving this notice
in person or within five days after it was deposited in the mail by giving written
notice of that termination to the owner, subdivider, or agent selling the property.

Date:

_____

If the Notice of Special Tax is delivered to the buyer after a purchase agreement has been signed, the buyer has the right to terminate the agreement within three days of delivery in person, or five days after delivery by mail. The buyer must provide written notice of termination of the agreement to the seller or the seller's agent.

Real estate agents must tell buyers that a project is subject to a Mello-Roos special assessment because their tax bill will be higher than if they only paid property taxes without the special assessment. The listing agent does not have an affirmative duty to discover a special tax district or assessment not actually known to the agent. [C.C. 1102.6b (e)].

However, information about Mello-Roos assessments may be obtained from the county tax collector's office. The Real Estate Commissioner can discipline a real estate agent for failure to provide a Mello-Roos disclosure. Failure to give notice to a buyer or lessee (if more than five years) before signing a sales contract or lease allows the buyer or lessee a three-day right to cancel after receiving the disclosure. [C.C. §1102.6a]

Property Taxes

Legislation effective January 1, 2006, requires a seller or his or her agent to deliver a disclosure notice to the prospective purchaser regarding supplemental property taxes. Supplemental taxes may be assessed whether a new loan is obtained or an existing loan is assumed to accomplish the purchase of the property or whether the property is purchased without financing.

Notice of Your 'Supplemental' Property Tax Bill

"California property tax law requires the Assessor to revalue real property at the time the ownership of the property changes. Because of this law, you may receive one or two supplemental tax bills, depending on when your loan closes. The supplemental tax bills are not mailed to your lender. If you have arranged for your property tax payments to be paid through an impound account, the supplemental tax bills will not be paid by your lender. It is your responsibility to pay these supplemental bills directly to the Tax Collector. If you have any question concerning this matter, please call your local Tax Collector's Office."

The disclosure notice requirements of this section may be satisfied by including the required information in the Mello-Roos disclosure. [C.C. §1102.6c]

Other Disclosures

Several disclosures must be considered. Not every one applies to every sale and this list is not exhaustive. This is, however, a good basic checklist to which you may add your own disclosure statements as need arises. Some of the disclosures are discussed after the list.

Other Disclosures

- Authorization to Order Inspections and Reports
- Supplemental Statutory and Contractual Disclosures
- Controlling Documents and Financial Statements – CIDs
- Database Disclosure
- Window Security Bars
- Water Heater and Smoke Detector Compliance
- Energy Conservation Retrofit and Thermal Insulation Disclosures
- Alien Status Tax Disclosures
- Pest Inspections
- Advisability of Title Insurance
- City Report
- Market Conditions Advisory
- Square Footage and Acreage Disclosure
- Tree Disease Disclosure

Controlling Documents and Financial Statements – CIDs

Specific requirements apply to common interest developments (CIDs). It is important for licensees to be aware of this, especially because CIDs comprise a large percentage of the salable homes in California, given their affordability and popularity. The owner (other than a subdivider) of a separate legal share in a **common interest development** (community apartment project, condominium project, planned development, or stock cooperative) must provide a prospective buyer with controlling documents and financial statements. [C.C. §§368, 1375, 1375.1(a)(1),(2),(3)]. An association has 10 days after receiving written request to provide the requested information.

Required Disclosures when Transferring Ownership in a CID

- A copy of the governing documents (operating rules and articles of incorporation, if any) of the common interest development.

- Age restriction statements and a statement that the restriction is only enforceable to the extent permitted by Civil Code §51.3 and a statement specifying the applicable provisions of §51.3.

- A copy of the most recent financial statement, operating budget, and most recent reserve study pursuant to Civil Code §1365.

- A written statement from an authorized representative of the association concerning the amount of the association's current regular and special assessments and fees, as well as any assessments levied upon the owner's interest, which are unpaid on the date of the statement, late charges, interest, and costs of collection which, as of the date of the statement, are or may become a lien on the owner's interest.

- Any change in the association's current and special assessments and fees that have been approved by the association's board of directors, but have not yet become due and payable.

- A copy of any notice previously sent to the owner that sets forth any alleged violation of the governing documents that remains unresolved.

- A copy of any construction defects and a statement that a final determination of the defects has yet to occur, including whether the list of defects is accurate and complete.

- A disclosure of any settlement agreement or other instrument between the association and the developer regarding construction defects.

- Information regarding any approved change in the assessments or fees that are not yet due and payable as of the disclosure date.

Database Disclosure (Megan's Law)

Every lease and sales contract is required to include a statutorily defined notice regarding the existence of public access to data base information regarding sex offenders in the neighborhood.

The first Megan's Law was passed in New Jersey in 1994 after the rape and murder of Megan Kanka by Jesse Timmendequas, a convicted sex offender who was living across the street from her. Since then, most of the country has adopted some form of Megan's Law. The website to search neighborhoods to determine whether registered sex offenders reside there is found at www.meganslaw.ca.gov.

The California Civil Code §2079.10a has specific language that must be provided concerning Megan's Law. It reads:

> **Notice:** The California Department of Justice, sheriff's departments, police departments serving jurisdictions of 200,000 or more and many other local law enforcement authorities maintain for public access a database of the locations of persons required to register pursuant to paragraph (1) of subdivision (a) of Section 290.4 of the Penal Code. The database is updated on a quarterly basis and a source of information about the presence of these individuals in any neighborhood. The Department of Justice also maintains a Sex Offender Identification Line through which inquiries about individuals may be made. This is a "900" telephone service. Callers must have specific information about individuals they are checking. Information regarding neighborhoods is not available through the "900" telephone service.

Window Security Bars

A seller must disclose on the Real Estate Transfer Disclosure Statement (TDS) or if mandated in the Local Option TDS, the existence of **window security bars** and any safety release mechanism on the bars. [C.C. §1102.16]

Water Heater Compliance

State law requires that all new and replacement **water heaters** sold in California on or after July 1, 1991 must be braced, anchored, or strapped to resist falling or horizontal displacement due to earthquake motion. The reason this is so important is because if not properly secured, during an earthquake a water heater that moves can rip out a gas line causing an explosion and fire and can also spill large quantities of water, causing further damage. The seller of any residential property must certify, in writing, to the buyer that all water heaters have been braced, anchored, or strapped in accordance  with local requirements. The certification can be included in a transaction document, including, but not limited to, the *Homeowner's Guide to Earthquake Safety*, the real estate purchase contract or receipt for deposit or the Real Estate Transfer Disclosure Statement.

Smoke Detector Compliance

State law requires that the seller of a single-family home must deliver to the prospective buyer a written disclosure statement indicating that the dwelling complies with state laws concerning **smoke detectors**. The State Building Code mandates that all existing dwelling units must have a smoke detector installed in a central location outside each sleeping area. In a two-story home with bedrooms on both floors, at least two smoke detectors would be required. New construction or any additions, alterations, or repairs exceeding $1,000 and for which a permit is required, must include a smoke detector installed in each bedroom and also at a point centrally located in a corridor or area outside the bedroom(s). This standard applies for the addition of one or more bedrooms, no matter what the cost. In new home construction, the smoke detector must be hard-wired, with a battery backup. In existing dwellings, the detector may be only battery operated.

Carbon Monoxide Detector Compliance

The **Carbon Monoxide Poisoning Prevention Act** requires that **carbon monoxide detectors** (CO detectors) must be installed in all dwelling units that contain a fossil fuel burning heater, appliance, or fireplace; or that have an attached garage. **Carbon monoxide** is an odorless gas produced whenever any fuel is burned. The Consumer Product Safety Commission recommends installing a CO detector in the hallway near every separate sleeping area of the home.

Sellers notify buyers on the Real Estate Transfer Disclosure Statement whether the property has carbon monoxide devices installed. No separate compliance certification is required. If the property does not have carbon monoxide devices, the buyer may negotiate with the seller for their installation as a condition of sale. [Health & Safety Code §13260 & §17926]

Energy Conservation Retrofit and Thermal Insulation Disclosures

State law prescribes minimum energy conservation standards for all new construction. Local governments also have ordinances that impose additional energy conservation measures on new and/or existing homes. Some local ordinances impose energy retrofitting as a condition of the sale of an existing home. The seller and/or agent should disclose to a prospective buyer the requirements of the various ordinances, as well as who is responsible for compliance. Federal law requires that a new home seller (including a subdivider) disclose in every sales contract the type, thickness, and **R-value** (resistance to heat loss) of the insulation that has been or will be installed.

Alien Status Issues

California is a state dealing with ever-increasing issues concerning foreign nationals taking up residence here. The beauty and desirability of our state is a huge draw for people from all over the world to come and enjoy the benefits of an idyllic setting and the opportunities that living here provides.

When non-citizens buy realty and sell realty, there are important considerations to take into account. For example, when the seller of real property is a foreign person, the IRS requires the buyer to withhold a portion of the sales price under both federal law and state law. The federal **Foreign Investment in Real Property Tax Act** (FIRPTA) requires that a buyer of real property must withhold and send to the Internal Revenue Service (IRS) 15% of the gross sales price if the seller of the real property is a foreign person. California law requires that if property is sold by a non-citizen of the United States or a resident of another state, the buyer must withhold 3 1/3% of the total sales price as state income tax and deliver the sum withheld to the State Franchise Tax Board.

A buyer's failure to withhold and deliver the required sum may result in penalties. Penalties might be levied against the escrow holder if he or she fails to notify the buyer.

There are exemptions, which vary between the state and federal levels. For instance at the federal level, if the buyer intends to live on the property at least fifty percent of the time and the purchase price is less than $300,000, then the buyer is exempt from the 15% withholding requirement. If the sales price is between $300,001 and $1,000,000, AND the property will be used by the buyer as a residence, then 10% of the sales price is withheld. At the state level, the home only has to be worth less than $100,000 for the exemption to apply. Obtaining appropriate documentation of citizenship or alien status can help licensees deal with these issues. A non-foreign affidavit will be necessary for persons who are not aliens.

Due to the number of exceptions and other requirements relating to this law, it is recommended that the IRS be consulted. Sellers, buyers, and the real estate agents involved who desire further advice should consult an attorney, CPA, or other qualified tax advisor.

Pest Control Inspection and Certification

The bane of existence for most homeowners in California is termites. Termites are not the only form of pest that can plague homeowners, but termites are highly destructive and can endanger a home's structural integrity. While disclosure is not required by statute, certification may be a condition of the contract or a requirement imposed as a condition of financing. Most prudent buyers will request one.

When an inspection is a requirement, there must be written certification attesting to the presence or absence of wood-destroying termites in the visible and accessible areas of the property, which is prepared and issued by a registered structural pest control company.

The company issuing the report must divide it into two categories: (1) to identify the portions of the property where existing damage, infection, or infestation are noted; and (2) to point out areas that may have impending damage, infection, or infestation. Lenders usually require that any infestation or damage discovered in part one of the report be corrected prior to close of escrow. The seller usually pays for the cost of correction. Since part two of the inspection report does not show actual infestation—just a potential, the seller is not obligated to correct it.

Generally, the real estate agent who obtained the offer is responsible for delivering the report unless the seller has given written directions regarding delivery to another agent involved in the transaction. Delivery of the required documents may be in person or by mail to the buyer. The real estate agent responsible for delivery must retain for three years a complete record of the actions taken to effect delivery.

Advisability of Title Insurance

In an escrow for a sale (or exchange) of real property in which no title insurance is to be issued, the buyer (or both parties to an exchange) must receive and sign the following notice as a separate document in the escrow:

Important: "In a purchase or exchange of real property, it may be advisable to obtain title insurance in connection with the close of escrow where there may be prior recorded liens and encumbrances which affect your interest in the property being acquired. A new policy of title insurance should be obtained in order to ensure your interest in the property that you are acquiring."

While the law does not expressly assign the duty, it is reasonable to assume that the escrow holder is obligated to deliver the notice. A real estate agent conducting an escrow also would be responsible for delivering the notice. [C.C. §1057.6]

SUMMARY

The purpose of disclosures is to ensure that the consumer, who is probably making the largest and most important investment of his or her lifetime, is making an informed decision. The law seeks to protect consumers from their own lack of expertise when making such important decisions. An important requirement of making disclosures fall upon members of the real estate professional, who are held to a high standard of care in ensuring that buyers have all pertinent facts concerning the investment at their disposal when making that decision. The benefit to the prudent professional is documentation of doing a thorough and professional job and, as a result, avoiding legal liability for problems that arise later.

Disclosures cover every conceivable condition that may be material to the sale—in other words, anything deemed to make the property desirable or salable. They cover the minutest electrical switch to such major issues as toxicity on the premises. Further, disclosures cover not only tangible things found on the premises, but less concrete items as well, such as dangerous conditions in the vicinity (such as sex offenders), deaths that may have occurred in the past, and noise (such as airports). Moreover, disclosures include financial information to educate the general consumer as to risks and expenses involved in the major commitment that is purchasing a home.

UNIT 14 REVIEW

Matching Exercise

Instructions: Write the letter of the matching term on the blank line before its definition. Answers are in Appendix A.

Terms

A. Agency Relationship Disclosure Act

B. asbestos

C. *caveat emptor*

D. common interest development

E. fault creep

F. flood hazard boundary maps

G. formaldehyde

H. hazardous waste

I. household hazardous waste

J. inundation map

K. lead

L. material facts

M. Mello-Roos District

N. mold

O. Natural Hazard Disclosure Statement

P. ordnance

Q. radon

R. Real Estate Transfer Disclosure Statement

S. red flag

T. R-value

Definitions

1. _____ Something that alerts a reasonably observant person of a potential problem

2. _____ Items that would affect the value or desirability of the property

3. _____ Act clarifying the relationships between sellers, brokers, and buyers

4. _____ Let the buyer beware

5. _____ Detailed statement telling what the seller knows about the condition of the property

6. _____ Prescribed statement warning prospective buyers about 6 specific hazards that may limit the ability to develop the real property, to obtain insurance, or to receive assistance after a disaster

7. _____ Maps identifying general flood hazards within a community

8. _____ Map indicating areas that may flood as the result of a dam failure

9. _____ Movement along an earthquake fault caused by stress and/or earthquake shaking

10. _____ Mineral fiber that causes lung and stomach cancer

11. _____ Colorless cancer-causing gas detected with a spectrometer

12. _____ Mineral that causes major health problems, especially learning disabilities

13. _____ Chemical organic compound found in building materials, which may be a carcinogen

14. _____ Chemicals, explosives, radioactive, or biological materials whose disposal is regulated by the EPA

15. _____ Consumer products (paints, cleaners, stains, varnishes, car batteries, motor oil, and pesticides) containing hazardous components

16. _____ Fungus that reproduces by means of spores

17. _____ Military weapons and ammunition

18. _____ Area with a special assessment imposed on real property owners within a Community Facilities District

19. _____ Name for community apartment project, condominium project, planned development, or stock cooperative

20. _____ Resistance to heat loss

Multiple Choice Questions

Instructions: Circle your response and go to Appendix A to read the complete explanation for each question.

1. A real estate agent's failure to provide disclosure could lead to:
    a. litigation.
    b. judgments entered against the agent.
    c. loss of license.
    d. all of the above.

2. Larry is the licensee who took a listing for Sally's home. He has Sally help him fill out the TDS. Sally fails to write down that the home suffered a crack in the wall during the last big earthquake, which Sally subsequently repaired. Larry brings the omission to Sally's attention and she pleads with him not to do anything that will make her house look less than completely desirable to a prospective buyer. What must Larry do?
    a. Larry must disclose the defect on the TDS and keep Sally as a client.
    b. Larry must convince Sally that she must make the disclosure or he will drop her as a client.
    c. Larry must drop Sally as a client immediately.
    d. Larry must do nothing that would adversely affect Sally's opportunities.

3. Kate is showing a property in which a death occurred. What is her disclosure responsibility to the buyer?
    a. A death is never considered a material fact, because properties cannot be stigmatized.
    b. It can be disclosed if the death occurred within 3 years prior to the buyer making an offer on the property.
    c. Kate can only disclose the information if the buyer asks a direct question about a death on the property.
    d. This is a material fact that must always be disclosed.

4. The Real Estate Transfer Disclosure Statement (TDS) is a document that the seller must provide to any buyer of residential property (one-to-four units). Which transfer is not exempt from the disclosure requirement?
    a. Transfers by a foreclosure sale
    b. Transfers by the administration of a probate estate
    c. Transfers from co-owners to a third party buyer
    d. Transfers from or to any governmental entity

5. Which of the following is NOT a required disclosure on the TDS?
    a. A cracked slab
    b. A notice of abatement against the adjacent property
    c. A pool located within the common area of a homeowners' association
    d. A shared driveway

6. Three years ago, a tornado tore through the town where Pam's home is. Luckily, Pam's home was unscathed. Does Pam have to disclose the fact that there was a tornado within the past three years on the NHD?

    a. Pam needs to disclose each natural hazard that occurred in the general vicinity, pursuant to the Civil Code.
    b. Pam needs to disclose every natural hazard that occurred within a five-mile radius, pursuant to the Civil Code.
    c. Pam needs to disclose only certain natural hazards on the NHD, and a tornado is not one of them.
    d. Pam would disclose this hazard in the Environmental Hazard Statement, not on the NHD.

7. What is the requirement for disclosing mold?

    a. Mold must be disclosed pursuant to the Toxic Mold Protection Act.
    b. Existence of mold must be disclosed on the TDS.
    c. Mold is disclosed on the Toxic Mold Disclosure Form.
    d. All of the statements are correct.

8. Sandra wishes to sell her home, which is located four miles across town from a large, well-known military base. Is Sandra required to make a special disclosure?

    a. No, because it is well-known that the base is located in the vicinity.
    b. No, because the base is no longer being used.
    c. No, because the base is four miles away.
    d. Yes, because the base is less than five miles away.

9. Which document is not required by statute when transferring ownership in a CID?

    a. A copy of the governing documents (operating rules and articles of incorporation, if any) of the common interest development
    b. A copy of the most recent financial statement, operating budget, and most recent reserve study
    c. A copy of the most recent pest control inspection and certification
    d. A disclosure of any settlement agreement or other instrument between the association and the developer regarding construction defects

10. Federal law requires that a new home seller (including a subdivider) disclose in every sales contract the type, thickness, and R-value of the insulation that has been or will be installed. What does R-value signify?

    a. Rating by Energy Star®
    b. Resistance to heat loss
    c. Retrofitting compliant
    d. Thickness of insulation

Residential Landlord-Tenant Law

Unit 15

INTRODUCTION

Property owners do not always use the property themselves. They sever their rights of exclusive use and rent that use to someone else creating a landlord-tenant relationship. This unit discusses the rental agreement between the property owner and the renter and their obligations and responsibilities. In addition, it describes the remedies for breach of contract if either party defaults on the agreement.

Learning Objectives

After completing this unit, you should be able to:

15A   identify the types of rental agreements.

15B   recognize clauses used in rental agreements.

15C   recall how rental agreements are terminated.

15D   specify the steps in the eviction process.

15E   indicate provisions of the Mobilehome Residency Law.

RENTAL AGREEMENTS

A rental agreement between the property owner and the renter is a complex legal document that spells out many aspects of their relationship. It details how the renter may use the property, services the owner will provide, the party responsible for utilities, required insurance, events that are considered default, and remedies of the parties. As a valid contract, it must have the same components as a legally enforceable contract—legally competent parties, mutual consent between the parties, a lawful objective, and sufficient consideration. The rental agreement is not only a contract; it is also a conveyance of a leasehold interest in real estate, which gives the renter a tenancy. **Tenancy** is the renter's right to take exclusive possession and use of the owner's rental unit in consideration for rent. A **rental unit** is the owner's house, duplex, condominium,

or apartment that is made available to a renter. **Rent** is payment for the use of a property under a lease or rental agreement. Although rent normally is paid as money, rent can take the form of some kind of non-monetary compensation, such as the tenant making repairs in exchange for the right to live on the property.

Rental agreements between the property owner and the renter for one year or less can be verbal or in writing. Leases for longer than one year (1 year plus 1 day) must be in writing. [C.C. §§1091, 1624(a)(3)]. However, all rental agreements should be in writing to clarify the duties and responsibilities of each party and reduce disagreements.

Types of Rental Agreements

California does not require owners to use a specific rental agreement; however, most use a periodic rental agreement or a lease.

Periodic Rental Agreement

A **periodic rental agreement** is an oral or written contract between the owner (**landlord**) and the renter (**tenant**) that states the length of time (days, weeks, months) between the rent payments, which is called the **rental period**. For example, a periodic rental agreement that requires one rent payment each month is a **month-to-month rental agreement**, and the tenancy is a month-to-month (periodic) tenancy. California law presumes that renting real property, unless the parties have agreed otherwise, is for a period of 30 days. [C.C. §1944]. A periodic tenancy automatically renews at the end of each period unless one party gives notice of termination to the other. The landlord can change the terms of the periodic rental agreement with proper written notice.

The rental period (days, weeks, or months) determines how often the rent is paid, e.g. every 30 days with a month-to-month agreement. The rental period also determines the amount of advance notice landlords and tenants must give each other if either decides to terminate the tenancy or if the landlord decides to change the terms of the periodic rental agreement (other than the amount of rent). [C.C. §§827(a)(b)].

> Example: For three years, Pat has rented an apartment on a written month-to-month rental agreement. She purchased a house and escrow is scheduled to close in 45 days. Because the rental period is 30 days, Pat must give her landlord at least 30-day's advance notice of her intent to terminate the periodic rental agreement. On the other hand, if Pat's rental period were only 7 days, she would only need to give the landlord a 7-day advance notice.

Lease

A **lease** is a rental agreement with a predetermined length of time between an owner (**lessor**) and a renter (**lessee**) which gives the lessee a tenancy. The tenancy, known as a **tenancy for years** (or tenancy for a fixed term), is often for six months or a year but sometimes longer. A lease states the total number of months that the lease will be in effect and has a beginning and an ending date. Since the end date is mutually agreed upon, the tenancy terminates automatically at the end of the specified rental period. As long as the lessee pays the rent and complies with other lease provisions, the lessor cannot evict the lessee, raise the rent, or change other terms of the tenancy during the lease.

Typical Rental Agreement Clauses

Whether the rental agreement is a periodic rental agreement or a lease, most clauses are the same. A rental agreement must clearly set forth all of its terms, conditions, obligations, and rights of all parties to the rental agreement. At a minimum, it needs to cover the basic terms of the tenancy, which include the names of the parties, rent amount, and duration of rental agreement. Sometimes the words **to let** or **to demise**, (another way to say to rent), will be found in a rental agreement, but those words are optional. The following discussion covers some of the more important clauses.

Names of All Tenants

The names of the landlord and all tenants must be documented on the rental agreement. Every adult who lives in the rental unit should be named as tenants and sign the rental agreement. By signing the rental agreement, each person is legally responsible for all terms, including the full amount of the rent and the proper use of the property.

The rental agreement must be signed by the landlord, but not necessarily the tenant. It is common practice for the tenant to sign the rental agreement, but the law requires only that the rental agreement be delivered to the tenant for it to be binding. The tenant's acceptance of the rental agreement by paying rent and taking possession of the property binds both parties to the terms of the rental agreement. A court may uphold a rental agreement if it is considered an implied contract.

> Example: A landlord signs the rental agreement, but the tenant moves in without signing it. After four months, the tenant decides not to pay rent. In court, he protests to the judge, "Your Honor, I never signed the rental agreement." The judge determines that he was the person who took possession of the described property and paid for the rental unit for four months. Therefore, the tenant is liable for the rent and must fulfill all the terms and obligations of the rental agreement.

Maximum Number of Occupants

Tenants who have signed a rental agreement are prohibited from allowing others to move in or to move out without securing the prior approval of the landlord. Too many people occupying a residence may violate housing and fire codes and can cause an unusual amount of wear and tear to the property. This clause gives the landlord grounds to evict a tenant who moves in a friend or relative, or sublets the unit, without permission.

Term of the Rental Agreement

Both a month-to-month rental agreement and a lease should have the beginning date, which may or may not be on the date the tenant actually occupies the premises. However, the date stated in the agreement as the beginning date is when the tenant becomes responsible to pay rent. A lease will have both beginning and ending dates and the duration stated in days, weeks, months, or years. A periodic rental agreement will state the rental period (week-to-week or month-to-month).

Rent

The amount of rent to be paid, when it is due, and to whom it is to be given must be clearly stated. Most periodic rental agreements and leases require rent to be paid by the first of the month. The acceptable methods of payment—personal check, cashier's check, or money order—must be indicated. [C.C. §§1961-1962.7]. Effective January 1, 2005, a landlord may not require tenants to pay rent in cash, except if the tenant has defaulted on the rent. If the landlord first gives a tenant written notice that the rent must be paid in cash, the landlord can only require up to three payments to be paid in cash.

Late Fees and Returned Checks

The date when rent is considered past due and the amount of the late fee is stated, as well as how to handle returned checks. The amount of late fees or returned check charges should not be excessive or a court might find them invalid as a forfeiture or penalty. [C.C. §1719(a)(1)].

Rent Increases

Rent cannot be increased during the term of a lease. With a periodic rental agreement, the rent can be increased with proper advance notice in writing. California law requires at least 30 days' advance written notice of a rent increase for a month-to-month periodic rental agreement. The requirement is 30 days' advance notice if the increase is 10% or less, and 60 days' advance notice if the increase is more than 10%. [C.C. §827(b)].

Rent Control

Some cities have rent control ordinances that limit or even prohibit rent increases. A landlord in a city with a rent control ordinance must follow specific procedures before increasing a tenant's rent.

Although rent control ordinances are challenged regularly in court, in fairly recent cases (e.g., California Supreme Court—*Kavanau* v. *Santa Monica Rent Control Board* (1997) 16 Cal.4th 761; U.S. Supreme Court and *Pennell* v. *City of San Jose* (1988) 485 U.S. 1), both high courts have re-affirmed that rent control itself violates neither the state nor federal constitution.

Because the courts have refused to invalidate rent control, property owners have turned to the California Legislature. For example, in *Nash v. City of Santa Monica* (1984) the California Supreme Court upheld the validity of a city ordinance that prohibited the removal of rental units from the housing market by conversion or demolition unless the property owner obtained a removal permit from the city's rent control board. In effect, Santa Monica's ordinance prohibited a landlord from going out of business without the city's permission. In response, the Legislature adopted what is known as the Ellis Act of 1985 [Govt. Code §§7060-7060.7]. It provides landlords the unconditional right to evict tenants in order to go out of the rental business by removing all the units in the building from the rental market. Under the Ellis Act, the apartments cannot be re-rented except at the same rate the evicted tenant was paying for five years following the eviction. The Act, however, imposes no restriction on the property then being converted to condominiums.

In 1995, property owners scored a similar success with the Costa-Hawkins Rental Housing Act [C.C. §§1954.50-1954.535]. Costa-Hawkins allows landlords to establish the initial rent for a unit or dwelling even if it is rent-controlled. So long as the same tenant stays in the unit, of course, the unit is subject to the rent control provisions for any increases in rent, but it will revert to market rate once the unit becomes vacant.

Fees and Deposits

The landlord often collects a deposit to cover such items as cleaning or potential damage to the property. The money collected may be non-refundable fees or refundable deposits.

Non-Refundable Fees

A **non-refundable fee** is a fee that will not be returned to the tenant under any circumstance, and this fee cannot legally be called a deposit. The landlord must provide the prospective resident a receipt for non-refundable fees. An example of a non-refundable fee is the application/credit check fee that must not exceed $30.00.

Refundable Deposits

A **security deposit** is a refundable deposit that the landlord requires the tenant to pay at the beginning of the tenancy. [C.C. §1950.5(m)]. The maximum deposit (whether called *security deposit*, *last month's rent*, *pet deposit*, *key fee*, or *cleaning fee*) allowed on an unfurnished property may not exceed the amount of two months rent. The maximum deposit allowed on a furnished property is not more than the amount of three months rent. A security deposit also includes any charges imposed at the beginning of the tenancy to reimburse the landlord for costs associated with processing a new tenant, other than application screening fees.

> Example: If rent on an unfurnished, 2-bedroom apartment is $900 per month and the landlord charged the tenant a $20 general processing fee, the maximum the landlord could collect up front is $2,700. The landlord can charge $900 for the first month's rent, $1,800 for the security deposit, and nothing for the general processing fee because it is considered part of the security deposit.

The landlord can use the security deposit for four purposes: (1) unpaid rent, (2) clean the unit, (3) repair damages, and (4) replace personal property, such as furnishings or keys, other than because of normal wear and tear. When cleaning the unit after the tenant moves out, the unit only needs to be as clean as it was when the tenant moved in. [C.C. §1950.5(b)(3) & §§1950.5(b)(e)].

The law is specific on the handling of residential security deposits—the security deposit must be returned to the tenant or transferred to the new owner, with notification to the tenant. The landlord has 21 calendar days after the tenant has moved out to return all unused portions of the security deposit, with a written itemized statement showing how the remainder was used (to clean, repair damage, replace windows, etc.). The landlord must include the receipts with the itemized statement. [C.C. §1950.5(g)(2)]. A landlord may only deduct from the security deposit the cleaning cost "necessary to return the unit to the same level of cleanliness it was in at the beginning of the tenancy." A landlord who keeps deposits without reason for more than 3 weeks after the tenant has moved may be subject to twice the amount of the security deposit in statutory damages in addition to actual damages. [C.C. §1950.5(l)].

Insurance

Standard rental agreement forms require the tenant to have liability and property insurance. Usually the tenant must give a copy of the policy to the landlord. The landlord may specify the specific dollar amount of liability coverage required by the tenant. The tenant's property insurance covers the personal property, fixtures, equipment, and any improvements made by the tenant.

An owner cannot refuse to rent to an otherwise qualified tenant because the tenant owns water-filled furniture, such as a waterbed. However, the owner can require such a tenant to carry special property damage insurance for leakage. [Civil Code §1940.5(a)].

Maintenance and Repairs

Both landlords and tenants have certain responsibilities regarding the cleanliness and maintenance of the property. This clause specifies who maintains and makes repairs to the premises.

Landlord's Responsibility

Because of the California Supreme Court case, *Green v. Superior Court*, every residential rental agreement in California contains an implied warranty of habitability. The **implied warranty of habitability** requires landlords to maintain their rental units in a condition that substantially complies with state and local building, health, and safety codes. [*Green v. Superior Court* (1974) 10 Cal.3d 616]. At the beginning of a rental agreement, the owner must ensure the property is free of trash, garbage, rodents, and insects. Furthermore, the property must have adequate heating, plumbing, and electrical  wiring (up to the current building code); waterproofing and weather protection; hot and cold running water; garbage receptacles; and safe floors, stairs, and railings. In addition, each unit must have a bathroom (with working toilet, sink, and tub or shower), natural lighting in every room, emergency exits, working deadbolt locks on entry doors, and working smoke detectors. [Health and Safety Code §§17900-17995, 116049.1, 116064, 13113.7].

Tenant's Responsibility

However, a landlord is not responsible to repair damage caused by the tenant or the tenant's pets or guests. [C.C. §§1929, 1941.2]. The tenant must take reasonable care of the rental unit and keep the premises "as clean and sanitary as the condition of the premises permits." Section 1941 of the Civil Code lists some of the tenant's responsibilities. For example, tenants must use gas, electrical, and plumbing fixtures properly, keep fixtures clean, dispose of trash and garbage in a sanitary manner, and use each portion of the premises in the manner for which it is intended.

Most rental agreements do not allow the tenant to make alterations, such as painting walls or adding built-ins without the landlord's permission. A tenant is liable for the cost of unauthorized alterations or damage upon termination of the tenancy, but not for "ordinary wear and tear" from normal use of the property.

Tenants must immediately notify the landlord of any problems with the plumbing or electrical systems or if the deadbolt locks or other security devices are inoperable.

Habitability Issues

If there is a repair problem involving the tenant's health, welfare, or safety, the landlord has a duty to make needed repairs under the implied warranty of habitability. The tenant should notify the landlord of the problem by a phone call, email, and a follow-up letter. After a reasonable time, if the landlord ignores the request or refuses to make the repair, the tenant may use one of the following remedies: repair and deduct, abandon the rental unit, or withhold rent. [C.C. §1942]. Before attempting to use any of these remedies, a tenant should obtain legal advice to determine the appropriateness of the remedy.

Repair and Deduct Remedy. The repair and deduct remedy is used to correct substandard conditions that affect the tenant's health and safety, such as a faulty water heater or broken thermostat. Under this remedy, the tenant may make the repairs and deduct the cost of the repairs (up to one-month's rent) from the rent when it is due. The tenant may do this only two times in any 12-month period.

Abandonment Remedy. If the cost to repair the substandard conditions exceeds the amount of one month's rent, the tenant may abandon the premises. Once the tenant abandons the property, he or she has no further responsibility to pay future rents.

Rent Withholding Remedy. Of the three remedies, this requires that the substandard defects or repairs that are needed must be more serious than would justify use of the repair and deduct and abandonment remedies. The defects must be serious enough to make the dwelling uninhabitable, such as exposed electrical wiring, collapsed ceilings, or a gas leak. In the rent withholding remedy, the tenant can continue to withhold the rent until the landlord makes repairs. The tenant should deposit the rent money into a separate account (escrow account). If the tenant ends up in court, this proves to the judge the willingness of the tenant to pay the rent.

Retaliatory Actions or Eviction

A landlord may not retaliate against a tenant by raising the rent or sending an eviction notice. California law recognizes that a tenant has the right to participate in a tenants' association or an organization advocating tenants' rights or if the tenant has "lawfully and peaceably exercised any rights under the law." [C.C. §1942.5(c)]. That last phrase covers such things as complaining to the owner or to a public entity about habitability problems (e.g., dangerous wiring) on the premises. It would also cover an eviction if the tenant exercised the repair and deduct provision of Civil Code §1942(a).

Pets

The rental agreement should state whether pets are allowed. Some properties have a "No Pets" policy. Others set aside several units that allow cats, dogs, or both. The landlord should have a clearly written  pet policy identifying any restrictions, such as breed or size of the pets, and a limit on the number of pets allowed per unit. Usually the pet policy requires a refundable pet deposit ($200-$1,000) and sometimes an additional monthly pet rent. Typical rent is $10-$15 per month for each cat and $15-$25 per month for each dog. Violation of the pet policy is grounds for eviction.

Rules & Regulations

The rental agreement or a separate document contains the rules and regulations prohibiting disruptive behavior, such as excessive noise, illegal activity, drug dealing, or participating in gang activities on or about the premises.

Right of Entry

During the term of a tenancy, the tenant is entitled to quiet enjoyment and can exclude the landlord from the property. However, in certain circumstances, the landlord has a limited right of entry. [C.C. §1954(a)].

The landlord must give the tenant reasonable advance notice in writing—usually 24-hours. The written notice may be personally served on the tenant, left with someone of suitable age, or posted on the property. If the notice is mailed to the tenant, mailing it at least six days before the intended entry is presumed to be reasonable. Advance written notice is not required in an emergency or if the tenant has abandoned the property.

Landlord's Limited Right of Entry

- Make necessary or agreed repairs or improvements. The repairs or other work can be performed only during normal business hours.

- Consent of the tenant upon less than 24-hours' notice

- Emergency. This does not require 24-hours' notice, but could subject the property owner to liability for a trespass if there is not truly an emergency (broken water pipe, fire, etc.).

- Tenant abandons or has surrendered the premises

- Court order

- Inspection by prospective or actual purchasers, or prospective tenants if the rental agreement is due to end

Although the landlord is entitled to make an entry in these situations, the landlord "may not abuse the right of access or use it to harass the tenant." [C.C. §1940.2(a)(4)]. If the landlord repeatedly enters the unit with the intention of influencing the tenant to move, the tenant has the right to sue the landlord in small claims court for a civil penalty of up to $2,000 for each violation. [C.C. §1940.2(b)].

Subletting or Assigning a Rental Agreement

Unless prohibited in the lease, a lessee may sublease or assign his or her leasehold interest in the property to another person.

Sublease

If the original lessee remains legally responsible for the lease, the new agreement is considered a sublease. A **sublease** is an arrangement in which a lessee rents his or her leasehold interest to another party called the **sublessee**. The sublessee is liable only to the original lessee (**sublessor**). The sublessor is still primarily liable for paying the rent to the owner under the original lease whether the sublessee makes the payments as agreed or not. A sublease is also known as a sublet or sandwich lease. A **sandwich lease** is so named because the original lessee is technically sandwiched between the new lessee and the lessor in the collection and payment of rent.

Example: Bob rents a two-bedroom apartment for $1,000 per month with a two-year lease from Donna. He lives there for six months until he is transferred to another part of the country. He has 18 months left on the lease before it expires. Bob knows the transfer is temporary and wants to return to his apartment at some time in the future.

Sam accepts Bob's offer to sublease the apartment for one year at $1,200 per month and moves in. Since Sam's sublease is with Bob, not the lessor, he sends his rent check for $1,200 to Bob each month. Bob pays rent of $1,000 to his lessor, Donna.

Bob is still responsible for his original lease with the lessor and keeps his interest as lessee in the property. Bob holds a sandwich lease in between the original lessor (Donna) and the sublessee (Sam).

Assignment

Unlike a sublease, a lessee can give up all rights to use or possess the rented property through an assignment. An **assignment** is the transfer of the entire leasehold estate to a new person, called an **assignee**. The original lessee (**assignor**) steps out of primary responsibility for the lease and the new assignee becomes responsible to the lessor for all the terms of the original lease. In order for a lease to be assigned, the lessor must approve the assignment and release the original lessee from liability. The written release is called a **novation**.

Unlike a sublease—in which the original lessee retains the right to retake the premises if the sublessee does not pay the rent—an assignment ends the lessee's relationship with the property and the assignee in effect "stands in the shoes" of the original lessee.

Example: Bob leases a two-bedroom apartment from Mike and lives there for six months until he is transferred to another part of the country. The term of the lease is one year, and he has six months left before it expires. Pat accepts Bob's offer of assignment of his lease and moves into the apartment when Bob moves out. Pat is responsible directly to the lessor (Mike) who also collects the rent. Bob no longer has any interest in the lease.

Default

The **default clause** pertains to the nonperformance of a duty or obligation in the contract (breach of contract) without a legal excuse. The rental agreement describes what constitutes an event of default, the tenant's right to cure (if any), and the landlord's remedies for tenant's default.

A tenant's default may be economic—failure to pay rent or assessments when due—or non-economic—improper use of the property, excessive number of people living in the unit, failure to follow the rules and regulations, or failure to adhere to the hours of operation.

Abandonment

When a lessee voluntarily gives up a lease before the expiration of its term, it is known as **surrender**. The lessee gives up any rights of possession and surrenders the rental unit back to the owner. If the lessor accepts the surrender, the lessee is no longer liable for rent. Sometimes a lessee just moves out or abandons the premises without doing a formal surrender. In this instance, the lessor has the option of demanding the balance of the rent due or rent due until the lessor finds another lessee.

A rental unit may be considered abandoned when rent on the property has been due and unpaid for at least 14 consecutive days and the lessor reasonably believes that the lessee has abandoned the property. If the evidence is strong that the rental unit has been abandoned, the lessor should give the lessee a **Notice of Belief of Abandonment**. The notice should provide the time in which the lessee has to reply, and it should state the consequences of the abandonment to the lessee. The notice can be personally delivered or sent by first class mail to the lessee at the last known address or to any other address where the lessee may reasonably be expected to receive the notice. [C.C. §1951.3].

TERMINATING RENTAL AGREEMENTS

Just as most property owners at some point decide to put their property on the market, most rentals of real property eventually end. In most cases, the end of the rental relationship ends amicably with little or no involvement with the legal system.

The majority of rental agreements end by the expiration of the agreed-upon term as in a lease or by mutual agreement between the landlord and tenant as in a periodic rental agreement. Other ways to terminate a lease are destruction of the premises, breach of conditions by either landlord or tenant, or eviction. A sale of the property during the term of the lease does not usually terminate the lease.

Even when the end of a rental relationship is orderly there are rules that must be followed so that everyone's rights are protected; the tenant moves out and the landlord can locate a new tenant.

Terminating a Lease

As noted earlier, a lease—a tenancy for a fixed term—ends automatically without either party having to give notice. At the expiration of the lease, if the tenant fails to vacate the rental unit, the owner can either commence eviction proceedings immediately or accept rent in what will thereafter be a month-to-month tenancy. Alternatively, the parties can use this occasion to re-negotiate a new rental agreement.

Terminating a Periodic Rental Agreement

To end a periodic rental agreement, a tenant must give the landlord proper written advance notice. Unlike a lease, a periodic rental agreement, such as a month-to-month agreement, has no fixed term. Therefore, it can run indefinitely as long as both parties are satisfied with the arrangement and neither does anything to breach the rental agreement. Therefore, while a fixed-term lease will have a definite end date, a party must take action to terminate a month-to-month rental agreement.

In order to terminate such tenancy in the absence of a dispute (e.g., the tenant has decided to relocate to accept a new job, or the landlord has decided to live in the rented premises) either party may give the other a **Notice of Termination of Tenancy**. [C.C. §789]. There are no particular "magic words" that must be used, but at a minimum the notice should state something to the effect that the party "hereby gives notice that the existing rental agreement for (identifying the address of the property) is terminated effective (date of effectiveness of termination)."

Advance Notice Required

Advance notice of the termination of tenancy is required by both tenant and landlord. The tenant's notice must be given at least the minimum number of days for which rent normally accrues, though no more than 30 days is required. [C.C. §1946].

A landlord can terminate a month-to-month tenancy by serving a written 30-day or 60-day notice on the tenant. A landlord can give the tenant a 30-day advance written notice if any tenant or resident has lived in the rental unit less than one year. [C.C. §1946.1(c)]. However, the landlord must give a 60-day advance written notice if tenant has lived in the rental unit for a year or more. [C.C. §1946.1(b)]. A landlord does not have to give a reason for giving a 30-day or 60-day notice of termination. If, however, the tenant suspects that the landlord has an ulterior motive that is unlawful, such as punishing the tenant for exercising rights under the law, then the tenant can raise the defense of retaliatory eviction when the matter eventually proceeds to court.

Serving the Notice

A tenant can use personal service to give the notice to the owner. **Personal service** is the actual physical delivery of a notice to the person named in the notice. However, the notice can be served by either party by sending a copy by certified or registered mail addressed to the other party. The tenant may send the mailed notice to the landlord's agent to whom the tenant has paid the rent for the month prior to the date of notice (or by serving the agent personally).

If the notice is being served by a landlord on a tenant, the notice should be served personally if possible. Otherwise, the notice can be delivered to a person on the premises of suitable age (which normally means someone at least 16 but preferably 18) at either the tenant's home or place of business, or by posting the notice on the property in a conspicuous place. [C.C.P. §§1162(1)(2)(3)].

If either of the two latter methods is used, Section 1162 also requires that the notice be mailed to the other party. Unfortunately, the statutes do not state when the service is effective if it is given by mail—some cases hold that it is effective when it is deposited in the mail, others that the tenant is allowed additional time to account for the mailing of notices (typically 5 days under Code of Civil Proc. §1013). In 1995, Section 1013 was amended to state that the extra time for mailing stated in that section apply unless a different rule is provided in another statute or a rule of court. This does not resolve the uncertainty, but suggests that landlords should wait those extra five days before going to court when the "substituted service" (including service by mail) is used.

Civil Code §1946 also provides that the notice does not have to be given on the first day that the rental period begins; it is effective 30 days after it is given regardless of when rent is normally paid.

While the 30-day provision is the minimum that must be given, nothing bars either party from giving more notice than necessary. In fact, if the parties are on good terms and it is practical to give more than 30 days' notice, the other party might well appreciate extra time to make new arrangements.

THE EVICTION PROCESS

The landlord has one legal remedy to remove a tenant—the eviction process using an unlawful detainer action. The landlord must use this court process to evict the tenant and not give in to frustration about the delinquent or remiss tenant by committing unlawful acts, such as changing the locks or bullying the tenant with threats of bodily harm.

Illegal Self-Help Remedies

- The landlord cannot turn off utilities, change the locks, remove outside doors or windows, or remove the tenant's personal property. If the landlord does any of the preceding, he or she will be liable for the actual damages of the tenant, plus $100 per day that it continues. [C.C. §789.3].

- The landlord cannot use threats or menacing conduct to interfere with the tenant's quiet enjoyment of the premises. The landlord is liable for $2,000 for each violation. [C.C. §1940.2].

The eviction process follows three main steps: (1) serving an eviction notice to terminate the rental agreement, (2) obtaining a judgment against the tenant in an unlawful detainer action, and (3) evicting the tenant by the sheriff under a writ of possession.

Eviction Notice

Simply violating the terms of the rental agreement does not actually terminate the agreement. To terminate the rental agreement, the landlord must serve the tenant an eviction notice (3-day notice) for cause asking the tenant to conform. [C.C.P. §1161]. A **three-day notice** instructs the tenant to either leave the rental unit or comply with the terms of the rental agreement within the three-day period. The 3-day notice gives the tenant **3 days** to pay the rent or take whatever action is required to cure the breach of the rental agreement. If the tenant fails to pay (or take the other action to cure the breach—e.g., to remove a non-permitted pet) within the three days, then the tenancy is terminated immediately, and the owner can proceed to court without further delay. [C.C.P. §12a].

Uses for 3-Day Notice to Quit

1. Tenant failed to pay rent when due.

2. Tenant violated any provision of the rental agreement.

3. Tenant damaged the rental property.

4. Tenant substantially interfered with other tenants.

5. Tenant used the rental property for an unlawful purpose.

If the tenant fails to pay rent, the owner gives the tenant a 3-Day Notice to Pay Rent or Quit. For breach of any conditions other than failure to pay rent, the owner uses a 3-Day Notice to Cure or Quit.

Three-Day Notice to Pay Rent or Quit

If the notice is a **Three-Day Notice to Pay Rent or Quit**, it must state the amount of rent that is owed. Even though the tenant presumably is aware of this sum, stating the full amount avoids disputes later if the tenant attempts to make only a partial payment. If the landlord wants to receive the rent within the 3 days, the notice must also have a street address where the tenant can deliver it; otherwise, the tenant can mail the rent within the 3 days and rely on the date of mailing.

Unlike the 30-day notice, the 3-day notice always gives the tenant some option to comply with whatever is demanded, assuming that the tenant has both the ability and willingness to comply. On the other hand, if the tenant complies but does not do so within the 3 days, the landlord has a choice to make.

> Example: Tom has a rental agreement that provides for the payment of rent on the first of every month. He fails to pay the rent on March 1 as agreed. On March 3, the owner, Linda, serves him with a Three-Day Notice to Pay Rent or Quit.

There are now three possible scenarios:

1. Tom pays within the three days. If he tenders the rent on March 4, 5, or 6, Linda must accept it and their rental relationship goes on as before. Absent further problems, Tom can remain on the premises under the same terms as if he had paid on March 1 as required.

2. Tom fails to pay by March 6. The tenancy is terminated, and Linda can immediately proceed to court. Even if Tom tenders the full rent, for example, on March 8, he cannot reinstate the tenancy without Linda's consent.

3. Tom fails to pay by March 6, but tenders a full month's rent on March 9. Linda could accept the overdue rent reinstating the rental agreement as before, or Linda could refuse to accept the rent, which terminates Tom's tenancy.

Because the tenant has the option of curing the default when served with a Three-Day Notice to Pay Rent or Quit, after one or more violations, a landlord may choose to serve a 3-day notice and a 30-day notice simultaneously. This gives the landlord the option to move to court immediately upon the expiration of the most recent 3-day notice (if the tenant fails to pay the rent within the 3 days) or to end the tenancy upon the expiration of the 30-day notice.

Example: Sam has a month-to-month rental agreement with Janet, the owner of the apartment building where he lives. Sam frequently has been late on his rent, which is due on the first of each month. For June, July, and August he waited until the Three-Day Notice to Pay Rent or Quit was served on him before paying it. Finally, when Sam failed to pay for the fourth consecutive month, Janet served the fourth Three-Day Notice to Pay Rent or Quit together with a 30-day notice on him on September 2. Even if Sam pays the rent on time, his tenancy will end on October 2 and Janet can thereafter initiate eviction proceedings.

If Sam and Janet have a LEASE instead of a MONTH-TO-MONTH TENANCY, Janet cannot evict him unless he fails to pay within the 3 days. She cannot terminate a lease with a 30-day notice as she could a periodic rental agreement. Unfortunately, even if the tenant is late month after month under a lease, all that the landlord can do is be diligent in getting the Three-Day Notice to Pay Rent or Quit served.

Three-Day Notice to Cure or Quit

Apart from failure to pay the rent, if the tenant fails to comply with another material term of the rental agreement (or is in violation of the law), the owner can serve the tenant with a **Three-Day Notice to Cure or Quit**. This notice is similar to the Three-Day Notice to Pay Rent or Quit, except that it must identify the tenant's activity that the owner believes violates the agreement with a directive to cease it within the time limit.

> Example: Sally has a rental agreement that provides that no commercial activities be conducted on the premises that she rents from Tom. The local zoning ordinance provides the same thing unless a use permit is obtained. Sally, however, begins to operate a chiropractic business from the property because commercial rents in her area are so high and the available space is limited. Neighbors notice many vehicles visiting the premises and one of Sally's clients even lets it slip that he has received treatment at her home.
>
> The local city planning department contacts Tom when it finds him listed as the owner of the property on the local tax roll. He, in turn, serves Sally with a Three-Day Notice to Cure or Quit. If he finds that she continues to see clients on the premises, he can declare that she has breached the agreement and, based upon her failure to abide by the Three-Day Notice to Cure or Quit, proceed immediately to court.

Proper Service of a Three-Day Notice

A landlord has three ways to serve a three-day notice on the tenant: by personal service, by substituted service, or by posting and mailing. It is better to have the tenant served with the notice personally, but serving a person of "suitable age" or posting to the premises (along with a mailing in either case) is sufficient to comply with the statute. [C.C.P. §§1162(1)(2)(3)].

Personal service. With personal service, the person serving the notice must hand the tenant the notice. The three-day period begins the day after the tenant received the notice.

Substituted service on another person. The landlord can use substituted service instead of personal service. The person serving the notice must leave the notice with a person of "suitable age and discretion" and also mail a copy of the notice to the tenant at home.

Posting and mailing. Assuming that the landlord cannot get personal or substituted service on the tenant, the next method is both to post the premises and to mail the notice. The notice can be served by taping or tacking a copy to the rental unit in a conspicuous place (such as the front door of the rental unit) and by mailing another copy to the tenant at the rental unit's address. The three-day period begins the day after the notice was posted and mailed.

Unlawful Detainer Action

An **unlawful detainer action** is a lawsuit to remove an unlawful holdover tenant (e.g. after the expiration of a 3-day or 30-day notice) and return the rental unit to its owner. An unlawful detainer proceeding moves relatively quickly (three to six weeks) compared to many other lawsuits (three months to one year), because they have calendar priority over all civil actions.

Summons and Complaint

The landlord will first draft a **complaint in unlawful detainer** and file it in the appropriate court. The complaint will usually be filed in the "limited division" of the superior court. An unlawful detainer case is a "limited civil case" if the total amount sought by the complaint is $25,000 or less. [C.C.P. §86(a)(4)].

Special court forms used to prepare this kind of lawsuit are available from the court for a nominal fee and usually involve only the checking of boxes or filling in short statements of fact. The landlord is only entitled to a judgment for possession of the premises, unpaid rent, and attorney's fees (if represented by an attorney). Other damages arising from the tenancy, such as physical harm to the rented property, must be adjudicated separately using a conventional lawsuit. The landlord must verify the complaint (sign it under penalty of perjury), attesting that all facts stated in it are true.

Once the complaint has been prepared and filed, the landlord will have the summons and the complaint served on the tenant by a peace officer (a marshal or sheriff depending on the county) or a registered process server.

Avoiding Risk

A tactic sometimes used by tenants resisting an unlawful detainer complaint was to have someone (an unnamed occupant) be on the premises when the sheriff was ready to evict the tenant after a court hearing had been completed. This unnamed occupant would claim that he or she was also a tenant (or subtenant) who had not been served with the lawsuit—stopping the eviction.

Therefore, when serving the summons and complaint, the peace officer or registered process server must make a reasonably diligent effort to determine if there are occupants who reside in the rental unit, but are not named in the complaint. If there are unnamed occupants, the peace officer or registered process server must serve them a prejudgment claim of right to possession, affix it to the premises, and then mail a copy to the same address by registered or certified mail. In this way, any such claims can be heard at the same time as the normal court hearing on the lawsuit itself.

Tenant's Response

Unlike the typical lawsuit where the defendant has 30 days to file a legal response, the tenant has only 5 CALENDAR DAYS to respond from the time the complaint is SERVED. If the fifth day falls on a Saturday, Sunday, or a holiday, the tenant has until the close of court business on Monday or non-holiday to file a legal response. [C.C.P. §1167].

When faced with a summons and complaint, the tenant may choose not to respond or may file a written legal response. If the tenant fails to file a written response, the court automatically enters a **default judgment** in favor of the landlord. The written legal responses available to a tenant are a motion to quash service of summons, a demurrer, or an answer.

Motion to Quash Service of Summons. A **motion to quash service of summons** is a legal response that a tenant can file if the tenant believes that the landlord did not properly serve the summons and complaint. For example, if the landlord miscounts and the 3-day or 30-day notice had not expired at the time the lawsuit was filed, that may require that a new notice be served and the whole process be started anew.

Demurrer. A **demurrer** is a legal response that a tenant can file to test the legal sufficiency of the charges made in the landlord's complaint. The landlord must abide by the strict procedural requirements in an unlawful detainer lawsuit. The tenant may respond with a demurrer if he or she believes that the complaint has some technical defect or does not properly allege the landlord's right for eviction.

If the tenant files a motion to quash service of summons or a demurrer, a hearing will be held. If the landlord loses, he or she must start over. If the tenant loses, he or she will file an answer and the Clerk of the Court will set a trial date.

Answer. Usually, the tenant responds to the complaint by filing an answer. The **answer** is a simple document to fill out; it is also a "checkbox" form with some spaces for longer answers if needed. It should be typed or neatly filled out in handwriting. In order not to lose any defenses that the tenant may have, the defenses must be written in the answer.

Typical Tenant Defenses to a Landlord's Complaint
- Inaccurate 3-day notice, such as requesting more rent than was actually due
- Breach of the warranty of habitability
- Retaliatory eviction

Green v. Superior Court

> Historically, the landlord's breach of this warranty was not a defense to an eviction for failure to pay rent; the tenant's only remedy was to sue the landlord for damages in a separate legal lawsuit. However, in *Green v. Superior Court* (1974) 10 Cal.3d 616, the California Supreme Court concluded that the tenant's obligation to pay rent was impliedly conditioned upon the rented premises being habitable. Therefore, even though the premises might be unsavory (or unsafe), the landlord could recover neither back rent nor the premises themselves if the owner breached this "warranty of habitability."

Breach of the warranty of habitability, of course, is a defense only to the tenant's failure to pay rent. If the basis for the unlawful detainer was based on a 30-day notice of termination, the landlord's breach is a defense only to the tenant's liability for any unpaid rent, not to the recovery of the premises.

Trial

After the tenant files a written answer, the Clerk of the Court sets the matter for trial and notifies the landlord and tenant of the date, time, and place. Unlawful detainer trials are normally set within two to three weeks of the request. Either party can request a jury trial, although in practice, a judge hears such cases in what is called a **bench trial**.

If the court decides in favor of the tenant, the tenant will not have to move, but will have to pay any rent that the court orders. The landlord may be ordered to pay the tenant's court costs and attorney's fees (if any). If the tenant fails to show up for the trial, or shows up but loses, the landlord will be awarded a judgment against the tenant and the eviction process proceeds to the final step.

Writ of Possession

In the tenant does not move out, the court will issue the landlord a writ of possession. [C.C.P. §715.020]. A **writ of possession** is the legal document issued by the court commanding the tenant to leave the premises within five days. The five days begin to run once the sheriff, marshal, or registered process server posts the writ of possession on the property. Upon expiration of the five days, the sheriff physically removes the tenant and gives the landlord possession. [C.C.P. §715.010(b)(2)]. At this time, the landlord may remove personal property of the tenant and change the locks.

Any property left by the tenant must be stored—at the tenant's expense—and can be sold by the owner at auction upon further notice to the tenant. [C.C.P. §§715.030, 1174(h)]. Alternatively, the tenant can reclaim the property after paying the lien for any storage charges. In practical terms, many property owners will give the tenant a limited additional amount of time (e.g., a few hours) to remove any property rather than go through the lien-sale notice and auction.

MOBILEHOME RESIDENCY LAW

Mobilehomes are treated with some of the same rules as other kinds of landlord-tenant dealings, but there are also some unique aspects of this relationship. A **mobilehome** is a structure designed for human habitation and includes a manufactured home, as defined in Section 18007 of the Health and Safety Code, and a mobilehome, as defined in Section 18008 of the Health and Safety

Code. [C.C. §798.3]. In a mobilehome park, the tenant (**resident**) owns the mobilehome (**coach**), which is personal property and the park owner owns the space beneath the coach, which is real property.

There are no fewer than five statutory schemes, several in the Health and Safety Code and one in the Civil Code that deal with various aspects of the ownership of mobilehomes. Some of these govern the construction, sale, and movement of mobilehomes; others cover the obligation of park owners  and operators of mobilehome parks; and one deals with the rights and duties of mobilehome parks and the residents of those parks. The following discussion will focus on the last of these, the Mobilehome Residency Law. Most of the provisions of the **Mobilehome Residency Law** (MRL) were enacted piecemeal over a number of years and eventually codified under Chapter 2.5 of the Civil Code §§798 et seq.

The MRL provides that a person who owns a mobilehome that is in a park cannot be charged a fee for anything other than rent, utilities, and incidental charges for services that are actually rendered to the owner of the unit. In addition, any such incidental charges must be listed in the rental agreement. Thus, even if services (e.g., watering of landscaping or trash removal) are actually rendered, the park cannot charge the resident for them if they are not listed in the rental agreement [C.C. §798.32(a)].

Other Provisions of the Mobilehome Residency Law
- Cost of capital improvements to the park that can be passed along to residents
- Restrictions on occupancy of the mobilehome by persons other than the owner and the owner's immediate relatives
- Notices that must be given by the park management to residents
- Duties of the parties with regard to the management of common areas

But, perhaps the most important part of the MRL from the resident's perspective is that it places significant restrictions on the park management's authority to evict the resident—which for all practical purposes means the eviction of the coach. Unlike the ordinary tenancy, which can be terminated at the will of either party upon the giving of the proper notices under law, the Legislature has declared that, given the expense and difficulty of relocating mobilehomes, the units cannot be evicted from a park except for the reasons stated in the MRL.

Those reasons include violation of reasonable rules of the park as set forth in the rental agreement; failure to pay rent; violation of local or state laws relating to mobilehome parks; or conviction of specified criminal offenses, most of which involve violence. [C.C. §798.56]. When the basis for eviction relates to violation of a park rule, the resident also must first be informed of the violation in writing and given an opportunity to correct the violation.

Taken together, these provisions come close to requiring the park to show "good cause" for eviction. Furthermore, assuming that the park management believes it has grounds to initiate an eviction that falls within one of the provisions of §798.56, it also must give the resident a minimum 60-day notice of the termination of the tenancy. The resident also has the option to sell the coach rather than move it out of the park.

SUMMARY

A rental agreement between the property owner and the renter is a legal document, which must have the same components as a legally enforceable contract—legally competent parties, mutual consent between the parties, a lawful objective, and sufficient consideration. A rental agreement must clearly set forth all of its terms, conditions, obligations, and rights of all parties to the rental agreement. At a minimum, it needs to cover the basic terms of the tenancy, which include the names of the parties, rent amount, and duration of rental agreement.

California does not require owners to use a specific rental agreement; however, most use a periodic rental agreement or a lease. A periodic rental agreement is an oral or written contract between the owner (landlord) and the renter (tenant) that states the length of time (days, weeks, months) between the rent payments, which is called the rental period. A lease is a rental agreement with a predetermined length of time between an owner (lessor) and a renter (lessee) which gives the lessee a tenancy.

Every residential rental agreement in California contains an implied warranty of habitability. The implied warranty of habitability requires landlords to maintain their rental units in a condition that substantially complies with state and local building, health, and safety codes. At the beginning of a rental agreement, the owner must ensure the property is free of trash, garbage, rodents, and insects. Furthermore, the property must have adequate heating, plumbing, and electrical wiring (up to the current building code); waterproofing and weather protection; hot and cold running water; garbage receptacles; and safe floors, stairs, and railings. In addition, each unit must have a bathroom (with working toilet, sink, and tub or shower), natural lighting in every room, emergency exits, working deadbolt locks on entry doors, and working smoke detectors.

The eviction process follows three main steps: (1) serving an eviction notice to terminate the rental agreement, (2) obtaining a judgment against the tenant in an unlawful detainer action, and (3) evicting the tenant by the sheriff under a writ of possession.

The Mobilehome Residency Law covers the obligation of mobilehome owners and the rights of mobilehome park residents.

UNIT 15 REVIEW

Matching Exercise

Instructions: Write the letter of the matching term on the blank line before its definition. Answers are in Appendix A.

Terms

A. assignment

B. implied warranty of habitability

C. lease

D. periodic rental agreement

E. rental period

F. rental unit

G. security deposit

H. sublease

I. tenancy

J. three-day notice

K. unlawful detainer action

L. writ of possession

Definitions

1. _____ Renter's right to take exclusive possession and use of the owner's rental unit in consideration for rent

2. _____ Owner's house, duplex, condominium, or apartment made available to a renter

3. _____ Month-to-month rental agreement

4. _____ Length of time (days, weeks, months) between the rent payments

5. _____ Rental agreement with a predetermined length of time

6. _____ Refundable deposit that the landlord requires the tenant to pay at the beginning of the tenancy

7. _____ Requirement of landlords to maintain their rental units in a condition that substantially complies with state and local building, health, and safety codes

8. _____ Arrangement in which a lessee rents his or her leasehold interest to another party

9. _____ Transfer of the entire leasehold estate to a new person

10. _____ Notice instructing tenant to either leave the rental unit or comply with the terms of the rental agreement

11. _____ Lawsuit to remove a tenant and return the rental unit to its owner

12. _____ Legal document issued by the court commanding the tenant to leave the premises within five days

Multiple Choice Questions

Instructions: Circle your response and go to Appendix A to read the complete explanation for each question.

1. Pam rents an apartment to Tom. The property is leased for the period from March 1 through December 31. He has paid his rent on time and has not violated any provisions of the rental agreement. If she wishes to evict him at the beginning of August to get a higher-paying tenant into the property, what must she do?
    a. Pam should serve him with a 3-day notice to quit.
    b. Pam cannot evict him as long as the rent is paid and he violates no terms of the lease.
    c. Pam should serve him with a 30-day notice.
    d. Pam should serve him with a complaint for unlawful detainer.

2. Bob owns an apartment building in a city that has a rent control ordinance. The ordinance provides that when a unit becomes vacant, Bob must apply to the local Rent Control Board to increase the rent before re-renting the unit. The requirement that Bob obtain approval to increase the rent before re-renting the unit:
    a. is a valid provision of the city's rent control law.
    b. will allow Bob to increase the rent no more than 15%.
    c. has been pre-empted since the adoption of the Costa-Hawkins Act.
    d. has been pre-empted by the adoption of the Ellis Act.

3. A tenant notified the landlord with a phone call and a follow-up letter that the water heater was not working properly. After two weeks of silence from the landlord, the tenant sent an email restating the problem with the water heater. Before repairing the water heater and deducting the cost of the repair from the next month's rent, the tenant should consult:
    a. the property owner.
    b. an attorney.
    c. other tenants on the property.
    d. the homeowners' association.

4. When does an owner have a right of entry onto the leased premises of a tenant?

    a. At any time, to verify that nothing illegal is happening on the property.

    b. At any time providing at least 6 hours' oral notice is given.

    c. If written notice is personally served on the tenant at least 24-hours prior to the entry.

    d. Whenever the tenant is not present.

5. Which of the following is correct as to assignments of leases?

    a. A lease may not prohibit assignment.

    b. Assignments of leases are illegal in California.

    c. Under an assignment, a lessee gives up all rights to use or possess the rented-property in the future.

    d. Under an assignment, the original tenant continues to have the right to retake the property at some point.

6. Default pertains to the nonperformance of a duty or obligation in the contract without a legal excuse. A rental agreement describes what constitutes default on the part of the tenant and the landlord's remedies for tenant's default. Which is a type of economic default?

    a. Following the rules and regulations

    b. Improper use of the property

    c. Non-payment of rent or assessments when due

    d. Two people living in a 2-bedroom unit

7. John has been leasing Sally's rental unit for a year. The term of the lease expires on March 31. Neither John nor Sally has given notice to extend the lease. If John is still living there on April 3 and refuses to leave, Sally:

    a. can remove him by filing an unlawful detainer lawsuit.

    b. can remove him by giving him a 3-day notice.

    c. can remove him by giving him a 30-day notice.

    d. cannot remove him under the facts as stated

8. Pat has lived in a rental house with a month-to-month rental agreement for nearly two years. The landlord's nephew is moving to town so the landlord is going to ask Pat to move and let the nephew live in the house. How much advance notice must the landlord give Pat?

    a. 3 days

    b. 5 days

    c. 30 days

    d. 60 days

9. Sam is the owner of a rental unit. Rent is customarily due on the first of the month. On October 4, Amanda, one of his tenants, has still not paid October's rent. What kind of notice should Sam give Amanda?

   a. Three-day notice to cure or quit
   b. Three-day notice to pay rent or quit
   c. Thirty-day notice to pay rent or quit
   d. Summons and complaint

10. According to the Mobilehome Residency Law, which service cannot be charged to the residents by the mobilehome park?

   a. Incidental charges for watering of landscaping
   b. Rent
   c. Trash removal that is listed in the rental agreement
   d. Utilities

APPENDIX A: ANSWER KEY

Unit 1: Overview of Law

Answers - Matching

1. M	5. C	9. T	13. H	17. B
2. E	6. K	10. N	14. A	18. L
3. D	7. Q	11. P	15. S	19. R
4. F	8. I	12. J	16. O	20. G

Answers - Multiple Choice

1. **(c)** The Code of Hammurabi is one of the first examples of codified law. After inscribing the law on the monolith, it became absolute and permanent. **Page 2**

2. **(b)** Six amendments: First, Third, Fourth, Fifth, Thirteenth, and Fourteenth pertain to real estate. **Page 3**

3. **(d)** All of the choices represent federal laws that affect the real estate industry. **Page 6**

4. **(a)** Administrative laws are written rules and regulations adopted by governmental agencies to enable the agencies to carry out regulatory duties. Regulations created by agencies carry the force of law. **Page 8**

5. **(b)** The two broad categories of law are civil law and criminal law. Civil law deals with private offenses, such as violations of contracts, and failure of professional duty. Criminal law concerns wrongs against persons or society. **Page 9**

6. **(d)** A crime is a violation of the federal or state criminal laws, typically punished by imprisonment, fines and/or community service. **Page 10**

7. **(b)** The highest court in California is the California Supreme Court. **Page 11**

8. **(d)** In the event of a dispute, some are settled out of court (arbitration and mediation) and some go to litigation to determine a remedy for the harmed party. **Page 14**

9. **(c)** Alternative Dispute Resolution is less costly than formal litigation and is usually quicker than litigation. ADR includes mediation or arbitration. **Page 15**

10. **(d)** A remedy refers to compensating the plaintiff for any injuries incurred. Remedies fall into two categories—legal and equitable. **Page 18**

Unit 2: Property & Legal Descriptions

Answers - Matching

1. F	6. G	11. T	16. V	21. R
2. P	7. H	12. Y	17. M	22. X
3. S	8. A	13. B	18. W	23. Q
4. J	9. C	14. L	19. D	24. N
5. I	10. K	15. U	20. O	25. E

Answers - Multiple Choice

1. **(c)** The right of transfer gives a property owner the right to dispose of the property in any way permitted by law. **Page 27**

2. **(c)** Land includes the surface, limited quantities of airspace above the surface, and the materials and minerals beneath the surface (subsurface). **Page 28**

3. **(b)** The ranch style home is an improvement and is real property. The wheat crop is fructus industriales and is personal property. The raspberry bushes are fructus naturales and are real property. The skylight is a permanently installed fixture on the roof of the cottage, which is an improvement. **Page 29**

4. **(a)** The first and primary factor is whether an agreement exists between the parties. If the buyers and sellers have not agreed that a particular item is included in a sale, the next step is to look at the method of attachment. **Page 31**

5. **(d)** Tenant-owned trade fixtures do not become the property of the landlord, even when attached to the real estate. However, the tenant must remove the trade fixtures, prior to the end of the lease without significant damage to the building. **Page 34**

6. **(b)** California's three classifications of groundwater are subterranean streams, underflow of surface waters, and percolating groundwater. Percolating groundwater has two sub-classifications: overlying land use and surplus groundwater. **Page 38**

7. **(a)** The doctrine of correlative rights allow landowners overlying percolating groundwater to use the water on an equal and correlative basis. **Page 38**

8. **(d)** A legal description is a description of a particular parcel of land that identifies it as precisely as possible, which should be written so that any person would be able to understand the description and determine the property location, with reasonable certainty. A street address is not sufficient for a legal description. **Page 42**

9. **(c)** Choice (c) is an informal reference, which is not a legal description. **Page 42**

10. **(d)** The Public Land Survey System uses the intersection of each principal meridian and base line to create grids, which form the basis for the surveys and measurement of all the lands within the territory that they control. **Page 47**

Unit 3: Real Property Interests

Answers - Matching

1.	R	7.	W	13.	J	19.	H	25.	AA
2.	Y	8.	L	14.	N	20.	G	26.	C
3.	Z	9.	M	15.	S	21.	BB	27.	E
4.	P	10.	U	16.	A	22.	T	28.	D
5.	K	11.	X	17.	DD	23.	B	29.	Q
6.	O	12.	CC	18.	V	24.	I	30.	F

Answers - Multiple Choice

1. **(b)** A fee (*not free*) simple absolute estate is a freehold estate that is also known as a perpetual estate. **Page 59**

2. **(b)** A nonfreehold estate is also known as a leasehold, which is a tenant's possessory estate in land or premises. **Page 66**

3. **(b)** A tenancy at sufferance occurs when a tenant "holds over" on the property after the expiration of a lease, without having signed a new lease agreement. **Page 68**

4. **(c)** A lien is an interest in real property owned by someone else that secures the payment of a debt or financial obligation. **Page 70**

5. **(c)** A deed of trust has three parties: the borrower (trustor), the lender (beneficiary), and a neutral third party (trustee). **Page 71**

6. **(a)** Ad valorem property taxes are imposed on real property as a percentage of the fair market value based on the most recent sale or improvement of the property. Special assessments are levied against property owners to pay for specific local improvements, such as underground utilities or water projects. **Page 76**

7. **(c)** Unlike an appurtenant easement, an easement in gross has a servient tenement burdened by the easement, but no dominant tenement. **Page 84**

8. **(d)** The right to enter another's land to remove soil or substances of the soil (water, minerals, timber, fruit, or other resource) is known as profit-à-prendre. **Page 95**

9. **(a)** Conditions are generally disfavored under modern law because the penalty—loss of title—is so harsh. **Page 97**

10. **(c)** The declaration of homestead protects real estate dwellings—not mobilehomes on leased land or other waterborne vessels. The automatic exemption protects houses, CIDs, mobilehomes, and waterborne vessels used as a residence. **Page 101**

Unit 4: Public Restrictions on Land Use

Answers - Matching

1. T	7. B	13. N	19. G	25. I
2. H	8. F	14. A	20. Q	26. E
3. R	9. S	15. X	21. C	
4. L	10. V	16. W	22. J	
5. Y	11. M	17. K	23. P	
6. Z	12. U	18. O	24. D	

Answers - Multiple Choice

1. **(c)** Police power allows the government to make and enforce laws and regulations for the safety, health, and welfare of the public. Zoning regulations, building codes, and fire codes are all enacted under the government's police power. **Page 112**

2. **(a)** In *Euclid v. Ambler Realty Co.*, the U.S. Supreme Court upheld the city's zoning ordinance as a valid exercise of the police power. The *Euclid* decision laid the foundation for modern land use regulation. **Page 115**

3. **(d)** Like the general plan, a zoning ordinance divides a city or county into different geographic zones, identifying what uses can and cannot be made on each parcel. **Page 116**

4. **(a)** Any uses that are not listed as either allowed or conditional are presumptively prohibited by the zoning code. Jeff's only choice is to find a different parcel to open a restaurant or to have the parcel re-zoned. **Page 120**

5. **(b)** A public entity can amortize a legal nonconforming use without the payment of compensation if it gives the landowner a period of time to continue the use, after which the owner must cease the activity without compensation. **Page 122**

6. **(b)** These are types of required maps under the Subdivision Map Act. **Page 125**

7. **(b)** The Lands Law does not apply to subdivisions that create four or fewer new parcels or to subdivisions creating parcels of 160 acres or larger. **Page 126**

8. **(c)** One kind of regulatory taking occurs if a law eliminates ALL economically viable use of a parcel. This has come to be known as a Lucas Wipeout. **Page 129**

9. **(b)** A categorical exemption means that the projects are small and will have little, if any, impact on the environment. Projects subject to a categorical exemption do not require further environmental analysis. **Page 134**

10. **(d)** The California Environmental Quality Act requires an environmental impact report (EIR). The National Environmental Policy Act requires an environmental impact statement (EIS). **Page 134**

Unit 5: Adjacent Owner Issues

Answers - Matching

1. C	4. A	7. B	10. L	13. D
2. J	5. N	8. H	11. I	14. F
3. E	6. G	9. K	12. O	15. M

Answers - Multiple Choice

1. **(b)**   Boundary lines are indicated by monuments (man-made objects, such as stakes or iron posts), by landmarks, or by common boundary improvements. **Page 144**

2. **(c)**   The property line of two parcels separated by a non-navigable waterway will be to the center or thread of the waterway. **Page 144**

3. **(d)**   Party walls are support walls for units in common interest developments. As such, an adjoining owner cannot remove or destroy a party wall without the consent of the other owner. **Page 145**

4. **(c)**   Line trees are trees whose trunks grow on the boundary line. **Page 146**

5. **(c)**   The house annoys the neighbors and it is probably an eyesore, the legal term is nuisance. **Page 147**

6. **(d)**   Trespass is an intentional and unauthorized entry upon another's real property. **Page 149**

7. **(b)**   Local government officials—not private individuals—are responsible to stop public nuisances. **Page 148**

8. **(b)**   An adjoining owner does not have the absolute right to cut encroaching roots and branches at the property line. The owner may prune tree limbs and remove roots from a neighbor's tree where they cross over the property line, but only if it will not damage the continued viability of the tree. **Page 153**

9. **(a)**   The location of the trunk of the tree determines ownership of the tree and therefore its fruit or nuts. The tree trunk is in David's yard, so the avocados belong to David who is the only one who may legally harvest the avocados. **Page 154**

10. **(b)**   California law follows the "first in time" rule. Whichever is first in time—the tree or the solar energy system—can remain. **Page 156**

Unit 6: How Ownership is Held

Answers - Matching

1. L	4. O	7. B	10. E	13. C
2. N	5. M	8. J	11. A	14. D
3. K	6. H	9. F	12. I	15. G

Answers - Multiple Choice

1. **(b)** A person who takes title in severalty often is described as "an unmarried man" or "an unmarried woman." **Page 164**

2. **(d)** The default method of holding co-owned title in California is the tenancy in common. **Page 166**

3. **(b)** Each cotenant is entitled to lease his or her share without the consent of the other cotenants. If the cotenant rents out only his or her share, the remaining cotenant(s) would not be entitled to a share of the rental payments. **Page 168**

4. **(c)** Due to the right of survivorship, a joint tenant may not will his or her share. **Page 171**

5. **(a)** When Kris sold her 1/3 interest to Sally, Sally became a tenant in common. Pat and Donna remained as joint tenants. When Pat died, Pat's third was automatically conveyed to Donna, who then became a 2/3 tenant in common with Sally. **Page 171**

6. **(a)** A joint tenancy requires equal interests. Community property ownership is also an equal 50/50 interest. **Page 175**

7. **(d)** In order for a couple to have community property rights, there must be a valid marriage. **Page 176**

8. **(d)** The owner of a sole proprietorship files one tax return, receives profits as income, and avoids double taxation. **Page 180**

9. **(d)** Planned development owners have fee title to their separately owned dwelling along with the lot underneath it. They do not directly own the common areas. **Page 186**

10. **(d)** Timeshare ownerships, which are also known as interval ownerships, are usually for specific blocks of time per year. **Page 188**

Unit 7: How Ownership is Acquired & Conveyed

Answers - Matching

1. C	7. M	13. CC	19. Y	25. W
2. G	8. DD	14. K	20. L	26. B
3. O	9. U	15. I	21. BB	27. A
4. AA	10. H	16. J	22. Q	28. D
5. N	11. V	17. P	23. R	29. F
6. S	12. Z	18. E	24. T	30. X

Answers - Multiple Choice

1. **(c)** Transferring title using a deed involves three steps: (1) execution of the deed by the grantor, (2) delivery of the deed to the grantee, and (3) the grantee's acceptance of the conveyance. Almost every real property transaction involves a fourth step: recording the deed with the county recorder's office as soon as possible. **Page 196**

2. **(c)**   The real property must be adequately described so that it is clear which parcel of land is being conveyed. It is not necessary to use a legal description. **Page 199**

3. **(a)**   A sheriff's deed is issued to a person who buys property sold via a sheriff's sale to satisfy a money judgment against the property owner. A tax deed is used by a public entity to convey title to tax-defaulted property from one person to another. A deed of trust can be used to convey title from the borrower when the borrower defaults on the loan. A quitclaim deed is executed by the person who has an interest in the property—not a third party. **Page 201**

4. **(d)**   Quiet title action is a court proceeding to establish an individual's right to ownership of real property against one or more adverse claimants. **Page 206**

5. **(d)**   Under the doctrine of dependent revocation, if a person revokes a prior valid will on the assumption that a subsequent will is valid, but it later turns out to be invalid for some reason, the law presumes that the testator would rather have had the prior valid will take effect instead of having the property pass by the law of intestacy. If it can be determined what the old will provided, a court can give effect to the prior, valid will. **Page 212**

6. **(a)**   A trust does not have to go through the probate process. Unlike a will, a trust can be signed only before a notary public and still is valid. **Page 214**

7. **(c)**   If no surviving relatives are found, the property escheats to the State. **Page 217**

8. **(b)**   The concept of adverse possession is based on the notion that land is too valuable to allow one person to own land without putting it to productive use. **Page 218**

9. **(a)**   In accretion and reliction, the landowner acquires title to the newly formed or exposed land on the bank. [C.C. §1014]. **Page 220**

10. **(b)**   In order to prevent an unscrupulous grantor from conveying the same parcel of land to more than one person, the grantee (buyer) should record the deed with the county recorder's office as soon as possible. **Page 221**

Unit 8: California License Law

Answers - Matching

1. E		5. P		9. G		13. A		17. I
2. O		6. M		10. R		14. F		18. C
3. N		7. B		11. H		15. S		19. Q
4. L		8. D		12. K		16. J		20. T

Answers - Multiple Choice

1. **(d)**   The two main purposes of the Real Estate Law is to protect consumers from loss because of dishonest or incompetent agents and to uphold the good standing of ethical agents from adverse publicity caused by unprincipled licensees. **Page 231**

2. **(d)**   A license is necessary for soliciting buyers, negotiating sales, and negotiating sales contracts or leases. **Page 233**

3. **(c)** Unless someone is involved in the direct sale or purchase of property for himself, a real estate license is a prerequisite for performing real estate work. **Page 234**

4. **(a)** CalBRE issues real estate broker and salesperson licenses for a four-year period. Occasionally, CalBRE issues restricted licenses. **Page 235**

5. **(d)** Licenses may be suspended, revoked, or otherwise restricted. Violators may be subject to civil injunctions, criminal penalties, or fines as the result of being found guilty of unethical conduct. **Page 246**

6. **(c)** The complaint is investigated by the Enforcement and Audit Sections of CalBRE. **Page 246**

7. **(b)** An Administrative Law Judge will preside over the hearing and make recommendations to the Commissioner for discipline after the hearing. **Page 247**

8. **(d)** Robert put the money into a trust fund and has not commingled his clients funds. **Page 249**

9. **(b)** A secret profit is the taking of a secret or undisclosed amount of compensation. **Page 250**

10. **(b)** A broker is subject to disciplinary action if the broker, or the officer designated by a corporate broker licensee, fails to exercise reasonable supervision over the activities of the broker's salespersons. Section 10177(h). **Page 253**

Unit 9: Agency Law

Answers - Matching

1. A	5. T	9. E	13. O	17. J
2. G	6. H	10. R	14. F	18. K
3. B	7. S	11. Q	15. L	19. P
4. N	8. D	12. M	16. C	20. I

Answers - Multiple Choice

1. **(a)** Statutory law agency is drawn from the statutes and rules created by various legislative and governing bodies. **Page 266**

2. **(d)** The people involved in an agency relationship are the agent, principal (client), and third party (customer). **Page 267**

3. **(d)** If the agency relationship is described in a written agreement, it is called actual authority. An implied agency is created through words, actions, and inference rather than a written agreement. **Page 268**

4. **(b)** Real estate brokers are involved in broker/client and broker/associate agency relationships. **Page 272**

5. **(d)** Both sales and broker associates may put their licenses with an employing licensed broker. **Page 272**

6. **(d)**   Agency relationships are created by agreement, ratification, or estoppel. **Page 274**

7. **(d)**   The typical ways to create a written agreement are by a power of attorney, listing agreements, and buyer representation agreements. **Page 274**

8. **(c)**   The duties that agents owe clients are obedience, loyalty, disclosure, confidentiality, accounting, and reasonable care. **Page 277**

9. **(c)**   Innocent misrepresentation refers to statements not known to be untrue at the time they are made and usually they carry no legal liability for an agent. **Page 284**

10. **(d)**   The client may unilaterally revoke a listing or buyer representation agreement to terminate an agency relationship. A property that is sold or closed terminates the agency relationship with the owner (or the buyer). In addition, incapacity or death of either the client or the broker terminates an agency relationship. **Page 290**

Unit 10: Fair Housing Laws

Answers - Matching

1.	B	5.	D	9.	G	13.	E	17.	F
2.	S	6.	J	10.	H	14.	A	18.	K
3.	Q	7.	C	11.	O	15.	M	19.	T
4.	I	8.	L	12.	R	16.	N	20.	P

Answers - Multiple Choice

1. **(a)**   The U.S. Supreme Court struck down racially restrictive covenants in *Jones v. Mayer*. The Unruh Act [C.C. §53] outlaws restrictive racial covenants and prohibits any attempt to bar the transfer of real property based on race and other characteristics listed elsewhere in the statute. **Page 300**

2. **(b)**   *Jones v. Mayer* prohibits discrimination based on race by upholding the 1866 Civil Rights Act and the 13th Amendment to the U.S. Constitution. **Page 301**

3. **(c)**   Title VIII of the Civil Rights Act of 1968 provided anti-discriminatory protection in education, housing, and employment for five protected classes of people based on their race, color, religion, sex, or national origin. **Page 302**

4. **(d)**   The federal Fair Housing Act does not apply to the sale of commercial or industrial property. **Page 304**

5. **(b)**   The 1866 law is both broader and narrower than the Fair Housing Act. The 1866 Act applies to race discrimination in the sale or lease of ALL real property. Thus, if someone refuses to sell commercial property because of the buyer's race, the 1866 law would allow the buyer to bring a lawsuit even though the Fair Housing Act would not. **Page 299**

6. **(b)**   Religious organizations are exempt under the federal Fair Housing Act. **Page 304**

7. **(d)**   The use of certain terminology in an advertisement is often a red flag. Describing a neighborhood as "integrated" (changing from one racial group to another) can be a violation of the Fair Housing Act. **Page 308**

8. **(a)** The FEHA prohibits discrimination in housing because of the source of a person's income. A property owner can consider the amount of a prospective tenant's income, but not its source. **Page 319**

9. **(d)** The California Supreme Court makes it clear that even sincerely-held religious beliefs do not excuse a person who offers rental property to the public from complying with California law, including the Fair Employment and Housing Act. A person who does not want to allow unmarried couples to rent property must either accept that the law requires this, or sell the property and invest the proceeds outside the real property rental market. **Page 319**

10. **(d)** All three of the major fair housing laws have exemptions for "seniors only" housing, including those that prohibit residency to those under the age of 62 if the development is constructed according to the terms of the law. **Page 320**

Unit 11: Consumer Protection Laws

Answers - Matching

1. N		6. X		11. F		16. G		21. A
2. L		7. U		12. C		17. W		22. S
3. O		8. B		13. V		18. R		23. K
4. J		9. H		14. E		19. D		24. P
5. M		10. Y		15. Q		20. I		25. T

Answers - Multiple Choice

1. **(b)** Group boycotting is the deliberate exclusion of a particular business or group from the benefits of competition and inclusion. **Page 331**

2. **(a)** Only public attorneys, such as the district attorney, Attorney General, or a citizen who alleges that he or she lost money or property or was injured as a result of the unfair business practice can bring a lawsuit under that law. **Page 335**

3. **(b)** Do Not Call rules apply to calls containing a commercial solicitation but not to calls made if an established business relationship already exists. **Page 336**

4. **(c)** Emails sent as part of an ongoing transaction, called transactional email messages, are excluded from the Act. **Page 339**

5. **(a)** The Equal Credit Opportunity Act (ECOA) requires banks and other creditors to extend credit equally to all creditworthy applicants with fairness, impartiality, and without discrimination on any prohibited basis. **Page 341**

6. **(c)** The Fair Credit Reporting Act promotes the accuracy, fairness, and privacy of the information collected and maintained by credit reporting agencies. **Page 344**

7. **(b)** The Fair and Accurate Credit Transactions Act allows consumers to obtain a free credit report once every 12 months from each of the three nationwide consumer-credit reporting companies—Equifax®, Experian®, and TransUnion®. **Page 345**

8. **(d)**   These are required disclosures under the Truth in Lending Act. **Page 348**

9. **(b)**   The Housing Financial Discrimination Act of 1977 (Holden Act) bans the consideration of the race or other defined characteristics of a borrower in making the decision on a real estate loan. The other choices are federal acts. **Page 354**

10. **(b)**   RESPA protects consumers by eliminating kickbacks and referral fees that unnecessarily increase the costs of settlement services. **Page 355**

Unit 12: Contract Law

Answers - Matching

1. H	5. N	9. I	13. Q	17. O
2. S	6. P	10. M	14. F	18. C
3. B	7. K	11. G	15. E	19. R
4. D	8. A	12. T	16. L	20. J

Answers - Multiple Choice

1. **(b)**   An example of an executory contract is a contract that has not yet closed or a contract that has not been signed by both parties. **Page 368**

2. **(b)**   "All persons are capable of contracting, except minors, persons of unsound mind, and persons deprived of civil rights." [C.C. §1556]. An emancipated minor is a person under 18 who is or has been married, is on active duty with the armed forces, or has been declared emancipated by the court. [Family Code §7050]. **Page 369**

3. **(b)**   An offer is terminated by lapse of time, death or incapacity of either party, destruction of the subject matter, revocation by the offeror, rejection by the offeree, and counteroffer by the offeree. **Page 373**

4. **(b)**   Destruction of the subject matter (by fire) terminated the offer. **Page 374**

5. **(c)**   Certain promises, although they may appear to be satisfactory to support a contract, are in fact only illusory promises because the promisor is agreeing to do something that is not, in fact, valid consideration. **Page 378**

6. **(d)**   Undue influence commonly involves a person who, although of sound mind, has become dependent on a caregiver and is pressured by that person to enter into agreements for the benefit of the caregiver. A court will carefully examine the consent given by a person who later claims undue influence. **Page 381**

7. **(c)**   Assuming that all elements of a real estate contract have been met and its terms are set forth in writing and signed by the parties to the agreement, the contract is valid. In *Seck* v. *Foulks* the contract between Seck and Foulks was valid even though it had been written on the back of a business card. **Page 384**

8. **(d)**   A broker who has procured a ready, willing, and able buyer according to the terms of the agreement would have satisfied the condition to find such a buyer, even if the seller ultimately decides not to go through with the sale. **Page 388**

9. **(d)** An unconditional release is a complete release and no further obligations are owed by either party. **Page 394**

10. **(c)** Once the statute of limitations has expired, any lawsuit that could have been brought to enforce one's contractual rights is terminated just as completely as if they had not existed in the first place. **Page 400**

Unit 13: Real Estate Contracts

Answers - Matching

1. O	4. D	7. L	10. I	13. M
2. B	5. F	8. N	11. G	14. J
3. C	6. H	9. E	12. A	15. K

Answers - Multiple Choice

1. **(d)** The broker is required to give a copy of an exclusive agency or exclusive right to sell listing agreement to the client at the time it is signed. The agreement is still enforceable, but the broker can be disciplined for not doing so. **Page 410**

2. **(d)** Brokers must keep copies of all listings, deposit receipts, canceled checks, trust records, and other documents executed by them or obtained by them in connection with any transaction for which a license is required to maintain for at least three years. [B&P §10148]. **Page 410**

3. **(c)** This is the no deal, no commission clause, which means the seller is not obligated to pay a commission unless a sale of the property is actually consummated. **Page 413**

4. **(d)** A safety clause entitles a broker to a commission even after the listing has ended if the seller consummates a sale within a stated period of time and the ultimate buyer is someone with whom the broker negotiated. **Page 414**

5. **(c)** The amount or rate of real estate commissions is not fixed by law. Exclusive listing must specify a definite termination date. [B&P §10176(f), §10147.5] **Page 414**

6. **(b)** Under an exclusive agency listing, the broker is entitled to a commission upon the procurement of a buyer meeting the requirements of that listing agreement, unless the owner finds a buyer on his or her own. **Page 416**

7. **(d)** All of the choices are multi-functions of the deposit receipt. **Page 420**

8. **(c)** If the seller ignores the offer, it will terminate due to lapse of time. **Page 420**

9. **(b)** Until an offer is accepted by the seller, the earnest money deposit belongs to the buyer, so the broker must return the money to the buyer. **Page 420**

10. **(c)** An option is a contract and must be supported by consideration. A gratuitous statement that an offer is irrevocable and is not supported by consideration does not give one party an enforceable option. **Page 422**

Unit 14: Disclosures in Real Estate Transactions

Answers - Matching

1.	S	5.	R	9.	E	13.	G	17.	P
2.	L	6.	O	10.	B	14.	H	18.	M
3.	A	7.	F	11.	Q	15.	I	19.	D
4.	C	8.	J	12.	K	16.	N	20.	T

Answers - Multiple Choice

1. **(d)** Failure to disclose can be financially devastating and can lead to lawsuits or a loss of license in some instances. **Page 429**

2. **(b)** A real estate licensee must disclose material facts. If the licensee conspires with the owner to conceal a material defect, then the licensee is liable to a prospective buyer. Rather than violate the law, a licensee must withdraw from employment. **Page 435**

3. **(b)** Civil Code §1710.2 states that the owner or the owner's agent do not have to disclose the occurrence of a death provided it occurred more than 3 years prior to the buyer's/lessor's offer to purchase or lease the property. **Page 436**

4. **(c)** A transfer from one co-owner to another co-owner is exempt, but not one to a third party buyer. **Page 438**

5. **(b)** A real estate licensee must disclose material facts, such as a shared driveway, damage to the foundation, or the existence of a homeowner's association. A notice of abatement against the adjacent property need not be disclosed. **Page 440**

6. **(c)** The natural hazards disclosure (NHD) requires disclose of six specific natural hazards that fall into three distinct areas: flooding, fire, and seismic risks. Tornados are not covered on the NHD. **Page 445**

7. **(b)** A transferor must disclose actual knowledge of mold on the property in paragraph II.C.1 of the Transfer Disclosure Statement. **Page 454**

8. **(c)** A seller must provide written disclose of former federal or state ordnance locations that are located within 1 mile of such a hazard. **Page 454**

9. **(c)** Pest control and certification is not required by statute, but may be imposed as a condition of financing. **Page 459**

10. **(b)** R-value signifies resistance to heat loss. **Page 461**

Unit 15: Residential Landlord-Tenant Law

Answers – Matching

1.	I	4.	E	7.	B	10.	J
2.	F	5.	C	8.	H	11.	K
3.	D	6.	G	9.	A	12.	L

Answers - Multiple Choice

1. **(b)** As long as the lessee pays the rent and complies with other lease provisions, the lessor cannot evict the lessee, raise the rent, or change other terms of the tenancy during the lease. **Page 471**

2. **(c)** The Costa-Hawkins Rental Housing Act now has pre-empted vacancy control provisions of local rent control ordinances. Costa-Hawkins allows landlords to establish the initial rent for a unit or dwelling even if it is rent-controlled. So long as the same tenant stays in the unit, of course, the unit is subject to the rent control provisions for any increases in rent, but it will revert to market rate once the unit becomes vacant. **Page 474**

3. **(b)** After a reasonable time, if the landlord ignores the request or refuses to make the repair, the tenant may use one of the following remedies: repair and deduct, abandon the rental unit, or withhold rent. [C.C. §1942]. Before attempting to use any of these remedies, a tenant should obtain legal advice to determine the appropriateness of the remedy. **Page 477**

4. **(c)** The lessor has a limited right to enter the rented premises to make necessary or agreed repairs or improvements. This requires 24-hours' written notice if the notice is personally served on the tenant, left with someone of suitable age, or posted on the property. **Page 479**

5. **(c)** A lessee who assigns all of his or her rights under a lease is known as an assignor and the person who takes over the property is the assignee. The original lessee's relationship with the property ends, and the assignee in effect "stands in the shoes" of the original lessee/assignor. **Page 480**

6. **(c)** A tenant's default may be economic—failure to pay rent or assessments when due—or non-economic—improper use of the property, excessive number of people living in the unit, failure to follow the rules and regulations, or failure to adhere to the hours of operation. **Page 481**

7. **(a)** At the expiration of the lease, if the tenant fails to vacate the rental unit, the owner can either commence eviction proceedings immediately or accept rent in what will thereafter be a month-to-month tenancy. **Page 482**

8. **(d)** The landlord must give a 60-day advance written notice if tenant has lived in the rental unit for a year or more. **Page 483**

9. **(b)** If the tenant is in default of any provision of the agreement, especially failure to pay rent, the owner can give a special 3-day notice to quit. If the tenant has failed to pay rent, the notice is called a 3-day notice to pay rent or quit. **Page 485**

10. **(a)** The MRL provides that a person who owns a mobilehome that is in a park cannot be charged a fee for anything other than rent, utilities, and incidental charges for services that are actually rendered to the owner of the unit. In addition, any such incidental charges must be listed in the rental agreement. Thus, even if services (e.g., watering of landscaping or trash removal) are actually rendered, the park cannot charge the resident for them if they are not listed in the rental agreement. **Page 492**

APPENDIX B:
INDEX OF COURT CASES

GLOSSARY

abandonment. The act of voluntarily surrendering or relinquishing possession of real property, without transferring title to someone else. Non-use of the property does not prove abandonment.

abandonment of homestead. A legal document that proves a homestead was abandoned. An owner must file an abandonment of homestead on the old property, in order to obtain a homestead on a new property.

abatement of nuisance. Legal process used to remove nuisances and code violations.

abrogation. The revocation, rescission, or annulling of a contract by mutual consent of the parties to the contract, or for cause by either party to the contract.

abstract of judgment. A document summarizing a court decision and is used to execute a judgment lien. It must be filed in all counties where the judgment debtor owns real estate.

acceptance. Unqualified agreement to the terms of an offer.

accession. The acquisition of title to additional land or to improvements, as a result of annexing fixtures or as a result of natural causes, such as alluvial deposits along the banks of streams by accretion.

accord and satisfaction. The discharge of an existing obligation by acceptance of a substitute agreement (accord) in which the creditor accepts less than the full amount owed as satisfaction of the debt.

accretion. A buildup of soil by natural causes on property bordering a river, lake, or ocean.

acknowledgment. A signed statement by a named person, made before a notary public, confirming that a document was signed voluntarily.

Act of God. An act attributable to nature without human interference. Such acts include tidal wave, flood, hurricane, volcanic eruption, earthquake, and fire. The occurrence of an act of God may temporarily or permanently relieve parties from the responsibilities of their agreement.

action. A lawsuit brought to court.

actual damages. Damages a court of law recognizes, as the result of a wrong.

actual fraud. An act intended to deceive another, e.g., making a false statement, making a promise without intending to perform it, suppressing the truth.

actual notice. Knowledge based on things actually seen, heard, read, or observed

addendum. An addition or change to a contract; a supplement. All addendums to an agreement should be dated and signed or initialed by all parties involved.

adjoining landowners. Pesons owning lands that share common boundaries and therefore have mutual rights, duties, and liabilities.

administrative law judge. Person who makes recommendations to the Commissioner concerning discipline, after a formal hearing.

adverse possession. A method of acquiring title to property by continued possession and payment of taxes, rather than by purchase or conveyance. Similar to prescription; however, prescription results in only a limited interest in the property and does not require the payment of taxes.

affidavit. A written statement or declaration made under oath before a licensed individual, such as a notary public.

affirm. To conform, to aver, to ratify, to verify.

affirmative easement. One that requires the owner of the servient estate to do something to benefit the dominant estate.

agency relationship. A legal and/or special relationship of trust by which one person (agent) is authorized to conduct business, sign papers, or otherwise act on behalf of another person (principal) when dealing with third parties. This relationship may be created by express agreement, ratification, or estoppel.

agent. A person who has the authority to act for and in the place of another, called a principal, for the purpose of affecting the principal's legal relationship with third persons.

agreed boundary line. Adjoining owners of property with an uncertain boundary set a new boundary line.

air rights. The rights in real property to the reasonable use of the air space above the surface of the land.

alienate. To voluntarilily or involuntarily transfer, convey, or sell property to another.

annual percentage rate (APR). The relationship of the total finance charge to the total amount to be financed, as required under the Truth in Lending Act.

answer. In law, a written pleading filed by a defendant to respond to a complaint in a lawsuit filed and served upon that defendant.

antitrust laws. The laws created to protect and preserve business competition.

appeal. The act of requesting a higher court of law to reconsider a decision made by a lower court, especially in order to reduce or prevent a punishment. Also, the request itself.

appropriative water rights. The right to take riparian surface water for a beneficial use on non-adjacent property.

appurtenance. All rights, privileges, and improvements that belong to and pass with the transfer of the property, but that are not necessarily a part of the actual property.

appurtenant easement. Easement that "runs with the land".

arbitration. A method of dispute resolution in which the claims are submitted to an objective third party (arbitrator), who renders a decistion.

"as is". Words in a contract signifying the property is being sold in its current state, and stating that the seller will not be responsible for the cost of repairing any defect. The seller must still disclose all known defects of the property to the buyer.

assignment. The transfer of an entire leasehold estate or a property's right, title, and interest to a new person.

avulsion. The sudden washing or tearing away of land by the action of water.

benchmark. A survey reference mark made on a monument indicating a known location and elevation, used in a metes and bounds survey.

bilateral contract. An agreement or contract in which each person or party promises to perform an act in exchange for another person's promise to perform.

blackletter law. Well-established legal principles. The term derives from the practice of printing law books in a bold, black Gothic type.

blockbusting. The illegal practice of causing panic selling by telling people property values in a neighborhood will decline because of a specific event, such as the purchase of homes by minorities.

bona fide. A Latin term meaning, in good faith. Actions that are done in good faith and honestly.

bona fide purchaser. Bona fide means good faith, so a bona fide purchaser is one who pays fair value for property in good faith, and without notice of adverse claims.

bona fide sale. The sale of property in a competitive market, at the current market price, where good faith between the buyer and seller is present in the transaction.

boundary line. Artificial or natural perimeter of a parcel of land, separating it from adjacent parcels of land.

boycotting. The deliberate exclusion of a particular business or group from the benefits of competition and inclusion.

breach of contract. Failure by one party to comply with all of the terms and conditions of contract.

bundle of rights. An ownership concept describing all the legal rights attached to the ownership of real property. The bundle of rights includes the right to use, possess, transfer, encumber, and enjoy property.

buyer representation agreement. Employment contract between a buyer and a broker.

caveat emptor. In Latin, means, "let the buyer beware." A buyer purchases property at his or her own risk and is responsible for determining its quality.

CC&Rs (covenants, conditions, and restrictions). Restrictions placed on certain types of real property, limiting the activities of owners. Covenants and conditions are promises to do, or not to do certain things. The consequence for breaking those promises may either be money damages, in the case of covenants, or the return of the property to the grantor, in the case of conditions.

civil law. Body of law imposed by the state or government for its citizens.

cloud on title. Any condition affecting the clear title of real property or minor defect in the chain of title which needs to be removed.

codicil. A change in a will before the maker's death.

codify. Compile, arrange, systemize, and write the laws of a given region into a code.

cold calling. The practice of making unsolicited calls to people you do not know in order to get new business.

collateral. Something of value given as security for a debt.

collusion. An agreement between two or more people to do something unlawful.

color of title. The false appearance of clear title, free of any clouds. The title actually has a certain defect, such as a forged deed, and as a result is invalid.

commercial e-mail message. Any electronic mail message whose primary purpose is the commercial advertisement or promotion of a commercial product or service.

commingling. The illegal practice of depositing client's funds in a broker's personal or general business account.

commission. A fee for services rendered, usually based on a certain percentage of the sales price of a property. The amount is agreed upon before the transaction takes place.

common interest development. A development of residential or commercial property that combines the individual ownership of dwellings or buildings with a shared undivided ownership of common areas and elements of the entire project. A homeowners' association usually governs the common areas.

common law. Body of law based on custom and judicial precedent rather than on codified statutes.

community property. Form of concurrent property ownership that exists only between spouses.

compensatory damages. Damages designed to compensate the injured party for the injury that was sustained.

complaint. The first document (pleading) that starts a civil action summarizing the plaintiff's case against the defendant including a demand for relief.

concurrent ownership. Ownership of a piece of property by two or more persons at the same time. Examples of concurrent ownership include joint tenants, tenants by entirety, tenants in common, and community property owners. Also known as co-ownership.

condition precedent. A condition which requires something to occur before a transaction becomes absolute and enforceable; for example, a sale contingent on the buyer obtaining financing.

condition subsequent. A condition which, if it occurs at some point in the future, can cause a property to revert to the grantor. For example, a condition subsequent in a grant deed may require the buyer to use the property only as a private residence. If they later use it for a business, it reverts to the original owner.

conditional use. A use that does not meet the current use requirements, but may be allowed by obtaining a special permit.

conditional use permit. Allows a land use that may be incompatible with other uses existing in the zone.

conditions, covenants, and restrictions. *See* CC&Rs.

condominium. A type of common interest development. An undivided interest in common in a portion of real property coupled with a separate interest in space called a unit.

consideration. Something of value—such as money, a promise, property or personal services; one of the essentials of a valid contract

constructive eviction. Conduct by a landlord that impairs tenant's possession of the premises, making occupancy impossible.

constructive notice. Knowledge, which the law presumes a person has, as in the case of documents which have been recorded as a matter of public record.

contingency. A provision in a contract requiring the completion of a certain act or the occurrence of a particular event, before the contract is binding.

contra proferentem. Ambiguous terms in a contract should be interpreted against the party drafting the document.

conversion. The appropriation of property or funds belonging to another; as in a broker using a client's money.

conveyance. The transfer of title to land by use of a written instrument from one person to another.

corporation. A legal entity or organization whose rights in business are similar to that of an individual. It exists indefinitely and has centralized management in a board of directors.

correlative water right. A law exercised in some states restricting riparian owners who share a common water source to taking a reasonable amount of the total water supply.

counteroffer. The rejection of an original purchase offer and the submission of a new and different offer.

criminal law. Wrongs against persons or society.

damages. Compensation a plaintiff may be paid as a result of injuries to himself or his property, through an act or default of another.

decedent. A person who has died.

declaration of homestead. The recorded notice to protect the equity in a home from forced sale by unsecured creditors.

dedication. The giving of land by its owner to a public use, and the acceptance for such use by authorized officials on behalf of the public.

deed. A written document used to convey an ownership interst in real property.

deed restrictions. Limitations in the deed to a property dictating certain uses that may or may not be made of the property.

default. (1) Failure to pay a contractual debt. (2) Failure to appear in court.

default judgment. A judgment entered in favor of the plaintiff when the defendant defaults, or fails to appear in court.

defeasible. Capable of being defeated. A defeasible estate having a condition attached to the title, which if broken causes the termination of the estate.

defendant. Person who sued in a civil proceeding or accused in a criminal proceeding.

deficiency judgment. A judgment against a borrower for the unpaid balance of a debt owed when the security or the loan is not sufficient enough to pay the debt.

definite and certain. Precise acts to be performed are to be clearly stated.

delivery. The unconditional, irrevocable intent of a grantor immediately to divest (give up) an interest in real estate by a deed or other instrument.

demand. The desire to buy or obtain a commodity.

demurrer. A written response to a complaint, which pleads for dismissal on the point that even if the facts alleged in the complaint were true, there is no legal basis for a lawsuit.

deposition. Live, oral testimony under oath that is reduced to writing.

disclaimer. A statement denying legal responsibility for the product sold. It is also a denial or renunciation of one's legal right to property.

disclosure statement. A required statement listing all the information relevant to a piece of property, such as the presence of radon or lead paint.

division fence. Fence lying exactly on the boundary line separating two properties.

doctrine of correlative user. A law exercised in some states, restricting riparian owners who share a common water source to taking a reasonable amount of the total water supply.

document. Legal instrument, such as mortgages, contracts, deeds, options, wills, bills of sale, etc.

dominant tenement. The property that benefits from an easement.

dual agency. An agency relationship in which a real estate broker represents both buyer and seller in a transaction. Some states require written consent before a broker may act as dual agent, and some states prohibit dual agency.

duress. The use of force to get agreement in accepting a contract.

easement. A non-possessory right to enter or use someone else's land for a specified purpose.

easement appurtenant. An easement connected to a particular property that transfers with the property when conveyed.

easement by prescription. Easement created by open, adverse, continuous, and uninterrupted use by a single party, for a number of years, as specified by law.

easement in gross. An easement that benefits a person, not a particular piece of land.

egress. The right to exit from a property using an easement.

emancipated minor. Someone who is under age, yet legally set free from parental control/supervision. Emancipation may be achieved by marriage or by court order.

emblements. Growing crops that are cultivated annually for sale; considered personal property.

eminent domain. The right of a local, state or federal government to acquire private property for public use after paying the owner fair market compensation for the acquired property.

encroachment. The unauthorized placement of permanent improvements that intrude on adjacent property owned by another.

encumbrance. An encumbrance is the legal term for a charge, claim, liability, or anything that affects or limits the title of a property or lessens its value. Encumbrances fall into two categories, those that affect the title, known as financial encumbrances, and those that affect the use of the property, known as non-financial encumbrances.

environmental impact report (EIR). Detailed report required by California Environmental Quality Act regarding projects potentially having significant environmental impacts.

environmental impact statement (EIS). Detailed evaluation required by National Environmental Policy Act regarding the environmental impact of a proposed development.

equitable title. The right to obtain absolute ownership to property when legal title is held in another's name.

erosion. The gradual wearing away of land by natural processes.

escheat. A legal process where property reverts to the state, because the deceased left no will (intestate) and has no legal heirs. The state must wait a number of years, as specified by state law, before trying to claim the property.

estate. The ownership right or legal interest in property, and the degree, quantity, nature, and extent to which a person has that right or interest.

estoppel. A legal doctrine which prevents a person from denying something to be true or a fact, if the denial is contrary to previous statements or actions made by that same person.

eviction. The legal process of removing a tenant from the premises for some breach or violation of the lease.

eviction notice. Written notice from the landlord to the tenant requesting that he or she move out of the property within the time specified by local or state law, or meet the landlord's requirements.

execute. To perform, complete, or sign.

executed contract. A contract in which the obligations have been performed on both sides of the contract, and nothing is left to be completed.

execution sale. The forced sale of a property to satisfy a money judgment.

executor/executrix. A person named in a will to handle the affairs of a deceased person.

executory contract. A contract in which obligation to perform exists on one or both sides.

express agreement. A written agreement, usually in the form of a listing contract, authorizing the broker to represent the seller in finding a ready, willing, and able buyer. A contract created when the parties declare the terms and put their intentions in words, either oral or written.

false promise. A false statement of fact.

fee simple. The most complete form of ownership of real property, which one can sell, pass to another by will or inheritance, do any other thing with real property allowed by law. Also known as fee simple absolute or an estate of inheritance.

fee simple defeasible. A fee simple estate that can be lost by violation of a condition or use restriction placed in the transfer by the grantor.

fee simple subject to condition subsequent. Any fee estate containing a condition that if violated, could lead to the termination of the estate and give the grantor a right of entry.

fiduciary. A person who holds assets in trust for a beneficiary, or who stands in a position of trust, confidence, and/or responsibility for another.

fiduciary relationship. A relationship that implies a position of trust or confidence.

final map. Map of a subdivision recorded in the county where the property is located.

fixture. Anything permanently attached to real property.

foreclosure. A legal procedure by which mortgaged property is sold to satisfy the debt.

forfeiture. Relinquishing rights to something, due to nonperformance of an obligation or condition. A delinquent borrower may lose the rights to property due to forfeiture.

forgery. The illegal falsification of a signature or document, making an entire contract void.

fraud. An act meant to deceive in order to get someone to part with something of value.

freehold estate. An estate or ownership rights in real property, continuing for an indefinite period of time.

fructus industrials. Annual crops produced by human labor, such as fruits, nuts, vegetables, and grains.

fructus naturales. Naturally occurring plant growth, such as grasses, trees, and shrubs as part of the real property.

future interest. An interest in real property that will take effect at a future time.

general lien. A lien affecting all the property owned by a debtor, rather than a specific property.

general partnership. Business entity established by two or more individuals or businesses, which join to operate a business for profit.

general plan. A comprehensive, master plan adopted by cities and counties that is used as a guide for long-term physical development. A general plan is implemented by decisions that direct the allocation of public resources and shape private development.

gift deed. Deed whose consideration is love and affection.

good faith. A bona fide act or an act done honestly, whether it is actually negligent or not. Recording laws protect good faith purchasers. Acts committed in bad faith are often punishable as a crime.

grant deed. A type of deed in which the grantor warrants that he or she has not previously conveyed the property being granted, has not encumbered the property, except as disclosed, and will convey to the grantee any title to the property acquired later.

granting clause. Words of purchase, such as grants, conveys, transfers, or sells contained in a deed or other instrument conveying the property.

groundwater. Water beneath the surface of the land filling the spaces and cavities between the rocks and soil.

habendum clause. The habendum clause begins with the words. to have and to hold, and defines or limits the ownership interest of the grantee.

heir. One who inherits property at the death of the owner or if the owner has died without a will.

holdover tenant. A tenant who retains possession of leased property after the lease has expired. The landlord agrees to the occupation by continuing to accept rent.

holographic will. A will, written in the maker's own handwriting, dated, and signed by the maker. The will is not witnessed and is not recorded.

homestead property. Home, occupied by a family, exempt from the claims of unsecured creditors.

implied warranty of habitability. The property will be maintained to meet basic living requirements.

in perpetuity. Of endless duration; forever.

incompetent. A person who is legally unfit to enter into a contract.

ingress. The right to enter onto a property.

injunction. A court order forcing a person to do or not do an act.

innocent misrepresentation. When a person unknowingly provides wrong information.

instrument. A formal legal document, such as a contract, deed, or will, setting forth the rights and liabilities of the parties involved.

interest. (1) The charge for the use of money. (2) Various rights, privileges, powers, and immunities with respect to real property.

interpleader action. A court proceeding initiated by the stakeholder of property, who claims no proprietary interest in it, for the purpose of deciding who among claimants is legally entitled to the property.

inter vivos trust. Trust in which the trustor is still alive when the trust is established.

intestate. Term describing a person who dies without leaving a valid will.

intestate succession. When a person inherits property, as the result of someone dying without a will.

inverse condemnation. When a private party forces the government to pay just compensation, if the property value or use has been diminished by a public entity.

involuntary alienation. Transfer of property against the wishes of the owner.

issue. Descendants of the testator.

joint and several liability. A legal term used in reference to a debt or a judgment for negligence, in which each debtor or each judgment defendant is responsible for the entire amount of the debt or judgment.

joint tenancy. Form of concurrent ownership providing for undivided ownership interests and automatic survivorship to remaining cotenants upon death of one of the joint tenants.

judgment. The final legal decision by a judge in a court of law, regarding the legal rights of parties to disputes in a civil case.

judgment creditor. Party to a lawsuit who obtains a money judgment against the other party.

judicial foreclosure. Foreclosure by court action.

just compensation. Fair and reasonable payment due to a private property owner, when his or her property is condemned under eminent domain.

kickback. An illegal payment made in return for a referral that resulted in a transaction.

laches. A legal doctrine stating that those who take too long to assert a legal right lose their entitlement to compensation.

land. A three-dimensional area of a parcel of the earth's surface, limited quantities of airspace above the surface, and the materials and minerals beneath the surface (subsurface).

landlord. Property owner. Under a lease, the property owner is termed a lessor.

latent defect. Defects in a home that may be hidden from a buyer, but known by a seller.

lateral support. Landowners' right to have their land in its natural condition held in place from the sides by adjoining land so that it will not fall away.

law. Body of rules and principles that every member of society must follow.

lease. A contract between an owner (lessor) and a renter (lessee), which gives the lessee temporary possession and use of the property.

leasehold. The lessee's interest in the leased property during the term of the lease.

legal description. A formal description of real property recognized by law, by which property can be definitely located by reference to metes and bounds, the Public Lands Survey method, or recorded maps.

legal notice. The legally required notification of others, as a result of property possession or document recordation.

legally non-conforming use. A property whose use was legal, according to the zoning requirements at the time of construction; however, the zoning has since changed, technically making the current property use illegal. When the use is still allowed, although does not conform to current zoning law, it is identified as a non-conforming use of property.

less-than-freehold estate. *See* non-freehold estate.

license. Permissive use of land, which may be revoked at any time by the grantor.

lien. A legal right, interest, or claim in the property of another for the payment of a debt.

life estate. An estate, limited in duration to the life of its owner or the life of a designated person.

life tenant. A person whose interest in real property lasts as long as they (or some other person) lives.

light and air easement. Negative easement created by grant preventing servient landowner from building a structure or planting trees that would prevent sunlight or air from reaching the dominant estate.

limited liability company (LLC). A business that has characteristics of both corporations and limited partnerships. The LLC offers its owners the advantage of limited personal liability (like a corporation) and a choice of how their business is taxed.

limited partnership. A partnership comprising a general partner and limited partners. The general partner operates the partnership and is fully liable for the debts of the firm. The limited partners' liability is limited to their original investment.

line trees. Trees or hedges whose trunks grow on the boundary line.

liquidated damages. An amount specified in advance of entering into an agreement, that must be paid as a penalty in the event of a breach of the contract.

lis pendens. A recorded notice that indicates pending litigation on a property, preventing a conveyance or any other transfer of ownership, until the lawsuit is settled and the lis pendens removed.

listing agreement. A written contract by which a seller (principal) employs and authorizes a broker (agent) to find a buyer (customer).

litigation. Process of bringing a lawsuit against someone.

littoral. Land bordering a lake, ocean, or sea.

lot, block, and tract system. A process developers use to divide parcels of land into lots. Each lot in a subdivision is identified by number, as is the block in which it is located. Each lot and block is in a referenced tract. Also known as lot and block system, subdivision system, or recorded map system.

marital property. A general term for property owned by a married couple.

material fact. Any fact likely to affect the judgment of the principal, when giving consent to the agent to enter into a particular transaction on the specified terms.

mechanic's lien. A lien placed against a property by anyone who supplies labor, services, or materials used for improvements on real property and did not receive payment for the improvements.

mediation. Process in which a neutral, uninterested third party helps the parties involved in a dispute to negotiate a settlement or other resolution.

menace. Using the threat of violence to get agreement in accepting a contract.

metes and bounds. A metes and bounds land description measures the dimensions of a property using direction and distance between landmarks and monuments. Metes mean measurements in length (measured in feet) from one monument to another. Bounds refer to the direction. The direction of the boundary lines are given in degrees, minutes, and seconds.

mineral rights. The right to search for, develop, and remove minerals from land.

minor. A person under 18 years of age and thus, not of legal capacity to enter into any legal contract.

mirror offer. An offer that matches all terms in the listing.

misrepresentation. Making a false statement or concealing a material fact, causing someone loss or harm.

mistake. (1) An error or misunderstanding. (2) The parties to an agreement have a misunderstanding about a fact that is material to the transaction.

monopoly. Person or group with exclusive control over a product or service within a given region.

month-to-month tenancy. A periodic tenancy in which the tenant pays rent for one period at a time. The tenancy continues until either the landlord or tenant gives notice of termination.

monument. A fixed landmark used in a metes and bounds land description.

mutual consent. An agreement between the parties in a contract, such as offer and acceptance. Also known as meeting of the minds.

mutual rescission. All parties to a contract agree to cancel the agreement and put themselves back where they started.

National Environmental Policy Act. A law passed by Congress in 1970 requiring a detailed environmental impact statement prior to any federal action that would affect the environment.

negative declaration. A finding by state or local agency that a proposed project will not have the potential to cause significant impacts to the environment.

negative easement. An easement preventing a servient landowner from using or improving the land in a certain way, because of the effect it would have on the dominant estate.

negligent misrepresentations. Untrue statements made without facts to back them up.

non-freehold estate. An estate in real property for the temporary and limited right of use in the real property, such as a tenancy for years, from period to period, at will, or at sufferance. It is an estate with a fixed or determinable duration. Also known as a leasehold estate.

non-judicial foreclosure. The power to foreclose on a property without court approval.

notice. An announcement of an event or fact. Notice may be written or oral. Most contracts contain a clause telling the parties how to give notice.

notice of default. A notice to a defaulting party that there has been a nonpayment of a debt.

notice to pay rent or quit. A written eviction notice from the landlord informing the tenant to meet the landlord's requirements or move out of the property within a specific number of days.

novation. The substitution of a new obligation for an old one; substitution of new parties to an existing obligation, as where the parties to an agreement accept a new debtor in place of an old one.

nuisance. An activity remaining outside the property or a land use that is incompatible or that interferes with surrounding land uses.

null and void. Of no legal validity or effect.

offer. A presentation or proposal to obtain acceptance and form a contract.

option. A contract to keep open, for a set period of time, an offer to purchase or lease real property. The option holder is not obligated to exercise the right.

oral contract. A contract made verbally without a writing.

ordinance. A law adopted by a local governing body. Typically, local governments issue ordinances establishing land usage and parking rules.

parcel map. Map showing a parcel of land that will be subdivided into less than five parcels or units, and shows land boundaries, streets, and parcel numbers.

parol evidence rule. In a dispute over a real estate transaction, the parole evidence rule refers to any evidence that is not written. Thus, any agreement between buyer and seller, made prior to or outside of the written sales contract, is inadmissible.

partition action. Court proceeding to settle a dispute between co-owners by dividing their interests in real property.

party wall. A wall erected on the boundary line between two adjoining properties, which are under different ownership, for the use of both parties.

patent defect. Observable defects in a home that must be disclosed by a seller.

percolating water. Underground water not flowing in a defined channel.

periodic tenancy. A form of tenancy in which the tenant pays rent one period at a time. The tenancy continues until either the landlord or tenant gives notice of termination. To terminate a periodic tenancy, advance notice equal to one rental period is generally required.

personal property. Anything movable that is not real property.

plaintiff. Person filing the civil suit in a court of law.

planned development. A type of common interest development with clustered single-family detached residences, townhouses, garden apartments, and other types of residences, with ample open space, community recreational facilities, and sometimes local shopping and employment centers.

plat map. A surveyor's map of land, showing natural and man-made boundaries, buildings, and other improvements.

point of beginning. Starting place for a legal description of land, using the metes and bounds method.

police power. The power of the state to enact laws, within constitutional limits, to promote the order, safety, health, morals, and general welfare of our society.

possession. Possessing or occupying property, whether actually or constructively. Actual possession is physically occupying the land. Constructive possession is legally possessing title to a property.

possessory interest. Present right to physically occupy land and to exclude others from that same land.

precedent. Concept of looking back at cases previously decided and following those decisions for the sake of consistency and fairness.

prescription. The process of acquiring an interest, not ownership, in a certain property.

present interest. Interest in land that can be exercised by the owner today.

price fixing. Agreement of one or more persons to set prices for goods or services.

prima facie. Latin meaning first sight, a fact presumed to be true until disproved.

priority. The order in which deeds and other instruments are recorded. Priority generally follows the order of recording. However, real property tax liens have priority over recorded liens, regardless of their date of recording.

private nuisance. Nuisance affecting only a few people.

private restrictions. A limitation on the use of property placed by private owners or developers.

probate. The legal process to prove a will is valid.

procuring cause. (1) A broker who produces a buyer ready, willing, and able to purchase the property for the price and on the terms specified by the seller, regardless of whether the sale is completed. (2) Person responsible for the ultimate sale of real property so as to be entitled to a commission.

profit-à-prendre. Right to enter another's land to remove soil, substances of the soil, or other resource.

proprietary lease. The lease used in co-op apartment buildings.

protected class. A class of people who are protected from discrimination by federal or state law.

Public Land Survey System. A method of legal land description, using east-west lines (base lines) and north-south lines (principal meridians). Additional lines, drawn six miles apart, are known as township lines (east-west) and range lines (north-south). Previously referred to as the U.S. Government Survey System or Rectangular Survey System.

public nuisance. Nuisance annoying the whole community in general.

public restrictions. Limitations on use of real property associated with government intervention.

pur autrie vie. For another's life. A life estate created on the life of a designated person.

quiet enjoyment. Right of an owner or tenant to the use of the property, without interference from the acts or claims of third parties.

quiet title action. Court proceeding to establish an individual's right to ownership of real property against one or more adverse claimants.

quitclaim deed. A deed with no warranties that transfers only that interest in the property in which the grantor has title.

ratification. The approval of a previously authorized act, performed on behalf of a person, which makes the act valid and legally binding.

real property. Real property includes the land, anything permanently attached to the land, anything appurtenant to the land, or anything immovable by law.

recording. The act of filing documents affecting the title to real property with the county recorder.

red flag. A warning. Something that indicates a potential problem and deserves further investigation.

redlining. The illegal use of a property's location to deny financing or insurance.

release of liability. An agreement that releases the borrower from obligation for repayment of a loan.

reliction. The exposing of previously covered land by receding water.

remedy. The means by which a right is enforced or by which the violation of a right is prevented or compensated. The four basic types of judicial remedies are (1) damages; (2) restitution; (3) coercive remedies; and (4) declaratory remedies.

rental period. Length of time (days, weeks, months) between the rent payments.

rescission. Legal action taken to repeal a contract, either by mutual consent of the parties, or by one party when the other party has breached a contract.

respondent superior. The superior is responsible for the acts of the subordinate.

restriction. A limitation on the use of property placed by private owners, developers, or the government.

retaliatory eviction. An eviction (usually illegal) made in response to a complaint made by the tenant.

reversionary interest. A future interest.

revocation. The canceling of an offer to contract by the person making the original offer.

rezoning. A change or amendment made to the zoning in a geographic area.

right of appropriation. The act of the government to divert water for public use.

riparian rights. The rights of a landowner, whose land is next to a natural watercourse (stream or river), to reasonable use of whatever water flows past the property.

safety clause. Clause protecting listing broker's commission, if the owner personally sells the property to someone who was shown the property or made an offer during the term of the listing.

sandwich lease. A lease agreement created when a lessee sublets the property to another person (sublessee), thus creating a sublessor-sublessee relationship.

scenic easement. An easement created to preserve a property in its natural state and prevent its development.

security deposit. Refundable deposit tenants are required to pay at the beginning of the tenancy.

service of process. The official act of notifying a defendant of an upcoming lawsuit, and the delivery of his or her summons. Service is usually performed by the sheriff.

servient tenement. The property that is burdened by an easement.

severalty. Ownership of real property by one person or entity.

sheriff's deed. A deed given to a buyer when property is sold through court action, in order to satisfy a judgment for money or foreclosure of a security instrument (deed of trust or mortgage).

solar easement. Easement for the purpose of receiving sunlight across real property of another for any solar energy system.

special assessment. Any tax or special charge levied against real property for specific, local public improvements.

specific performance. A court action brought about by one party to force the other (breaching) party to fulfill the conditions of the contract. Specific performance is an alternative to a judgment for money.

spite fence. Fence exceeding 10 feet in height erected for the purpose of annoying a neighbor.

spot zoning. Zoning changed for a single parcel without considering the larger planning context.

statute. A law.

statute of frauds. A state law that requires certain contracts to be in writing and signed, in order to be valid and enforceable and also to prevent fraud in the sale of land or an interest in land.

statute of limitations. A statute limiting the period of time during which legal action may be taken on a certain issue. The statute attempts to protect against outdated claims, about which a true and just outcome may be difficult to determine.

steering. The illegal practice of directing people to specific locations for housing accommodations, depriving them of choice. Steering is a violation of fair housing laws.

subjacent support. Absolute right of the property owner to have his or her land supported from beneath its surface.

sublease. Transfers less than the entire leasehold interest, with the original lessee being primarily liable for the lease.

subpoena. A subpoena is a written order to appear in court.

subrogation. In regard to a legal right or obligation, replacing one person with another.

substitution of liability. *See* novation.

subsurface rights. Rights to the natural resources, such as minerals, oil, and gas below the surface.

succession. The legal transfer of a person's interest in real and personal property to his or her named heirs or beneficiaries, under the laws of descent.

summons. Written request that establishes the plaintiff's position in filing a complaint and calls for the defendant to answer or appear in court.

surface rights. The rights to use the surface of land, including the right to drill or mine through the surface when subsurface rights are involved.

surrender. When a tenant voluntarily gives up a lease, before the expiration of its term.

survey. The process by which a parcel of land is measured and its area is ascertained.

tax lien. A lien placed on property when income or property taxes are not paid. A tax lien remains with the property until the taxes are paid, even if the property is conveyed to another person.

tax sale. Forced sale of real property by the county to satisfy delinquent taxes.

tenancy. (1) The interest of a person holding property by any right or title. (2) A mode or method of ownership or holding title to property.

tenancy at sufferance. The interest of a tenant has when he or she continues to occupy the property after the expiration of a lease.

tenancy at will. A written or oral agreement, allowing a tenant to use or occupy property with the permission of the owner. The term of the tenancy is unspecified and the tenant may leave at any time, or at the request of the owner.

tenancy for years. A tenancy created by a lease for a fixed period of time. If the tenancy is for more than one year, the agreement must must be in writing.

tenancy in common. Ownership of property by two or more persons, each of whom has an undivided interest, without the right of survivorship.

tenant. The person who possesses or occupies a property under a tenancy agreement.

tender. An offer by one of the parties to a contract to carry out his or her part of the contract.

tentative map. Map showing the conceptual design of the proposed subdivision and the improvements that will go along with it.

testate. A person who dies leaving a valid will.

three-day notice to pay rent or quit. The initial notice given to a tenant to begin the eviction process, in the event of non-payment of rent. The tenant must pay the amount owed, or vacate the property.

time is of the essence clause. A clause in a contract that emphasizes punctual performance as an essential requirement of the contract.

title. Evidence that the owner of land is in lawful possession of land, publicly recorded in the county where the property is located.

tort. Legal wrong (other than breach of contract) for which civil remedies for injuries or damages are provided.

township. An area of land, as described by the Public Land Survey System. One township measures 6 miles-by-6 miles (36 square miles) and contains 360 sections, each one being one mile square.

trespass. Intentional and unauthorized entry upon another's real property.

trust. A legal arrangement, in which property or money is transferred from the grantor (trustor) to a trustee, to be held and managed by that person for the benefit of a third party, or beneficiary.

trustee's sale. The forced sale of real property, by a lender, to satisfy a debt. The sale is the final step in the foreclosure process.

undivided interest. A special form of property ownership, in which an interest is held under the same title by two or more people or entities, whether their rights are equal or unequal in value or quantity.

undue influence. Using unfair advantage to get agreement in acceptance of a contract.

unenforceable contract. A contract that was valid when made, but either cannot be proved or will not be enforced by a court.

unilateral contract. A contract in which a party promises to perform, without expectation of performance by the other party.

unilateral rescission. Legal action taken to repeal a contract by one party, when the other party has breached a contract.

unity. Equal right of possession or undivided interest.

unjust enrichment. A benefit obtained by one person at the expense of another, without a legal justification for it.

unlawful detainer action. The legal remedy to remove a tenant and return the rental unit to its owner.

unrecorded contract. A written document that creates a legal relationship between parties, but does not encumber any property. It is not publicly recorded.

usufructuary right. Right that allows the reasonable use of property that belongs to another.

valid contract. A contract with all required elements and is therefore binding and enforceable.

variance. An exception granted to existing zoning regulations to allow the building of a structure or a use that is not otherwise acceptable under current zoning law.

vesting. The way title will be taken.

vicarious liability. Liability that does not result from an individual's personal actions, but from his or her relationship to the party creating the liable situation. For example, brokers are vicariously liable for the actions their associate licensees, even if the broker has done nothing wrong personally.

void contract. A contract that has no legal effect, due to lack of capacity of one of the parties to the contract or an illegal subject matter.

voidable contract. An agreement that is valid and enforceable on its face, but may be rejected by one or more of the parties.

waive. To abandon a right or to refrain from insisting on a right or a formality.

will. A written instrument, whereby a person makes a disposition of his or her property to take effect after their death.

witnessed will. Will usually prepared by an attorney and signed by the maker and two witnesses.

writ. The formal order of a court, which directs a person or persons to do or refrain from doing something in particular.

writ of attachment. The document recorded in the public record, by which the court holds the real or personal property of a defendant as security for a possible judgment, pending the outcome of a lawsuit.

writ of execution. An order for a sheriff to seize and publicly sell a person's property in order to satisfy a judgment.

writ of possession. A document that is executed at an eviction hearing that authorizes the sheriff's office to evict the tenant.

zoning. The regulation of structures and uses of property within selected districts. Zoning laws affect the use of land, lot sizes, types of permitted structures, building heights, setbacks, and density.

zoning districts. Areas showing all of the possible classifications that might be given to any particular parcel of land.

INDEX

A

B